Situating the Feminist Gaze
and Spectatorship in Postwar Cinema

Situating the Feminist Gaze and Spectatorship in Postwar Cinema

Edited by

Marcelline Block

Situating the Feminist Gaze and Spectatorship in Postwar Cinema, Edited by Marcelline Block

This book first published 2008. The present binding first published 2010.

Cambridge Scholars Publishing

12 Back Chapman Street, Newcastle upon Tyne, NE6 2XX, UK

British Library Cataloguing in Publication Data
A catalogue record for this book is available from the British Library

ISBN (10): 1-4438-2226-4, ISBN (13): 978-1-4438-2226-8

For my parents

TABLE OF CONTENTS

II: Theorizing Terror

III: Postfeminist Interventions

IV: (Re)Inscribing the Female Subject in History

PREFACE

"MULVEY WAS THE FIRST…"

JEAN-MICHEL RABATÉ

Why is film theory so organically connected with psychoanalysis? Can this be attributed to Jacques Lacan's lasting impact on late twentieth century culture, or to intelligent adaptations of his theories of the eye, the gaze and the screen by notable theoreticians like Laura Mulvey, Joan Copjec and Slavoj Žižek? Or is it because the subjective situations involved by psychoanalysis and the experience of watching a film in a theater are so close? When we are in the dark and watch in a rapt stupor a flow of animated images, we do more than follow a pleasant narrative or discover new vistas, we are led to indulge our deepest fantasies and reenact traumas that we would not want to be reminded of in real life. Whether this is done in the community of an anonymous crowd of spectators or in the relative solitude of a patient brought back piecemeal to past memories and hidden associations by the active silence of the psychoanalyst, soon the room gets crowded, at least at an imaginary level. All the roles of one's life can be acted out by the most famous actors or by humdrum figures: Ava Gardner, mother, John Malkovich, father, Tipi Hedren, sister, Groucho Marx, brother, Monica Vitti, aunt, Javier Bardem, uncle, all taking on diverse parts, all to be endowed with specific legends. And just as psychoanalysis teaches us to come to terms with the "mother in us" instead of fighting with the real mother, similarly, films give us access to Gardner or Bardem in us.

Most of the authors gathered in this exciting collection would seem to agree with the first hypothesis—the impact of Lacanian reworkings of Freud is determining—and they would all state, like Molly Bloom: "Mulveys was the first…"[1] Let us note that "Mulveys was the first" does not exactly mean "Mulvey was the first." In *Ulysses,* when Molly ruminates on her past, she remembers that it was Mulvey, her first real lover back in Gibraltar, who had been the first man ever to send her a love letter. By alluding in this oblique way to Laura Mulvey's groundbreaking 1975 essay on "Visual Pleasure and Narrative Cinema," an essay that is being discussed by almost all the contributors of this volume, at times to contest it, at times to apply it differently, I mean that we are all aware that Mulvey had been the first to send us a letter about love as perceptible in the cinematographic dialectics of visuality linking audience to plot and characterization, or rather, to use a technical vocabulary that she would prefer, a letter about libidinal and gendered investments in classical film; the letter's message has not been forgotten.

It was a fitting coincidence that 1975, the year when Laura Mulvey was able to successfully systematize the interaction between psychoanalytic conceptions of gender and a feminist critique of the male gaze following a trend relayed by *Screen,* the leading British magazine applying French structuralism, from Roland Barthes to Christian Metz, to literature, social issues and above all film analysis, was also the year when Chantal Akerman produced her first masterpiece, *Jeanne Dielman, 23 Quai du Commerce, 1080 Bruxelles*. At the time, the film was thought shocking, less because it depicted the apparently senseless murder of a customer by an occasional prostitute than because the audience had to follow the process of boiling water or peeling potatoes in real time. Prostitution did not seem worse than doing daily chores, forgetting one's dish in the oven or taking care of a rebellious son. The grinding repetition of daily activities highlighted how tenuous Jeanne Dielman's control over her life was, while suggesting something like a feminist *Waiting for Godot,* with the difference that the final twist turned to sudden horror. Just when Mulvey was denouncing the domination of the male gaze in Hollywood films depicting women as objects of desire and subjugation, a female director was turning the tables (kitchen tables, no doubt) on the male setup of voyeurism and dominance.

I take Akerman as a good example of that generation of feminist filmmakers who did not follow in the paths of their male elders, but also refused to paint themselves in the corner of "experimental" or "avant-gardist" cinema. One could illustrate this with two films which were released almost at the same time, Akerman's *La Captive* (2000), a modernized adaptation of Marcel Proust's *La Prisonnière* section of *In Search of Lost Time,* and Raúl Ruiz's acclaimed 1999 *Time Regained*. Both directors came to Proust with a reputation as formal experimenters, and both decided wisely that since they could not adapt the whole novel, they would concentrate on a limited segment. While Ruiz seemed more interested in comparing the whole world conjured up by Proust with that of the French and even international cinema, with Odette played by Catherine Deneuve, Gilberte by Emmanuelle Béart, Morel by Vincent Perez, Albertine by Chiara Mastroianni, Charlus by John Malkovich,

Akerman focuses on the issues at hand, namely the impossibility of love, the paradoxes of desire and the ambivalence of gender. Ruiz makes sense for readers who already know Proust and thus recognize instantly famous scenes, but his decision to move back and forth in time blurs anything like a narrative sequence. Finally, he had to rely on visual pyrotechnics calling up surrealist techniques to evoke the magic of Proust's style, and one can only conclude that the visual is no match for the written word. By contrast, Akerman's minimalism, anti-naturalism, stylized interactions, her Hitchcock-like insistence on voyeuristic exchanges and perverse innuendoes, along with her choice of a modern setting and relatively unknown actors (except for Sylvie Testud as the highly enigmatic Ariane a.k.a. Albertine), end up highlighting the very meaning of Proust's oeuvre in so far as at its very core there lurks an obsession with deviant sexuality. Thus Akerman's narrative thread is accessible to viewers who have never opened *La Recherche*. It is undeniable that Akerman has been successful in creating a stunning visual experience that leaves room for thought, thus prolonging in an original manner Proust's own interrogations, even when they are most disturbing, while Ruiz remains decorative, awed by a book he attempts to summarize, which in the end leads one to conclude that he has not discovered the secrets of Time—the pages of the novel remain massively forbidding and time is never really "regained."

Should one ascribe this sharp contrast in tones, styles and techniques to gender difference? I believe so, and appreciate the fact that it was Akerman's "lesbian" approach that allowed her to universalize Proust much more than Ruiz's polite fascination for a cultural monument of modernism. With Ruiz, Proust's work remains a monument, nothing but a monument, with Akerman we are at times bored but we are haunted by questions about love, jealousy, dehiscence between other-sex and same-sex patterns. My attribution of a certain superiority to Akerman's being a woman may smack of essentialism, and one might want to query any identification of Akerman's film with a "feminine" point of view and Ruiz's film with a "male" and totalizing gaze. However, it is my belief that these equations are indispensable fictions that we will need to elaborate in order to talk about gender in film. The best theories are those one can disagree with after having used them productively, because they begin by simplifying issues. Mulvey's simplification was deliberate, and she could not ignore that the chain of equivalences linking Hollywood, the male gaze, voyeuristic aggression facing a female body always presented as that of an exploited victim could not be sustained seriously as a universal paradigm.

The contributors to this collection nevertheless decide to revisit the paradigm, not to prove that it was after all quite true but that it still yields new and important insights. This is due to a changed discursive field, in which the names of Lacan, Kristeva and Deleuze are now regularly quoted together (whereas they were seen as enemies one decade ago) and in which a later feminism has been reconciled with a revised Freud. No doubt, Lacan himself had to absorb a powerful and militant new wave of French feminism and he did it with remarkable brio when he presented his "formulae of sexuation" in the seventies as a way of combing his earlier stress on castration with an optional sexual divide in which both men and women could choose to be impacted differently by castration. Freud himself, when studied closely or with different lenses, resists simple dichotomization based on gender roles. Even if Freud tends to identify femininity with passivity and masculinity with activity, as soon as he works with fantasy—which is, after all, what Mulvey is doing all the time—he appears at his best, capable of understanding the complex grammar that declines sentences such as "a child is being beaten," "my father is beating the child," "I am being beaten by my father," in a spectrum going from the equivalence of "beating" with "hating" and then with "loving." Such reversals underpin his general metapsychology of fantasy, a metapsychology defined by a pervasive lability of investments and of gendered roles. Freud concludes his essay on "A Child is Being Beaten" in a very measured way: "In the last resort we can only see that both in male and female individuals masculine as well as feminine instinctual impulses are to be found, and that each can equally well undergo repression and so become unconscious."[2]

Feminist film theory presented in the lucid critical polyphony gathered with unerring critical instinct by Marcelline Block will insist upon such a dynamic and mobile attitude facing the gaze. As the case of *Jurassic Park* clearly shows, it is the very discourse of science facing gender—when it attempts to control reproduction, to regulate the biology of gender choice, and to vanquish time by returning to archaic pre-history—that creates monsters. It would be too simple to say that these voracious dinosaurs embody our terrifying "fathers of the horde" or our always domineering and castrating mothers... Similarly, when we witness today a fascination for "slasher" films shared by male and female audiences, we may want to qualify the idea that it is produced for the exclusive enjoyment of a male gaze. It might be more productive to stress, as Angela Carter did in her groundbreaking *Sadeian Woman,*[3] that fantasy, no matter how transgressive, monstrous or repulsive it may be, is no gender's or sex's property, and that perversion, especially when filmed, once it is located firmly within the realm of fantasy, can provide subjective empowerment for all of us.

JEAN-MICHEL RABATÉ
VARTAN GREGORIAN PROFESSOR IN THE HUMANITIES
UNIVERSITY OF PENNSYLVANIA

Works Cited

Carter, Angela. *The Sadeian Woman and the Ideology of Pornography.* New York: Pantheon Books, 1979.

Freud, Sigmund. "A Child is Being Beaten." In *Sexuality and the Psychology of Love*, edited by Philip Rieff. New York: Collier Books, 1978.

Joyce, James. *Ulysses, The 1922 Text.* Edited by Jeri Johnson. Oxford: Oxford University Press, 1993.

Notes

[1] James Joyce, *Ulysses, The 1922 Text*, ed. Jeri Johnson (Oxford, Oxford University Press, 1993), 710.

[2] Sigmund Freud, "A Child is Being Beaten," in *Sexuality and the Psychology of Love*, ed. Philip Rieff (New York, Collier Books, 1978), 131.

[3] Angela Carter, *The Sadeian Woman and the Ideology of Pornography* (New York, Pantheon Books), 1979.

ACKNOWLEDGMENTS

I wish to express my deepest gratitude to Professor Jean-Michel Rabaté, whose invaluable mentorship allowed me to complete this anthology. I also wish to acknowledge my gratitude to those who read previous versions of this manuscript and generously gave me their good advice: Karen Beckman, Immanuel Ness, Gabriel Riera, and David Sterritt.

My profound gratitude goes to the truly inspirational professors who guided my studies from Harvard University to New York University and Princeton University, as well as to the Richard and Mica Hadar Foundation, the John L. Dales Fellowship of the Screen Actor's Guild Foundation, the Mensa Education and Research Foundation, and the Jacob K. Javits Fellowship, all of which contributed immensely to my education. The professors I would like to thank in particular are April Alliston, Carol Armstrong, David Bellos, André Benhaim, Martine Benjamin, Sacvan Bercovitch, Leo Bersani, Göran Blix, Eduardo Cadava, Tom Conley, Daniel Heller-Roazen, Patrice Higonnet, Stanley Hoffmann, Denis Hollier, Marie-Hélène Huet, Kiki Jamieson, Stephen Kargère, Sarah Kay, Jeffrey Mehlman, Suzanne Nash, François Rigolot, Avital Ronell, P. Adams Sitney, Susan R. Suleiman, Richard Terdiman and Thomas Trezise. My unending gratitude goes to my wonderful friends Daisy and David Paradis, for their sincere and welcome encouragement, which means so much to me.

Teaching at Princeton University has been a truly rewarding experience, since my students and colleagues are a source of support, friendship and inspiration.

Last but not least, I wish to acknowledge my indebtedness to Amanda Millar and Carol Koulikourdi of Cambridge Scholars Press, for their diligent help, unforgettable patience and kindness throughout the publication of this book.

Marcelline Block
Manhattan
Summer 2008

INTRODUCTION

DISSIDENTS OF PATRIARCHY

MARCELLINE BLOCK

Situating the Feminist Gaze and Spectatorship in Postwar Cinema examines films made in the United States, Europe and Russia.[1] Contributors to this volume engage with and readdress classic tenets of feminist film theory. Several chapters explore its interaction with other critical perspectives such as psychoanalytic, queer, disability, postfeminist, quantum, trauma and chaos theories.

This volume is divided into four sections. The five essays in "De-Gendering the Gaze," the first section, depart from and extend the concept of the male gaze discussed by Laura Mulvey (see below), in order to foreground gendered looking relations and theories of the gaze from various critical perspectives including the quantum gaze, female voyeurism, the poly-gaze, the queering of the gaze, and the female director's gaze. The second section, "Theorizing Terror," includes two essays on thriller and horror films, which are staples of feminist film critique. The two essays of the third section, "Postfeminist Interventions," focus on the interaction between feminism and postfeminism.[2] The final section, "Re-Inscribing the Female Subject in History," includes essays that address the formation, development and representation of female subjecthood within the framework of the politico-historical contexts of Belgian, British, French, and Russian films.

Most of the contributors take Laura Mulvey's "Visual Pleasure and Narrative Cinema" (1975) as a starting point, while also engaging with the works of other theorists. According to Mulvey,

> In a world ordered by sexual imbalance, pleasure in looking has been split between active/male and passive/female. The determining male gaze projects its fantasy onto the female figure...In their traditional exhibitionist role women are simultaneously coded for strong visual and erotic impact so that they can be said to connote *to-be-looked-at-ness*...The man controls the film fantasy and also emerges as the representative of power...: as the bearer of the look of the spectator, transferring it behind the screen to neutralize the

extra-diegetic tendencies represented by woman as spectacle...The image of woman as (passive) raw material for the (active) gaze of man takes the argument a step further into the structure of representation, adding a further layer demanded by the ideology of the patriarchal order as it is worked out in its favorite cinematic form—illusionistic narrative film...Film has depended on voyeuristic active/passive mechanisms.[3]

As stated above, Mulvey's discourse on looking relations, scopophilia, the male gaze, female *to-be-looked-at-ness*, and the fragmentation/fetishization of the female body on screen propels a feminist revision of film. Feminist film theorists have incorporated, revised, and critiqued Mulvey's "Visual Pleasure," which P. Adams Sitney considers "the most influential text of feminist film theory."[4] Some critics who have modified Mulvey's binarism—proposing different theories such as the possibility of many gazes and shifting subject positions among spectators—include Janet Bergstrom, Carol Clover, Barbara Creed, Mary Ann Doane, Cynthia Freeland, Jane Gaines, E. Ann Kaplan, Teresa de Lauretis, Tania Modleski, Constance Penley, Trinh T. Minh-ha, B. Ruby Rich, Vivian Sobchak, Jackie Stacey, and Gaylyn Studlar, among others. Yet, "Visual Pleasure" remains the urtext, "the single most reprinted essay in the field of feminist film theory."[5] In 1981, Mulvey revisited her "Visual Pleasure" in "Afterthoughts on 'Visual Pleasure and Narrative Cinema' Inspired by King Vidor's *Duel in the Sun*,"[6] in which she addressed the female spectator position as well as cinepsychoanalytic constructions of femininity.

Several contributors to *Situating the Feminist Gaze and Spectatorship in Postwar Cinema* propose, in turn, theories of the transgendered gaze as well as what I would like to call the Versailles gaze (modeled on the Lacanian "crowd's gaze") and the gaze of History, among others.

In the first chapter, Lisa DeTora writes:

Mulvey notes that Hollywood narrative films construed looking relations, or more properly, the investment of pleasure in looking relations as relying on the operation of a gendered binary, with man as 'bearer of the look' and woman as 'object of the gaze.' Today, this observation informs readings of nearly all visual media, despite the advances that Mulvey, among others, have noted in technologies that have profoundly altered what can be packed into a second of screen time.[7] Feminist film theorists such as Barbara Creed, Cynthia Freeland and Sue Thornham have long worked to account for different gazes and subject positions in order to supplement and/or problematize the heteronormative binary of Mulvey's theory of subject-object looking relations. (4-5)

Elizabeth Gruber, in the twelfth chapter, states that,

There are certain dangers in adhering too rigidly to the masculine-looker/feminine-object schema. An especially cogent critique of this formulation is presented by Jane Gaines, who argues: 'the male/female opposition, so seemingly fundamental to feminism, may actually lock us into modes of analysis which will continually misunderstand the position of many women.'[8] (229)

Yet, Rachel Ritterbusch, in the second chapter, notes that, "critics who focus on the weaknesses of Mulvey's arguments overlook the intent of her article, which is to call for radical change...to create the conditions for an alternative cinema...that provides an authentic position for the female subject" (35-36).

Along with confronting patriarchy of mainstream cinema and the politics of phallocentrism—which, according to Susan R. Suleiman, is the "submission to the rule of logic, syntax, linearity, homogeneity, and realist representation"[9]—several essays in *Situating the Feminist Gaze and Spectatorship in Postwar Cinema* seem written in response to E. Ann Kaplan's queries: "is the gaze *necessarily* male...Or would it be possible to structure things so that women own the gaze?...What does it mean to be a female spectator?...Is it possible for there to be a female voice, a female discourse?"[10] Posed in 1983, Kaplan's questions continue to generate responses, thus showing their relevance to today's feminist film scholars seeking to subvert patriarchy's enduring biases.

In 2004, Kaplan re-asserted that we are not yet "'beyond the gaze' (either male or imperial)..."[11] In April 2008, at the Museum of Modern Art (MoMA) in Manhattan, the Feminist Future Series program featured a conference entitled "Gender and Film: Resituating the Past in the Present." The speakers—Laura Mulvey, Chantal Akerman and Trinh T. Minh-ha—took stock of the current state of feminist film theory and filmmaking, and Mulvey reasserted the continued importance of feminist film theory for cinema and media studies. Mulvey considers that the present moment metaphorically approximates the shape of a threshold, a space to maintain previous and new theories together in which the past, present and future co-exist as in a Deleuzian rhizome, cartographically rather than archeologically. It was in 1975 that Mulvey's essay "Visual Pleasure and Narrative Cinema" and Akerman's film *Jeanne Dielman, 23 Quai du Commerce, 1080 Bruxelles* were acclaimed as innovative, making 1975 a memorable year, a year that also saw the publication of Hélène Cixous's "Le rire de la Méduse" ("The Laugh of the Medusa") and the release of Marguerite Duras's film *India Song*: "Akerman the filmmaker came of age at the same time as the new age of feminism."[12] It was also in 1975 that Michel Foucault published *Surveiller et punir: Naissance de la prison*

(*Discipline and Punish: The Birth of the Prison*). At the time of this writing, it has been thirty-three years since "Visual Pleasure..." and *Jeanne Dielman* (and also *Surveiller et punir*). April 2008 at the MoMA is another important date for feminist film criticism as its past conflates with its promising future.

I: De-Gendering the Gaze

In "'Life Finds a Way': Monstrous Maternities and the Quantum Gaze in *Jurassic Park* and *The Thirteenth Warrior*," Lisa DeTora explores the representation of the monstrous-feminine in the screen adaptations of two bestselling novels by the late Michael Crichton. Female dinosaurs newly created by a team of cinescientists—who have reassembled various DNA materials from frogs and mosquitoes to that effect—exemplify the monstrous-feminine in *Jurassic Park*.

Jurassic Park's cinescientists—in the tradition of the Hollywood "mad scientist"—reproduce copies of dinosaur DNA of which they do not have the original genetic code, therefore creating copies of copies without an original. According to DeTora,

> The reduction of the already overly simplistic binary of *nature=good, science=bad* into *science=hubris=bad* presents a highly troublesome moralism that Stephen Jay Gould has noted as characteristic of cinematic—but not of novelistic—portrayals of scientists and that Gallardo-Torrano sees as Promethean disaster...(9)

The cinescientists' "hubris centers on the idea that they can control their creations" (9). According to Jean-Michel Rabaté, "it is the very discourse of science facing gender—when it attempts to control reproduction...—that creates monsters" (see the preface of *Situating the Feminist Gaze and Spectatorship in Postwar Cinema*, xiii).

Jurassic Park, an amusement theme park located on a fictitious island inspired by Disneyworld, soon becomes a dystopia. The dinosaurs, created only to be female, soon rebel against their breeders by swapping sexual identity with each other. In order to reproduce, some females become males. Gender switching and reproduction occur when the female dinosaurs stage a mutiny and escape the carceral gaze of the high-tech scientists in charge of breeding them.

E. Ann Kaplan's statement that motherhood "is a place to start rethinking sexual difference"[13] can be applied to the diegesis of *Jurassic Park*, where monstrous mothers are capable of gender mutability. Avital Ronell's statement that "mother [is] exposed by equipment linked to surveillance and medicine, [she] has been probed and analyzed, sectioned and scanned, measured and standardized by the pressures of the technological grid,"[14] is also relevant to *Jurassic Park*, where procreation of dinosaur mothers must be controlled by scientists through electronic devices. According to DeTora, the monstrosity of dinosaur maternity has "to do with a violation of looking relations—and the inherent wresting away of the reproductive process from any primary male intervention" (19).

The behavior of *Jurassic Park*'s dinosaurs is reminiscent of that of humans who behave "well" in public, yet might not do so in private. DeTora states that, "the forbidden sight does not exist until it is gazed upon" (23). Unlike Jacques Lacan's sardine can—which cannot gaze back and therefore is not threatening—Jurassic Park's female Tyrannosaurus and Diplodocus return the gaze with threatening eyes. DeTora presumes a connection between gazing, violence and masculinity. The dichotomy between public and private spheres recalls Jeremy Bentham's Panopticon discussed by Michel Foucault in *Surveiller et punir* (*Discipline and Punish*), thus adding another dimension to the examination of science fiction and horror film. For DeTora, *Jurassic Park* and *The Thirteenth Warrior*

> construct maternity as monstrous by demonstrating that female reproduction deeply violates looking relations, defying definition outside the narrow confines of particular gazes...In both films, maternity remains hidden, maintaining mystery through disguise, sublimation, and transformation into animal monstrosity...The most frightening aspects of the consuming, maternal monsters that inhabit these films reside in their ability to be several things at once, to shift physical attributes and positions, until they are fixed in a gaze. (21-23)

DeTora makes use of the quantum gaze to further her contention about the connection between looking relations and monstrous maternity in *Jurassic Park* and *The Thirteenth Warrior*: "quantum theory indicates that the act of observation actually changes these physical circumstances, snapping the particle into a specific state at the moment it is trapped by a gaze" (18). The fluidity and interchangeability of sexes among the dinosaurs that were bred to be only female concurs with the argument that gender is mainly performative. According to Judith Butler in *Gender Trouble* (1990),

> In a sense, *gender* is not a noun, but neither is it a set of free-floating attributes, for we have seen that the substantive effect of gender is performatively produced and compelled by the regulatory practices of

gender coherence. Hence, within the inherited discourse of the metaphysics of substance, gender proves to be performative—that is, constituting the identity it is purported to be. In this sense, gender is always a doing, though not a doing by a subject who might be said to preexist the deed... there is no gender identity behind the expressions of gender; that identity is performatively constituted by the very 'expressions' that are said to be its results.[15]

Slavoj Žižek states that in *Jurassic Park*, the dinosaurs' "destructive fury merely materializes the rage of the paternal superego."[16] DeTora shows that the film is about the maternal, and the dinosaurs' refusal to allow scientists to manipulate their reproduction. Yet, within the discourse of science itself, breaches had already fractured the optimistic outlook of the park's future, since one of the cinescientists visiting Jurassic Park, Ian Malcolm (Jeff Goldblum), a chaos theoretician, doubts the success of the operation:

[The] chaos theoretician and promiscuous father Ian Malcolm...critiques [the] genetic process not as such but as uncontainable. Malcolm rejects the reassurance that an all-female group cannot mate, because he recognizes that chaos is likely to intervene. His comment 'life finds a way' is echoed throughout the film as life, indeed, does find a way to escape both scientific and theme park containment, creating a monstrous maternal abject...Malcolm's critique evokes the specter of hubris [and] the failure of science. (8)

Ultimately, *Jurassic Park* is about the triumph of female ingenuity—that of female dinosaurs, a female scientist and a little girl—females who "find a way" over chaos, hubris, and misogyny.

Rachel Ritterbusch's "Shifting Gender(ed) Desire in Anne Fontaine's *Nathalie...*" examines a film that at first appears to be about the relationship of two females and a male, a clichéd[17] triangular romance reconfigured with a "feminist twist" (29). Catherine (Fanny Ardant), a middle-aged physician, suspecting her husband Bernard (Gérard Depardieu) of infidelity, hires a prostitute whom she renames "Nathalie" (Emmanuelle Béart) in order to tempt and test her husband. The film's diegesis departs from a banal storyline as it becomes the site "'of women reclaiming power' rather than...a tale of adultery"[18] (29). The two female protagonists— one mature, the other young; one financially secure, the other struggling; one in a green suit, the other in a red dress—become confidants, and their friendship leads to intimate encounters.

Although Rachel Ritterbusch is well aware of the ambiguities inherent in the perception of "'women's cinema'...and [that] more importantly, there is no consensus about what constitutes a feminine practice" (27), she concludes that because *Nathalie...* treats questions about marriage, adultery and female sexuality, it can be classified as a "feminist film text" (28). Ritterbusch moreover writes that Anne Fontaine's "feminist stance is evident not only in the film's content but also...in its visual form" (34). As Ritterbusch notes, in the 1970s, early feminist film critics encouraged and influenced filmmakers to "develop 'a new language of desire' capable of speaking woman's reality"[19] (34).

In this respect, in "problematizing the voyeuristic mechanisms inherent in mainstream cinema" (34) by showing that a mature female physician is not only bearer of the voyeuristic gaze but is also the site of unavowed desires that become more explicit as the story unfolds, *Nathalie...* reverses the expectation of patriarchy, perhaps even neutralizing it, and displays— although softly rather than militantly—an openness in giving voice to female desire. All possible turmoil that could result from such important reversals of societal expectations and emotional re-balancing is glossed over in an atmosphere of social drinking, *bon chic, bon genre* outfits, and a color coordinated decorating scheme, as well as unintrusive background music. In Stanley Kubrick's *Eyes Wide Shut* (next chapter), the male physician protagonist loses possession and control of the gaze. In *Nathalie...*, it is Catherine, the female physician, who is uncontestably bearer of the gaze, thus deviating from Laura Mulvey's gaze theory. Therefore, this film provides an affirmative answer to E. Ann Kaplan's query: "would it be possible to structure things so that women own the gaze?"[20]

Pondering whether art imitates film theory or whether film theory imitates art, one wonders if without the feminist film theorists of the 70s, *Nathalie...* would have been made. Careful to avoid the pitfall of essentializing women, Ritterbusch is in agreement with Sandy Flitterman-Lewis, who in *To Desire Differently: Feminism and the French Cinema* (1996), coined the term "feminist cinema" to describe the content and form of films that challenge dominant patriarchal cinema. In Flitterman-Lewis's words,

> A feminist cinema will attempt to restore the marks of cinematic enunciation so carefully elided by the concealing operation of patriarchal cinema [and] it will foreground sexual difference...focusing on the status and nature of the representation of the woman—her desire, her images, her fantasms.[21]

Nathalie...'s two main female characters draw on opportunities for individual women to express desire and fantasies yet unstereotyped.

M. Hunter Vaughan's "*Eyes Wide Shut*: Kino-Eye Wide Open," seems written in response to Dziga Vertov's concept of the "kino-eye" (or the "ciné-oeil"), "that which the eye doesn't see" or "the decoding of life as it is."[22] According to Vertov,

> The weakness of the human eye is manifest. We affirm the kino-eye, discovering within the chaos of movement the result of the kino-eye's own movement; we affirm the kino-eye with its own dimensions of time and space, growing in strength and potential to the point of self-affirmation.[23]

Vaughan examines Stanley Kubrick's unfinished controversial film, in which the male protagonist, Dr. Bill Harford (Tom Cruise), tries but fails to access a forbidden sphere of knowledge, eroticism and power, thus demonstrating the "weakness" of his eyes and his inability to discover the truth. That the title of the film refers to closed eyes tends to indicate that the gaze is absent from either the cinematic apparatus or from the film's protagonist. Dr. Harford, an insecure character mystified by his wife's adulterous thoughts, is also incapable of discovering the circumstances surrounding the death of a prostitute whom he had met in a nightmarish encounter.

Vaughan claims that *Eyes Wide Shut* reverses Mulvey's gender binaries. According to Gilles Deleuze,

> There is as much thought in the body as there is shock and violence in the brain. There is an equal amount of feeling in both of them. The brain gives orders to the body which is just an outgrowth of it, but the body also gives orders to the brain, which is just a part of it: in both cases, these will not be the same bodily attitudes nor the same cerebral gest. Hence the specificity of the cinema of the brain, in relation to that of the cinema of bodies. If we look at Kubrick's work, we see the degree to which it is the brain which is *mis en scène*. Attitudes of body achieve a maximum level of violence, but they depend on the brain. For in Kubrick, the world itself is a brain, there is identity of brain and world. [24]

In *Eyes Wide Shut*, Harford's wife Alice (Nicole Kidman) wears glasses at the start of the film, thus indicating that she appropriates the gaze. Mary Ann Doane claims that "the female recourse for appropriating the gaze" is to wear glasses:

> The woman who wears glasses constitutes one of the most intense visual clichés of the cinema. The image is a heavily marked condensation of motifs concerned with repressed sexuality, knowledge, visibility and vision, intellectuality and desire...glasses worn by a woman in the cinema

do not generally signify a deficiency in seeing but an active looking, or even simply the fact of seeing as opposed to being seen. The intellectual woman looks and analyzes, and in usurping the gaze she poses a threat to an entire system of representation. It is as if the woman had forcefully moved to the other side of the specular. The overdetermination of the image of the woman with glasses, its status as a cliché, is a crucial aspect of the cinematic alignment of structures of seeing and being seen with sexual difference. The cliché, in assuming an immediacy of understanding, acts as a mechanism for the naturalization of sexual difference.[25]

Recall that in Alfred Hitchcock's *Strangers on a Train* (1951), glasses play an important part in the plot. Barbara Morton (Patricia Hitchcock), the "brainy little girl" who wears glasses, perceives that she reminds the psychopath Bruno Antony (Robert Walker) of the glasses-wearing Miriam Haines (Kasey Rogers), the woman he had already murdered. Moreover, the murder is reflected in Miriam's glasses, which had been knocked off her face when Bruno attacked her, leaving her defenseless and without the possibility of a gaze.

In one of the earliest scenes of *Eyes Wide Shut*, Alice looks directly at the camera. Appearing to return the viewer's gaze, Alice becomes de-objectified. She is not the passive object of the male gaze, but rather, becomes an active gazer herself. Akin to the female physician Catherine in *Nathalie…* (chapter two), Alice seizes and owns the gaze. In this respect, she also affirmatively replies to E. Ann Kaplan's inquiry, "would it be possible to structure things so that women own the gaze?"[26]

In analyzing scenes from the film featuring nude or scantily clad women, Vaughan claims that *Eyes Wide Shut* demonstrates that female nudity can be displayed on screen without (intentionally) provoking scopophilia nor the arousal expected from a heterosexual male spectator. Nudity, then, becomes mere nakedness, a sight/site more abject than alluring.

Vaughan's discussion of Stanley Kubrick recalls Chantal Akerman and Sofia Coppola, whose films foreground the fragmented and/or nude female body on screen without objectifying or fetishizing it (chapters eight and fourteen). In Vaughan's estimation, Kubrick's final film "suggests how cinema can struggle against the principal characteristics aptly described in much of feminist film theory…Mulvey's male gaze works on a multitude of levels, each of which is accentuated, though frequently subverted, by *Eyes Wide Shut*" (44-45).

Vaughan eschews the male/active female/passive binary in making a claim for the "poly-gaze": "the representation of sexual difference through the institution of multi-sexual gazes…both on the level of the cinematic apparatus as well as among the characters in the film" (49). Kubrick's *Eyes Wide Shut* illustrates Deleuze's claim that "the brain is no more reasonable a system than the world is a rational one."[27]

When as a child Ian Scott Todd, along with his father, was watching Alfred Hitchcock films on television, little did he know that, according to Avital Ronell, "after a hard day's work on *Psycho*, Alfred Hitchcock used to doze in front of the TV, claiming that TV, unlike film, was soporiferous."[28]

In "Hitchcock's 'Good-Looking Blondes': First Glimpses and Second Glances," Todd's nostalgic description of his early encounters with the Master of Suspense on the small screen in his living room contrasts with how Hitchcock made use of the televisual medium. Obviously, at the time of *Psycho*, Hitchcock could not yet have been acquainted with Jacques Lacan's televised interview which, according to Shoshana Felman, "originally aired on French television in January 1973, destined to be published simultaneously as a book entitled *Télévision…*in which [Lacan] invites [the viewer] not to take 'the little screen for granted.'"[29] Evidently, Todd did not take television for granted, as demonstrated by his childhood experience related in his essay, in which he seems to have been following Lacanian prescriptions *avant la lettre*. Deleuze's claim that television's "image remains so regrettably in the present unless it is enriched by the art of cinema"[30] also directly impacts Todd's discussion of watching Hitchcock's motion pictures on television. Todd was not watching programs made for television, but rather, was engaging with masterpieces of cinema on the small screen, which became his own surrogate movie theater.

Hitchcock's "good-looking blondes" (52) even if seen mainly on television, kept Todd and his father gaping in awe: these blondes had survived not only the transfer from the silver screen to the TV screen— from the public cinematic sphere to the private sphere of home theater— but also remained alluring in spite of drastic size reduction from their overinflated image on the big screen to the diminutive TV screen where they shrank to the proportions of Barbie dolls.

With "Hitchcock's 'Good-Looking Blondes': First Glimpses and Second Glances," Todd proposes queering the gaze in order to reposition the spectator, thus eroding Mulvey's molar gender binaries. Drawing upon his memories of watching Hitchcock films in youthdom with a heterosexual father, Todd investigates his own spectator/subject position and subjectivity as a gay male, a feminist, and a gender studies scholar. Through his analysis of the representation of women in Hitchcock films, Todd investigates what queering the gaze might offer to feminist film theoreticians and spectators. He proposes a theoretical model in which the personal and the political run parallel, or intersect, since he discusses queer and feminist film theories as they relate not only to images of women in Hitchcock's films, but also to images from his private life and personal experiences in a culture that feeds on images and their manifold reproductions: photos, clichés, pictures, cartoons, graffiti and other visual traces. Todd's father enjoyed the actresses' looks, which he had already admired on the silver screen. Inviting his son to share in his scopic euphoria, was the father aware of—or disappointed by—Todd's failure to respond appropriately (read: "erotically")? Todd's lack of expected masculine response allows him to undermine the heteronormativity enmeshed in patriarchy, while still enjoying the glamour of Hitchcock's women in a non-objectifying way.

For Todd, queering the gaze gives a less "reductionistic model of spectatorship" (56) as well as a new way of looking at Hitchcock's female characters that refuses a monolithic categorization, since Hitchcock's female characters are multi-faceted rather than only good-looking and only blonde: "the process of queering the male gaze inaugurates significant possibilities for the ways in which images of women and men" (57) emerge, are produced and assimilated. According to Tania Modleski, "what both male and female spectators are likely to see in the mirror of Hitchcock's films are images of ambiguous sexuality that threaten to destabilize the gender identity of protagonists and viewers alike."[31] P. Adams Sitney considers that in *Vertigo*, the male protagonist becomes an object of the gaze,[32] thus partially reversing Mulvey's theory of gendered looking relations.

Todd therefore demonstrates why Hitchcock's "films continue to function as objects of our desire"[33] for all spectators, regardless of their sexual identities:

> Following Foucault, queer theory argues that because there is no essential truth of human sexuality, it is not a matter of contesting existing sexual norms in the name of a preexistent sexual identity or of liberating repressed or silenced sexualities. Rather in the name of sexual identities yet to be created it urges an ethic of exploration that mobilizes the heterogeneity of forces present in every individual.[34]

For Gilles Deleuze, French New Wave filmmakers "pouvait être dite à bon droit hitchcocko-marxienne, plutôt que 'hitchcocko-hawksienne'"[35] ("could be said to be indeed hitchcocko-marxian rather than hitchcocko-hawksian"). In this vein, following Deleuze's model, Ian Scott Todd would be, due to his feminist/queer outlook, "hitchcocko-foucauldian."

Noëlle Rouxel-Cubberly, in "Family Resemblances: Engendering Claire Denis, Nicole Garcia and Agnès Jaoui's Film Titles," discusses three French female filmmakers. She states that film titles "are an incentive to rethink and question language through gender" (80), performing what Annette Kuhn calls "a feminist politics of intervention at the levels of language and meaning, which may be regarded as equally applicable to the 'language' of cinema as it is to the written and spoken word."[36] For Kuhn, this concern is predicated on the notion that in a patriarchal and/or misogynistic society,

> Women have no language of their own and are alienated from culturally dominant forms of expression...The issue of a non-patriarchal language immediately raises the question of the relationship between such a language and feminism. Although it is clear that the question of women and language could not be raised in the ways it has been without the impetus of feminist politics, the nature and provenance of such a language remains rather more problematic.[37]

According to Rouxel-Cubberly, for Denis, Garcia and Jaoui's films,

> the title reflects an intention to create another order of things, to rethink the imaginary. More than discussing [topics] common to the feminine imaginary—love, family, redefinition of space and time—their titles speak against a set order of things. (79-80)

The titles of these three female directors can be taken as forms of resistance to the phallogocentric structure of patriarchal language. These titles demonstrate "how to fight the 'unconscious structured like a language' (formed critically at the moment of arrival of language) while still caught within the language of the patriarchy,"[38] to cite Laura Mulvey discussing Lacan. Directors whose titling practices form an important part of their cinematic production play with the delayed effect of a postponed title upon the audience. This shifting of the traditional title display challenges the viewer's expectations, thus allowing for a different interaction with the film text. "Raymond Queneau, referring to the phallic power of the title, talked about the 'titre cache-sexe' ('G-string title')"[39] (77). The titling practices of these female directors are evidenced in films such as Garcia's *Un week-end sur deux* (*Every Other Weekend*, 1990); Denis' *Beau travail* (*Good Work*, 1999); and Jaoui's *Comme Une Image* (*Look At Me*, 2004). These titles offer the spectator another "reading of the world: a female reading" (81) at the juncture where the title intersects with the diegesis. Within Denis' *Beau travail*, an untranslatable play on the words "belle trouvaille" ("beautiful find") occurs, thus effectively feminizing a male protagonist (72-73).

Rouxel-Cubberly reconsiders the triangular conversation, a kind of conference call between film, title and spectator, and she interrogates why these titles attest to their authors' *féminitude* and allude to a feminine cinema. Like Sharon Lubkemann Allen, Georgiana M. M. Colvile and Sandy Flitterman-Lewis, who in the last section of this volume discuss the morcellation of female identity and women's life experiences, Rouxel-Cubberly stresses the fragmentary quality of the film title as it relates to a female experience with language. The title, a semiotic fragment, should be attractive. Rouxel-Cubberly compares film titles to witticisms, brief and tightly condensed, which force the viewer to uncover what is only partially revealed.

Titles can be riddles, such as that of Denis' 1988 film *Chocolat*, which takes place in Africa, "where riddles commonly invite, through the symbolic transposition of banal realities, to get to the heart of things" (71). The *modus operandi* of witticisms, riddles, and titles is brevity. Denis' *Chocolat* "speaks of the cocoa exportation through a slave system, of Europe feeding on Africa...*Chocolat*'s savor lies at the crossroad of the mythical dimensions of chocolate and Africa" (72) where cocoa beans are cultivated and processed. Both African slaves and chocolate—an agricultural product of the African continent—forcibly serve a colonial system that exploited the land together with its native inhabitants (male as well as female) because of the pleasures they provided to a white, European patriarchal culture and market. In her discussion of this film title, Rouxel-Cubberly highlights the racist connotations inherent to the term "chocolat" during France's (not so distant) colonial past:

> Chocolate—a colonial food—conjures up a whole racist imagery with corresponding three-syllable chocolate brands such as Bamako or Banania, and the derogatory term 'chocolat,' by extension, referred, until the end of the 19th century, to an African man. (72)

Rouxel-Cubberly discusses another meaning of the word "chocolat." In French, the colloquial expression "être chocolat" means, "'to be had, to be cheated'"[40] (71). This adds another dimension/savor to the film, in which a Caucasian French woman—aptly named France (Mireille Perrier)—recalls the injustices committed against as well as the sexual commodification of the African population at the hands of European imperialists in colonized Cameroon.

Coincidentally, in 2000, 12 years after Claire Denis' *Chocolat*, the Swedish cineaste Lasse Hallström directed a film also entitled *Chocolat*

(adapted from Joanne Harris's 1999 eponymous best-selling novel). Hallström's *Chocolat* narrates the story of a free-spirited single mother (Juliette Binoche) in a French village circa 1950. Although Hallström's film's ideology diverges from that of Denis' *Chocolat*, one wonders why two feminist films have the same title: could it be that the semiotic associations of chocolate conflates diverse female subjectivities, tying them together? In these two films, the pleasure provided by chocolate— also considered to be an aphrodisiac—appeals to characters as well as spectators. Hallström's *Chocolat* depicts the physical, emotional and spiritual renewal of a small town, through a nomadic mother-daughter pair. These two female characters transform an entrenched patriarchal structure into a more tolerant community.

Although the two films entitled *Chocolat* have little in common in terms of aesthetics and thematics, they converge in denouncing racism. In Hallström's version, ethnically ostracized gypsies and their leader (Johnny Depp), are prevented from entering a French village whose inhabitants also ostracized the single mother protagonist. While in Denis' film chocolate symbolizes the oppressiveness of the racist colonial patriarchal system, in Hallström's, chocolate represents liberation from domestic patriarchy and racism.

II: Theorizing Terror

In "Return of the Female Gothic: the Career-Woman-in-Peril Thriller," Monica Soare demonstrates that the Female Gothic, exemplified by Ann Radcliffe's 18th century novels which created the template for this genre, is reformulated in late 20th century cinema. Soare inaugurates the "career-woman-in-peril thriller" (CWPT), which foregrounds the continuing significance of the Female Gothic to current cinematic preoccupations: "in classic Female Gothic form, career-woman-in-peril thrillers stage an exploration of female fantasy via the heroine's (and female spectator's) engagement with the affect of fear" (90). Fear, in Gothic terms, is always ultimately the fear of death[41] or extinction, which, according to Paul Wells—cited in this book's opening chapter—"has informed horror productions since the earliest examples of Gothic literature" (7). According to Soare, the term CWPT is probably her own; it conflates elements from horror, slasher, detective, noir, and erotic thriller films. This contemporary cinematic perspective bridges the gap between the pre-cinematic 18th century and the 21st, which is engulfed in the primordiality of pictorial representation.

The CWPT portrays its female protagonist's relationship with a father figure, in contrast to several films discussed in this anthology—for example, those directed by Chantal Akerman, Sofia Coppola, Marguerite Duras, Anne Fontaine, Christophe Gans, Neil Marshall, Steven Spielberg, Quentin Tarantino and Agnès Varda—whose preoccupations are centered (or de-centered) around the mother figure and the mother-daughter configuration, while marginalizing the father figure. Soare problematizes the father-daughter relationship, arguing that the female protagonist of the CWPT "often inherits her career and sense of self from her father or a father figure [and] her relationship to him is mirrored in her interaction with the criminal man," (88) who is often a serial killer. Soare explores the female protagonist's interest in the male serial killer, whom she is investigating, fleeing and/or dating: in Jean-Michel Rabaté's words, serial killers "allow themselves absolute mastery over the lives of others."[42]

Soare claims that in Jonathan Demme's *The Silence of the Lambs*, it is Hannibal Lecter (Anthony Hopkins) who allows Clarice Starling (Jodie Foster) to access the sublime. Hannibal Lecter, in Slavoj Žižek's words, "is a sublime figure in the strict Kantian sense...in *The Silence of the Lambs*, Lecter is truly cannibalistic, not [only] in relation to his victims but in relation to Clarice."[43]

Drawing upon feminist film theory—and occasionally writing against some of the predominant views on feminist horror film scholarship— Soare discusses, among other films, Richard Marquand's *Jagged Edge* (which she considers the first CWPT), Jane Campion's *In the Cut*, Philip Kaufman's *Twisted* and Bernard Rose's *Candyman*. Soare's analysis of the female spectator's engagement with the semiotics of fear as a means of reaching the sublime recalls Slavoj Žižek:

> [The] secret of the Kantian sublime: if beauty is a symbol of morality (of the good), the sublime announces evilness *qua* ethical stance—this is the power discernible in what Kant calls the 'dynamical sublime,' the power that an image of terrifying unruly nature evokes by way of its very failure to represent it adequately: an ethical (principled, implacable), yet radically evil rage...[44]

Prior to Žižek, Gilles Deleuze had mentioned the moment of the sublime, which "met with the infinite within the spirit of evil...Kant used to distinguish two kinds of Sublime, mathematical and dynamical."[45] The CWPT is exciting not only because of the pleasurable dose of adrenaline that its fear-inducing sublime images send through the viewer's system, but also because of its representation of the imagined "real world" as dangerous and "masculine...hostile and challenging" (106) for women.

In these films, peril and maleness represent a forbidden and desirable sphere for women. The guilty, scopophilic voyeurism inherent to visual sadistic violence is shared across the spectatorial horizon regardless of gender. Soare heralds the return of the Female Gothic and also, uncannily, the return to and of a Freudian/Lacanian patriarch, watching.

In *"Mille Genres*: Woman and women, Horror Film and Horror Films,"* Chuck Robinson considers the representation of women in *Silent Hill* (Christophe Gans, 2006) and *The Descent* (Neil Marshall, 2005). Writing against previous feminist horror film scholarship, which, in his opinion, essentializes women, Robinson stresses that, "a fundamental problem of psychoanalytically influenced feminist approaches to horror film is that they concern themselves with 'the Woman'" (120). In examining *Silent Hill* and *The Descent*, Robinson challenges Barbara Creed's concept of the "monstrous-feminine," since in his estimation, "the monolithic term 'monstrous-feminine' corresponds to a molar, essentialized concept of *the* woman" (125). Gilles Deleuze's writings and Anna Powell's *Deleuze and Horror Film* (2005) are Robinson's points of departure for releasing horror film from essentialist feminist pronouncements: "these two films serve as staging grounds for a Deleuzian approach to viewing and reading horror film…The protagonists in both films can be considered feminists in a molecular sense. Both are totally unconcerned with essences" (132).

In viewing *Silent Hill* and *The Descent* as exemplary film texts in spite of their "lowbrow" status as B-movies, Robinson proposes Deleuzian becomings such as "becoming-birthday" in *The Descent*, "a film about transformation that occurs in a world where gender is a relic and what one is becoming is more interesting than what one is" (130).

Silent Hill's ghost town brings to mind Deleuze's statement that, "the city—deserted. The city absent from itself, will continue to haunt cinema, as if it were keeping a secret."[46] *Silent Hill* is predicated upon the female protagonist searching for her lost daughter through snow-covered empty streets. Furthermore, *Silent Hill* seems to illustrate Jean-Michel Rabaté's statement that silence constructs meaning:

> The problematics of silence can offer an approach which would go beyond the facile antagonism between the surface realism of the stories and the suggestions, allusions, and quasi-symbolist tactics of inferring by cross-references…Meaning is thus only a limit imposed onto this silence, a border helping to define the diseased mother…silence begs the question of textual hermeneutic, for its disturbing effect is the epiphany of meaning.[47]

At the conclusion of his essay, Robinson proposes another look at horror film—"creepy horror"[48] (in Rabaté's words)—through laughter: "observing how phallicizing, oedipalizing, vaginalizing horror film images exposes the ridiculous, laughable, and perhaps inescapable ideologies of the gendered body" (134).

Bergsonian references are found in Robinson's remarks about the multiple causes for laughter emanating from the horror film audience as a response to fear, anguish, embarrassment, or a mechanism for releasing tension. Here Robinson seems to bring back the established Freudian theory of the unconscious, through the reflex of laughter. Of course, laughter can reveal an evil streak among a spectatorship reveling in horror. Nevertheless, Robinson's essay on two contemporary horror films challenges the taboos as well as the *poncifs* of horror film scholarship: "horror films have more to give viewers, thinkers, and feminists than the same old psychoanalytic platitudes" (134).

III: Postfeminist Interventions

Amy Woodworth's "A Feminist Theorization of Sofia Coppola's Postfeminist Trilogy"—*The Virgin Suicides* (1999), *Lost in Translation* (2003) and *Marie Antoinette* (2006)—explores the postfeminist debate and brings together a feminist and postfeminist point of view. Woodworth's purpose is to "offer an analysis of Coppola's aesthetic…and…to evaluate how early feminist film criticism" (142) might impact it. Since commercially successful American films still tend to exhibit the inner fantasy of patriarchy, Woodworth concludes that feminist film theory challenges and deconstructs the filmmaking industry. Woodworth bridges the gap between early feminist film theory and 21st century film production, arguing convincingly that feminist film theory enriches readings of contemporary films. Coppola's films question the gendered spectatorial position and offer the possibility of correcting patriarchal portrayals of women, suggesting that the male spectator might also identify with a female subject position. In Woodworth's estimation, Coppola's *Marie Antoinette* has "inherited some of the politics of second-wave feminism, [including] its revisions to the camera angles, focus, and framing formerly used to objectify women" (159).

Coppola's *Virgin Suicides* and particularly *Lost in Translation* are her most acclaimed films. *Marie Antoinette* was not as well received, although this third panel of her triptych is successful in many ways. It depicts the atmosphere in which the eponymous young queen was plunged after her marriage. Pastel colors, evocative of Fragonard, Boucher and Watteau's paintings—especially pink and powder blue—in which Coppola dresses the female characters of *Marie Antoinette*, reflect a postfeminist aesthetic. Coppola sketches the frivolous attitude of the Versailles courtesans during this gilded time capsule. Self-centeredness, indifference, a desire to beautify oneself, as well as to play are symptomatic of life at Versailles as well as life in Western postfeminist culture. Woodworth discusses how the fragmentation of the female body in Coppola's cinema deemphasizes their sex appeal. Coppola's biopic of Marie Antoinette stops short of the looming French Revolution, allowing the French queen's biographical timeline to end shortly before her insouciant palatial world collapsed. The guillotine is a long way from Coppola's preoccupations when she depicts an aristocratic female in her teenhood, trying on "frou-frou...dresses."[49] What unnerved film critics is how this film deconstructs extra-diegetic horror, substituting it with a semiotics of futility (frivolous wigs, shadowed eyes and a few applied beauty spots).

Marie Antoinette's world was uncertain until she produced an heir to France, which was her main *raison d'être* at Versailles. Under the gaze of Versailles and under her mother's supervisory gaze emanating from her admonishing letters, Marie Antoinette attempted to fulfill her queenly duties of motherhood. Versailles' gaze upon Marie Antoinette is a variation of Lacan's "crowd's gaze" that he discusses in *Télévision*.[50] The gaze of Versailles recalls the gaze of the scientists in *Jurassic Park* as discussed in the first chapter: the cinescientists intended to control the reproduction of dinosaur mothers. But whereas *Jurassic Park*'s dinosaurs were bred to produce only female offspring, Versailles was hoping that Marie Antoinette would bear male offspring ("an heir and a spare"). In a muted voice, after her daughter's birth, Marie Antoinette whispers in the infant's ear that although France demands a male heir, she loves her baby girl just the same. Lisa DeTora, among others, has compared Jurassic Park to the Panopticon, a comparison that circles back to Versailles, where the Panopticon concept probably originated.[51] At the Versailles court, everyone was at once object of the gaze and active gazer. Beyond this cross-gazing, however, everyone gazed at Marie Antoinette—mainly at her belly. Another variation on the Panopticon infuses Coppola's *Virgin Suicides*, in which a draconian mother of five girls sought total control over them. The five daughters, virtual prisoners in their home, killed themselves.

The first shot of Coppola's *Lost in Translation*, a close-up of the female protagonist's *derrière* glimpsed through pink translucent clothing as she reclines on a hotel bed in Tokyo, disinvites eroticism in spite of the fragmentation of her body that, in other contexts, would objectify her.

Although the representation of a reclining female—nude or partially clad—is a staple of Western art inviting scopophilia, in *Lost in Translation*, that reclining female brings no scopophilic pleasure; rather, this enlarged shot of her *derrière* is laughable. Woodworth notes how in Coppola's postfeminist rendition, the promise of an "erotic spectacle" is cancelled, not only in this opening scene, but also throughout most of this film, which is about a young female protagonist's bittersweet experiences abroad. Another instance of missed scopophilia is when the female protagonist performs karaoke in a scene recalling the atmosphere of Federico Fellini's Roman nights in *La Dolce Vita* (1960) and Michelangelo Antonioni's Milan in *La Notte* (1961): her "singing voice (thin and stumbling) and the pink wig…seem to ironize or deflate what would traditionally work as erotic spectacle"[52] (148).

In "*Laisse tomber les filles*: (Post)Feminism in Quentin Tarantino's *Death Proof*," Jeremi Szaniawski analyzes Tarantino's 2007 film from the perspectives of recent postfeminist as well as classic feminist film theory, in particular through Carol Clover's work on horror films and slashers.

Szaniawski's essay seeks to collapse what Woodworth calls the "feminist-postfeminist binary" (139) and to apprehend *Death Proof* from both theoretical frameworks: "*Death Proof* constitutes a postfeminist effort" (184), yet "there lies a more complex dimension, which might surprisingly reconnect Tarantino with feminism" (170). Writing against the grain of feminist and postfeminist scholarship about Tarantino and horror film, Szaniawski shows how *Death Proof* resemantizes Clover's classic concept of the Final Girl:

> Clover's claim is that the female victim-hero must be the victim before she becomes the hero and therefore she always carries an element of monstrosity (the aforementioned 'Final Girl').[53] Yet this is not quite the trajectory followed in Tarantino's film…While Clover argues that the Final Girl is not so much a proto-postfeminist figure as a return to an earlier discourse—the 'one sex reasoning' discourse challenged by psychoanalysis but prominent until the 18th century,[54] Tarantino's Final Girls seem indeed to embody and champion the truly postfeminist pendant of the concept. (181)

The film's psychopath villain, Stuntman Mike (Kurt Russell), murders young women by crushing them with his "death proof" car until one group of females resists and attacks him back. While Stuntman Mike is but one example of how Tarantino's film rewrites, in the 21st century, the plots of the slashers, exploitation films and B-movies of the last quarter of the 20th century, this representation of the male serial killer recalls Jack the Ripper, a haunting figure of Western artistic and literary tropes. According to Jean-Michel Rabaté,

> Jack the Ripper was the first of the famous serial killers, the original psychopathic murderer who transformed his crimes into paradoxical mementos of popular culture, monuments to an inflated egocentrism, doubtful shrines to a widespread fascination for male outrage on women.[55]

Stuntman Mike similarly situates his "male outrage on women" within popular culture, when he claims to have worked on classic road race films such as *Vanishing Point* (1971), from which he draws his murder weapon: a "death proof" car. Stuntman Mike's car is used for voyeurism as well as murder:

> [He is] characterized not only by his car, but also by his voyeuristic function as [a] shot reveals him injecting drops into his eyes. This underscores...his voyeurism...Furthermore, it is noteworthy that this initial shot of Stuntman Mike's eyes are not framed directly, but rather are reflected in the tiny mirror of the visor. This reflexive device collapses the viewer with the voyeur...He is the active bearer of the male gaze as he objectifies and photographs the women he will eventually kill. These women are not only passive objects of his gaze, but soon also will become his passive victims. (173-174)

Rescripting Jack the Ripper's horrific schemes, *Death Proof* acknowledges undercurrents of the Gothic, along with "grindhouse," road race B-movies and psycho-killer thrillers. Monica Soare notes the Gothic's far-reaching implications into 21st century cinematic culture (for a reformulation of the 18th century Female Gothic invention, see chapter six). However, the 21st century re-embodiment of Jack the Ripper is subverted in the second part of *Death Proof* as a group of would-be female victims fiercely fights back and beats the psychopath to death in a display of "angry girl power...with a re-establishment of feminist politics" (178).

This "re-establishment of feminist politics" is emphasized by Tarantino's insistence upon the figure of the single mother throughout his oeuvre, perhaps a biographical trace of his own upbringing by Connie McHugh-Zastoupil, his teenaged single mother: "it is this figure of the single mother, far more than the male father figure, who is the true place of inspiration; she is the mother of and in these films, alive in them and through them" (186-187). This statement is supported by the endings of both *Kill Bill* and *Death Proof.* In *Kill Bill*, the unbeatable Beatrix Kiddo (Uma Thurman)—who has slaughtered all of her attackers, including the father of her daughter—spends the final scene of the film in blissful domesticity, watching cartoons on television with her young daughter.

A single-mother figure's appearance occurs in the last scene of *Death Proof*, which features single-mother Abernathy (Rosario Dawson) kicking the psychopath Stuntman Mike even more violently than the two other female characters—who are not mothers—catapulting the filmic ending with a close-up of her foot. *Death Proof*'s ending, which "captures the dwarfed position of the male confronted with these empowered female figures who boast simultaneously masculine and feminine characteristics, in a climactic gesture of (post)feminist retaliation" (178), can also be conflated with feminist film theories such as Barbara Creed's "monstrous-feminine" and the Final Girl theorized by Carol Clover. "Encrypted in" Tarantino's *Kill Bill* and *Death Proof* "is above all...the independent, strong single mother" (186). Tarantino's emphasis upon the figure of the mother reconstructs other discussions about mythical mothers as trope in this volume: monstrous maternity in *Jurassic Park* and *The Thirteenth Warrior* (chapter one); a strong-willed mother in *Silent Hill* and an ambivalent mother in *The Descent* (chapter seven); the tragic mother of *The Virgin Suicides* (chapter eight) and moreover, the fragmentary love-hate mother-daughter relationship imbued with misrepresentations and violence in Marguerite Duras's works (chapter ten). In Julia Kristeva's words,

> Like an archetype of the madwomen who fill Duras' universe, the madness of the girl's mother, in *The Lover*, towers with dismal Gothic force...hatred grips daughter and mother in a passion-driven vise that turns out to be the source of the mysterious silence that striates writing.[56]

A variation on the mother-daughter *tangage*, enmeshed in nomadism—a version of which also traverses Lasse Hallström's *Chocolat*—emanates throughout Chantal Akerman's exilic nostalgia (chapter fourteen).

IV: Re-Inscribing the Female Subject in History

Georgiana M. M. Colvile's "Duras Ravaged, Ravished...Ravishing," is an intratextual psychoanalytic study of Marguerite Duras's texts and films. Dudley Andrew comments that

> Many of the situations and characters originating in Duras's prose fiction began to reappear in the cinema. *La Femme du Gange* (1974; *Woman of the Ganges*), combining characters from several earlier novels, in turn served as the basis for a play from which another film, her most famous,

was made: *India Song* (1975). The mesmerizing soundtrack of *India Song* in turn generated still another film.[57]

Colvile, however, examines Duras's cycle of creation and destruction throughout her oeuvre. According to Colvile, "the destruction perpetuated from one film to the next occurs...and yet, each time, the precursor text remains [as] a trace" (208). This destructive quality of Duras's work is especially notable in her "Indian cycle," a group of texts and films that start in 1964 with a novel, *Le Ravissement de Lol V. Stein* (*The Ravishing of Lol Stein*) and ends with the film *Son Nom de Venise dans Calcutta désert* (*Her Venetian Name in Deserted Calcutta*, 1976): "Duras claimed each film destroyed the corresponding novel. She completed the obliteration of the entire cycle by making the final film, *Son Nom de Venise dans Calcutta désert*" (205).

Moreover, this "destructive mechanism" (205) of Duras's cinema is also inscribed upon the faces of her female characters, which become ravaged surfaces. In *Son Nom de Venise*, the depiction of the Rothschild chateau emblematizes the Nazi era: during the occupation of France, the chateau was requisitioned by Göring and subsequently destroyed. It then becomes a trope of Duras's *modus operandi*, a Deleuzian "any-space-whatever." Colvile's semantization of Duras's close-ups of the chateau's "cracked walls, broken mirrors, gaping doors, windows, and fireplaces—in short, empty spaces devoid of human presence" (205), conflates with Deleuze:

> The fact is that, in Europe, the post-war period has greatly increased the situations which we no longer know how to react to, in spaces which we no longer know how to describe. These were 'any spaces whatever,' deserted, inhabited, disused warehouses, waste ground, cities in the course of demolition or reconstruction...Marguerite Duras's first films were marked by all the powers of the house, or of house and ground together, fear and desire, talking and being quiet, going out and coming back, creating the event and burying it, etc. Marguerite Duras was a great filmmaker of the house, such an important theme in cinema, not simply because women 'inhabit' houses, in every sense, but because passions 'inhabit' women... The house-grounds undoubtedly already had most of the properties of an any-space-whatever, the voids and the disconnections. But the house had to be left, abolished, so that the any-space-whatever could only be constructed in flight, at the same time as the speech-act had to 'get out and away.'[58]

In examining "the voids and the disconnections," in Duras's oeuvre, Danielle Bajomée, cited by Colvile, writes that "everywhere, morcellation, discohesion, and disaggregation dominate and are inscribed, again and again, in recurring scenes, that show how the child relates to the mother and the mother to the child."[59] Chantal Akerman's fragmentation and Duras's insistence on morcellation echo each other in foregrounding the estrangement of the female in a patriarchal world that marginalizes her and renders her invisible. The history of colonized Vietnam (Indochina and Cochinchina),[60] as well as the catastrophes of World War II—including the Nazi Occupation of France, the Shoah and the nuclear bombing of Hiroshima[61]—are constantly alluded to in Duras: for Kristeva, "Auschwitz and Hiroshima have revealed that the 'malady of death,' as Marguerite Duras might say, informs our most concealed inner recesses."[62] These events are not merely a background, but rather form a permanent presence in Duras's "phenomenal corpus (around a hundred works: novels, essays, plays, screenplays, films)" (194).

According to Kristeva,

> If Duras uses the screen in order to burn out its spectacular strength down to the glare of the invisible by engulfing it in elliptical words and allusive sounds, she also uses it for its excess of fascination, which compensates for verbal constriction. As the characters' seductive power is thus increased, their invisible malady becomes less infectious on the screen because it can be performed: filmed depression appears to be an alien artifice.[63]

Of this "verbal constriction" and polyphonic "disjunction" between sound and image in her films, Duras, when discussing *La Femme du Gange*, writes:

> 'There are two films, the film of the image and the film of the voices…the two films are there, with total autonomy…neither are (the voices) voices-off, in the conventional sense of the term: they do not facilitate the unrolling of the film: on the contrary, they hamper and disturb it. They ought not to be linked with the film of the image.'[64]

Duras's use of sound and image is described by Deleuze as follows:

> In the disjunction between the sound image become pure speech-act, and the visual image become readable or stratigraphic, what distinguishes the work of Marguerite Duras from that of the Straubs? A first difference would be that, for Duras, the speech-act to be reached is total love or absolute desire. It is this which can be silence, or song, or shout like the shout of the vice-consul in *India Song*. It is this which has control over memory and forgetting, over suffering and hope. And it is above all this which is creative story-telling coextensive with the whole of the text from

which it tears itself, constituting an infinite writing deeper than writing, an unlimited reading deeper than reading.[65]

Colvile demonstrates that Duras's films tear themselves from their original texts, destroying them and often themselves as well. According to Colvile, this creation-destruction process is inherent to Duras's work, in which "the death drive is sometimes expressed through the self-destructive work of her films" (201). Duras decided not to shoot any more films after *Les Enfants* (*The Children*, 1984). She told an interviewer: "'I said to myself that that was enough, what with my films in tatters, dispersed, without a contract, lost.'"[66] As part of her analysis of Duras's cycle of creation/destruction, Colvile draws upon Louis Marin's text *Détruire la peinture* (*To Destroy Painting*, 1977), in particular, how Marin's discussion of Caravaggio relates to Duras's film *Détruire, dit-elle* (*Destroy, She Said*, 1969). For Colvile, "the phrase [*Détruire, dit-elle*], now almost synonymous with Duras, reverberates through the corpus of criticism surrounding her work" (196). To cite Jane McLelland's review of *Détruire la peinture*, "all history, in writing a past, rewrites previous history,"[67] a claim applicable to the progression of Duras's works from novel to film, from creation to destruction, that Colvile calls "textual fabrics that fray and self-destruct at their creator's will, under the gaze of the fascinated reader-spectator" (194).

In considering three films by Agnès Varda—the "grandmother of French New Wave cinema"—Sandy Flitterman-Lewis seems caught in the dilemma that feminist film theorists debate. The goal of such theorists is to avoid essentializing women when discussing Woman, women, femininity, *féminitude, écriture féminine*, woman's films, women's cinema, and their "different voice(s)." Jean-Michel Rabaté states that, "the best theories are those one can disagree with, after having used them productively, because they begin by simplifying issues" (see the preface of *Situating the Feminist Gaze and Spectatorship in Postwar Cinema*, xii).

Flitterman-Lewis proposed the term "feminist cinema" and she specifically coined "filmer en femme" (214) for Varda in her 1996 book *To Desire Differently: Feminism and the French Cinema*. Flitterman-Lewis interprets the implications of Varda's recent installation within the exhibit *Hommage aux Justes de France* (*Homage to the Righteous of France*, Panthéon, Paris, January 18, 2007). She links this installation to an earlier film that Varda made in 1958, almost 50 years before, entitled *L'Opéra-Mouffe*. Varda's third film discussed by Flitterman-Lewis is *Les Glaneurs et la Glaneuse* (*The Gleaners and I*, 2000), also exemplary of *filmer en femme*.

In Varda's 2007 installation at the Panthéon, Flitterman-Lewis discovers the infiltration of the feminine in two of the most celebrated monuments to patriarchy, the Panthéon in Paris and the Old Testament, through the Book of Ruth. Flitterman-Lewis shows how the Panthéon, bastion of phallocentrism, is challenged by Varda's work. An epigraph engraved on the frontispiece of the Panthéon—"the grand patriarchal institution par excellence" (217)—reads, "*Aux grands hommes la patrie reconnaissante* (*To the great men, the grateful nation*)." What about the "*grandes femmes*" (the "*great women*")? Is not the nation grateful to them, too? In reply to these implicit queries, Varda installed the "idea of a feminine consciousness" (217) under the inscription "*Aux grands hommes...*"

Twice in her career, Varda has debunked the Panthéon's patriarchy: in *L'Opéra-Mouffe*, Varda filmed marginalized Parisians haunting a then-impoverished section of Paris, the rue Mouffetard, situated at the Panthéon's feet, almost directly under the epigraph "*Aux grands hommes...*" For Patrice Higonnet, "a Parisian monument is expected to propose a broader message, one that is simultaneously civic and universal and therefore more apt to express the readable and representative myths that the capital incarnates."[68] The feminist finger pointing at the Panthéon's epigraph which ignores women's contributions to France can be considered an assault—or at least a protest—against the patriarchal hegemony inscribed within its "universal" monumentality from which the feminine has been evacuated.

The 2007 installation in *L'Hommage aux Justes de France* (*Homage to the Righteous of France*) heralds the return of Varda to the Panthéon with her continued insistence on placing the female subject alongside the accepted male subject. Varda's multimedia installation has symbolically taken the Panthéon—"an impossible monument,"[69] in Higonnet's words—down from its utopian representation of masculine splendor to the street level inhabited by the Other, embodied by the feminine. In *L'Opéra-Mouffe* and in her installation within the *Hommage aux Justes de France*, Varda empowers women—women who had previously been invisible—giving them access to visibility. Varda commemorates marginalized beings, such as Jews, among others deported from Vichy France.

Varda's decision to "humanize" the Panthéon recalls an event that occurred in Paris in August 1970, when a group of "liberated" women attempted to peacefully lay a wreath under the Arc de Triomphe, another great monument to patriarchy, that Higonnet, however, considers "a less politicized and more national structure"[70] than the Panthéon. Under the Arc de Triomphe lays the Tomb of the Unknown Soldier, lit up by a flame eternally burning in memory of soldiers who died for France. Daring an unparalleled reversal, the posse of liberated women did not bring the wreath for the Unknown Soldier this time, but rather, for "his wife." According to them, the Unknown Soldier's wife "was even more unknown than he was,"[71] he, the Unknown Soldier, supreme symbol of unsung self-sacrifice, the unnamed, *innomable*, anonymous. Of course, in 1970, the French police cut short that brave yet aborted ceremony, preventing the women from laying their wreath, but the press saluted their homage, which is now encrypted within the history of the French women's liberation movement (*Mouvement de libération des femmes* or *MLF*). In her installation, Varda "recasts History in feminine terms while she simultaneously conceives of the feminine in historical context…She posits the historical feminine subject" (217-218), writing against what Jean-François Lyotard calls the "grand narratives" and what Georges Perec, in an untranslatable pun, calls "L'Histoire avec une grande hache" ("History with a capital 'H'/a big hatchet").

Michael Herr, quoted by Avital Ronell in "TraumaTV," writes,

It took the war to teach…**that you were as responsible for everything you saw as you were for everything you did**. The problem was that **you did not always know what you were seeing until later,** maybe years later, that a lot of it never made it in at all, it just stayed stored there, in your eyes.[72]

Commenting on Michael Herr, Avital Ronell states:

What might especially interest us here is the fact that responsibility no longer pivots on a notion of interiority. **Seeing, *itself*, without the assistance of cognition or memory, suffices to make the subject responsible.** It is a responsibility that is neither alert, vigilant, particularly present, nor informed.[73]

Agnès Varda's installation seems to illustrate Avital Ronell's statement, since it recognizes those who, during the Nazi Occupation of France, saw injustice and acted upon it. In Alain Resnais' 1959 film *Hiroshima mon amour* (screenplay by Marguerite Duras), "He," the Japanese male protagonist (Eiji Okada) accuses "She," the French female protagonist (Emmanuelle Riva) of the following: "you saw nothing in Hiroshima. Nothing," to which She replies, "I saw *everything*. *Everything*."[74] He/She, a binary bared to its simplest enunciation, complemented by the adverbial binary nothing/everything, paradigmatically captures the polarization of male/female that declines masses of unacceptable, diffused clichés about maleness and femininity.[75] In the context of a Japanese city pulverized by a nuclear attack, the accusation "you saw nothing" impresses upon us that we are not only responsible for what we have seen and for what we see—as Michael Herr states—but also responsible for what we have not seen. This ethics of responsibility pervades Varda's work.

Flitterman-Lewis sees in the figure of Varda's *Glaneuse* no less than the Old Testament figure of Ruth, whose name, in Hebrew, means "friend." In the Old Testament there are only two books named after women: Esther and Ruth. The Book of Ruth narrates Ruth's friendship with her mother-in-law, Naomi. Eschewing the irony inherent in the fact that in Western culture, mothers-in-law and daughters-in-law are often viewed as nemeses, the bond between Ruth and Naomi centers upon the concepts of responsibility and care. Flitterman-Lewis cites Carol Gilligan's *In a Different Voice* (1982), in which she coined the expression "ethic of care."

Varda's multimedia installation—four screens simultaneously showing films and displaying photographs of Holocaust victims and their rescuers, the "Righteous" women—therefore, would in itself become a non-patriarchal "monument" to feminism as humanism, if such a monument were possible. The viewer's gaze upon these films and photographs seems to be returned by a gaze trapped in the installation itself, which is none other than the gaze of History. Varda's cinematic oeuvre in its fluidity escapes most categorization, except for one: it could be called the "cinema of responsibility." Varda's *Sans toit ni loi* (*Vagabond*, 1985), is another film about gleaning, but with a tragic ending that interrogates and accuses a narcissistic world, a non-Levinasian society disengaged from the "ethic of care." For Tom Conley, Mona (Sandrine Bonnaire), the protagonist of *Sans toit ni loi*, "like Duras's heroines…is born of the sea—*la mer, la mère*—is thus gratuitous, and has no reason for being where she is or where she goes."[76] Mona's short life ends in a wintry ditch, where she expires, alienated and lost.

In her 2007 installation, Varda portrays victims of the Shoah, alongside portraits of the "Righteous," those "ordinary" citizens who saved lives. Stanley Hoffmann's schoolteacher and his wife are among the Righteous. Of his experiences during World War II, Hoffmann writes:

> In my memory, the schoolteacher…who taught me French history, gave me hope in the worst days…gave false papers to my mother and me so that we could flee a Gestapo-infested city…He and his gentle wife were not Resistance heroes, but if there is an average Frenchman, it was this man who was representative of his nation.[77]

Hoffmann's schoolteacher and his wife epitomize Varda's 2007 installation.

Paying attention to the gender politics of the Restoration stage in England, in "'No Woman Would Die Like That': *Stage Beauty* as Corrective-Counterpoint to *Othello*," Elizabeth Gruber discusses a possible "feminist intervention" to Shakespeare's play. The film *Stage Beauty* (Sir Richard Eyre, 2004) depicts the performance of *Othello* during the Restoration at a time when women were becoming actors in public theatrical productions. Previously the British theater had employed all-male casts, with men playing the roles of female characters. In *Stage Beauty*, an aspiring actress named Maria Hughes (Claire Danes), who is about to take over the part of Desdemona from male star Ned Kynaston[78] (Billy Crudup) insists that a woman "would not die" in the exaggeratedly passive way in which Ned had interpreted her character in the play's murder scene. Maria, in insisting that "no woman would die like that," thus corrects not only Ned's interpretation of the role of Desdemona, but also by extension, Shakespeare: according to Gruber, "if Ned's Desdemona exhibits pliancy or surrender...this is because he [Ned] adheres closely to the text of *Othello*, which does indicate the heroine's acquiescence to her murder" (233). Therefore Maria challenges both the theatrical conventions of her day and Shakespeare's play. Gruber demonstrates that Maria's insistence on playing Desdemona as a woman who resists her attacker and struggles against him rather than willingly yielding to the murderous assault, raises questions relevant to contemporary feminist film theories as well as "dislodges" (235) the masochistic aspect of Desdemona's acceptance of her tragic fate. According to Gruber, Maria confronts dominant scopic politics—then and now—when she demands that a woman not be represented as an idealized spectacle of eroticism and sadomasochism for the voyeuristic pleasure of the male spectator. In cinematic and theatrical productions today, female roles—while no longer played by men—are still nevertheless often influenced by patriarchal male fantasies.

Chen Kaige's 1993 film *Farewell my Concubine* addresses transvestism and gender performativity in classical Chinese opera in which male actors/singers played female roles. *Farewell my Concubine* investigates, among other topics, a psychological trauma, the drama that transgendering on stage might inflict upon the male actor impersonating a woman if he were to identify too closely with the character. For Judith Butler, gender is inherently performative:

> Gender ought not to be construed as a stable identity or locus of agency from which various acts follow; rather, gender is an identity tenuously constituted in time, instituted in an exterior space through a *stylized*

repetition of acts. The effect of gender is produced through the stylization of the body and, hence, must be understood as the mundane way in which bodily gestures, movements, and styles of various kinds constitute the illusion of an abiding gendered self.[79]

In her discussion of *Stage Beauty*, Gruber refers to Butler's theories of performativity and the fluid layerings of gender: "femininity is acutely stylized, emerging as a series of specific practices and gestures, a point that tends to corroborate the constructedness of gender roles" (232).

Although in *Stage Beauty* and *Farewell my Concubine*, gender interchangeability in stage productions involves men playing women's roles, there are notable theatrical exceptions such as *Peter Pan*, whose eponymous leading character was traditionally played by a woman (yet, as Gruber notes, a shift in gender has intervened, and men are now playing Peter Pan). Another cinematic reference to the interchangeability of gender—this time, involving women impersonating men and how it relates to postfeminism—occurs in Quentin Tarantino's *Death Proof* (chapter nine):

Marcy…impersonates the part of a fictional man named Barry. The embodiment of the male fantasy through the body of the otherwise utterly feminine Marcy has a double effect. First the female character taking on the attributes of a man evokes the interchangeability of gender, a postfeminist dimension of the film upon which its finale will be based. Thus, traits and characteristics typically associated with the male, including the bet and the will to prove oneself, but most conspicuously Marcy taking on the part of the fictitious 'Barry,' are embodied by female characters. (173)

The aestheticization/fetishization of the female corpse in *Othello* as it is performed in *Stage Beauty* is a prevalent trope not only in Shakespeare's day but is also a "central enigma" (233) of Western visual culture and literature according to Elisabeth Bronfen in *Over Her Dead Body: Death, Femininity and the Aesthetic* (1992). In this text, Bronfen considers how

femininity and death serve as western culture's privileged topoi and tropes for what is superlatively enigmatic…Owing to the prevalence of representations of beautiful dead women during this particular historical moment, my textual corpus begins with the mid-eighteenth century…and ends with contemporary texts.[80]

One exemplar of the artistic rendering of the dead woman as enigma is found in Marcel Duchamp's installation *Etant Donnés: 1˙ la Chute d'eau, 2˙ le gaz d'éclairage (Given: 1˙ The Waterfall, 2˙ The Illuminating Gas,* 1946-1966) exhibited at the Philadelphia Museum of Art since 1969. In this installation, the viewer looks through a small peephole in a wooden door at a bluish, naked, dead female body, spread-eagled towards the viewer, thus inviting the voyeuristic gaze. Jean-Michel Rabaté in *Given: 1˙ Art, 2˙ Crime: Modernity, Murder and Mass Culture* (2007) extensively discusses this installation, claiming that with it, "Duchamp forces spectators to come to terms with a calculated sense of voyeurism."[81] Another exemplary moment of necrophilic voyeurism in cinema is found in Hitchcock's *Vertigo*; according to P. Adams Sitney, the "limp and defenseless body" of Madeleine Elster/Judy Barton (Kim Novak) arouses a "necrophilic passion" in the male protagonist (James Stewart).[82] The connections drawn between voyeurism and necrophilia examined by Bronfen, Rabaté and Sitney, are also evidenced in Shakespeare's *Othello*, which "arguably dabbles in necrophilia, in its presentation of Desdemona's murder" (227). Othello's menacing words, "I will kill thee/And love thee after,"[83] reveal the morbid limitlessness of unbridled patriarchal empowerment.

Feminist film theorists' struggle against patriarchal representations of women on screen is reminiscent of that of Maria in *Stage Beauty* when she challenges the interpretation of Desdemona by a male actor. Maria's stance was radical in her day and still is in the 21st century, since we are not yet "'beyond the gaze'"[84] (in E. Ann Kaplan's words). Feminist film theorists wonder—as Maria did—why women are so often portrayed as masochistic, passive victims and how this portrayal can be corrected (see the next chapter). Gruber argues that Maria's attempts to correct Desdemona's representation—to "recast erotic politics" (235) and move away from depicting women as incompetent, incapable of agency and/or self-determination—are still valid. This remains a contemporary object of inquiry for feminist theorists, female filmmakers and the sociologist Pierre Bourdieu, among others.

In "Dis-Abling the Sadistic Gaze and Deaf Prostitutes in Aleksei Balabanov's *Of Freaks and Men* and Valerii Todorovskii's *Land of the Deaf*" (both 1998), Izabela Kalinowska considers two post-Soviet Russian films that "foreground looking at women" (240). The depiction of female characters in these films is significant since it bridges the gap between older Soviet and current Russian cinema:

In previous epochs, Soviet cinema's portrayal of women provided an indication of changing ideological and aesthetic styles...The female body presents one of the surface manifestations of the search for a new aesthetics that is quite apparent in recent Russian cinema as well. (240-246)

Preoccupation with the female body as surface is shared with Western postfeminist cinema (chapter nine). Most of the female protagonists in these two films are physically challenged. In *Of Freaks and Men*, there are at least three disabled characters: a blind mother and her adopted Siamese twins; in *Land of the Deaf*, there are two: a hearing-impaired stripper/prostitute and another female character who loses her hearing after gunfire detonation.[85] These disabilities add to the two women's marginalization/estrangement from Russian society at a time when "old ideas were being reevaluated and new ideas were forged amidst the ongoing search for a new aesthetic" (240). According to Kalinowska, Balabanov's film contends that "cinema begins…as a calculated appeal to voyeuristic desire" (241) and that the cinematic medium itself is but a pretext for male scopophilic gratification, since any representation of women in photography or in film is presumed to enhance erotic feeling in the heterosexual male spectator. Can Hitchcock's films be viewed as proceeding along similar lines? P. Adams Sitney states:

> Some of Hitchcock's films even imply that filmgoing and filmmaking themselves arise from a propensity to sin—to see and identify with acts of sex and violence, at the price of moral blindness. Hitchcock seems to have considered sinful the fundamental voyeurism driving both the desire to see films and the desire to make them. While his films often provide occasions to indulge violent fantasies and imagine erotic scenarios, they question the moral consequences of such indulgence.[86]

The "moral blindness" to which Sitney refers is literally and metaphorically evidenced in Balabanov's *Of Freaks and Men*, as it is embodied by the moral and sexual corruption of the blind woman through her encounter with a Western filmmaker who objectifies her in his home-made pornographic films, in which she stars: "the blindness of Dr. Stasov's wife serves as an external sign of her flawed character. She is not only physically, but also spiritually crippled: …she is…drawn onto a path that destroys her as well as her entire family" (252).

For Kalinowska, in spite of Balabanov's ambition to trace the history of Russian cinema, the film's "political message bears witness [only] to contemporary Russia" (241). Not only men, but women, too, are corrupted/corruptible through the viewing of obscene images. Kalinowska discusses the film's overdetermination through the "checkered past" of the

Western filmmaker/pornographer, Yohan (Sergei Makovetskii), who has come to Russia from abroad with his filmic equipment in a mysterious suitcase: "the poison that spread from Yohan's checkered suitcase... thoroughly contaminated Russia's 'innocents'" (243). Moreover, Yohan's assistant, Victor Ivanovich (Viktor Sukhorukov), his protégé, is also "dressed in checkers from head to toe" (241).

These two photographers soon take, reproduce and disseminate images of females

> in poses [conveying] strong sadomasochistic overtones such as women with exposed buttocks who are subjected to a thrashing...the entire world within Balabanov's film becomes corrupted by pornographic images of women. (241-243)

For Balabanov, woman is certainly, in Lacan's words, "the symptom of man." These misogynistic views are further expressed since the female is ontologically viewed as "the epicenter of a brewing disaster" (241). Balabanov's portrayal of the depravity of the male gaze upon the objectified female subject recalls and even surpasses Mulvey's binary of the gaze: "Balabanov exposes the relations of power present in gendered looking in a manner akin to second-wave feminism" (242). He denounces cinema as a medium for "illicit pornographic" (241) trade.

In Russia, the cinematic medium—from Sergei Eisenstein and Dziga Vertov to the present—has been used for the dissemination of political ideologies. Contemporary Russian narrative film and documentary might still be a template for propaganda while simultaneously seeking a new aesthetic. Eliot Borenstein, cited by Kalinowska, writes:

> On a scale surpassing both the libertinism of the *fin-de-siècle* 'boulevard' and the eroticized battlefield of the Russian Civil War and New Economic Policy, Russian culture in all its manifestations would appear to have become thoroughly and overtly sexualized...Many voices have spoken against the sexual saturation of Russian popular culture. One man's utopia is another's apocalypse, and the numerous critiques of sexual 'excess' suggest that it is only a small step from scatology to eschatology. [87]

In *Of Freaks and Men*, the Russian people's enthusiasm for everything Western is symbolized by a young woman named Liza (Dinara Drukarova), who longingly looks at trains leaving a railroad station. She wishes that she, too, could leave Russia and go West, although she has been warned against it. In the film's moral universe, her focus on the West is depicted through her excitement over pornography, which leads to her downfall and consequently to her father Radlov's (Igor Shibanov) death:

upon discovering sexually explicit photos in his daughter's possession, the unfortunate father drops dead. In *Of Freaks and Men*, the sustained suspicion of the West as embodied by its cinematic culture reappears in the entrenched politico-historical paradox of Russian society.

Kalinowska draws upon disability theory since both films "place the figure of a crippled woman at their centers" (252) and she discusses how a hearing impaired female named Yaya (Dina Korzun) constructs her own sense of self in relation to deafness:[88]

> Yaya's loss of hearing results from the abuse she suffered as a child. But female bodies in Todorovskii's film no longer 'document their owners' suffering and degradation.'[89] Instead, Yaya views herself as different rather than crippled. (252)

In demonstrating that Yaya fashions her identity independently from her gender and disability, *Land of the Deaf* represents "a move away from determined models of femininity and cultural iconography sanctioned by the dominant culture towards a female rediscovery of the self" (249).

Sharon Lubkemann Allen's final essay of this volume stresses Chantal Akerman's treatment of "the commonplaces of exile, emigration, diaspora, and nomadism" (270) along with states of exilic displacement and linguistic discontinuity—the whole paraphernalia of "postmodern homelessness" (273). According to Gilles Deleuze,

> Since the new wave, every time there was a fine and powerful film, there was a new exploration of the body in it. Starting with *Jeanne Dielman*, Chantal Akerman wants to show 'gestures in their fullness.' Enclosed in the bedroom, the heroine of *Je Tu Il Elle* links involutive refuge- and infantile postures in a mode which is that of waiting, counting the days: a ceremony of anorexia. Chantal Akerman's novelty lies in showing in this way bodily attitudes as the sign of states of body particular to the female character, whilst the men speak for society, the environment, the part which is their due, the piece of history which they bring with them, (*Anna's Rendezvous*). But the chain of states of female body is *not* closed: descending from the mother or going back to the mother, it serves as a revelation to men, who now talk about themselves, and on a deeper level to the environment, which now makes itself seen or heard only through the window of a room, or a train, a whole art of sound. In the same place or in space, a woman's body achieves a strange nomadism which makes it cross ages, situations, and places (this was Virginia Woolf's secret in literature).[90]

The title and thematics of *Demain on déménage* (*Tomorrow We Move*, 2004), attests to the instability of the female characters' domestic set-up anchored in Buñuelesque frustration: "both a mother's and an artist's everyday feature constantly in Akerman's films. Indeed, the desire to extricate the artist's quotidian from the mother's banality is one of the impelling forces in Akerman's dry transmutation of daily life."[91]

Akerman's films show women in their everydayness, which "transgenders the camera, as it were, through its redirected and formally redefined focus on women's [daily] existence" (258). For example, in *Jeanne Dielman*, Akerman recontextualizes the prostitute's trade as the eponymous Jeanne (Delphine Seyrig, acclaimed actress of the nouvelle vague) is shown in her kitchen, slicing potatoes, among other menial tasks. The potato chore is recuperated in Claire Denis' *Beau travail* (*Good Work*, 1999), in which men are shown peeling potatoes with great concentration. Van Gogh's 1885 painting *The Potato Eaters* launched the tuber into the art world. For Akerman, the filmed potato becomes a gesture that ricochets intertextually in Denis' transgendered gest. According to B. Ruby Rich,

> *Jeanne Dielman*...is the first film to scrutinize housework in a language appropriate to the activity itself...Nearly devoid of dialogue, the film charts Jeanne Dielman's breakdown via a minute observation of her performance of household routines...until...she permanently disrupts the patriarchal order by murdering her third client.[92]

For Jean-Michel Rabaté, "the grinding repetition of daily activities highlighted how tenuous Jeanne Dielman's control over her life was, while suggesting something like a feminist *Waiting for Godot*, with the difference that the final twist turned to sudden horror" (see the preface of *Situating the Feminist Gaze and Spectatorship in Postwar Cinema*, xi). The representation of housework as drudgery infuses Akerman's cinema, from her earliest work, *Saute ma ville* (1968), filmed when she was eighteen, in which

> brushes, spaghetti, water and soap dance animistically with Akerman...*Saute ma ville* presents, in swift succession—as if they all pertained to the same order of events—cleaning, cooking, and committing suicide...enhancing these actions' paradoxical equivalence.[93]

For Janet Bergstrom, housework through these

> dislocated activities is the despairing prelude to [a] suicide...A sound-image carried over from this scene opens the film *Jeanne Dielman*: before the names appear in the credits, the loud sound of a jet of gas can be heard, a noise repeated every time Jeanne turns on the stove,[94]

thus threading an umbilical cord between *Jeanne Dielman* and *Saute ma ville*, which challenges the heterogeneity ruling each work. Housework as chore is scripted at the inception of *Jeanne Dielman* while the title and credits are rolling, thus epitomizing the female director's gaze in the apparatus (see Noëlle Rouxel-Cubberly's discussion of the displacement of credits and titles in films created by women, chapter five). The explosion of sound from *Saute ma ville* carried over to the opening of *Jeanne Dielman*'s credits makes the two films interact retroactively and sequentially. The disjunction between sound and image fragments the diegesis, emphasizing the nomadism and transportability of the heterogeneous female body. It is as if *Jeanne Dielman* were rewritten on a palimpsest, a re-edition, an expansion and correction of the adolescent vision in *Saute ma ville*, progressing from suicide—which psychoanalysis interprets as a would-be murder of another—to the actual murder of the Other. In the second edition of Akerman's narrative, the criminal act moves outward, from introversion to extroversion, from murder of the self to murder of the other. For Ivone Margulies, "*Saute ma ville* announces literally with a bang Akerman's entry into artistic adulthood."[95] She adds: "it is well known that suicide is a favorite subject of adolescents' first films."[96] Margulies's comment also applies to Sofia Coppola's first feature-length film, *The Virgin Suicides*, in which five sisters commit suicide (chapter eight).

One cannot ignore Akerman's engagement with time and the "marginalized" (often female) subject's relationship to the quotidian as well as the dance with history and estrangement from patriarchal authority: "more than a depiction of historical events, everyday time can register these historical traces of women's lives, of exiles' and illegal immigrants' lives, of all sorts of lives on cultural margins" (276), which recalls Agnès Varda (chapter eleven).

Akerman's "transhistorical" (266) work, according to Allen, is exemplified by *Sud* (*South*, 1999), one of her "documentaries on racial and ethnic discrimination,"[97] such as *D'Est* (*From the East*, 1993) and *De l'autre côté* (*From the Other Side*, 2002). In *Sud*, Akerman approaches the southern United States, placing its history of racial violence in dialogue with European genocide and current racism:

> Akerman attests that as she registers racial divides in the American South, she is both recalling Stalin's purges and the Holocaust as well as speaking to contemporary racism in Europe…Akerman notes not only literary subtexts (Faulkner and Baldwin) for her representation of the American South, but also transcultural and transhistorical connections to cultures and violent practices of exclusion…Lingering on solitary trees at crossroads,

her camera seeks to remind us of a history of lynching in the South. (273; 266)

In this respect, "Akerman's project seems to be precisely to re-member the past in the present and the present in relation to the past" (277) and she "concerns herself with the 'performative nature of the human body and the nomadic constitution of female identity'…'enmeshed' in the present" (261-262).

Akerman's films are steeped in silence and incommunicability between characters, performers and spectators: "one of the central concerns and strategies of [her] cinema is silence" (269). In her ten minute silent film *La Chambre* (1972), where a female character in bed—Chantal Akerman herself—gazes at the cinematic apparatus, the "camera surveys a small apartment in a continuous circular motion."[98] When the camera focuses on her, she repeats the same motion, rocking back and forth. Samuel Beckett's minimalist one-woman play-poem *Rockaby* (1980) uncannily recalls Akerman's *La Chambre*.

La Captive (2000), "traversing Proust's ample understanding of the insufficiencies of the quotidian to animate desire…renews Akerman's investment in obsession as a dynamic force."[99] With *La Captive*, Akerman revisits suicide, but unlike in *Saute ma ville*, where the unnamed female character is in a manic phase, in *La Captive*, Arianne (Sylvie Testud) commits suicide while in an apparent depressive phase. The insecure Arianne, quietly staggering under the carceral gaze of an obsessive male, Simon (Stanislas Merhar), finally manages to free herself and escape her panoptical surroundings, abandoning her captor Simon, and disappearing from the screen,[100] thus paradoxically confirming Deleuze's statement that Akerman's films "develop a female gest which overcomes the history of men and the crisis of the world."[101]

Works Cited

Akerman, Chantal. "Chantal Akerman on *Jeanne Dielman*." *Camera Obscura*, no. 2 (1977): 118-19. Quoted in Teresa de Lauretis, "Rethinking Women's Cinema: Aesthetics and Feminist Theory." In *Issues in Feminist Film Criticism*, edited by Patricia Erens, 288-308. Bloomington and Indianapolis: Indiana University Press, 1990.

Andrew, Dudley. "On Certain Tendencies of the French Cinema." In *A New History of French Literature*, edited by Denis Hollier, 993-1000. Cambridge: Harvard University Press, 1989, 1994.

Armel, Aliette. "Dossier Marguerite Duras et interview de l'écrivain." *Magazine Littéraire* 278 (1990): 16-59.

Armstrong, Carol. "Pink." In "Fates and Futures of Feminism," eds. Johanna Burton and Suzanne Hudson. Special Issue, *Critical Matrix: The Princeton Journal of Women, Gender and Culture*, vol. 16 (Fall 2007): 18-25.

Bajomée, Danielle. "Veiller sur le sens absent." *Magazine Littéraire* 278 (1990): 32-34.

Bergstrom, Janet. "The Innovators 1970-1980: Keeping a distance." *Sight and Sound: The International Film Magazine* (November 1999). http://www.bfi.org.uk/sightandsound/feature/196/.

Borenstein, Eliot. "About That: Deploying and Deploring Sex in Postsoviet Russia." *STCL* 24 no. 1 (Winter 2000): 51-83.

Bronfen, Elisabeth. *Over Her Dead Body: Death, Femininity and The Aesthetic*. Manchester: Manchester University Press, 1992.

Butler, Judith. *Gender Trouble: Feminism and the Subversion of Identity*. London: Routledge, 1990.

Chion, Michel. "The Impossible Embodiment." In *Everything You Always Wanted to Know about Lacan (But Were Afraid to Ask Hitchcock)*, edited by Slavoj Žižek, 195-207. London: Verso, 1992.

Clover, Carol J. *Men, Women and Chainsaws: Gender in the Modern Horror Film*. Princeton, NJ: Princeton University Press, 1992.

Conley, Tom. *Film Hieroglyphics: Ruptures in Classical Cinema*. Minneapolis: University of Minnesota Press, 2006.

Deleuze, Gilles. *Cinéma 1: L'Image-Mouvement*. Paris: Les Editions de Minuit, 1983.

—. *Cinema 2: The Time-Image*. Translated by Hugh Tomlinson and Robert Galeta. Minneapolis: University of Minnesota Press, 1989.

Doane, Mary Ann. "Film and the Masquerade: Theorizing the Female Spectator." In *Issues in Feminist Film Criticism*, edited by Patricia Erens, 41-57. Bloomington and Indianapolis: Indiana University Press, 1990.

Duras, Marguerite. *Hiroshima mon amour*. Translated by Richard Seaver. New York: Grove Press, 1981.

Erens, Patricia, ed. *Issues in Feminist Film Criticism*. Bloomington and Indianapolis: Indiana University Press, 1990.

Evans, Martha Noël. *Masks of Tradition*. Ithaca: Cornell University Press, 1987.

Felman, Shoshana. "Lacan's Psychoanalysis, or The Figure in the Screen." *October* vol. 45 (Summer 1988): 97-108.

"Feminism in France since 1970." *Contemporary France Online* (3/20/2002). http://www.well.ac.uk/cfol/feminism.asp (accessed September 18, 2008).

Flitterman-Lewis, Sandy. *To Desire Differently: Feminism and the French Cinema.* New York: Columbia University Press, 1996.

Foucault, Michel. *Surveiller et punir: Naissance de la prison.* Paris: Gallimard, 1975.

Gaines, Jane. "White Privilege and Looking Relations: Race and Gender in Feminist Film Theory." In *Issues in Feminist Film Criticism*, edited by Patricia Erens, 197-215. Bloomington and Indianapolis: Indiana Univ. Press, 1990.

Goscilo, Helena. *Dehexing Sex. Russian Womanhood During and After Glasnost.* Ann Arbor: University of Michigan Press, 1996.

Hodgdon, Barbara. *The Shakespeare Trade: Performances and Appropriations.* Philadelphia: University of Pennsylvania Press, 1998.

Higonnet, Patrice. *Paris: Capital of the World.* Translated by Arthur Goldhammer. Cambridge, MA and London: Harvard University Press, 2002.

Hoffmann, Stanley. "On *The Sorrow and the Pity*." *Commentarymagazine.com*, September 1972, http://www.commentarymagazine.com/viewarticle.cfm/on--the-sorrow-and-the-pity--5118.

Kaplan, E. Ann. "Global Feminisms and the State of Feminist Film Theory." In "Beyond the Gaze: Recent Approaches to Film Feminisms," eds. Kathleen McHugh and Vivian Sobchack. Special issue, *Signs: Journal of Women in Culture and Society* 30, no. 1 (2004): 1236-1248.

—. "Is the Gaze Male?" In *Powers of Desire: The Politics of Sexuality*, edited by Ann Barr Snitow, Christine Stansell, Sharon Thompson, 309-326. New York: Monthly Review Press, 1983.

Kuhn, Annette. "Textual Politics." In *Issues in Feminist Film Criticism*, edited by Patricia Erens, 250-267. Bloomington and Indianapolis: Indiana University Press, 1990.

—. "The Body and Cinema: Some Problems for Feminism." In *Feminisms*, edited by Sandra Kemp and Judith Squires, 403-409. Oxford and New York: Oxford University Press, 1997.

Kristeva, Julia. *Black Sun: Depression and Melancholia.* Translated by Léon Roudiez. New York: Columbia University Press, 1982.

Lapsley, Robert and Michael Westlake. *Film Theory: An Introduction.* Manchester and New York: Manchester University Press, 1998, 2006.

Lauretis, Teresa de. "Rethinking Women's Cinema: Aesthetics and Feminist Theory." In *Issues in Feminist Film Criticism*, edited by Patricia Erens, 288-308. Bloomington and Indianapolis: Indiana University Press, 1990.

Lyotard, Jean-François. *The Postmodern Condition*. Minneapolis: University of Minnesota Press, 1984.

Margulies, Ivone. "La Chambre Akerman: The Captive as Creator." *Rouge* (December 2006). http://www.rouge.com.au/10/akerman.html.

Modleski, Tania. "Hitchcock, Feminism, and the Patriarchal Unconscious." In *Issues in Feminist Film Criticism*, edited by Patricia Erens, 58-74. Bloomington and Indianapolis: Indiana University Press, 1990.

Mulvey, Laura. "Afterthoughts on 'Visual Pleasure and Narrative Cinema' Inspired by *Duel in the Sun*." In *Feminism and Film Theory*, edited by Constance Penley, 57-79. New York: Routledge, 1996.

—. "Visual Pleasure and Narrative Cinema." In *Feminism and Film Theory*, edited by Constance Penley. New York: Routledge, 1996.

—. "Visual Pleasure and Narrative Cinema." In *Issues in Feminist Film Criticism*, edited by Patricia Erens, 28-40. Bloomington and Indianapolis: Indiana University Press, 1990.

Queneau, Raymond. *Bâtons, chiffres et lettres*. Paris: Gallimard, 1950.

Rabaté, Jean-Michel. *Given: 1˙ Art, 2˙ Crime: Modernity, Murder and Mass Culture*. Brighton: Sussex Academic Press, 2007.

—. *James Joyce: Authorized Reader*. Baltimore and London: The Johns Hopkins University Press, 1991.

Rich, B. Ruby. "In the Name of Feminist Film Criticism." In *Issues in Feminist Film Criticism*, edited by Patricia Erens, 267-287. Bloomington and Indianapolis: Indiana University Press, 1990.

Riviere, Joan. "Womanliness as Masquerade." In *Formations of Fantasy*, edited by Victor Burgin, James Donald, and Cora Kaplan, 35-44. London: Methuen, 1986.

Ronell, Avital. "Haunted by Metaphysics." In *Thirteen Alumni Artists*, edited by Emmie Donadio, 15-22. Middlebury, VT: Middlebury College Museum of Art, 2000.

—. "TraumaTV: 12 Steps Beyond the Pleasure Principle." In *The ÜberReader: Selected Works of Avital Ronell*, edited by Diane Davis, 63-88. Urbana and Chicago: University of Illinois Press, 2008.

Seacroft, Sheila. Review of *Nathalie...* by Anne Fontaine. *Flotation Suite* (December 14, 2004). http://www.floatationsuite.com/index.php?option=com_content&task=view&id=162&Itemid=45.

Shakespeare, William. *Othello. The Riverside Shakespeare*. Edited by G. Blakemore Evans. Boston: Houghton Mifflin, 1997.

Sitney, P. Adams. "'Let Me Go Into the Church Alone': The Roman Catholic Subtext of *Vertigo*." In *The Hidden God: Film and Faith*, edited by Mary Lea Bandy and Antonio Monda, 249-259. New York: Museum of Modern Art, 2003.

Suleiman, Susan Rubin. "(Re)Writing the Body: The Politics and Poetics of Female Eroticism." In "The Female Body in Western Culture: Semiotic Perspectives," ed. Susan Rubin Suleiman. Special issue, *Poetics Today* 6, no. 1/2 (1985): 43-65.

Tasker, Yvonne and Diane Negra, eds. *Interrogating Postfeminism: Gender and the Politics of Popular Culture*. Durham and London: Duke University Press, 2007.

—. Introduction. "In Focus: Postfeminism and Contemporary Media Studies." *Cinema Journal* 44, no. 2 (Winter 2005): 107-110.

Thornham, Sue, ed. *Feminist Film Theory: A Reader*. New York: New York University Press, 1999.

Vertov, Dziga. *Kino-Eye: The Writings of Dziga Vertov*. Edited by Annette Michelson. Translated by Kevin O'Brien. Berkeley, CA: University of California Press, 1984.

Žižek, Slavoj. *Enjoy Your Symptom! Jacques Lacan in Hollywood and Out*. London: Routledge Classics, 2008.

—. ed. *Everything You Always Wanted to Know about Lacan (But Were Afraid to Ask Hitchcock)*. London: Verso, 1992.

Notes

[1] Gilles Deleuze in *Cinema 2: The Time-Image*, trans. Hugh Tomlinson and Robert Galeta (Minneapolis: University of Minnesota Press, 1989), asks: "Why is the Second World War taken as a break? The fact is that, in Europe, the post-war period has greatly increased the situations which we no longer know how to react to, in spaces which we no longer know how to describe. These were 'any spaces whatever'…Situations could be extremes, or, on the contrary, those of everyday banality, or both at once: what tends to collapse, or at least lose its position, is the sensory-motor schema which constituted the action-image of the old cinema…the relations and disjunctions between visual and sound, between what is seen and what is said, revitalize the problem and endow cinema with new powers for capturing time in the image" (xi-xiii). Of the aftermath of World War II, Julia Kristeva in *Black Sun: Depression and Melancholia*, trans. Léon Roudiez (New York: Columbia University Press, 1982), writes that "a tremendous crisis of thought and speech, a crisis of representation, has indeed emerged; one may look for analogues in past centuries…or for its causes in economic, political, and

juridical bankruptcies. Nonetheless, never has the power of destructive forces appeared as unquestionable and unavoidable as now, within and without society and the individual...While political and military cataclysms are dreadful and challenge the mind through the monstrosity of their violence (that of a concentration camp or of an atomic bomb), the shattering of psychic identity, whose intensity is no less violent, remains hard to perceive...one of the major stakes of literature and art is henceforth located in that invisibility of the crisis affecting the identity of persons, morals, religion or politics...Such a new apocalyptic rhetoric was carried out in two seemingly opposite, extreme fashions that complement each other: a wealth of images and a holding back of words. On the one hand, the art of imagery excels in the raw display of monstrosity. Films remain the supreme art of the apocalypse, no matter what the refinements, because the image has such an ability to 'have us walk in fear,' as Augustine had already seen...within this image/words dichotomy, it falls to films to spread out the coarseness of horror or the external outlines of pleasure, while the literature becomes internalized and withdraws from the world in the wake of the crisis in thought" (221-224).

[2] According Yvonne Tasker and Diane Negra in their edited volume *Interrogating Postfeminism: Gender and the Politics of Popular Culture* (Durham and London: Duke University Press, 2007), 1: "postfeminism broadly encompasses a set of assumptions, widely disseminated within popular media forms, having to do with the 'pastness' of feminism, whether that supposed pastness is merely noted, mourned or celebrated. Crucially for us, postfeminism suggests a more complex relationship between culture, politics and feminism than the more familiar framing concept of 'backlash' allows." For further discussion of the definition of postfeminism, see the essays by Amy Woodworth and Jeremi Szaniawski in this volume's third section, "Postfeminist Interventions."

[3] Laura Mulvey, "Visual Pleasure and Narrative Cinema" in *Issues in Feminist Film Criticism*, ed. Patricia Erens (Bloomington and Indianapolis: Indiana University Press, 1990), 33-34, 38-39. Mulvey's essay was originally published in *Screen* 16 (3): 6–18.

[4] P. Adams Sitney, "'Let Me Go Into the Church Alone': The Roman Catholic Subtext of *Vertigo*," in *The Hidden God: Film and Faith*, eds. Mary Lea Bandy and Antonio Monda (New York: Museum of Modern Art, 2003), 253.

[5] Patricia Erens, ed., *Issues in Feminist Film Criticism* (Bloomington and Indianapolis: Indiana Univ. Press, 1990), 3.

[6] Originally published in *Framework* 15-16-17 (Summer 1981): 12-15.

[7] Laura Mulvey, "Afterthoughts on 'Visual Pleasure and Narrative Cinema Inspired by King Vidor's *Duel in the Sun*" and "Visual Pleasure and Narrative Cinema" in *Feminism and Film Theory*, ed. Constance Penley (New York: Routledge, 1996), 57-79.

[8] Jane Gaines, "White Privilege and Looking Relations: Race and Gender in Feminist Film Theory," in *Issues in Feminist Film Criticism*, ed. Patricia Erens, (Bloomington and Indianapolis: Indiana Univ. Press, 1990), 210.

[9] Susan Rubin Suleiman, "(Re)Writing the Body: The Politics and Poetics of Female Eroticism," in "The Female Body in Western Culture: Semiotic Perspectives," ed. Susan Rubin Suleiman, special issue, *Poetics Today* 6, no. 1/2 (1985): 52.

[10] E. Ann Kaplan, "Is the Gaze Male?" in Ann Barr Snitow, Christine Stansell, Sharon Thompson, eds., *Powers of Desire: The Politics of Sexuality* (New York: Monthly Review Press, 1983), 312-313.

[11] E. Ann Kaplan, "Global Feminisms and the State of Feminist Film Theory," in "Beyond the Gaze: Recent Approaches to Film Feminisms," ed. Kathleen McHugh and Vivian Sobchack, special issue, *Signs: Journal of Women in Culture and Society* 30, no. 1 (2004): 1244.

[12] Janet Bergstrom, "The Innovators 1970-1980: Keeping a distance," *Sight and Sound*, November 1999: http://www.bfi.org.uk/sightandsound/feature/196/.

[13] E. Ann Kaplan, "Is the Gaze Male?" 323.

[14] Avital Ronell, "Haunted by Metaphysics," in *Thirteen Alumni Artists*, ed. Emmie Donadio (Middlebury, VT: Middlebury College Museum of Art, 2000), 21.

[15] Judith Butler, *Gender Trouble: Feminism and the Subversion of Identity* (London: Routledge, 1990), 33.

[16] Slavoj Žižek, new preface to *Enjoy Your Symptom! Jacques Lacan in Hollywood and Out* (London: Routledge Classics, 2008), xiii.

[17] Gilles Deleuze questions the cliché about the cliché: "Where is the end of the cliché, and where is the beginning of the image? [...] if images have become clichés (clichéd) inside as well as outside, how can we extract an image from all of these clichés, 'just an image'? What is an image that will not be a cliché?" Gilles Deleuze, *Cinéma 1: L'Image-Mouvement* (Les Editions de Minuit, 1983), 298 (translation mine).

[18] Sheila Seacroft, review of *Nathalie...* by Anne Fontaine, *Flotation Suite* (December 14, 2004), http://www.floatationsuite.com/index.php?option=com_content&task=view&id=162&Itemid=45.

[19] Laura Mulvey, "Visual Pleasure and Narrative Cinema," in *Narrative, Apparatus, Ideology*, ed. Philip Rosen (New York: Columbia University Press, 1986), 200.

[20] E. Ann Kaplan, "Is the Gaze Male?" 312.

[21] Sandy Flitterman-Lewis, *To Desire Differently: Feminism and the French Cinema* (New York: Columbia University Press, 1996), 22-23.

[22] Dziga Vertov, *Kino-Eye: The Writings of Dziga Vertov*, ed. Annette Michelson, trans. Kevin O'Brien (Berkeley, CA: University of California Press, 1984), 16, 41.

[23] Ibid., 49.

[24] Gilles Deleuze, *Cinema 2: The Time-Image*, trans. Hugh Tomlinson and Robert Galeta (Minneapolis: University of Minnesota Press, 1989), 205.

[25] Mary Ann Doane, "Film and the Masquerade: Theorizing the Female Spectator" in *Issues in Feminist Film Criticism*, ed. Patricia Erens (Bloomington and Indianapolis: Indiana University Press, 1990), 50.

[26] E. Ann Kaplan, "Is the Gaze Male?" 312.

[27] Deleuze, *Cinema 2: The Time-Image*, 206.

[28] Avital Ronell, "TraumaTV: 12 Steps Beyond the Pleasure Principle," in *The ÜberReader: Selected Works of Avital Ronell*, ed. Diane Davis (Urbana and Chicago: University of Illinois Press, 2008), 79.

[29] Shoshana Felman, "Lacan's Psychoanalysis, or The Figure in the Screen," *October* vol. 45 (Summer, 1988): 97.

[30] Deleuze, *Cinema 2: The Time-Image*, xiii.

[31] Tania Modleski, "Hitchcock, Feminism, and the Patriarchal Unconscious," in *Issues in Feminist Film Criticism*, ed. Patricia Erens (Bloomington and Indianapolis: Indiana University Press, 1990), 62.

[32] According to Sitney, "in the last third of the film, he [Scottie] becomes the object of our gaze—although Hitchcock does not quite effect the reciprocal shift of identification with Judy" (255).

[33] Žižek, *Enjoy Your Symptom!* 228.

[34] Robert Lapsley and Michael Westlake, *Film Theory: An Introduction* (Manchester and New York: Manchester University Press, 1998, 2006), 243.

[35] Gilles Deleuze, *Cinéma 1: L'Image-Mouvement*, 289.

[36] Annette Kuhn, "Textual Politics," in *Issues in Feminist Film Criticism*, ed. Patricia Erens (Bloomington and Indianapolis: Indiana University Press, 1990), 258.

[37] Ibid., 258-259.

[38] Laura Mulvey, "Visual Pleasure and Narrative Cinema," 29.

[39] Raymond Queneau, *Bâtons, chiffres et lettres* (Paris: Gallimard, 1950), 129.

[40] Judy Stone, "'Chocolat': Bittersweet Memoir of Colonial Africa," *San Francisco Chronicle*, April 21, 1989, 47.

[41] For Montaigne, in his 19th essay, "Que Philosopher, c'est apprendre à mourir" ("That to Philosophize is to Learn how to Die") every fear is fundamentally a fear of death, and if we can control that, we would not be afraid of anything else.

[42] Jean-Michel Rabaté, *Given: 1˙ Art, 2˙ Crime: Modernity, Murder and Mass Culture* (Brighton: Sussex Academic Press, 2007), 111.

[43] Žižek, *Enjoy Your Symptom!* 209.

[44] Ibid.

[45] Deleuze, *Cinéma 1: L'Image-Mouvement*, 79 (translation mine).

[46] Ibid., 120 (translation mine).

[47] Jean-Michel Rabaté, *James Joyce: Authorized Reader* (Baltimore and London: The Johns Hopkins University Press, 1991), 20-21.

[48] Rabaté, *Given*, 111.

[49] Carol Armstrong, "Pink," in "Fates and Futures of Feminism," eds. Johanna Burton and Suzanne Hudson, special issue, *Critical Matrix: The Princeton Journal of Women, Gender and Culture*, vol. 16 (Fall 2007): 18.

[50] According to Felman, "for there is another aspect that the seminar and television have in common: both are spectacles in which Lacan feels watched by, and exposed to, the crowd's gaze" (Felman: 100).

[51] See Michel Foucault, *Surveiller et punir: Naissance de la prison* (Paris: Gallimard, 1975) for a discussion of the possible roots of the Panopticon in Versailles, in particular Le Vaux's menagerie.

[52] The concept of femininity as masquerade was first theorized by Joan Riviere in her article "Womanliness as Masquerade," now anthologized in *Formations of Fantasy*, eds. Victor Burgin, James Donald, and Cora Kaplan (London: Methuen, 1986). As a psychoanalyst, Riviere discovered this mechanism of masquerade while studying intellectual or authoritative women. According to Riviere, femininity is a mask that can be put on and taken off, and women typically wear it as a defense mechanism when they have usurped "too much" masculine cultural power. For more on the masquerade as used in feminist film criticism, see Mary Ann Doane's "Film and the Masquerade: Theorizing the Female Spectator" in *Feminist Film Theory: A Reader*, ed. Sue Thornham (New York: New York University Press, 1999).

[53] Carol J. Clover, *Men, Women and Chainsaws: Gender in the Modern Horror Film* (Princeton, NJ: Princeton University Press, 1992), 9.

[54] Ibid., 15.

[55] Rabaté, *Given*, 111.

[56] Julia Kristeva, *Black Sun: Depression and Melancholia*, trans. Léon Roudiez (New York: Columbia University Press, 1982), 242.

[57] Dudley Andrew, "On Certain Tendencies of the French Cinema," in *A New History of French Literature*, ed. Denis Hollier (Cambridge: Harvard University Press, 1989, 1994), 999.

[58] Deleuze, *Cinema 2: The Time-Image*, xi, 257-258.

[59] Danielle Bajomée, "Veiller sur le sens absent," *Magazine Littéraire* 278 (1990): 32.

[60] For a comprehensive history of the history of French Indochina, see Daniel Hémery, "Indochina During the Age of Extremes: Protests and Revolutions (19th-20th centuries)," trans. Marcelline Block, in Immanuel Ness, ed., *The International Encyclopedia of Revolution and Protest, 1500-the Present* (Boston : Blackwell Synergy, 2009).

[61] See "The Time is Out of Joint: Temporal Deconstruction in *Hiroshima Mon Amour*" (unpublished paper) by contemporary filmmaker Julia Kots. Kots's unpublished essay on Rainer Werner Fassbinder, "The Rebuilding of Germany: Space and Architecture in *The Marriage of Maria Braun*," examines the rise and fall of a young woman in post-World War II Germany.

[62] Kristeva, 221.

[63] Ibid., 227.

[64] Duras, cited in Deleuze, *Cinema 2: The Time-Image*, 251.

[65] Deleuze, *Cinema 2: The Time-Image*, 258.

[66] Duras, cited by Arliette Armel, "Dossier Marguerite Duras et interview de l'écrivain," *Magazine Littéraire* 278 (1990): 31.

[67] Jane McLelland, review of *Détruire la peinture* by Louis Marin, *Modern Language Notes* 95, no. 4 (May 1980): 1114.

[68] Patrice Higonnet, *Paris: Capital of the World*, trans. Arthur Goldhammer (Cambridge and London: Harvard University Press, 2002), 158

[69] Ibid., 159. According to Higonnet, "Some Paris monuments must therefore be counted as relative failures because they are too intimately intertwined with a particular ideology rather than associated with the more general identity of the nation and its metropolis…The Pantheon is 'an impossible monument,' because the great men to whom (according to the inscription on the building) the *patrie* owes a debt of gratitude are essentially men on the left: symbolically, on November 11, 1920, the Chamber of Deputies simultaneously voted to place the heart of Gambetta (a republican politician) in the Pantheon and to inter the remains of the unknown soldier under the Arc de Triomphe…" (158-159).

[70] Ibid, 159.

[71] "Feminism in France since 1970," *Contemporary France Online* (3/20/2002), http://www.well.ac.uk/cfol/feminism.asp (accessed September 18, 2008).

[72] Michael Herr cited in Ronell, "TraumaTV," 63, emphasis mine.

[73] Ronell, "TraumaTV," 63, emphasis mine.

[74] Marguerite Duras, *Hiroshima mon amour*, trans. Richard Seaver (New York: Grove Press, 1981), 15.

[75]

He	She
Nothing	Everything
Nothing	Everything
Male	Female
---	+++

[76] Tom Conley, *Film Hieroglyphics: Ruptures in Classical Cinema* (Minneapolis: University of Minnesota Press, 2006), 193.

[77] Stanley Hoffmann, "On *The Sorrow and the Pity*," *Commentarymagazine.com*, September 1972, http://www.commentarymagazine.com/viewarticle.cfm/on--the-sorrow-and-the-pity--5118.

[78] It should be noted that both Maria Hughes and Ned Kynaston were two of the best-known actors of the Restoration period and the films' characters are modeled on them.

[79] Butler, 179.

[80] Elisabeth Bronfen, *Over Her Dead Body: Death, Femininity and The Aesthetic* (Manchester: Manchester University Press, 1992), 13.

[81] Rabaté, *Given*, 33-34: "Marcel Duchamp's last work of art, the posthumously unveiled *Given 1: The Waterfall, 2: The Illuminating Gas* […] contains a riddle, if it is not a riddle itself […] They [the museum visitor] face a wide double door, hermetically closed, an old barn door framed in bricks. Only on further inspection does one realize that the door is part of the artwork, that one has to come closer and peer through two tiny pinholes that allow one to discern what is behind […] Is this the scene of a crime? But everything there is real, hyper-realistic even, and also totally unreal. What was Duchamp's point? Since the piece is made up of two elements, the flat barn door and the three-dimensional diorama, it stages its own

rapport to the viewer's gaze and perspective. Duchamp forces spectators to come to terms with a calculated sense of voyeurism: in fact, we all become peeping toms."

[82] Sitney, 257.

[83] Shakespeare, *Othello. The Riverside Shakespeare*, ed. G. Blakemore Evans (Boston: Houghton Mifflin, 1997), 5.2.18-19.

[84] E. Ann Kaplan, "Global Feminisms and the State of Feminist Film Theory," 1244.

[85] One might wonder if Valerii Todorovskii's *Land of the Deaf* is a nod to the silent film, since the icon of the silent film, Sergei Eisenstein, was after all, Russian. According to Deleuze in *Cinema 2: The Time-Image*: "The silent film was not silent but only noiseless, as Mitry says, or only 'deaf,' as Michel Chion says" (225).

[86] Sitney, 249.

[87] Eliot Borenstein, "About That: Deploying and Deploring Sex in Postsoviet Russia," *STCL* 24, no.1 (Winter 2000): 55, 61.

[88] The interest in disability is another portal to the 18th century—this time, not only an opening onto the Gothic, but to a scientific interest in the handicapped who were referred to sometimes as monsters (see Denis Diderot, *Lettre sur les aveugles/An Essay on Blindness,* 1749 and *Lettre sur les sourds et muets/Letter on Deaf-Mutes*, 1751).

[89] Helena Goscilo, *Dehexing Sex. Russian Womanhood During and After Glasnost* (Ann Arbor: University of Michigan Press, 1996), 89.

[90] Deleuze, *Cinema 2: The Time-Image*, 196.

[91] Ivone Margulies, "La Chambre Akerman: The Captive as Creator," *Rouge* (December 2006), http://www.rouge.com.au/10/akerman.html.

[92] B. Ruby Rich, 273.

[93] Margulies.

[94] Janet Bergstrom, "The Innovators 1970-1980: Keeping a distance," *Sight and Sound: The International Film Magazine* (November 1999), http://www.bfi.org.uk/sightandsound/feature/196/.

[95] Margulies.

[96] Ibid.

[97] Margulies.

[98] Bergstrom.

[99] Margulies.

[100] *La Captive*'s opening and closing scenes recall Federico Fellini's *La Strada* (1954): in the first scene of Akerman's film, a group of women—Arianne and her girlfriends—are shown frolicking on the beach. This recalls Gelsomina (Giulietta Masina) and her sisters in the first scene of *La Strada*. In the closing moments of both films, the camera returns to sea—"la mer, la mer, toujours recommencée"/ "the sea, the sea, always renewed" (Paul Valéry, "Le Cimetière marin"/"The Cemetary by the Sea" (1920) in *Charmes ou poèmes* (1922))—to follow lonely male perpetrators who have caused the deaths of "their" women (Gelsomina, Arianne). These male protagonists, dejected and isolated, are depicted as lost in

thought: one facing the unquiet waters, the other moving away from them. For a discussion of *La Strada*'s Gelsomina, see Kenneth Camacho's "The Failure of Male Communities and the Sacrificial Female in Fellini's *La Strada*" (unpublished, revised version of a paper presented at the 2007 NeMLA convention).

[101] Deleuze, *Cinema 2: The Time-Image*, 196.

I:

DE-GENDERING THE GAZE

CHAPTER ONE

'LIFE FINDS A WAY': MONSTROUS MATERNITIES AND THE QUANTUM GAZE IN *JURASSIC PARK* AND *THE THIRTEENTH WARRIOR*

LISA DETORA

And if my work is marked by a certain hunger to see what should not be seen, to show what should not be shown, the beginning of the appetite may be…struggling in my mother's arms because I was forbidden the sight.[1]
—Clive Barker

Michael Crichton's best-selling novels have been the basis for several high-grossing and influential films, such as his 1990 novel *Jurassic Park*, which was made into a 1993 film of the same title directed by Steven Spielberg. Much of Crichton's work is notable for its participation in popular discourses of current scientific topics. For example, Crichton's recent novel, *State of Fear* (2004), has been recognized as a substantial account of the consequences of global warming. Among his earlier works, *The Andromeda Strain* (novel 1969; film 1971, directed by Robert Wise) was acclaimed for its portrayal of the potentially ill effects of genetics research, a theme he reprises in several other books, including *Jurassic Park*. Crichton's novels sometimes feature rapacious or consuming woman figures which feminists would consider misogynist, as in *Eaters of the Dead* (1976) and *Jurassic Park*. In this essay, I consider the operation of looking relations in the representation of maternity as a site of the monstrous in the film versions of *Jurassic Park* and *Eaters of the Dead,* which was adapted to the screen as *The Thirteenth Warrior* (directed by John McTiernan, 1999). I chose these films because they each rely on a figurative mother for the operation of the horrific in their narratives and because this figure defies both verisimilitudinous and horror film expectations in looking relations. Neither film has been the subject of a detailed feminist reading.[2]

Not only are these two films of interest from a feminist perspective, but also, each film has a global social significance. Spielberg's *Jurassic Park* was among the top grossing films of all time, and it has been followed by two sequels: *The Lost World: Jurassic Park* (1997, directed by Spielberg, based on a 1995 Crichton novel) and *Jurassic Park III* (2001, directed by Joe Johnston). The original film is arguably one of the most influential documents of United States popular culture not only because of its box office success, but also because of its participation in scientific discourses of genetics and paleontology. In fact, the film *Jurassic Park* has become an important referent in popular scientific writings about advances in the discovery of dinosaurs, to be discussed further. *The Thirteenth Warrior*, in contrast, is considered notable largely because of its creative re-adaptation of *Beowulf* and its refiguring of Grendel from an individual monster into a large tribe of primitive cave-dwellers.[3] This cinematic adaptation of *Beowulf*—one of the most important texts of English literature—has been examined largely as a twentieth century depiction of medieval Viking culture.

The possible connections between the *Jurassic Park* trilogy and the scientific community tend to focus on the original film, Spielberg's *Jurassic Park*. For example, in an article entitled "Breathing Life into Tyrannosaurus rex," Gregory M. Erikson writes, "Spielberg's *Jurassic Park*...boasted the most accurate popular depiction of dinosaurs ever."[4] Erikson's article was published in *Scientific American* in 1999, six years after the film's initial theatrical release, and two years after the sequel, *The Lost World: Jurassic Park* appeared in theaters. Erikson credits Spielberg's original production crew with an impressive feat in the realms of popular science and Hollywood cinematic technology: developing an accurate series of dinosaur models and images that remained noteworthy for years afterward. Erikson's article was published before the BBC miniseries *Walking with Dinosaurs* (1999) was available in the United States. This series built on technologies like those employed in the making of *Jurassic Park*.

Moreover, the linkage with real-life science can also be seen in the concurrence of the film's initial production period and the controversy surrounding Tyrannosaurus Sue, the largest specimen of the species, which was unearthed in 1990. After disputes erupted over ownership of the remains of this dinosaur, the US government seized the fossil and a group of corporate and artistic partners banded together to help Chicago's Field

Museum purchase Sue, ensuring that she would be available to the public gaze in perpetuity.[5] While this circumstance might appear only superficially significant to the film, the partners who purchased Sue for the Field Museum included Walt Disney Studios and McDonald's. Walt Disney Studios later animated the dinosaurs of *Jurassic Park III* and, according to Pere Gallardo-Torrano in his recent work about *Jurassic Park*, McDonald's is credited with the banalization of culture worldwide.[6] This grouping of Disney and McDonald's with the dinosaur firmly grounds the public discourse of this particular Tyrannosaurus, and by extension all examples of the species, in terms of family life. Such family orientation is commonly understood to characterize Disney films, and not surprisingly, *Jurassic Park III* has the strongest nuclear family narrative of any of the films in this series. Furthermore, this partnership evokes the many obvious parallels drawn between Jurassic Park and Disneyland, the lack of propensity for pirates as opposed to dinosaurs to eat the audience notwithstanding.

Both *Jurassic Park* and *The Thirteenth Warrior* can be classified as horror or action films with an additional identification as science fiction sometimes made for each, but more commonly for *Jurassic Park*. This play between possible genres is potentially interesting because the films, especially *Jurassic Park*, are not necessarily classified similarly in previous scholarly readings. For the purposes of the current discussion, I will consider the way each of these films can be seen to operate within the horror genre. This identification is especially important when considering the monstrous, because monsters propel the action in most horror films. In the following pages, I provide a brief overview of the feminist theory on which I draw, along with related theories of the horror genre as well as previous feminist readings of *Jurassic Park* before presenting a new reading of these films in terms of the monstrous mother and her placement vis-à-vis the gaze.

Visual Pleasure in Twenty-first Century Narrative Cinema

Laura Mulvey's work launched the field of feminist film theory in the 1970s. Mulvey's foundational essay "Visual Pleasure and Narrative Cinema" (1975) explained the impact of visual relations and gender in celluloid and formed the basis for most subsequent psychoanalytic readings of women in film. Specifically, Mulvey notes that Hollywood narrative film construed looking relations, or more properly, the investment of pleasure in looking relations, as relying on the operation of a gendered binary, with man as "bearer of the look" and woman as "object of the gaze." Today, this observation informs readings of nearly all visual media, despite the advances that Mulvey, among others, have noted in technologies that have profoundly altered what can be packed into a second of screen time.[7] Feminist film theorists such as Barbara Creed, Cynthia Freeland, and Sue Thornham have long worked to account for different gazes and subject positions in order to supplement and/or problematize the heteronormative binary of Mulvey's theory of subject-object looking relations.[8]

Considerations of the gaze in feminist psychoanalytic readings can also work against a primary circumstance of power formation. The distinction between who—or what—is doing the looking and who—or what—is being observed is an important binary. In his 1975 *Surveiller et punir* (translated in 1977 as *Discipline and Punish*), Michel Foucault identified the function of this binary through the social operation of carceral and educational authority. Foucault's figural Panopticon, like Jeremy Bentham's literal prison design, deprives certain subjects of any gaze, transforming looking relations into power relations, an ability to discipline and punish without physical violence or bodily disfiguration.[9] This binary also evokes Lacan's sardine can, which is seen as an object precisely because it does not possess a gaze with which to look back at the seeing subject. By considering power or function separately from gender, one can problematize the unspoken assumption that an attractive woman will be the powerless object of the gaze in narrative films. For example, Linda Williams notes that female subjects in horror films often have the first access to a gaze that incorporates a view of the monster, but this gaze translates into victimization, a circumstance that Cynthia Freeland sees as symptomatic of the bleak horizon for feminist studies of horror.[10] I would like to suggest that, if not a recuperation, at least a revision of Freeland's claim is possible.

Although Mulvey's work is well-established, recent scholars evince a certain impatience with the earlier models of feminist film theory. The current state of feminism in film studies allows for readings like those Vivian Sobchak has observed as characterizing twenty-first century treatments of gender analysis. For Sobchak, the use of cultural studies as an intellectual method allows scholars to consider gender in all types of inquiry, obviating the need for an originary feminist agenda in critical work. Sobchak expresses concern that feminist ideology is now so widely accepted that the historical context for the initial development of theories that may now seem dated or dogmatic may be lost. Sobchak further indicates that cultural studies encourages intellectuals to eschew binaries in favor of differentiation, particularly when considering gender, which may indicate that any looking binary is incorrect, reductive or simplistic.[11] However, when considering this binary as inherently problematic, such a reading might allow for a new consideration of the ways that looking relations operate in terms of monstrous maternity.

Mother figures in *Jurassic Park* and *The Thirteenth Warrior* transform into monsters when they are not available to any gaze, and this invisibility is the key to both their generative and deadly powers. Visual pleasure in these narratives is undercut and the tension of horror (the desire to simultaneously look and not look) is introduced by the ability of certain figures to disappear into the filmic and diegetic underbrush, escaping from both the psychoanalytic and the carceral gaze, thus violating a series of looking relations that are intended to have been gendered exactly as Mulvey described in 1975. Given that both *Jurassic Park* and *The Thirteenth Warrior* rely heavily on the workings of monstrosity and can therefore be classified as horror films, a consideration of the operation of this binary may be especially important in the context of Freeland's work.

As noted, Sobchak comments on a current state of feminist film studies that underwent some revision during the twenty-first century. One important feature of these newer feminisms is a recognition that, as Sue Thornham indicates, "the category 'all women' has itself become suspect" necessitating a careful reconsideration of the motives and identifications of individual theorists and critics.[12] My consideration of these films, therefore, is informed by my own white, suburban, heteronormative upbringing, subsequent higher education in English and women's studies, and several years of working in the medical sciences. Consequently, I value the discourses of science and take seriously their claims that certain cultural products are more important than others in the realm of the popular imagination. Furthermore, my self-identification as a feminist produces a desire to poke at the edges of representations to see what subtle discourses of gender might be lurking, monstrous and veiled, in the underbrush.

Monstrosity, Horror, and the Hidden

Monsters are the most crucial inhabitants of the forests, mists, and other spaces of the horror genre. Monsters are figures that embody cultural and psychological anxieties that cannot always be spoken aloud. Like science fiction, which Donna Haraway identifies as a site for working out current social issues,[13] horror provides a space within which society can be metaphorically examined. Paul Wells notes that horror films, like most other works in the horror genre—novels, shorts stories, plays—draw heavily on figures or creatures from a "primordial world" to create their monsters.[14] He further states that horror narratives borrow tropes and plots from fairy tales and myths that are powerful means of attempting to make sense of reality. Along these lines, *Jurassic Park* and *The Thirteenth Warrior* draw on a series of Paleolithic or paleontologic monsters in order to create a space within which to consider the social dangers of an unlimited and/or uncontrollable generation of older species in modern settings. Ironically, in these films, the uncontrolled generation of animals or entities that should be extinct drives the key anxiety of each film—none other than the fear of death—which, as Wells notes, has informed horror productions since the earliest examples of Gothic literature. Since the fear of death, or extinction, comes about because of the unlimited proliferation of previously extinct creatures, the monsters in these films simultaneously threaten and embody this fear while also perverting the very process that should mitigate the horror of death—the generation of new life. This narrative trajectory was prefigured in certain horror films of the early Cold War—*Them!* (1954), *Food of the Gods* (1976), and *Godzilla* (1954)—which featured uncontrollable generation or growth as a result of nuclear or radiant contamination, a cultural anxiety which has been gradually subsumed into concerns about genetics and disease, as noted by Daniel Dinello, who describes the scientists of *Jurassic Park* as inept but good-hearted.[15]

Genetics and disease are the basis for creating fictitious monsters, like Godzilla, giant ants, or the Incredible Hulk, that were supposedly formed as a result of radioactive contamination. Monsters like the Swamp Thing, Jason, or The Mummy often have mutilated, decayed, altered, abject, or mutated bodies, which evoke fears of death, dismemberment, radioactivity, and disfiguration. As Anna Powell observes in *Deleuze and Horror Film,* Gilles Deleuze and Félix Guattari posit that a body without organs is a means of "remapping" the terrain of the body in horror films, allowing for a series of amoeba-like transformations. Powell refers to this circumstance as "becoming anomalous," a state that deprives many seemingly essential terms of existence, like gender or species, of any meaning. These shape shifters undercut the very basis for identity and individual subjectivity.[16] Both *Jurassic Park* and *The Thirteenth Warrior* contain monsters that push the boundaries of identity, shifting shapes seemingly at will and evoking the threat of universal anomaly/amorphousness.

Barbara Creed notes that the "central ideological project" of horror film is confronting the abject, which Julia Kristeva identifies as a fundamental threat to boundaries and systems, in order to reject it and restore order, ejecting the monstrous feminine. According to Creed, the "archaic" mother in these films is characterized by "the voracious maw" that symbolizes both uncontrollable generation and castration while simultaneously threatening to consume the universe.[17] This maw can be seen in the *Alien* films and Hitchcock's *Psycho* (1960), which Creed uses as examples to support her interpretation of the monstrous-feminine as a thematic and experiential phenomenon for audiences, and the central figure that must be repressed to restore order in horror films. For Creed, "the horror film stages and re-stages a constant repudiation of the maternal figure," strongly indicating the terms of male—while overlooking the terms of female—desire.[18] When considering *Jurassic Park* and *The Thirteenth Warrior,* a similar central ideological project can be identified as the characters must restore order in the face of a monstrous feminine.

Unauthorized Breeding and Its Discontents

The film *Jurassic Park*, like *The Andromeda Strain*, describes the results of genetic experimentation gone awry. In a prehistoric zoo *qua* theme park—which is likened to a carnivorous Disneyland and set on an isolated island off the coast of Costa Rica—a group of hired scientists has extracted deoxyribonucleic acid (DNA) from a series of Mesozoic creatures through the medium of mosquitoes trapped in amber and unearthed by a crew of obliging Spanish-speaking miners. A group of white-coated scientists takes this DNA and, through the magic of recombinant genetics, creates a series of dinosaur embryos. In this scenario, the maternal is transformed into the paternal. John Hammond (Richard Attenborough), the creator of Jurassic Park, insists on imprinting with each of the baby dinosaurs as they are "born," or rather, hatch. The lab-coated scientist, Dr. Henry Wu (B.D. Wong), assures both Hammond and his scientific guests that no "unauthorized breeding" can take place in Jurassic Park because all dinosaur embryos are left in the default "female" gender, therefore without a male to inseminate them.

In this scene, chaos theoretician and promiscuous father Ian Malcolm (Jeff Goldblum) critiques this genetic process not as such but as uncontainable. Malcolm rejects the reassurance that an all-female group cannot mate because he recognizes that chaos is likely to intervene. His comment "life finds a way," is echoed throughout the film as life, indeed, does find a way to escape both scientific and theme park containment, creating a monstrous maternal abject that undercuts all order on the island. More significantly, Malcolm's critique evokes the specter of hubris, the failure of science to consider what it should do rather than what it can do, thus articulating this narrative into a discourse of the "mad scientist" that dates back at least to Victor Frankenstein's "den of filthy creation."[19] The reduction of the already overly simplistic binary of *nature=good, science=bad* into *science=hubris=bad*, presents a highly troublesome moralism that Stephen Jay Gould has noted as characteristic of cinematic—but not of novelistic—portrayals of scientists, and that Gallardo-Torrano sees as a Promethean disaster.[20] Of course, as Dinello notes, the scientists of Jurassic Park are not aspiring evil warlords set on universal domination, but rather, are a team trying to build the world's coolest theme park, complete with rides, cartoons, ice cream and cuddly toys.[21] These men want to make good on their promises, and they feel uneasy when workers are eaten by velociraptors. Their hubris centers on the idea that they can control their creations after releasing them into a newly fabricated "natural" environment.

It is perhaps more interesting, however, to consider other subtle problems of the gleaming white and highly polished technology den of creation in Jurassic Park. According to the informational cartoon Hammond presents to the scientists at the visitor's center, Jurassic Park's geneticists extract DNA from mosquitoes trapped in amber and fill in the missing pieces with frog DNA in order to replicate dinosaurs. This version of "science" is too simplistic for the expert visitors, who demand to know more. Oversimplification is hinted at by the collapse of the crew of Central American workers seen earlier in the film into a lone Caucasian geologist shown in the cartoon version. The park thus begins its own narrative by leaving out the messy details and sanitizing the filthier aspects of creation for the protection of its audience. Additional loose ends become evident when Drs. Sattler (Laura Dern), Grant (Sam Neil) and Malcolm stop the ride and escape into the incubation laboratory, arriving just in time to witness a hatchling emerge from its shell. Hammond, chiding Wu for not warning him of the happy event, insists that his presence is necessary at the "birth" of each of the park's dinosaurs, so that they can imprint on him.

Ultimately, life "finds a way" to circumvent the breeding laboratory—and its politics—by spontaneously transforming females into males, which results in more dinosaurs than initially planned. In a consideration of Crichton's 1990 novel *Jurassic Park*, James J. Miracky notes that the initial Jurassic Park dinosaurs are not actually copies of the originals, but adapted and genetically altered simulacra. He also considers the park and its operation as "hyperreal" following Jean Baudrillard's reading of Disneyland.[22] While Miracky's points work in the context of the novel, the hyperreal operates somewhat differently in the context of the film. First, the idea of the hyperreal can be seen in Dennis Nedry's (Wayne Knight) Barbasol can of embryos, presumably buried for a future paleontological disaster; the can is one of millions of non-original copies. However, and more interestingly, although Jurassic Park functions like Disneyland, trying to be more real than reality, DNA is the actual site of the most dangerous hyperreality in the park. Baudrillard notes that the double helix represents the ultimate copy without an original, a circumstance made more acutely dangerous by the continual manipulation of DNA by the park's scientists. In effect, these scientists are not quite certain what they are copying because they had no originals and they supplemented their source materials with DNA from frogs. These dinosaurs, then, even before they start to shift from feminine to masculine genders, were created as organless bodies, subject to great mutability, the signifiers carefully placed on their cryogenic embryonic storage capsules notwithstanding. Furthermore, the function of hyperreality in the form of "unauthorized 'breeding'" extends beyond the dinosaurs to the park itself, which seems to reproduce, amoeba-like, as a series of unauthorized backups in subsequent installments of the story. Apparently, the hyperreal transcends individuals in Jurassic Park, allowing for the production of copies *ad infinitum*, none of which are based on an original.

The control of breeding through genetic research in Jurassic Park has important implications for feminist positioning in the film. In their essay "'There is No Unauthorized Breeding in Jurassic Park': Gender and the Uses of Genetics," (2000) Laura Briggs and Jodi I. Kelber-Kaye examine *Jurassic Park* (1990 and 1993) and *Gattaca* (1997) as cultural depictions of the public debate about genetics at the turn of the twenty-first century. Briggs and Kelber-Kaye see these films as representative of essential and conservative antifeminist stances that inform popular discourse around this public debate, suggesting that Hollywood film and the popular novel identify genetics research as an "unnatural" form of reproduction. Thus, this discourse calls for a return to natural modes of mothering while omitting a discussion of women, a stance that Briggs and Kelber-Kaye see as highly problematic, and not only because of its antifeminism:

> Women enter the discourse of genes only unevenly and irregularly…Yet questions of genes and genetics are primarily about reproduction, a subject that traditionally has been inescapably imbricated in cultural negotiations of gender, family, and feminism. Where did this cultural baggage of reproduction go?[23]

Briggs and Kelber-Kaye discover through their readings of *Jurassic Park* (1990) and *Gattaca* that conservative antifeminist values valorize the "traditional" nuclear family and its unique model of domesticated mothering "unencumbered by feminism or careerism."[24] The critique of genetic manipulation is also read here as a general criticism of

> science, which is imagined as something done only by men, and contrasted with 'natural' maternity, in which women (who do not do science, and presumably stay home to act as good mothers) bear good children, enclosed within a heterosexual nuclear family.[25]

The authors further note that these stories evoke additional frightening images, such as uncontrollable "third world" reproduction in the case of Crichton's novel *Jurassic Park.*

Briggs and Kelber-Kaye read the film version of *Jurassic Park* as fundamentally more simplistic as compared to the novel. They specifically note that the film removes or minimizes the discourses of race and uncontrollable third-world procreation that form an important part of the novel's critique of genetics research. Furthermore, the simplification of the novel's thematics when rendered onto the silver screen is conjoined to what they term a "softening" of Crichton's "misogyny" through shifts in the representation of the two important female protagonists, Ellie Sattler and Lex Murphy (Ariana Richards).[26] This reading of the film is limited because it concentrates on the book and the thematic concerns of genetics and does not consider the visual aspects of the film systematically, if at all. This may account for the apparent "simplicity" of their view of the film narrative's thematics, which would necessarily be complicated by a meaningful visual discourse. Briggs and Kelber-Kaye also omit the type of psychoanalytic film reading one might expect in a feminist analysis of the film, but not the novel, on which they concentrate. However, these authors are primarily worried about the real-life implications of a simplistic discourse of genetics that reinscribes the "inherent" and "natural" recuperative value of the heteronormative nuclear family as the only appropriate site for reproduction, a theme also treated by Rajani Sudan in "Technophallia" and Constance Balides in "Jurassic post-Fordism: Tall Tales of Economics in the Theme Park."[27]

Two points deserve some comment. In their analysis of the novel *Jurassic Park*, Briggs and Kelber-Kaye specifically state that women do not (or should not) do science, while the film shows Ellie Sattler performing science actively. In contrast, Alan Grant either disrupts science practice (as in their introductory scene when the electronic tools cease to function around him) or engages in a sort of natural observation *qua* tour for Hammond's grandchildren, during which he actually discards the only artifact of "real" paleontology in the park. In fact, aside from speech, which is certainly informed by science, neither Grant nor Malcolm engage in scientific activity and only does Grant engage in constructive action within the "natural" world of the park. Ellie, on the other hand, interacts successfully with the paleontology site; with the electronics in the Jurassic Park hatchery that malfunction when Grant approaches; with the living dinosaurs, and with the park's security technology. Ellie Sattler is the only character that successfully bridges all of these scientific and technological spaces in the course of the film. This circumstance, rather than invalidating Briggs and Kelber-Kaye's point, may provide evidence that Jurassic Park is constructed as an island in crisis, where only female figures can dependably transcend the disorder.

Another point in Briggs and Kelber-Kaye's argument that is worth noting is the bending of the nuclear family dynamic and the overt discourse of Ellie's feminism throughout the film.[28] However, this feminism is only acceptable because she maintains at once her nurturing stance throughout the film and also manages to outdo all the men on the action hero paradigm. That Grant is encumbered by the two children— significantly, only the boy suffers some physical damage during this journey—seems inconsequential when considering that Ellie not only becomes nurse to Malcolm, the injured chaos theoretician, but also must risk her life in order to reactivate the park's electric system, waging a feminist battle in the process. Dr. Ellie Sattler, an attractive, feminist scientist, is a nurturing woman who will not allow the elderly handicapped John Hammond to risk his life on the premises that chivalry always prevails.

Reading Gender as Horror in *Jurassic Park*

I noted above that one of the central projects of horror films is the containment of a monstrous feminine, at least according to Barbara Creed; however, the application of this central project to *Jurassic Park* requires some consideration. In my research, I found two specifically feminist readings of *Jurassic Park* that did not focus on capitalism, the more recent of which I considered immediately above. In the earlier "Feminist Frameworks for Horror Films," Cynthia Freeland notes that until the mid-1990s, most feminist analyses of horror films were psychodynamic and therefore emphasized "viewers' motives and interests in watching horror films, and…the psychological effects such films have,"[29] a description that would most likely include Creed's 1993 essay. Freeland notes that these analyses typically rely on psychoanalysis, and "presume some connection between gazing, violent aggression, and masculinity,"[30] then summarizes a general feminist psychoanalytic reading of the typical, mass-market horror film:

> The tension between the viewer's desire to look and the ongoing narrative of a film is especially acute in the horror film. Typically in horror, the woman or visual object is also the chief victim sacrificed to the desire to know about the monster. Horror flirts directly with the threat of castration underlying the fetish or visual appearance of the woman, and this means that looking (visual pleasure) is even more immediately at odds with narrative in horror films than in other mainstream Hollywood movies. The woman's flesh, the reality behind the surface appearance, *is* made visible, and horror shows the 'wound' that we are revolted to look upon. To make up for this horror, this account continues, the viewer must turn attention to the narrative thrust of the investigator, typically a male, who will complete the story for us.[31]

Freeland goes on to critique this model of feminist psychoanalysis, questioning the default use of Lacan and Kristeva as central theorists and the also highly gendered assumptions that drive most readings of the gaze in this work.

Freeland then uses *Jurassic Park* as one example of a film that can yield a feminist reading that considers women and their roles in the film's plot, rather than the psychodynamics of viewer experience. In her reading, women must remain "pretty, flirtatious and nurturing" even while they are being "brave and smart," and furthermore, since all of the "active agents" that move the film's plot are male, women and girls tag along as helpers.[32] Freeland sees the ending of this film as forming a happy and idealized Caucasian nuclear family, having excised all of the ethnically "other" people who otherwise inhabited the film, but in fact only appear at the beginning as obliging workers who find the mosquitoes trapped in amber and possibly end up being devoured by velociraptors. Thus, despite Ellie Sattler's overt criticism of the masculine order in Jurassic Park, the film according to Freeland ultimately yields a fairly depressing reenactment of the very worst sort of reductive gender representation.[33]

I would like to suggest that *Jurassic Park* provides a more complex terrain, and a more vexed conclusion, than Freeland indicates. First, the narrative structure of the film does not parallel Freeland's brief description in several important ways. In *Jurassic Park*, all of the human sacrifices to the monsters that inhabit the park are men: an unidentified Costa Rican "worker," Dennis Nedry, Mr. Arnold (Samuel L. Jackson), Robert Muldoon (Bob Peck), and Donald Gennaro (Martin Ferrero). The woman's body, which arguably should represent the threat of castration, is not strongly visible, although the threat of consumption by gigantic, and presumably female, dinosaurs is overpowering: a series of voracious, toothy maws emerging from the simulated primeval forests. Also, no coherent male investigator appears and the narrative explanation of what went wrong is abandoned, like the island, in a mad scramble to keep Hammond's grandchildren from being devoured by velociraptors.

In Freeland's alternative reading, the all-white nuclear family is problematic because it excludes the native ethnic people who previously inhabited the island. I agree with Freeland, but not for the same reasons she suggests. In my view, it is significant that the white heteronormative family that leaves the island is comprised entirely of individuals who were imported in the first place. In other words, this nuclear family and its third-order dinosaur simulations had no reason to be on the Isla Nublar in the first place, and should rightfully be ejected. Therefore, there is no reason to expect that the local workers—who only appear briefly and are presumably evacuated during the storm—will be on the helicopter with Hammond and his hired scientists. The nuclear family is an alien import, potentially a monster itself, or at the very least a harbinger of a highly disturbing abject. This brings me to a more interesting point, that Hammond's desire to insert nuclear families into the park creates many of the difficulties that propel the film's plot. My reading here deviates from those of Balides and Sudan, who see the insertion of the nuclear family into the technological and capitalist spaces of the theme park as an ideological band-aid intended to right all wrongs.

Instead, I see the insertion of the nuclear family into the experimental milieu of genetics as the originary problem that creates monsters. The initial impetus for finding a group of scientists to evaluate Jurassic Park is due to the fact that a velociraptor unexpectedly ate a local worker during a routine, although very high-tech, dinosaur transportation mission. The velociraptor proved to be too intelligent for standard zoo procedures and the rules of the InGen corporation. This corporation developed the dinosaur in question and since it owns the park, is liable for the death of the worker. In true US corporate style, the investors threaten to withdraw their funds unless the park's mastermind, John Hammond, is able to prove that the park is going to be safe for the tourists who are supposed to generate revenue. It is assumed that these tourists will be well-to-do families with children. Hammond and his lawyer, Donald Gennaro, each bring a scientist or two to the park to see if the displays would be acceptable for the average touring nuclear family. Well, they aren't.

The real problem with the nuclear family vis-à-vis Jurassic Park may be that Hammond cannot seem to discern the binaries that should be helping him create usable boundaries between danger and safety. By removing the workers and scientists who keep control over the park, Hammond makes the park into a family scene, and it is this action—this failed attempt to construct a nuclear family-friendly amusement park inhabited by voracious human-imprinted predators—that brings about calamity. Hammond conflates fantasy and reality, simulacra and originals, family and work, creating potential sites of the abject which require the restoration of order or boundaries. The film abounds with scenes in which Hammond melds work and family relationships, such as when he chides rather than fires Dennis Nedry, an act of indulgent parenting in the face of adolescent rebellion that indirectly results in general mayhem and death. Since Hammond functions as the site of the park's collapsed boundaries— between corporate concerns, work, family, and dinosaurs—then this fatal flaw in Jurassic Park actually exists prior to the film's plot, and it is only brought to the surface when the major scientific infrastructure of the park disappears. Therefore, the nuclear family cannot "fix" the park, but rather, must be saved from it.

Another possible area of inquiry is in the constitution of this "nuclear" family. In the final exit from the park, Dr. Ellie Sattler does indeed smile at Alan Grant and the children sleeping together. However, she smiles from her seat between Hammond, the children's actual grandfather, and Ian Malcolm, who has presumably not given up on her as a potential "future ex-Mrs. Malcolm." At best, the film provides an extended family with Ellie as the possible mother of Hammond's grandchildren or possibly the unseen multimothered brood of the ex-Mrs. Malcolms. Although Ellie Sattler may want Alan Grant to have children, she is separated from the "nuclear family" Freeland sees at the end of the narrative, following the suggested model in which Malcolm has children, but does not remain involved with their mothers. Furthermore, the parallel scene showing Grant with the sleeping children occurs earlier in the film, at a moment when Sattler and Hammond eat ice cream together while their loved ones are out in the park being hunted by dinosaurs. The final scene in the helicopter is therefore a replay of an earlier scene of danger. Finally, the nuclear family of Grant and the two children also bears an unfortunate resemblance to the "family" of velociraptors, which is comprised of a dominant female and two younger, but unrelated, individuals. In all, the "idealized" nuclear family that Freeland finds so troublesome poses more problems than those of Sattler's place in this equation.

In addition, Freeland supports the idea that the agents running the film's action are male. However, a convincing argument can be made that the agents running the film's action are, in fact, dinosaurs, in which case, the viewer does not know what gender they are, as these creatures imbued with frog DNA can change sex at will when no one is looking. As I noted above, the plot twist that brings the outside experts to Jurassic Park is the initial scene of a man being eaten by a dinosaur, with investigation being warranted not because of the tragedy, but rather because of the threat of litigation. This suggests that capitalism is another powerful plot driver, a theme treated by Miracky, Sudan and Balides. Dennis Nedry's scheme to sell dinosaurs is thwarted when he is killed (and devoured) by a dilophosaurus, allowing the dinosaurs to escape. The animals go on to drive all of the further action in the film—including chasing cars and munching on lawyers—providing both the monstrous threat and the *deus ex machina* that demonstrate how little the human nuclear family actually matters in a world where monsters can change gender at will in order to reproduce.

Significantly, only so long as dinosaurs are kept in forced interaction with humans are they a threat to human existence. Although this point is never made explicitly in the film, many of the dinosaurs, particularly the meat eaters, are kept in isolation from other species and are fed a daily diet of modern mammals by their human caretakers. As far as these dinosaurs are concerned, the universe is populated only by them and by their human captors. Yet, these same dinosaurs are consistently distracted from their interactions with humans by the presence of other dinosaurs, such as when the Tyrannosaurus opts to eat a velociraptor, thus allowing Sattler, Grant and the children to escape. Similarly, the Gallimimus herd ignores Grant and the children even before the seemingly ubiquitous tyrannosaurus attacks, and the brachiosaurus responds to the members of its herd when called, once again leaving the humans behind. Only the velociraptors band together to hunt humans; however, they forego this activity when faced with a larger meat eater, which is their first encounter with another dinosaur. This indicates that Hammond's insistence on imprinting hatchlings on humans has unforeseen consequences, not least of which is a blood stained trail of dead men.

A final point complicating the idea that the agents who drive the film's plot are men is that men do not "fix" anything, although they do help in the process of fleeing from the island. Throughout the film, men consistently try to take action, but the dinosaurs are stronger and often overpower them. While Malcolm is merely injured after his attempt to distract a Tyrannosaurus, other men do not fare as well. Gennaro is eaten, as are Muldoon and Arnold, indicating a sense of impotence—and a possible castration complex—in the men who work on Isla Nublar. Hammond himself cannot even read a park map to Ellie, requiring that the injured yet hyperfertile Malcolm make himself useful, once again proving that he is stronger than the men employed by the park. Ultimately, the hands-on fixing is done by Ellie—who reboots the electrical systems after Mr. Arnold is dismembered in his attempt to fix it—and Lex, who reboots the computer, thus enabling everyone to flee safely. Therefore, although this film is inhabited by a monstrous feminine, a masculine agency is not the sole means of escape and no human women are sacrificed during the film. Thus, *Jurassic Park* presents a very intriguing discourse of gender, despite the limitations that Freeland notes in her analysis.

The Quantum Gaze and Monstrous Mothers

I suggested above that Mulvey's theory of the gaze, when considered in terms of both gender and power relations, might shed some light on the question of monstrous maternity in *Jurassic Park* and *The Thirteenth Warrior*. I will consider *Jurassic Park* here and add a discussion of *The Thirteenth Warrior* below. In *Jurassic Park,* the idea of gendered looking relations is somewhat vexed. Certainly, Ellie Sattler is the object of Ian Malcolm's gaze, as he looks for a new ex-wife, and Grant's refusal to look at Ellie and Ian in the jeep indicates that something is not quite right in the paleontologists' romantic relationship. It would seem that Grant needs to take up his role as bearer of the look in order for the nuclear family plot to prosper. However, these looking relations seem to cease abruptly once Dennis Nedry deactivates the park's security systems and the dinosaurs begin to escape. Instead of repeated voyeuristic glimpses of Ellie's nubile flesh while she is pursued by monsters, which might be expected given Freeland's analysis, the audience is treated to several dinosaur-eye-views of other characters in the film.

The most significant examples of dinosaur-informed shots are during stalking or chase sequences. For example, the famous scene in which the passenger mirror cautions that "objects are closer than they appear" captures both Malcolm's and the tyrannosaurus's gaze, even though the audience presumes that only Malcolm can read the mirror. Later, as the velociraptors chase Lex and Tim through the Jurassic Park kitchens, the point of view shifts between an omniscient third person gaze, the children's gaze, and the velociraptors' gaze. This shifting allows for the shock when the velociraptor, not understanding reflections, dashes headlong into a mirror rather than capturing Lex. Finally, the raptor's eye view hones in on Robert Muldoon's proud whisper, "clever girl," just before he is killed and eaten by his erstwhile charges. Each of these scenes demonstrates power relations in terms of this gaze—the character or creature doing the looking is invariably in control of the action until the camera's vantage shifts, thus changing the point of view to which the audience has access. This circumstance hints that power is more significant than gender in these particular looking relations.

While this reading is potentially interesting, it also mirrors standard horror genre tropes that place the audience in the monster's shoes, a move that contributes to the psychodynamics of horror that were of such interest to feminist critics of past decades.[34] I suggest that an even more interesting process involving power and the gaze is at work in this film. I borrow Freeland's language and presume some connection between gazing, violence and masculinity, and I frame my contention in terms of a popular scientific discourse worthy of Crichton's oeuvre: Schrödinger's cat. This echoes Stephanie Turner's analysis of genetics in the novel *Jurassic Park* as "virtual," following Schrödinger's code script metaphor when considering the meaning of life.[35] Schrödinger's cat is a thought experiment put forth by Erwin Schrödinger to illustrate the paradoxical physical relationship between quantum particles and larger entities, such as household pets. It is commonly accepted—at least by people who understand quantum physics—that a superposition of states is possible for subatomic particles. In other words, these particles may simultaneously be in several distinct physical states, one superimposed on another. Quantum theory indicates that the act of observation actually changes these physical circumstances, snapping the particle into a specific state at the moment it is trapped by a gaze. Schrödinger suggested that circumstances where the state of a subatomic particle was in question might result in an extension of superposition over nearby objects, such as cats. If, for example, a cat was trapped in a box in which poisonous gas may or may not have been released by the flux of subatomic particles, the cat would not be alive or dead until an observer looked at the particles in question. In the real world, this supposition is preposterous and Schrödinger's cat is understood as a paradox.[36] I suggest, however, that such a supposition may explain exactly why the dinosaurs in the film version of *Jurassic Park* are so monstrous.

The dinosaurs in Jurassic Park appear to have been well behaved as long as they were in sight. However, after they are enclosed in opaque spaces, their behavior is significantly less tractable. Thus, when their presence is demanded to entertain the park's visitors, the dinosaurs disappear into the forest and emerge only when the protective fencing malfunctions. The spontaneous mutation of some females into males also takes place in the hidden recesses of the jungle, out of sight of prying scientific eyes. One of the most disturbing aspects of this ability to hide behind fences, trees, and foliage is that the dinosaurs who most resist being subject to the scientific and/or carceral gaze are the predatory meat-eaters: dilophosaurus, velociraptor, and tyrannosaurus. In contrast, herds of docile herbivores wander up to cars and allow themselves to be petted by humans. Thus, the meat eaters behave when under scrutiny—such as the velociraptor hatchling—but mutate freely when not being watched, leaving behind only tangential evidence of their activities: broken egg shells, dead workers, and mutilated harnesses. In short, Jurassic Park allows these dinosaurs to exist in a quantum-like state when they are not trapped in a scientific gaze. They take on a definite size, shape, and gender only when they are under direct observation. These circumstances indicate that the monstrosity of dinosaur maternity in the film has more to do with a violation of looking relations—and the inherent wresting away of the reproductive process from any primary male intervention—than the gaping voracious maws that threaten literal castration, dismemberment, and consumption, the usual elements of previous psychoanalytic treatments of horror. These superpositional shifts allow for what Dr. Wu claimed to be impossible, namely, breeding among a group of females.

Another implication of this state shifting among dinosaurs is the failure of Hammond's big-happy-family model of the park. Because the act of observing actually changes and fixes the object being observed, the watchful eye of the laboratory geneticists and field zoologists is vital for maintaining order on the island. As soon as these workers leave the island and stop keeping an eye on things, the dinosaurs are free to do what they like. The monsters remanufacture themselves through hidden processes, transcending the structure of enforced homosexual homogeneity to take on masculine gender and engage in "unauthorized breeding." This discourse of gender creates the most truly horrific monsters, unauthorized female males who are breeding with their sisters without the help of the largely male scientific staff. These dinosaurs then take on the identity of a monstrous-feminine because they reject mandatory female identity and controlled reproduction in favor of a return to the "natural" modes of maternity that Briggs and Kelber-Kaye identify as valorized in discourses of genetics research. This narrative conflicts with the obvious moral of the film, that a "natural" maternity is superior to genetic manipulation. However, such a narrative dovetails with feminist film theories, like those of Carol Clover, that posit shifting subject positions, following the work of LaPlanche and Pontalis.[37]

Squandered Days

In the pages above, I have concentrated on providing a series of new feminist readings of *Jurassic Park* in the context of previous scholarly work, ending with the idea that a superposition of states allows for the most disturbing aspects of the monstrous mothers that inhabit Isla Nublar. In order to show that this reading is not particular to Spielberg's 1993 film and its sequels, I will briefly consider the operation of this "quantum gaze" in *The Thirteenth Warrior,* which, as I have indicated above, shares certain characteristics with *Jurassic Park.*

The narrative of John McTiernan's *The Thirteenth Warrior* describes how a character named Ibn Fahdlan Ibn Al Abbas Ibn Rashid Ibn Hamad, or "the Arab" (Antonio Banderas) becomes a man through his interactions with a group of Viking warriors and a series of fearsome monsters, the Wendol. Before this trip, Ibn Fahdlan had "squandered his days," dallying with women, writing poetry, and seducing another man's wife, which ultimately leads him to be named ambassador to the Vikings. In Viking country, Ibn Fahdlan becomes a man when he is incorporated into a group of warriors charged with killing a nameless monster, later called "the Wendol." The coding of the specifically feminine monstrous is very strong in the film because the Wendol are ruled by a figure called "the Mother" (Susan Willis) symbolized by a corpulent and fecund-looking fertility idol so repugnant to the Vikings that they cannot even look at it. The lead warrior, Buliwulf (Vladimir Kulick) conscripts the Arab since his foreign sensibilities bring a different set of assumptions to looking relations and horror. Fahdlan is the only character who can bear to look at the idol or discern the identity of the monsters that come in the night, kill Vikings and gnaw on their remains. Only Ibn Fahdlan can see that these creatures are not animals, but men, fixing their identity as such with his foreign gaze.

Viking superstition does not fully account for the inability of Buliwulf's warriors to see the Wendol and their "Mother" for what they are. The Wendol blend into the surrounding countryside, the earth, the caves, and the mist, emerging in various emanations, unseen in the night or reconstituted as a "fire worm" or dragon, configurations that defy the symbolic limitations of Viking language. There are simply no words to describe this particular monstrous creature. All the elements of horror—a monstrous-feminine, blood, cannibalism, bodies without organs, the gaping maw—are here fragmented, shifting endlessly between states until fixed in Fahdlan's gaze. Ironically, the humor used in the film—such as when a warrior comments that he would rather fight a real dragon than the hordes of torch-bearing Wendol who comprise the "fire worm"—indicates that the enemy is proportionally more monstrous and horrifying as it becomes less mysterious.

Like *Jurassic Park, The Thirteenth Warrior* does not follow the standard horror narrative that Freeland describes. In fact, Buliwulf is the first and only person to see the Mother, and he is the one who is sacrificed, killed by a phallic, poisonous instrument that mimics the teeth of the Mother's fragmented maw. While an argument could be made for a beefcake aspect of voyeuristic pleasure in the film, it is significant that the semi-clad and nubile woman who inhabits the cave is, in fact, the most monstrous creature in the story rather than an intended object of scopophilia. Her monstrosity is profound because the gaping maw Creed describes is here fragmented into a thousand pieces which can emerge unpredictably, creating a situation of continued horror, a monstrous-feminine and organless body changing states at will. In other words, the nubile flesh Buliwulf sees and the claw that kills him are only a tiny portion of the teeth that make up the Mother's jaws. This figure is so fragmented that it is not enough to kill her: the remaining Viking warriors must battle to eliminate the claw-bearing Wendol warriors up to the very last one. The film ends with what should be a resolution, Ibn Fahdlan writing his account on a voyage back to his home. However, this account, which is intended to immortalize Buliwulf, in fact also immortalizes the monstrous mother: the horror of her shifting form returns endlessly in the most disturbing manner.

Conclusion: Monster Mothers and Quantum Gazing

The two films discussed above construct maternity as monstrous by demonstrating that female reproduction deeply violates looking relations, defying definition outside the narrow confines of particular gazes. In both films, women appear relegated to helping roles: in *The Thirteenth Warrior* they are sex objects, queens, crones, or servants whereas in *Jurassic Park* human females clean up for others and female dinosaurs dominate the narrative. In both films, maternity remains hidden, maintaining mystery through disguise, sublimation, and transformation into animal monstrosity. It is important to note that in *Jurassic Park*, maternity is distinct from reproduction, which only becomes monstrous once any potential mothers enter the mix. In both films, maternity is hidden, deep in a cave or behind the laboriously reconstructed Jurassic vegetation.

Maternity in these films is often monstrous because it appears to excise the masculine in order to reproduce uncontrollably. That *Jurassic Park* and its sequels depict unauthorized reproduction as specifically maternal potentially implants the idea of the uncontrolled—and uncontrollable—nature of genetics in the public imagination. Lest this idea seem far-fetched, both subsequent films hinge on the idea of generation and reproduction. In *The Lost World: Jurassic Park,* Ian Malcolm actually brings the monsters from a secondary Jurassic Park island site to the Western, developed urban world in his quest to save a "future ex-Mrs. Malcolm." *Jurassic Park III* is about a lost child, stranded on yet another Jurassic Park site. Ultimately, the nuclear family in this film is saved when Ellie, no longer a scientist, but staying at home with her children like the good mother Briggs and Kelber-Kaye describe, mobilizes the armed forces to save those who are in danger on the island site, thus demonstrating the power of appropriate maternity. This final narrative reinforces the power of a particular type of motherhood that trumps all other relationships and social conventions. Simultaneously, the film naturalizes the young Erik Kirby's (Trevor Morgan) ability to survive by negotiating technological and reconstituted natural spaces, a parallel to Lex rebooting the Jurassic Park computers after coming to terms with "veggiesaurs"—like the tree-eating brachiosaurus—and velociraptors. For both children, seemingly innate and instinctive behaviors allow them to survive in conditions of extreme danger that thwart their adult companions.

Erik and Lex's successful negotiations illuminate an important point in all of these Crichton-based film narratives: survival in these spaces hinges on pragmatism and the ability to successfully manage the realms of nature and technology. The films demonstrate that those whose knowledge is overly cerebral (Malcolm), intellectual (Tim, Grant), linguistic or text-based (Ibn Fahdlan) can only manage monsters once they take on additional skills, much the way that Ellie, Lex, and Erik do. For example, Ibn Fahdlan, the only literate person in the Viking realm, employs a blacksmith's force to reconstitute Viking weaponry into a form he can wield, allowing him to fight alongside the Viking warriors. Similarly, Malcolm steps out of his highly cerebral chaos theory and into a practical mode in *The Lost World: Jurassic Park*. Oddly enough, Grant never manages to adopt technology and must therefore rely on support and salvation from Ellie, Lex, and Erik. His knowledge makes him valuable, but he is unsuccessful as an action hero because he cannot close the loop.

Briggs and Keller-Kaye note that

> Bestsellers and Hollywood films 'work' because they...offer rather familiar re-workings of stories that the culture as a whole can assent to, consume, and enjoy...[We] think of genes as what Bruno Latour calls 'hybrids,' objects that we as a culture make sense of in equal parts through the laboratory, the technologies we produce with them, and the stories we tell to make sense of the social change they bring.[38]

In this essay, I, too, have tried to make sense of the social changes brought about by genetics and paleontology as constructed through film adaptations of best selling novels. This essay considers the working of the monstrous and the anxieties about maternity in *Jurassic Park* and *The Thirteenth Warrior* through a visual trope—the gaze—that has not been used in previous analyses of these two films. Furthermore, I placed this gaze in dialogue with the superposition of subatomic particles as a way of understanding the dangers of the indefinite and indeterminate in popular conceptions of sciences such as genetics. The most frightening aspects of the consuming, maternal monsters that inhabit these films reside in their ability to be several things at once, to shift physical attributes and positions, until they are fixed in a gaze. In effect, the unviewable, forbidden sight does not exist until it is gazed upon. The young Clive Barker's struggles, when looked at, are truly disturbing.

Works Cited

Balides, Constance. "Jurassic post-Fordism: Tall Tales of Economics in the Theme Park." *Screen* 41 (2000): 139-60.

Baudrillard, Jean. *Simulations.* New York: Semiotexte, 1986.

Bihlmeyer, Jaime. "Novel, Script, Image: A Case Study of the Phallic (M)Other in Mainstream Culture." In *Images and Imagery: Frames, Borders, Limits: Interdisciplinary Perspectives*, edited by Leslie Boldt-Irons, Corrado Federici, Ernesto Virgutli. New York: Peter Lang, 2005.

Briggs, Laurie, and Jodi I. Kelber-Kaye. "'There is No Unauthorized Breeding in Jurassic Park': Gender and the Uses of Genetics." *NWSA Journal* 12 (2000): 92-113.

Clover, Carol J. "Her Body, Himself: Gender in the Slasher Film." In *Feminist Film Theory: A Reader*, edited by Sue Thornham. New York: NYU, 1999.

Creed, Barbara. "Horror and the Monstrous Feminine: An Imaginary Abjection." In *Feminist Film Theory: A Reader,* Sue Thornham. New York: NYU, 1999.

Crichton, Michael. *Eaters of the Dead.* New York: Knopf, 1976.

—. *Jurassic Park.* New York: Knopf, 1993.

—. *State of Fear.* New York: Harper Collins, 2004.

—. *The Andromeda Strain.* New York: Knopf, 1969.

—. *The Lost World.* New York: Knopf, 1997.

Dinello, Daniel. *Technophobia: Science Fiction Visions of Posthuman Technology.* Austin: Texas, 2005.

Douglas, Gordon. *Them!* Warner Bros, 1954.

Erickson, Gregory M. "Breathing life into Tyrannosaurus rex." *Scientific American* 281 no. 3 (1999): 42-49.

Foucault, Michel. *Discipline and Punish: The Birth of the Prison.* Translated by Alan Sheridan. New York: Vintage, 1995.

Freeland, Cynthia A. "Feminist Frameworks for Horror Films." In *PostTheory: Reconstructing Film Studies,* edited by David Bordwell and Noel Carroll, 195-218. Madison: U Wisconsin Press, 1996.

Gallardo-Torrano, Pere. "The McDonaldization of the Modern Prometheus: Michael Crichton's *Westworld* and *Jurassic Park.*" *Letterature D'America: Revista Trimestrale.* 24 (2004): 137-59.

Gordon, Bert I. *Food of the Gods,* 1976.

Gribbin, John. *In Search of Schrödinger's Cat.* New York: Bantam, 1984.

Honda, Ishiro. *Godzilla.* Toho Film, 1954.

Johnston, Joe. *Jurassic Park III.* Amblin, 2001.

Lacan, Jacques. *The Four Fundamental Concepts of Psychoanalysis,* edited by Jacques-Alain Miller, translated by Alan Sheridan. New York: Norton, 1998.

McTiernan, John. *The Thirteenth Warrior.* Touchstone, 1999.

Miracky, James J. "Replicating a Dinosaur: Authenticity Run Amok in the Theme-parking of Michael Crichton's *Jurassic Park* and Julian Barnes' *England, England.*" *Critique* 45 (2004):163-171.

Mulvey, Laura. "Afterthoughts on 'Visual Pleasure and Narrative Cinema' Inspired by *Duel in the Sun.*" In *Feminism and Film Theory*, edited by Constance Penley, 57-79. New York: Routledge, 1996.

—. "Visual Pleasure and Narrative Cinema." In *Feminism and Film Theory*, edited by Constance Penley. New York: Routledge, 1996.

Powell, Anna. *Deleuze and Horror Film.* Edinburgh: Edinburgh University Press, 2005.

Sobchak, Vivian. "'Presentifying' Film and Media Feminism." *Camera Obscura* 21 (2006): 64-68.

Spielberg, Steven. *Jurassic Park.* Universal, 1993.

—. *The Lost World: Jurassic Park.* Amblin, 1997.

Sudan, Rajani. "Technophallia." *Camera Obscura* 40-41 (1997): 105-128.

Thornham, Sue, ed. *Feminist Film Theory: A Reader.* New York: NYU,1999.

Turner, Stephanie J. "Jurassic Park Technology in the Bioinformatic Economy: How Cloning Narratives Negotiate the Telos of DNA." *American Literature* 74 (2002): 887-909.

Wells, Paul. *The Horror Genre: From Beelzebub to Blair Witch.* New York: Wallflower, 2000.

Williams, Linda. "Film Bodies: Gender, Genre, and Excess." In *Feminist Film Theory: A Reader*, edited by Sue Thornham, 267-281. New York: NYU, 1999.

Notes

[1] Clive Barker quoted by Paul Wells in *The Horror Genre: From Beelzebub to Blair Witch* (New York: Wallflower, 2000), 112.

[2] Two brief feminist readings of Jurassic Park have been published: Laura Briggs and Jodi I. Kelber-Kaye, "'There is No Unauthorized Breeding in Jurassic Park': Gender and the Uses of Genetics," *NWSA Journal* 12 (2000): 92-113, and Cynthia A. Freeland, "Feminist Frameworks for Horror Films" in *Post-Theory: Reconstructing Film Studies*, ed. David Bordwell and Noel Carroll (Madison: U Wisconsin P, 1996), 195-218.

[3] Jaime Bihlmeyer, "Novel, Script, Image: A Case Study of the Phallic (M)Other in Mainstream Culture" in Leslie Boldt-Irons, Corrado Federici, Ernesto Virgutli, eds., *Images and Imagery: Frames, Borders, Limits: Interdisciplinary Perspectives* (New York: Peter Lang, 2005), 153-64.

[4] Gregory M. Erickson, "Breathing life into Tyrannosaurus rex," *Scientific American* 281 no. 3 (1999): 42.

[5] Field Museum, "Sue at the Field Museum": http://www.fieldmuseum.org/sue/about.

[6] Pere Gallardo-Torrano, "The McDonaldization of the Modern Prometheus: Michael Crichton's *Westworld* and *Jurassic Park*," *Letterature D'America: Revista Trimestrale* 24 (2004): 137-59.

[7] Laura Mulvey, "Afterthoughts on 'Visual Pleasure and Narrative Cinema Inspired by King Vidor's *Duel in the Sun*" and "Visual Pleasure and Narrative Cinema" in *Feminism and Film Theory*, ed. Constance Penley (New York: Routledge, 1996), 57-79.

[8] Cynthia A. Freeland, "Feminist Frameworks for Horror Films." Barbara Creed, "Horror and the Monstrous Feminine: An Imaginary Abjection" in *Feminist Film Theory: A Reader*, ed. Sue Thornham (New York: NYU, 1999), 251-265.

[9] Michel Foucault, *Discipline and Punish* (New York: Vintage, 1995).

[10] Cynthia A. Freeland, "Feminist Frameworks for Horror Films." Linda Williams, "Film Bodies: Gender, Genre, and Excess" in *Feminist Film Theory: A Reader,* ed. Sue Thornham (New York: NYU, 1999), 267-281.

[11] Vivian Sobchak, "'Presentifying' Film and Media Feminism," *Camera Obscura* 21 (2006): 64-68.

[12] Sue Thornham, introduction, *Feminist Film Theory: A Reader* (New York: NYU Press, 1999), 1.

[13] Cited by Briggs and Kelber-Kaye, 92-113.

[14] Paul Wells, *The Horror Genre: From Beelzebub to Blair Witch* (New York: Wallflower, 2000), 13.

[15] Daniel Dinello, *Technophobia: Science Fiction Visions of Posthuman Technology* (Austin: Texas, 2005).

[16] Anna Powell, *Deleuze and Horror Film* (Edinburgh: Edinburgh UP, 2005).

[17] Creed, 261.

[18] Ibid., 265.

[19] Briggs and Kelber-Kaye, whose essay is discussed below, also make this point and connection.

[20] "The McDonaldization of the Modern Prometheus," 137.

[21] Dinello, 198.

[22] James J. Miracky, "Replicating a Dinosaur: Authenticity Run Amok in the Theme-parking of Michael Crichton's *Jurassic Park* and Julian Barnes' *England, England*," *Critique* 45 (2004): 163-171.

[23] Briggs and Kelber-Kaye, 95.

[24] Ibid., 94.

[25] Ibid..

[26] Ibid., 92-113.

[27] Rajani Sudan, "Technophallia," *Camera Obscura* 40-41 (1997): 105-128. Constance Balides, "Jurassic post-Fordism: Tall Tales of Economics in the Theme Park," *Screen* 41 (2000): 139-60.

[28] Briggs and Kelber-Kaye, 92-113.

[29] Freeland, 195.

[30] Ibid., 195-6.

[31] Ibid., 196.

[32] Ibid..

[33] Ibid.

[34] See Freeland and Sobchak.

[35] Stephanie J. Turner, "Jurassic Park Technology in the Bioinformatics Economy: How Cloning Narratives Negotiate the Telos of DNA," *American Literature* 74 (2002): 887-909.

[36] John Gribbin, *In Search of Schrödinger's Cat* (New York: Bantam, 1984).

[37] Carol J. Clover, "Her Body, Himself: Gender in the Slasher Film" in *Feminist Film Theory: A Reader,* ed. Sue Thornham (New York: NYU, 1999).

[38] Briggs and Kelber-Kaye, 93.

CHAPTER TWO

SHIFTING GENDER(ED) DESIRE IN ANNE FONTAINE'S *NATHALIE*...

RACHEL RITTERBUSCH

The critical reception of creative endeavors is not impartial: the race, gender, age, and sexual orientation of an artist all influence how his/her work is perceived. With regard to gender, for instance, critics often present and discuss the work of women as distinct from that of men. As a result, novels by women authors are frequently treated as an example of *écriture féminine*, a way of writing that inscribes female difference in language and text, instead of being judged independently from the gender of its author. Similarly, films by women directors are often labeled as "women's films" or "women's cinema." Such pigeonholing is problematic for two reasons. First, the terminology implies that only women are capable of creating texts/films that challenge phallocentric norms, when in reality a feminine practice of writing/filmmaking is accessible to men as well. Second, and more importantly, there is no consensus about what constitutes a feminine practice. Consequently, the term "women's writing" or "women's cinema" is problematic.

Given the ambiguity of such terms, it is not surprising that contemporary French director Anne Fontaine (b. 1959) attacks those who categorize her dramas as "women's films." In fact, Fontaine insists that when she writes and directs, she does so not as a woman, but as a blank slate. For instance, when critics called her 1997 film *Nettoyage à sec* an insightful "woman's film," Fontaine replied as follows: "I don't know what that means. I think that to be a filmmaker, as far as sexuality, it's something that is really de-sexualizing...during the shooting, you're neither a man nor a woman, you're really something strange and very ambivalent."[1]

Clearly, Fontaine rejects the term "woman's film" because of the way it links gender to artistic creation. Indeed, as E. Ann Kaplan stresses, being "female" or "male" does not signify any necessary social stance vis-à-vis dominant cultural attitudes: "[B]iological women are not necessarily more progressive or forward looking than are biological men, and the terms 'male' and 'female' do not automatically link biological sex to masculine or feminine behaviours or to certain film genres."[2] For this reason, it is imperative to use terminology that avoids the essentializing overtones of "women's cinema" and "woman's film." In her *Women's Pictures*, Annette Kuhn suggests using the term "feminine film text," which she defines as a text that is highly conscious and disrespective of the illusionist viewing strategies and gendered pleasures embedded in the dominant male cinema. By using the term "feminine" rather than "woman," Kuhn shifts the focus from the gender of the filmmaker to specific textual and enunciative processes that position the work as alternative cinema. Sandy Flitterman-Lewis does the same in her *To Desire Differently*, where she proposes the term "feminist cinema" for those films whose content and form challenge the norms of dominant cinema: "a feminist cinema will attempt to restore the marks of cinematic enunciation so carefully elided by the concealing operations of patriarchal cinema [and] it will foreground sexual difference…, focusing on the status and nature of the representation of the woman—her desire, her images, her fantasms."[3]

Fontaine would no doubt find this neutral language more acceptable than the older, weighted terms. Yet whether one chooses to speak of "women's films" or "feminist film texts," the question remains: how can one determine whether the work of a given filmmaker actualizes the counter-cinema envisioned by feminist film critics of the 1970s such as Laura Mulvey and Claire Johnston? Is there for instance something about the content and form of Fontaine's dramas that causes critics to treat them as feminist cinema? In the following discussion, I will attempt to answer these questions by analyzing *Nathalie...* (2003), a film which continues the exploration of female sexuality and desire undertaken in Fontaine's earlier dramas *Nettoyage à sec* (1997) and *Comment j'ai tué mon père* (2001).

Emphasizing the Positive: the Role of Female Friendship and Intimacy in *Nathalie...*

The story presented in *Nathalie...* is a simple one. The film's protagonists, Bernard (Gérard Depardieu) and Catherine (Fanny Ardant), are well-to-do professionals who have been happily married for twenty years. However, their perfect world is shattered when Catherine accidentally discovers that Bernard has been cheating on her. Catherine is hurt, but instead of demanding a divorce or having a fling of her own, she goes to a sex club and hires a prostitute named Nathalie (Emmanuelle

Béart) to seduce her husband and report what takes place. Catherine no doubt hopes to discover what drives Bernard to be unfaithful. But after a few meetings, Catherine and Nathalie begin to develop a relationship that goes beyond the client-prostitute contract. As the film progresses, it appears that it is Catherine rather than Bernard, who is having an affair with Nathalie. The women's intimate bond is subsequently broken when, in an unexpected twist, Catherine learns that Nathalie is not actually having an affair with Bernard as she claims: she is merely pretending to do so in order to be paid by Catherine. In fact when Nathalie tried to seduce Bernard, he showed no interest in her.

Film critics are divided about *Nathalie*...: for each one who praises the director's depiction of female sexuality, there is another who attacks it. For example, Jamie Russell lauds Fontaine for tackling voyeurism and desire from a woman's viewpoint, while Jake Wilson slams the film as "a wish fulfillment fantasy for middle-age women."[4] While Fernando López feels that recounting the sexual act rather than showing it heightens the film's erotic charge, Rich Cline finds the film "overtalky and...strangely sexless."[5] Who is right? The film's advocates, its detractors, or both? The following explores the merits of each position.

Let us begin with those critics who emphasize Fontaine's feminist stance. Anton Bitel, for example, calls attention to the unexpected way Fontaine treats the dynamics between husband, wife, and lover, calling it "a new feminist variation on this theme."[6] Bitel is correct in this assessment because in most films about infidelity, the person that disturbs the dyad of the married couple is a rival. This is true regardless of the interloper's gender: in the Hollywood classic *The Postman Always Rings Twice* (dir. Tay Garnett, 1946), it is a man who supplants the husband, while in François Truffaut's *La Femme d'à côté* (1981) it is a woman who comes between her former lover and his second wife. In Fontaine's film, however, the third party is not an intruder. On the contrary, since it is Catherine, the wife, who orchestrates the affair, Nathalie is an accomplice rather than a rival. She and Catherine share the satisfaction of fooling the clueless Bernard. Furthermore, the fact that the two women are sexually attracted to each other constitutes another feminist twist, one already explored by Josiane Balasko in *Gazon maudit* (1995), albeit in a comedic, rather than serious, vein.

Like Bitel, critic Sheila Seacroft finds much to praise in *Nathalie*.... Yet she chooses to read the film as "a picture of women reclaiming power" rather than as a tale of adultery.[7] For Seacroft, the real focus of Fontaine's drama is the two female protagonists and the intimacy they develop over time. There is a great deal in the film to support this interpretation. For instance, Bernard has very little on-screen time when compared to the women. There is, of course, a technical explanation for the husband's minor role: the film's events are focalized through Catherine, who is therefore present in almost every scene. Since the camera follows her everywhere, and since she has very little contact with Bernard, viewers hardly see him. The married couple is only shown together briefly during meals or in the evening, as they get ready for bed.

Consequently, the couple that dominates the screen is Catherine/Nathalie and not Catherine/Bernard or Nathalie/Bernard. At the onset of the film, the locations of the women's meetings are limited to the sex club or a nearby bar, where they talk about Nathalie's encounters with Bernard. Soon, however, a more personal relationship develops, which is signaled by a shift in the locations where the women meet. One afternoon, for example, Catherine seeks out Nathalie at the beauty salon where she works during the day, and invites her for coffee. Although their conversation still centers on sex, Bernard is no longer the main topic of conversation, but rather, a young waiter with whom Catherine recently had a one-night stand. This is the first time that Catherine speaks of herself, and as these *confidences intimes* develop, the two women are brought closer together.

The degree of intimacy deepens further when the dialogue between them moves from the public to the private sphere. One day, when Catherine's reclusive mother wants a haircut but refuses to leave her house, Catherine asks Nathalie to visit her mother and to cut her hair. As afternoon becomes evening, Catherine asks Nathalie to stay over for dinner and spend the night with them. The scene in Catherine's girlhood bedroom is reminiscent of an adolescent sleep-over: the two women smoke, try on each other's jewelry, and talk about old boyfriends. Against all odds, it seems that the prostitute hired to seduce the philandering Bernard has becomes his wife's best friend.

This unlikely friendship is further highlighted by the film's color scheme. Red, which is normally associated with sex and passion dominates the sex club's décor. It is Nathalie's color of choice, both at work and during her meetings with Catherine. Green is the color of Catherine's world. Its calm, cool tones pervade her wardrobe and even her bedroom's decorating scheme. The contrast between these two colors recalls the differences between the two female protagonists: hot/cold, young/old, lower-class/upper-class. Yet as the relationship between Catherine and Nathalie progresses, the complementary nature of the two colors is foregrounded. Together, these friends form a harmonious whole: Nathalie helps Catherine rediscover her passion for life, while Catherine has a matronly, calming influence on the younger woman. As the film reaches its denouement, Catherine is clad in red, but Nathalie sports some green outfits.

Nonetheless, the women's nurturing friendship is only a fraction of the story. As Seacroft notes, the friendship evolves into "something new, which might well feel very menacing to the male viewer."[8] This "something new" is the sexual attraction between the two women which, as it grows, causes Catherine to exhibit all the behaviors typical of a cheating spouse. First, she starts lying about where she goes, how she spends her time, and whom she sees. Next, she feigns some indispositions in order to avoid social commitments and sneaks off to spend time with Nathalie, who has become central to her daily life. Later, when Nathalie loses the lease of her apartment, Catherine rents one for her, just as a man would for his mistress. Finally, when Bernard goes to London on business, the two women have a night out of drinking and dancing, a scene that is an ironic pendant to the film's opening scene in which Bernard has a fling while on business in Zurich.

However, the "affair" between the two women cannot simply be reduced to a series of plot elements. What truly creates the sexual charge that might seem threatening to the male viewer is the *mise en scène*, the cinematographic techniques used to present their relationship. Consider, for example, the use of point-of-view shots during the first encounter between the two women. As Catherine enters the club, the camera zooms in on her face, thus establishing her as the focalizing figure. What the camera reveals next is scantily clad female hostesses and their overweight balding male clients, all of which is seen from Catherine's eyes. Once Catherine sits down, her eyes (the camera's lens) continue to scan the room, looking for the right woman for her purpose, which is the seduction of her husband. Catherine's gaze moves slowly from one prostitute to another, lingering first on a dark-skinned beauty then moving on to a buxom brunette and then looking at a red-head as she leads her client upstairs. At this moment, Nathalie comes into view. From then on, the camera focuses exclusively on Nathalie and Catherine, tracking Nathalie as she moves toward the bar, then cutting back to Catherine who seems fascinated by this sultry blond. The following reverse shot reveals Nathalie gazing back at Catherine. By using point of view here, Fontaine pinpoints the instant attraction between the two women.

In later scenes, slow motion is employed to further highlight this attraction. Take, for instance, the sequence in which Nathalie recounts her second invented sexual encounter with Bernard. As Catherine enters the hotel room where the encounter supposedly took place, a point-of-view shot reveals Nathalie's naked body through the glass of the shower stall, a sight which—like the rumpled bed sheets and the empty wine glasses—visibly disturbs and excites Catherine. Catherine's agitation continues to mount as Nathalie, clad only in a towel, tells her tale of seduction in great detail.

When Nathalie describes Bernard's climax, the mood of the scene abruptly shifts. There was no extradiegetic soundtrack before this scene, but now soft piano music begins to play. Then, as Nathalie describes how she caressed the sleeping Bernard with hand cream, the action moves into slow motion. Nathalie holds up her hand for Catherine to smell, then leans forward, her body pressing against Catherine's back. Catherine's eyes close, the music swells slightly and then Nathalie stretches out on the bed in a pose mirroring that of the reclining Venus hanging on the wall. By assuming this seductive pose, Nathalie brings the sexual tension between the women to a high point.

This use of slow motion is somewhat surprising in a film that otherwise offers little in the way of cinematographic tricks. Yet that is probably why it is so effective. Fontaine uses slow motion only twice more after the hotel room scene, first during the sleep-over sequence and later as the two women dance together in a disco. Because it is used sparingly, this technique is effective in highlighting the bond between the female protagonists. During those brief moments when Catherine and Nathalie are united in their desire for each other, time almost seems to stop.

Highlighting the Negative: Deception and Manipulation in *Nathalie...*

My discussion so far seems to support the interpretation of critics such as Seacroft who view *Nathalie...* as a film about the liberating force of women's friendship. However, such a positive interpretation of the film willfully elides the economic contract governing the women's relationship. They can never simply be friends or lovers because Catherine is paying Nathalie for certain services. The client-prostitute relationship, based as it is on monetary exchange, cannot fail to affect how the two women interact. Indeed, once Nathalie reveals that she never actually slept with Bernard, the viewer begins to wonder if her affection for Catherine is as fictitious as her sexual exploits.

This point of view is borne out by certain shots that focus on the contractual nature of their relationship. Consider, for instance, their first encounter at the sex club. Having caught Catherine's eye, Nathalie approaches her and proceeds to serve her a drink. During this sequence, the camera espouses Catherine's point of view, focusing first on Nathalie's long blond hair, then on her hands, and finally on her face, where it lingers on her heavily rouged lips. Feminist film critics such as Mulvey have identified this fragmentation and fetishization of the female body as typical of the dominant male gaze. Why, then, would a woman gaze at another woman in this objectifying way? In Catherine's case, one could argue that she is trying to see Nathalie through her husband's eyes and wondering if this is a woman who would appeal to him. Yet there is another reason: Catherine, like the men who come to the club, is a client with money to spend. She is therefore in a position of control over Nathalie, whose role is to serve and please.

This power differential between the two women is emphasized in each of their meetings. During their first encounter, no money exchanges hands although a contract is clearly established. After serving Catherine, Nathalie remains standing. She only sits down after Catherine offers her a drink, an action that signals her willingness to pay for services rendered. During their next encounter, which again takes place in the sex club, Nathalie recounts her first meeting with Bernard. During this narration, the camera moves back and forth in a predictable shot-countershot pattern. As soon as the tale ends, however, this rhythm changes. The camera tilts down and zooms in on Catherine's hands as she opens her purse and extracts an envelope, which she gives to Nathalie. By focusing on this exchange of money, Fontaine emphasizes that however authentic the bond between the two women may seem, in reality it is an artificial one, an illusion borne of Catherine's desires and fed by her assets. Like a modern-day Scheherazade, Nathalie tells stories night after night for Catherine's pleasure and entertainment. However, the parallel ends there, for while Scheherazade spins tales to save her life, Nathalie invents stories to earn a living. When she is with her clients—male or female—she tells them what they want to hear: "Je fais semblant. C'est mon métier" ("I fake it. It's my job.")

Nevertheless, it would be inaccurate to depict Nathalie as the conniving manipulator and Catherine as the gullible victim because, as Andrew O'Hehir notes, the relationship between the women is mutually manipulative.[9] Like Pygmalion who falls in love with the statue he sculpts, Catherine falls in love with an illusion she creates. For one must never forget that Nathalie is a fictional character whose name and appearance are carefully selected by her creator, Catherine. Nathalie is in fact not the prostitute's real name, but rather the one given to her by Catherine who disapproves of the prostitute's *nom de guerre* Marlène, which evokes the sultry *femmes fatales* played by Marlene Dietrich.[10] Thanks to its soft "ie" ending, the prostitute's new name sounds innocent and chaste. First names such as Nathalie, Virginie, or Sylvie evoke "good" girls raised in proper, affluent, bourgeois families. And this is exactly what Catherine wants. Nathalie should have nothing about her that says "tramp": her clothing should be modest and her make-up subtle. When Nathalie is with Bernard, she should pretend to be "une fille normale," a Parisian university student.

As we have seen, it is this "fille normale" with whom Catherine falls in love, becoming increasingly dependent on Nathalie for companionship and intimacy. Fontaine stresses the illusory nature of this infatuation by showing the viewer occasional images of Marlène-Nathalie when she is neither whore nor "good girl," but rather, when she is truly herself. For example, in one sequence the camera follows her as she meets two girlfriends at a shopping mall. The three women talk and laugh as they stroll past the shop windows and then go ice-skating together. Marlène-Nathalie swoops gracefully around the rink, smiling with a kind of *joie de vivre* visible nowhere else in the film, no doubt because here—at least for a few hours—she is not controlled by the desire of others.

Fontaine's Cinematography: Challenging the Dominance of the Male Gaze

The way in which *Nathalie...* deals with issues of marriage, infidelity, and female desire categorizes it as a feminist film text. The director's feminist stance is evident not only in the film's content but also—and just as importantly—in its visual form. As we will see, Fontaine problematizes the voyeuristic mechanisms inherent in mainstream cinema, thus rising to the challenge issued by feminist film critics of the 1970s who called on filmmakers to develop "a new language of desire" capable of speaking woman's reality.[11]

Although over thirty years have passed since the publication of Laura Mulvey's "Visual Pleasure and Narrative Cinema" (1975) followed by its 1981 revision, the debate sparked by her theory of spectatorship continues unabated. Using Freudian psychoanalytic theories, Mulvey argued that the visual pleasure of classical Hollywood cinema is based on voyeuristic and fetishistic forms of looking. Because of the ways these looks are structured, the spectator necessarily identifies with the male protagonist and his objectification of the female figure. Thus, according to Mulvey, the construction of woman as spectacle is built into the apparatus of dominant cinema, and the spectator position produced by the film narrative is necessarily a masculine one, regardless of the sex of the actual moviegoer.

Mulvey's position generated considerable controversy amongst film theorists. Many criticized her fixed alignment of passivity with femininity and activity with masculinity. Yet the most prevalent objection raised by critics such as Mary Ann Doane (1982) and E. Ann Kaplan (1983) concerned Mulvey's failure to account for the female spectator. Since both the subject of the gaze and the narrative are defined as male, this leaves the female spectator with only two equally unsatisfactory possibilities: transvestite identification and narcissistic identification. In the first, the female spectator identifies with the male protagonist and thus experiences the freedom of action and control over the diegetic world that he enjoys. In the second, the female spectator identifies with her counterpart within the diegesis and experiences the masochistic pleasure of objectification.

When taken to their logical conclusion, Mulvey's arguments deny authentic female spectatorship. Theorists have found different ways out of this impasse. Some such as Ilaria Serra and Elizabeth Cowie returned to psychoanalytic theory in order to develop a more flexible concept of cinematic spectatorship. For example, Ilaria Serra used Deleuzian schizoanalysis to free the spectator from the constrictive male-female binarism of Freudian psychoanalysis, while other feminist critics turned to Laplanche and Pontalis's "fantasy theory" which presents the processes of identification as shifting and multiple rather than confined by boundaries of biological sex or cultural gender.

However, another group of critics decided to look elsewhere for a way to explain the spectator-screen relationship. Some, such as Jackie Stacey, chose to focus on the responses of actual spectators rather than theoretical questions of subject positioning, while others, such as Christine Gledhill, used theories drawn from the work of the Italian Marxist Antonio Gramsci to argue that cultural texts are the sites of struggles over meaning. The dominant order will always seek to impose their classification of the social and cultural world through such texts, but these meanings will, to some extent, remain open to contestation. This process of negotiation ensures that the film spectator is not as fixed by the structures of a film as Mulvey's analysis suggests.

As can be seen from this brief summary, Mulvey's theory of spectatorship has come under attack from all sides. Yet critics who focus on the weaknesses of Mulvey's arguments overlook the intent of her article, which is to call for radical change. The military vocabulary she employs is significant: terms such as "weapon," "attack," "destroy," and "strike the first blow" show that Mulvey in no way condones the masculinization of spectatorship which she discusses. On the contrary, she sees the objectification of women for male visual pleasure as something to be attacked, and psychoanalytic theory is her weapon of choice: "There is no way in which we can produce an alternative out of the blue, but we can begin to make a break by examining patriarchy with the tools it provides, of which psychoanalysis is not the only but an important one."[12] Her goal is to expose how mainstream film manipulates visual pleasure and, in doing so, to create the conditions for an alternative cinema, one that provides an authentic position for the female subject.

How might such a cinema function? According to Mulvey, in order to subvert the conventions of dominant cinema, one must "free the look of the camera into its materiality in time and space and the look of the audience into dialectics, passionate detachment."[13] As Mulvey explains at the end of "Visual Pleasure," there are three different looks associated with the cinema: that of the camera, that of the spectator, and that of the characters in the diegesis. In order to maintain the illusion necessary for the fulfillment of the male spectator's scopophilic drive, the conventions of narrative film deny the first two looks and subordinate them to the third. Consequently, what Mulvey wants is a cinema that highlights the act of showing and, in doing so, creates a distancing awareness in the audience.

Foregrounding the Look of the Camera

This is precisely what Anne Fontaine does in *Nathalie...* by repeatedly calling attention to the presence of the camera. The first such foregrounding occurs during the credit sequence. Here, the camera is located outside Catherine's house. It peers at her through the window, moving first to the left then back to the right in order to keep her in its gaze. Through the process of primary identification (defined by Christian Metz as identification with the viewing apparatus), the spectator is positioned with the camera: we are outside, looking in at a group of people who ignore our presence. In this context, the window frame—which echoes both the camera's viewfinder and the screen itself—calls the spectator's attention to his/her role as a voyeur. However, at the end of the credit sequence, the camera "enters the house," and the materiality of the recording process is downplayed.

Another foregrounding of the viewing process occurs about fifteen minutes into the film, when Nathalie first meets Bernard. The sequence begins with Catherine telling Nathalie where to find her husband and how to recognize him: every morning he drinks his coffee and reads the paper in the same café. At this point, the camera cuts to a shot of Nathalie walking purposefully towards the café. When she enters, the camera remains outside, looking through the large plate glass windows. The spectator is positioned with the camera, watching as Nathalie approaches the unsuspecting Bernard to ask him for a light. Thus, in this scene a window again functions as a framing device that emphasizes the pleasure of looking without being seen, which, according to Metz, may be related to the guilty pleasure of the primal scene, when a child watches the parents making love.

It is significant that Catherine is excluded from this act of viewing. She has orchestrated the meeting between Bernard and Nathalie at the café and would like to be in the position of voyeur, but this pleasure is denied her. Instead, she must depend on Nathalie to find out what takes place in her absence.

Telling Rather than Showing

This brings us to an important characteristic of Fontaine's film: the sexual act is verbalized rather than visualized. Obviously, the choice between mimesis and diegesis is one that must be made by both writers and filmmakers, but what showing and telling entail varies according to medium. In written narrative, all actions and gestures are rendered in words. In showing, events are presented directly; the narrator seems to disappear (as in drama), and the reader is left to draw his own conclusions from what he "sees" and "hears." Conversely, when events are told in narrative texts, they are mediated by a narrator who comments on and summarizes them. In filmic narrative, on the other hand, the distinction between showing and telling concerns the means of enunciation, not the degree of narrative mediation: filmic events can be shown visually as they are unfolding or recounted verbally after the fact. The question I raise is why Fontaine chose to talk about sex rather than show it.

One could argue that Fontaine did not choose at all and that telling is the only option given the fact that Nathalie and Bernard are not actually having sex. However, to focus on this narrative constraint is to miss the point. Within the diegesis, Nathalie does everything in her power to maintain the illusion that she and Bernard are having an affair. As previously mentioned, she even rents a hotel room and creates a convincing post-coital disarray for Catherine's benefit, complete with scattered pieces of clothing and half-empty wine glasses. Given this "proof" of Bernard's philandering, neither Catherine nor the spectator suspects that the stories told by Nathalie are pure fiction. Both assume that something is taking place which they cannot witness. However, whereas Catherine accepts this limitation of her knowledge, the spectator does not. For although events are generally presented from Catherine's point of view, the camera is occasionally omniscient, revealing things she cannot see, such as the meeting between Bernard and Nathalie in the café. Accordingly, the spectator may feel cheated, and may believe s/he is being denied the voyeuristic pleasure of watching the sexual act.

Support for this assertion is provided by the reactions of a specialized group of spectators, that of film critics. Almost all critics comment on Fontaine's decision not to show the sexual act. It is significant to note how their reactions vary according to gender. Whereas critics of both genders praise Fontaine for using the erotic power of the spoken word to stimulate the spectator's imagination, the strong negative reactions are almost exclusively male. For instance, Rich Cline of *Shadows on the Wall* says that, "[f]or all the talk of sex, the film is strangely sexless."[14] Jake Wilson of *Urban Cinefile* echoes this sentiment, stating that "*Nathalie* could be described as feeble arthouse porn, except that it has little art and (sadly) even less porn."[15] Michael Mackenzie of *DVD Times*, who is frustrated by the lack of sex in *Nathalie...*, argues that "Fontaine's approach of *tell* rather than *show* does it no favours, as the act of telling adds nothing that simply showing the process would not have achieved, and at least then the film could potentially have succeeded in being a steamy erotic thriller."[16] Mackenzie and other irate male critics missed the point, since the approach of tell rather than show achieves something quite important: it denies these male spectators (as well as others) the visual pleasure they have come to expect.

Woman as Spectacle

Although *Nathalie...* manages to deny the male spectator the gratification of his scopophilic drive where the sexual act is concerned, it cannot prevent him from gazing at and objectifying the female body presented on screen. For as Mulvey reminds us, the cinematic apparatus functions in such a way that "women are simultaneously looked at and displayed, with their appearance coded for strong visual and erotic impact so that they can be said to connote *to-be-looked-at-ness*."[17] Nonetheless, there are ways to subvert this presentation of woman as spectacle. One possibility is highlighted in a recent article by Phil Powrie entitled "Transitial Woman: New Representations of Women in Contemporary French Cinema." Here Powrie notes that while women are still displayed as sexual objects in many French films, certain women directors are creating heroines who seemingly escape specularity: "The gaze constructed in these films no longer seems clearly voyeuristic, or caught in the sadistic/fetishizing binary."[18] For example, such films as *Y aura-t-il de la neige à Noël?* (1996) by Sandrine Veysset and *Rosetta* (1999) by Jean-Pierre and Luc Dardenne present "ordinary women," unglamorized either by costume or by cinematographic style.

Anne Fontaine does not go this route in *Nathalie...*. On the contrary, both female protagonists present a spectacularized allure. Although Catherine can be considered sexy in a refined bourgeois way, it is clearly Nathalie (played by French sex symbol Emmanuelle Béart) who is cut to the measure of male desire. Everything about her appearance as a prostitute is designed to please the male gaze: provocative outfits that leave little to the imagination, high-heeled shoes, and heavy makeup that accentuates her sultry beauty. It would thus seem that Fontaine is presenting the male spectator with an erotic spectacle *par excellence*. However, Nathalie's role as a sexual object is problematized through the use of subjective camera work.

As mentioned earlier, almost the entire film is shown from Catherine's point of view. Occasionally, however, the spectator is invited to share the male point of view. Consider, for example, the two sequences in which Nathalie dances for male clients. In the first sequence, Fontaine foregrounds the voyeuristic pleasure of the male gaze by including Nathalie's client at the lower right of the frame. This creates a certain distance between the spectator and the female spectacle on the screen because we are made aware of the looking relations in play. At the same time, we are aware of our position as spectator: we are watching a man look at a woman. Our voyeuristic pleasure is thus called into question. The same effect is created in the second sequence. Here, the client's head is initially visible in the lower left of the screen. Yet soon the camera shifts, and Nathalie appears to be looking directly at the spectator, who is thus put in the place of the male voyeur.

Both sequences seem to present the classic paradigm highlighted by Mulvey: the male is the active bearer of the look while the female is the passive object of this look. Yet I argue that Nathalie is actually in control. She is an object of desire, but she determines who can look at her and when. In a certain sense, then, it is not her body that Nathalie sells, but rather her image. This observation suggests a parallel between prostitution and film production: in both cases, the act of viewing is commodified. Like Nathalie's clients, the spectators of Fontaine's film must pay for the privilege of the gaze. But Fontaine's foregrounding of the male point of view problematizes the act of looking and thus prevents us from satisfying our scopophilic drive the way that the male characters in the diegesis do.

What happens, however, when Nathalie is the subject of a female rather than a male gaze? To answer this question, let us consider the sequence discussed earlier, in which Catherine goes to the hotel room where Nathalie ostensibly seduced Bernard. As the sequence begins, the spectator sees Nathalie's naked body reflected and framed in the bathroom mirror, then the camera pulls back to reveal Catherine as the subject of the gaze. How strongly Catherine desires Nathalie becomes increasingly apparent as the scene progresses. For instance, when Nathalie describes how she used face cream to caress Bernard, she leans in toward Catherine to let her smell the cream's scent. As noted before, the sexual tension of this moment is emphasized through soft extradiegetic music and the use of slow motion: the women are as if frozen in a moment of erotic attraction.

It would therefore seem that the presence of a female gaze changes the dynamics between subject and object. For in this scene Nathalie is open and vulnerable rather than distanced and harsh. Instead of leather or vinyl she wears only a towel, and the mask of make-up that creates her sex club persona has been washed away. Yet one must not forget that Catherine is a paying client, not a female friend. Consequently, the image that Nathalie presents to Catherine here is just as consciously produced as the one she sells to male clients, a fact that is subtly emphasized by an element of the *mise-en-scène*. The hotel room is decorated with a painting in keeping with its function as a trysting place, that of a reclining nude and winged cherub, one of the many "Venus and Cupid" compositions produced during the baroque period. It is no coincidence that when Nathalie lies down on the bed, the position of her proffered body mirrors that of the nude hanging above her: she is provocatively displayed for Catherine's gaze just as Venus is for the spectator. These elements demonstrate that when a woman looks at another woman, objectification can occur in the same way as when a man looks at a woman.

Nathalie...: A Feminist Film Text?

Can *Nathalie...*, be considered an example of feminist cinema? Perhaps. *Nathalie...* not only focuses on the representation of woman—her desire, her images, her fantasms—but also problematizes the voyeuristic mechanisms inherent in mainstream cinema. On the other hand, the intimate bond between Catherine and Nathalie is undermined by the contractual nature of their relationship, with the compliant prostitute telling the well-to-do client exactly what she wants to hear.

Some critics, such as Seacroft, choose to ignore the ambiguity of the women's friendship in order to find a feminist message in Fontaine's drama, heralding it as a picture of women reclaiming power. However, I would argue that it is precisely this ambiguity that informs the film. Just like Fontaine, who insists that she is neither man nor woman when making a film, *Nathalie...* is neither dogmatically feminist nor blatantly sexist but rather, to quote Fontaine, "a bizarre thing...something strange and very ambivalent."[19] Hence, it is not a "women's film" in the accepted sense of the term, but rather a film about women, a film that surely both male and female spectators will find intriguing in its approach to human relationships as far as gender, sexuality and power are concerned.

Works Cited

Bitel, Anton. Review of *Nathalie...* by Anne Fontaine. *Movie Gazette.* http://www.movie-gazette.com/cinereviews/837.

Cline, Rich. Review of *Nathalie...* by Anne Fontaine. *Shadows on the Wall* (April 21, 2004). http://www.shadowsonthewall.co.uk/04/arth.htm#nath.

Comment j'ai tué mon père. Directed by Anne Fontaine. Paris: Ciné B, 2001.

Cowie, Elizabeth. *Representing the Woman: Cinema and Psychoanalysis.* Minneapolis, MN: Minnesota University Press, 1997.

Doane, Mary Ann. "Film and the Masquerade: Theorising the Female Spectator." In *Film Theory and Criticism*, edited by Gerald Mast, Marshall Cohen, and Leo Braudy, 758-772. New York: Oxford University Press, 1992.

Flitterman-Lewis, Sandy. *To Desire Differently: Feminism and the French Cinema.* Urbana, IL: University of Illinois Press, 1990.

Fontaine, Anne. "Sexual Politics and 'Dry Cleaning' with Directrice Anne Fontaine." Interview by Eve-Laure Moros. *IndieWIRE* (March 16, 1998). http://indiewire.com/people/int_Fontaine_Anne_980316.html.

Gledhill, Christine. "Pleasurable Negotiations." In *Female Spectators: Looking at Film and Television*, edited by E. D. Pribam, 64-89. New York: Verso, 1988.

Kaplan, E. Ann. "Is the Gaze Male?" In *Feminism and Film*, edited by E. Ann Kaplan, 119-138. New York: Oxford University Press, 2000.

—. "Women, Film, Resistance: Changing Paradigms." In *Women Filmmakers: Refocusing*, edited by Jacqueline Levitin, Judith Plessis, and Valerie Raoul, 15-28. Vancouver: UBC Press, 2003.

Kuhn, Annette. *Women's Pictures: Feminism and Cinema.* 2nd ed. New York: Verso, 1994.

López, Fernando. "Sensualidad femenina en el espejo." Review of *Nathalie...* by Anne Fontaine. *La Nación* (August 26, 2004).

espectáculos:
    http://www.lanacion.com.ar/Archivo/nota.asp?nota_id=630477.
Mackenzie, Michael. Review of *Nathalie...* by Anne Fontaine. *DVD Times*
    (December 7, 2004).
    http://www.dvdtimes.co.uk/content.php?contentid=55463.
Metz, Christian. *Le signifiant imaginaire: psychanalyse et cinéma.* Paris:
    Union Générale d'Éditions, 1977.
Mulvey, Laura. "Afterthoughts on 'Visual Pleasure and Narrative Cinema'
    Inspired by King Vidor's *Duel in the Sun* (1946)." In *Feminist Film
    Theory*, edited by Sue Thornham, 122-130. New York: New York
    University Press, 1999.
—. "Visual Pleasure and Narrative Cinema." In *Narrative, Apparatus,
    Ideology*, edited by Philip Rosen, 198-209. New York: Columbia
    University Press, 1986.
Nathalie.... Directed by Anne Fontaine. Paris: France 2 Cinéma, 2003.
Nettoyage à sec. Directed by Anne Fontaine. Paris: Cinéa, 1997.
O'Hehir, Andrew. Review of *Nathalie...* by Anne Fontaine. *Salon.com*
    (April 13, 2006).
    http://www.salon.com/ent/movies/review/2006/04/13/btm/index3.html
Powrie, Phil. "Transtitial Woman: New Representations of Women in
    Contemporary French Cinema." *L'Esprit créateur* 42, no. 3 (Fall
    2002): 81-91.
Russell, Jamie. Review of *Nathalie...* by Anne Fontaine. *BBC-Films* (June
    9, 2004).
    http://www.bbc.co.uk/films/2004/06/09/nathalie_2004_review.shtml.
Seacroft, Sheila. Review of *Nathalie...* by Anne Fontaine. *Flotation Suite*
    (December 14, 2004).
    http://www.floatationsuite.com/index.php?option=com_content&task
    =view&id =162&Itemid=45.
Serra, Ilaria. "The Female Spectator's Laughter: *Anti-Oedipus* to Free
    Female Spectatorship." *theory@buffalo 8: Deleuze and Feminism*
    (2003): 100-122.
    http://wings.buffalo.edu/theory/archive/pdfs/Serra.pdf.
Stacey, Jackie. *Star Gazing: Hollywood Cinema and Female
    Spectatorship.* New York: Routledge, 1994.
Wilson, Jake. Review of *Nathalie...* by Anne Fontaine. *Urban Cinefile.*
    http://www.urbancinefile.com.au/home/view.asp?a=8783&s=Review.

Notes

[1] Anne Fontaine, "Sexual Politics and 'Dry Cleaning' with Directrice Anne Fontaine," interview by Eve-Laure Moros, *IndieWIRE* (March 16, 1998), http://indiewire.com/people/int_Fontaine_Anne_980316.html.

[2] E. Ann Kaplan, "Women, Film, Resistance: Changing Paradigms," in *Women Filmmakers: Refocusing*, edited by Jacqueline Levitin, Judith Plessis, and Valerie Raoul (Vancouver: UBC Press, 2003), 25.

[3] Sandy Flitterman-Lewis, *To Desire Differently: Feminism and the French Cinema* (Urbana, IL: University of Illinois Press, 1990), 22-23.

[4] Jamie Russell, review of *Nathalie...* by Anne Fontaine, *BBC-Films* (June 9, 2004), http://www.bbc.co.uk/films/2004/06/09/nathalie_2004_review.shtml; Jake Wilson, review of *Nathalie...* by Anne Fontaine, *Urban Cinefile*, http://www.urbancinefile.com.au/home/view.asp?a=8783&s=Reviews.

[5] Fernando López, "Sensualidad femenina en el espejo," review of *Nathalie...* by Anne Fontaine, *La Nación* (August 26, 2004), espectáculos, http://www.lanacion.com.ar/Archivo/nota.asp?nota_id=630477; Rich Cline, review of *Nathalie...* by Anne Fontaine, *Shadows on the Wall* (April 21, 2004), http://www.shadowsonthewall.co.uk/ 04/art-h.htm#nath.

[6] Anton Bitel, review of *Nathalie...* by Anne Fontaine, *Movie Gazette*, http://www.movie-gazette.com/cinereviews/837.

[7] Sheila Seacroft, review of *Nathalie...* by Anne Fontaine, *Flotation Suite* (December 14, 2004), http://www.floatationsuite.com/index.php?option=com_content&task=view&id=1 62&Itemid=45.

[8] Ibid.

[9] Andrew O'Hehir, review of *Nathalie...* by Anne Fontaine, *Salon.com* (April 13, 2006), http://www.salon.com/ent/movies/review/2006/04/13/btm/index3.html.

[10] One could go farther and note that "Marlene" is a contraction of Marie Magdalene, the name of the disciple of Jesus Christ identified by Pope Gregory as a "sinful woman" and later decried by Church fathers as a prostitute.

[11] Laura Mulvey, "Visual Pleasure and Narrative Cinema," in *Narrative, Apparatus, Ideology*, edited by Philip Rosen (New York: Columbia University Press, 1986), 200.

[12] Ibid., 199.

[13] Ibid., 209.

[14] Cline, review of *Nathalie...*.

[15] Wilson, review of *Nathalie...*.

[16] Michael Mackenzie, review of *Nathalie...* by Anne Fontaine, *DVD Times* (December 7, 2004), http://www.dvdtimes.co.uk/content.php?contentid=55463.

[17] Mulvey, "Visual Pleasure," 203.

[18] Phil Powrie, "Transtitial Woman: New Representations of Women in Contemporary French Cinema," *L'Esprit créateur* 42, no. 3 (Fall 2002): 81.

[19] Fontaine, "Sexual Politics."

CHAPTER THREE

EYES WIDE SHUT: KINO-EYE WIDE OPEN

M. HUNTER VAUGHAN

Eyes Wide Shut (1999), Stanley Kubrick's final film, is a psychological thriller that graphically explores eroticism and sexuality. It is a film focused on masquerade and based on the cleavage between reality and unconscious motivations. This film is a combination of esoteric art cinema and popular culture, since it boasts two of the most famous actors in Hollywood, Tom Cruise and Nicole Kidman, under the directive helm of one of cinema's most notoriously cerebral directors, Stanley Kubrick. At first glance it appears to be a feminist film theorist's dream come true, at least as far as the dominant strand of 1970s feminist film theory and other theories of gender and representation are concerned. Yet *Eyes Wide Shut* manages to challenge monolithic attempts at analyzing the portrayal of gender in cinema. By subverting traditional conventions of what Laura Mulvey dubs the "male gaze,"[1] *Eyes Wide Shut* demonstrates the lengths to which this staple of feminist film criticism is both applicable to Hollywood film practices while, at the same time, revealing the shortcomings of this construct.[2] Initially appearing to romanticize the male gaze, only to overthrow its psychological and social association through formal and narrative subversion, *Eyes Wide Shut* suggests how cinema can struggle against the principal characteristics aptly described in much of feminist film theory.

The male gaze, constituted in the groundbreaking essay by Laura Mulvey entitled "Visual Pleasure and Narrative Cinema," is a cornerstone of feminist film theory. Mulvey uses this term to describe the underlying patriarchal domination of Hollywood and its consequent division of representation by gender. Popular American cinema has served as a bastion for the social status quo and is a subtle vessel for dominant patriarchal ideology. Primarily, the male gaze for Mulvey represents a visual metaphor—both cause and result—for the systematic objectification of women in classical Hollywood cinema. This includes woman as an object of representation and also as a spectatorial position. Referring to the representation of women on screen—and thus *through* the eye of the camera—as well as to the portrayal of male-female relations postulated in conventional film narratives, the patriarchal system can be seen to prevail. Mulvey's male gaze works on a multitude of levels, each of which is accentuated—though frequently subverted—by *Eyes Wide Shut*.

Consider the cinematic apparatus itself, the eye of the camera as an extension of particular socio-cultural values. Based on Sigmund Freud's theory of the objectifying gaze, Mulvey applies *scopophilia*—looking as a source of pleasure in and of itself—to the representation of women in cinema. As men have traditionally held the means of production in the film industry, Mulvey argues that the representation of women has been derived from a heterosexual male pleasure found in looking at them. Part of a representational symbiosis, the male pleasure found in looking at women coincides with the representation of the female desire to be visually objectified, what Mulvey calls the woman's "to-be-looked-at-ness."[3] In Mulvey's estimation, in dominant heteronormative codes of cinematic as well as other forms of audio-visual mass media, men desire women by displacing them as an object of vision, whereas female desire is found in the status of being this object.

Based on fascination with sexual difference, this act of looking, this trajectory or "gaze," reflects a problem of alienation or difference that the male psyche (re)solves in one of two ways: investigation, such as in film noir, or fetishization, such as in the voyeuristic principle of mainstream pornography.[4] The former genre involves a narrative problem in which *woman* acts as a symbolic marker and an epistemological article of knowledge to be acquired as well as possessed through the solving of a mystery. In these types of films, the male psyche deflects the threat of female Otherness, whereas in pornographic movies, female Otherness becomes the focus not of inquiry but of alienation and exoticization.[5]

Both facets of the male gaze play an important role in *Eyes Wide Shut*. However, this is no longer classical Hollywood: in a challenge to the very roots of Mulvey's concept, *Eyes Wide Shut* removes the conditioning sexual orientation of the gaze itself. Investigation—which Mulvey suggests is necessary for the subsequent devaluation of the object (in other words, the woman)—is the catalyst for the narrative of *Eyes Wide Shut*. Investigation in this film is central to subverting the traditional representation of sexual relations and, in particular, the gendered constructions of the woman as passive and looked-at while the male is the active viewer. This film could be placed in the tradition of the post-

Classical suspense thriller that rose to prominence with the post-war films of Alfred Hitchcock and, to cite French philosopher Gilles Deleuze, the crisis of the *image-mouvement*.[6]

Eyes Wide Shut centers around Dr. Bill Harford (Tom Cruise), whose investigation into the death of a prostitute leads him to discover nothing save for his own lack and inability to reduce human beings to objects as well as his impotence in a sexually charged environment. Bill's role as the source of *narrative thrust* initially supports yet ultimately subverts Mulvey's analysis of the male protagonist and star as narrative manifestation as well as source of the male gaze. Instead, *Eyes Wide Shut* presents a de-centered filmic subjectivity that can no longer be traced to a particular active source of identification such as a character, nor a specific mode of interpretation, in other words, an implied spectator.[7]

The question of subjectivity is crucial to feminist—and most post-structuralist—theory. As Kaja Silverman notes: "subjectivity is by no means an ideologically innocent condition, but one which reflects dominant cultural values."[8] Silverman argues that it is the responsibility of *semiotics* to examine the ways in which sexual difference provides the impetus for signification, and most feminist film theory considers the role of subjectivity in representation and the use of signs to generate meaning. In traditional mainstream cinema, according to Jackie Stacey's extension of Mulvey's argument in "Desperately Seeking Difference,"[9] the character who controls the narrative—conventionally a man—defines the spectator's mode of identification and objectivity.[10]

However, a significant generic aspect of noir that Mulvey appears to have overlooked is the chaotic world of the almost always male protagonist. In film noir, the protagonist is a pawn in an uncontrollable context, an often frustrated and ill-fated archetype originally embodied by Humphrey Bogart and then extended in Hitchcock's films of the 1950s, such as *Rear Window* (1954) and *Vertigo* (1958). While Bill is the "protagonist" of *Eyes Wide Shut*, his inability to conclude his investigation symbolizes his incompetence, and by extension his *impotence*, thus rendering him symbolically *castrated* and therefore feminized, thereby subverting the traditional male-driven narrative. This is often a central contradiction of post-World War II film noir: the spectator is led through narrative frequency—who gets the most screen time, whose actions and reactions are central to the plot's events—to identify with a male ego that is lacking in true subjective agency and unable to produce meaning. In other words, Bill fails as a detective to discover the truth of the prostitute's death as well as of other mysterious encounters he experiences during his night-long quest throughout Manhattan and its surrounding areas.

An alternative to investigation, according to Mulvey, is the fetishization of the female body, which is another staple of feminist film criticism that is subverted in this film. From its very opening, *Eyes Wide Shut* appears to be focused on the role of the cinematic gaze and its inherent process of objectification and fetishization, especially of the female body. The film opens with a shot of Bill's wife Alice (Nicole Kidman) undressing. Not only does this initial scene reflect Mulvey's concept of scopophilia, but it also supports her derivative point about the fetishization of the female star. Yet, *Eyes Wide Shut* prevents the spectator from enjoying Kidman's body: when she is joined by her husband, Kidman glances directly into the camera, breaking the distance that had guaranteed the spectators' safety in objectifying her body for their own pleasure. By looking directly into the camera, Kidman demonstrates agency, and becomes a fully formed subject rather than an object of voyeuristic desire.

The fetishization and objectification of the human body remains this film's central preoccupation. Though there is an abundance of female nudity, *Eyes Wide Shut* is not pornographic. A Mulveyan analysis of the cinematic gaze in this film is inadequate because it cannot render the way the film breaks the fundamental binary oppositions that form the basis of the Mulveyan argument. First, the film presents a stylistic motif in which female nudity is desexualized. In the opening sequence Bill must save a woman who has overdosed on drugs—the woman who later ends up murdered—her naked body pale blue and compressed through flat lighting. This aesthetic rejection of eroticism is reflected in the narrative sterility because Bill is a medical doctor who approaches this body as if it were a series of symptoms and medical signs rather than if it were eliciting erotic stimulation. Similarly, in the perfunctory crosscutting sequence of daily life, Bill routinely examines female patients; this is juxtaposed against shots, back in Bill and Alice's home, of his wife getting dressed/undressed in front of their daughter. In these instances the female body is de-fetishized, de-eroticized and is not a site of scopophilia for either the spectator or the characters in the scenes.

Beyond this lack of female fetishization/erotization is its reversal, a possibility neglected by Mulvey but acknowledged by Jackie Stacey: that of the male character as a fetishized object.[11] In this instance, Mulvey's theory of the male gaze is subverted. Tom Cruise—perhaps the best example of a modern-day romantic leading man aimed at the heterosexual female spectator—is objectified in this film as well.[12] Frequently showing this male star in suggestive ways contradicts the male gaze on two levels: not only does it throw into question the sexual bias of the camera, but it also sutures in a signifying position of viewership for the heterosexual female and gay male spectator.[13] Moreover, Bill as a castrated protagonist trumps Mulvey's analysis of the male star's characteristics as being "not those of the erotic object of the gaze, but those of the more perfect, more complete, more powerful ideal ego..."[14] The film not only reveals the male star—Cruise—as object of the gaze, but it also reveals his character—Bill—as a weak and incomplete ego, thus castrating him yet again.

Not only is the notion of the male gaze subverted by the de-fetishization of the female body, the objectification of the male star and the generic destruction of the male hero, but also the film's narrative and theoretical approach to masquerade is at the heart of *revisionist* concepts of the gaze as reconsidered by Mary Ann Doane in "Film and the Masquerade: Theorizing the Female Spectator."[15] In considering the role of masquerade in concealing female identity and distancing the female spectator, Doane initially concurs with Mulvey that mainstream Hollywood traditionally attaches male subjectivity to the gaze, and that the male gaze requires sexual difference. In other words, masquerade—much like the Bakhtinian notion of the carnivalesque—provides a certain overthrow of traditional hierarchies and processes of differentiation.

Doane views masquerade as a device necessary to grant the female spectator distance enough to identify with the characters, which *Eyes Wide Shut* does for a multi-gendered spectatorship. *Eyes Wide Shut* considers masquerade's relation to identity and sexuality since the film relies upon masquerade as a central device. For example, the narrative climax of the film takes place during an elaborately costumed and masked orgy. Whereas Doane views masquerade as a way of hiding female identity, the film uses it to distract the gaze and to liberate the apparatus, characters, and spectators from any engendered identity. Still, Doane's appropriation of Hélène Cixous's adage that "women are body"[16] applies to the representation of both women and men at this costumed orgy: since they are wearing only masks, they are metaphorically beheaded and are only body. While one might argue that in this case they are reduced to the fundamental characteristics of sexual difference—and that this difference cannot, in this situation, be seen as a basis for signification or anything beyond the purpose it serves—they are only sexual beings when practicing sex. Liberating the body, *Eyes Wide Shut* seems to create a world based on trying to achieve an equal distribution of the sexes.

This masquerade subverts the sexual divide discussed in feminist film criticism. Seen through the subjectivity of Bill's narrative, and from his point of view, there is no gendered preference given to sexual images. Since Bill is the only character who does not perform sexual acts, he is again castrated. The formal rhetoric provided by the shooting of this scene is reminiscent of Orson Welles' reclamation of spatial and temporal unity, praised by André Bazin as essentially "realist." The orgy scene is shot in deep-focus long-takes, revealing an asexual point of view of the cinematic apparatus.[17] The camera itself rejects any particular preference for one object of viewing over another, and permits instead the visual content to evolve and flow in and out of the frame without a value judgment.

Eyes Wide Shut is, however, anything but asexual; indeed, it challenges traditional representation of sexual difference through the institution of multi-sexual gazes, which I will call the *poly-gaze*, both on the level of the cinematic apparatus as well as between characters in the film. Not only does the apparatus itself reveal the fetishization of male and female stars and characters alike, thus providing spectatorial positions for both male and female spectatorship of any sexual orientation; but, within the film, the subjective point-of-view and third-person glance, such as the exchange of glances from one character to another, are thrown from all perspectives and at all characters. Employing both critically-analyzed methods such as Doane's analysis of the female recourse for appropriating the gaze—Alice's wearing glasses—and formal devices including eye-line matches and shot/reverse-shot, *Eyes Wide Shut* presents a world in which eyes are anything but shut.

Men gazing at women, women gazing at men, women gazing at women and men at men, disembodied gazes as well as masked faces atop seemingly headless bodies: *Eyes Wide Shut* renders male and female characters as lost bodies roaming through a confusing world beyond the scope of monolithic gender- or sex-based difference. Moreover, the film embraces the gaze self-consciously, both by revealing its limits and by making it at once subject and object of the film. *Eyes Wide Shut* reveals cinema's intrinsic capacity for acknowledging, manipulating, and moreover subverting the patriarchal traditions of Classical Hollywood. While *Eyes Wide Shut* seems at first glance to fit into Mulvey's quintessentially feminist criticism, it ultimately provides an array of deviations from the traditional norms of sexual difference as represented in cinema.

Works Cited

Baudrillard, Jean. *Le Système des objets*. Paris: Editions Gallimard, 1968.
Bazin, André. *Qu'est-ce que le cinéma?* Paris: Les Editions du Cerf, 2002.
Deleuze, Gilles. *Cinéma I: l'image-mouvement*. Paris: Les Editions de Minuit, 1983.

Doane, Mary Ann. "Film and the Masquerade: Theorizing the Female Spectator." In *Issues in Feminist Film Criticism*, edited by Patricia Erens, 41-57. Bloomington and Indianapolis: Indiana University Press, 1990.

Gledhill, Christine. "Recent Developments in Feminist Criticism." In *Film Theory and Criticism*, edited by Leo Braudy and Marshall Cohen, 251-72. New York/Oxford: Oxford University Press, 1999.

Mulvey, Laura. "Visual Pleasure and Narrative Cinema." In *Film Theory and Criticism*, edited by Leo Braudy and Marshall Cohen, 833-44. New York and Oxford: Oxford University Press, 1999.

Silverman, Kaja. *The Subject of Semiotics*. New York: Oxford University Press, 1983.

Stacey, Jackie. "Desperately Seeking Difference." In *Issues in Feminist Film Criticism*, edited by Patricia Erens, 365-79. Bloomington and Indianapolis: Indiana University Press, 1990.

Notes

[1] Laura Mulvey, "Visual Pleasure and Narrative Cinema," written in 1975, reprinted in ed. Leo Braudy and Marshall Cohen, *Film Theory and Criticism* (New York/Oxford: Oxford University Press, 1999), 833-844.

[2] We have here a practice reminiscent of the works of Jean-Luc Godard, whose films often walk the fine line between reaffirming mainstream patriarchal tendencies and reflexively criticizing and trying to deconstruct such codes of representing sexual difference.

[3] Mulvey, 837. It is worth noting that Kaja Silverman, in *The Subject of Semiotics* (Oxford University Press: New York, 1983), explains this division clearly: active masculine scopohilia and passive female exhibitionism. However, as I hope constantly to affirm in these pages, such descriptions are not of inherent characteristics but, instead, are descriptions of our conventional codes of audio-visual representation.

[4] Mulvey, 840.

[5] In *Le Système des objets*, Jean Baudrillard performs a striking analysis of the intersection between fetishization and epistemological possession, a conjunction he argues to be specific to mass media capitalist culture.

[6] See Gilles Deleuze, *Cinéma I: l'image-mouvement* (Les Editions de minuit: Paris, 1983).

[7] Again we are returned here to the manifestation of an historical progression, which can be traced through the socio-historic crisis in masculinity that the male ego suffered in the wake of World War II. This crisis—including the futility of masculine characteristics proposed by the horrors and destruction of the aforementioned war, and the subsequent degeneration of conventional values and hierarchies in the 1950s and 1960s—can be argued to be contiguous in the post-

war evolution of Deleuze's image-temps, which charts a gradual disintegration in the division between inside and outside, subjective and objective, that is stipulated by traditional codes of filmic subjectivity.

[8] Silverman,125.

[9] Reprinted in *Issues in Feminist Film Criticism*, ed. Patricia Erens (Bloomington and Indianapolis: Indiana University Press, 1990), 365-79.

[10] Stacey, 366.

[11] Stacey, 366.

[12] This point is of particular interest in light of the overwhelming gossip and speculation concerning Cruise's sexual orientation. In films starring Cruise such as *Risky Business* (1983) and *Top Gun* (1986), Cruise has been molded as an icon of such stalwart conventionalism as to mirror the thematic centerpieces of his films (such as American military supremacy). *Eyes Wide Shut* turns this persona against itself, or rather interweaves it into a text in which everyone objectifies everyone else, and no gaze is given superior positioning.

[13] For the question of suture, I would direct any reader toward Silverman's chapter on this subject in *The Subject of Semiotics* (especially pp. 195-204).

[14] Mulvey, 838.

[15] Reprinted in *Issues in Feminist Film Criticism*, ed. Patricia Erens (Bloomington and Indianapolis: Indiana University Press, 1990), 41-57.

[16] Doane, 46.

[17] See André Bazin, "L'évolution du langage cinématographique," in *Qu'est-ce que le cinéma* (Les Editions du Cerf: Paris, 2002), 63-80.

CHAPTER FOUR

HITCHCOCK'S 'GOOD-LOOKING BLONDES': FIRST GLIMPSES AND SECOND GLANCES

IAN SCOTT TODD

As a child I grew up watching Alfred Hitchcock movies with my father; together we looked at one classic Hitchcock blonde after another as she seduced and eluded her obsessed male love interest. I distinctly recall coming across Hitchcock's *Marnie* (1964) one night while flipping through the channels with my dad. Although I was only about ten years old, I was already intrigued by any film that bore Hitchcock's name, which I associated with mystery, suspense, and beautiful women. Once we began watching *Marnie*, we could not stop, not least because of Tippi Hedren who was the type of woman my father would classify as a "good-looking blonde." According to feminist film theory, such female characters exist as objects of the "male gaze" through which men experience scopophilia. According to Laura Mulvey, the binary gazer/object of the gaze is divided along gender lines: the male looks at the female who is imbued with "to-be-looked-at-ness," to be discussed further.

Hitchcock's films are replete with "good-looking blondes," from Hedren and Grace Kelly to Kim Novak and Doris Day, among others. I found myself mesmerized by Hitchcock's women: not only were they indeed "good-looking," but also they had a quality of blitheness and intelligence. Yet something subtle and mysterious always remained beneath their immaculately groomed surfaces, a secret that Hitchcock's male heroes spend the duration of his films trying to unravel.

As a gay man now revisiting Hitchcock's work with a more critical eye, I remain fascinated and compelled by the women in his films: they exude a magnetic presence that extends beyond their potential sex appeal or attractiveness. Part of my attempt in writing this is to reclaim Hitchcock's heroines as something other than the fetishized objects proposed by some feminist critics. I suggest instead that, when examined through a queered gaze in which non-heterosexual subjectivities interrogate the films at hand and disrupt their purported cohesion, these female characters are more complicated. In queering the act of gazing at Hitchcock's heroines, we see at work the radical potential of queer spectatorship to problematize and re-frame traditional ways of understanding gender and sexuality in seemingly heteronormative film texts. In other words, how can queer readings free Hitchcock's blondes— as well as other characters—from an overly reductionist understanding of gender and spectatorship?

Before delving further into these questions, it is necessary to clarify some terms. First, let us consider the range and diversity of Hitchcock's female characters, since they differ so widely from one another in personality, temperament, and appearance that it is impossible to make a claim about them as a collective unit. Much of what makes these women so appealing is their diversity of character from film to film. It is already problematic, then, to make any monolithic claims about Hitchcock's female characters because they resist analogous comparison. The female characters of Hitchcock's Universal period, for example, such as Melanie Daniels (Tippi Hedren) in *The Birds* (1963) and Lisa Fremont (Grace Kelly) in *Rear Window* (1954), are sly, assertive, glamorous, and capable of getting what they want. Other characters from this period, such as Madeleine Elster/Judy Barton (Kim Novak) in *Vertigo* (1958) and the title character in *Marnie* (Tippi Hedren), are alternately duplicitous and easily victimized. Featured in what are arguably Hitchcock's best-known and most commonly studied films, these are perhaps the "good-looking blondes" who come to mind when one mentions him. Yet even among this group of women, the lines between power and passivity as well as subject and object begin to blur, so that those who appear to serve the same role actually have very little in common aside from their iconic blondeness.[1]

Furthermore, lest one argue that Hitchcock's women are only stylish glamour goddesses, the films of his earlier periods present women of very different ages, classes, and personae, not to mention hair colors. *The 39 Steps* (1935), possibly the best film of Hitchcock's British period, not only features Pamela (Madeleine Carroll), a prim but high-spirited heroine in the "good-looking blonde" paradigm, but also brunette Margaret (Peggy Ashcroft), the Scottish crofter's wife who, in about five minutes of screen time, communicates unspoken desires and dreams of a forsaken life. In *Shadow of a Doubt* (1945), from the earlier half of his Hollywood period, the viewer is presented with three radically different female characters within the same family: twentyish brunette Charlie Newton, who develops from a trusting innocent into a mature woman; her precocious younger sister, Ann, one of Hitchcock's "brainy little girls" (to cite Peter

Bogdanovich)[2]; and their doting, chatty, emotionally fragile mother, Emma. Thus, to speak of the women in Hitchcock's work as though they are all variations on the same "type" is to ignore the subtlety and care with which each of them was created, not only through Hitchcock's direction, but also by his various screenwriters (in particular, Ben Hecht and John Michael Hayes) and perhaps chiefly through the actresses who brought them to life.

The diversity of female characters in Hitchcock's *oeuvre* is helpful in understanding their relationship to feminist and queer theory. As Tania Modleski notes, "when one is reading criticism defending or attacking Hitchcock's treatment of women, one continually experiences a feeling of 'yes, but...'"[3] Every female victim objectified by men within the film's narrative finds her double in a scheming sexual aggressor; every glamorous socialite corresponds to a pragmatic, clear-headed working woman; mothers—always crucial female figures in Hitchcock—are menacing and gentle, overbearing and distant, calculating and scatterbrained.[4] Hitchcock's women are sometimes platonic friends with—rather than love interests of—his male protagonists: the scenes between Scottie (James Stewart) and Midge (Barbara Bel Geddes) in *Vertigo* reveal how complicated friendship between a man and a woman can be. Although the women in Hitchcock's films are often considered in terms of their beauty or sex appeal, a sense of humor—which has often gone unnoted by critics who tend to downplay the sly comedy of much of his work—is arguably the one link they share. Whether engaging in wisecracks, deadpan asides, or manipulative flirtation, at times they recall the merry yet strong-willed heroines of the screwball era.

This strength and humor initially drew me to Hitchcock's women and it still does today. Hitchcock's female characters defy categorization and simplistic, definitive readings: they are never simply victims or objects. As I matured as a film viewer, as a gender studies scholar, and as an adult gay male, I have discovered that the dimension of Hitchcock's female characters refutes any kind of essentializing—a notion that feminist film critics like Modleski have also discussed.[5] Modleski's work is particularly helpful in suggesting more complicated ways of thinking about women in Hitchcock's films than has previously been done, to be discussed further.

Thus, although Hitchcock revisited the same themes throughout his work—such as mistaken identity, sexual frustration, voyeurism, and violent crime, among others—his female characters were and still remain fresh, unique, and almost never only the variations on a stock type that they are often claimed to be. In her short story "Fat Man My Love" (2006), for instance, Joyce Carol Oates imagines a kind of chain of

Hitchcock actresses, collectively referred to as the "Icy Blondes," all with similar-sounding names such as Gigi, Mimi, and Pippi. It is as though these women served identical functions, were devoid of individual personalities, and fulfilled interchangeable roles in each of Hitchcock's films.[6] While fictionalized, Oates's exaggeration of the Hitchcock blonde as archetypal recalls Mulvey's dismissal of the women in Hitchcock's films as enacting the part of the passive object. From Mulvey through Oates, it is possible to trace a line of response to Hitchcock's treatment of women that indicates an unwillingness on the part of many critics to see beyond generalizations about his female characters.[7] I would like to suggest not only that Hitchcock's women deserve a less dismissive reading than they have usually been granted, but also that a queer reading of Hitchcock can be useful. Looking at Hitchcock's women from a queer perspective allows them to be considered in ways that transcend conventional paradigms that are employed to analyze gender in film. As developments in the field have shown, queer criticism involves more than the process by which queer people—those who identify outside of heteronormative categories of gender and sexuality—respond to texts and films that seem to have been created with only straight audiences in mind. Rather, queer theory has the potential to reappropriate these texts and films in subversive or radical ways by problematizing notions of spectatorship altogether. By this process, we might further complicate our understanding of women characters within Hitchcock's films and begin to think about them in ways that move beyond the divides of the active/passive, gazer/object-of-gaze paradigm.

In discussing queer spectatorship, I return to the circumstances in which I first encountered these films. I watched them as a boy with my father, a scenario that may supply some preliminary complications to the ways in which it is possible to read women in Hitchcock's work. This scenario points out some of the limitations of Mulvey's original theory of the "male gaze" in classical Hollywood cinema. In her essay "Visual Pleasure and Narrative Cinema," the foundational text of psychoanalytic feminist film theory, Mulvey identified narrative cinema as a means by which audience members are invited to gaze at women, who act as objects of aesthetic and/or voyeuristic pleasure: "as the spectator identifies with the main male protagonist, he projects his look onto that of his like, his screen surrogate, so that the power of the male protagonist as he controls events coincides with the active power of the erotic look."[8] Mulvey specifically cites Hitchcock's films, with their heavy use of subjective point-of-view shots and alternation (shot/reverse shot), as invitations to the male viewer to identify with the male protagonist, joining him in gazing at the objectified woman within the film.

Many feminist and queer critics writing since Mulvey, while acknowledging their indebtedness to her, have identified the various ways in which her theory relies upon somewhat essentialist and totalizing assumptions about gendered spectatorship. Queer theorists in particular have been quick to take up the question of the eroticized gaze as identified by Mulvey. Modleski has traced the attempts of feminist film theorists such as Linda Williams, Mary Ann Doane, as well as herself to extend and complicate Mulvey's theory.[9] I will not restate these arguments here, nor do I purport to be the first to raise such questions about the possible limitations of Mulvey's early work in gaze theory. Indeed, so much has already been written in response to Mulvey that it seems almost redundant to attempt to problematize her work here, especially since she has gone on to re-assess her own theory in later writings.[10] Rather, I will read these theories of gendered spectatorship *through* my own experiences of watching Hitchcock's films in youthdom and in doing so will hopefully make a case for the adoption of a less reductionistic model of spectatorship.

The act of watching, with my father, these films on television would seem, at first, to match perfectly Mulvey's paradigmatic scenario in which men gather to gaze at women on screen. Crowding around our television set that Saturday night, watching *Marnie* together, my father and I would seem to have acted as the male "bearer[s] of the look" as defined by Mulvey.[11] On the verge of becoming an adolescent, I might even read myself at that moment as undergoing unconscious indoctrination into a prescribed code of masculine behavioral expectations. The image of my twelve-year-old self, planted in front of a Hitchcock film, encouraged by my father to gaze at the foregrounded "good-looking blondes," tantalizingly invites comparison to Mulvey's staging of the viewing experience as defined by men's gathering to watch women.

This initial reading of the situation obscures, however, the contradictory nature of my response to Hitchcock's women. Gazing at Tippi Hedren in masculine company, I do not remember having experienced any strong sexual reaction, either positive or negative. Still existing in a kind of pre-sexual obliviousness, I neither desired to look at Tippi Hedren nor preferred looking at Sean Connery—the film's leading man and her love interest—and thus did not experience a sexual identity crisis. At the time, Tippi Hedren existed for me, the male viewer, simply as the woman playing the compelling central character of the film. It later became clear that I would never gaze at Tippi Hedren, or Grace Kelly, or any other Hitchcock blonde with the erotic desire that narrative cinema encourages of the male viewer according to Mulvey. I began to realize that although I had grown up taking pleasure in watching Hitchcock's women, I had enjoyed watching them in the "wrong" way, so to speak, and for reasons which would seem different from those expected of me-as-male-viewer, again according to Mulvey's model. Although the elements of her scenario had been in place—men gazing at women—they had not followed through to the expected result as far as I am concerned. An awareness of my sexual identity as a gay person had not yet occurred. Women inspired no erotic desire in me, and therefore, I did not take pleasure in gazing at Hithcock's blondes in this manner. Yet, while I had not experienced a specifically erotic or sexual pleasure in gazing at these women, I nevertheless enjoyed *another kind* of scopophilic pleasure, which is difficult to define or explain.

The realization that I had largely been resistant to the patriarchal invitation to desire Hitchcock's women inspires me to consider the extent to which queer spectatorship is capable of undermining the dimensions of heteronormativity embedded within mainstream culture. Mulvey insists that narrative cinema perpetuates a *certain kind of looking*; it presumes to speak to an implied male viewer, urging him to look at "these women" in "this way." What I find exhilarating and subversive about queer responses to heteronormative film texts—those which appear to have been designed about and for the "average" (i.e., heterosexual male) viewer—lies in their transgressive refusal to follow any such rules of looking. The queer viewer responds by looking in a different way than prescribed by the heteronormative text and its creator(s). The queer viewer looks at and fantasizes about characters of the same rather than the opposite sex. Alexander Doty suggests that queer theory involves the "non-straight work, positions, pleasures, and readings of people who do not share the same 'sexual orientation' as that articulated in the text they are producing or responding to."[12] Doty has aptly posited that a queer reading "subversively or secretly reinterprets products not made with [queer viewers] in mind."[13] My looking at Hitchcock's women in this way frees them, and myself, from the heteronormative expectations and assumptions put forth by most mainstream films as well as from the constraints of the restrictive Mulveyan model of gendered spectatorship in which men and women are assumed to occupy specific spectatorial positions. The process of queering the male gaze inaugurates significant possibilities for the ways in which images of women and men may be decoded.

Recent feminist and queer scholarship takes up these premises in an attempt to question and extend our understanding of gendered spectatorship. Carol J. Clover's groundbreaking study of the slasher film genre claims that spectators of these films occupy a multivalent viewing position in which they are invited to identify across gender. Spectatorship of slasher films involves a process of continual shifts in identification from female would-be victim to male predator, both of whom often signify androgyny. This drifting in and out of spectatorial positions renders "masculinity and femininity...more states of mind than body."[14]

In her study of Hitchcock, Modleski similarly "problematize[s] *male* spectatorship and masculine identity in general" by suggesting that Hitchcock's films invite men to identify with his female characters while at the same time facilitating their objectification.[15] According to Rhona J. Berenstein, Modleski's work "explores the concept of double identification, in which men identify with characters of both sexes."[16] Berenstein has further complicated queer spectatorship by exploding the binary model of gendered identification. She posits that the lines between male and female are constantly blurred within the act of spectatorship, and that rather than merely facilitating identification as/with male or female, spectatorship allows these categories to register in seemingly contradictory ways at the same time:

> Although recent gay and lesbian work has focused on homosexual subjectivity, the thorny question of the equivalence of a spectator's everyday identity with viewing positions has yet to be addressed fully. Having raised the issue, queries emerge: is it possible for a male homosexual viewer to both identify with and desire a female character? Or, for that matter, is it possible for a heterosexual male to both identify with and desire a hero? While it is important to theorize a cinematic and social space in which gays and lesbians access and are accorded the rights to express same-sex desire, doing so does not exhaust all possibilities for the viewer, gay or otherwise.[17]

Through her theory of "spectatorship-as-drag," Berenstein attempts to explore "the possibility that spectators also identify *against* themselves" by occupying a multivalent viewing position in which various identifications, desires, and other gendered behaviors are simultaneously performed.[18]

As Berenstein points out in the passage quoted above—and as Clover has noted in her work as well—nearly all audience members of any gender or sexual orientation may participate in such acts of cross-gender identification and desire, thus suggesting the need for new models predicated on a specifically queer understanding of gendered spectatorship. Critics like Berenstein and Clover have effectively queered

Mulvey's initial theory of the gaze as tied to various binary oppositions (male/female, active/passive, gazer/object-of-gaze) by making available the possibility of spectators, regardless of their gender or sexual orientation, to cast themselves into shifting spectatorial roles. Such alternative models become particularly useful when attempting to unpack the various ways in which queer viewers respond to heteronormative texts. In my own example, it is possible that although I resisted playing the role of the male gazer for whom Hitchcock's women are supposedly designed to act as fetishized erotic objects, I nonetheless found that I am the bearer of a different male gaze, one that still takes pleasure in looking at Tippi Hedren. In order to comprehend fully the extent to which Berenstein has problematized gaze theory, we must accept that queer spectatorship is quite capable of subverting *as well as* complying with assumed ways of looking.

When I watch *Rear Window*, I find myself shuttling between several contradictory viewing positions in the way that Berenstein has suggested. I watch at once as a student of film theory, as a feminist, and as a queer theorist, actively interrogating the spectacle in terms of its ideology, its latent meanings and/or its coded messages about gender and sexuality. I also watch to be entertained, hoping to *forget* my critical work. I treasure the moments of technical precision and visual beauty in Hitchcock's films that drew me to them long before they held any academic interest for me. In certain respects, I still watch them as I did in childhood. Now, as a gay man, I am conscious that the male actors and characters within the film are imbued with erotic appeal.

Another part of me identifies with Grace Kelly's character, Lisa; I bristle along with her when, arguing with her, Jeff (James Stewart) seems to become too cruel, and I wonder about their pairing as onscreen lovers: it seems that Lisa could find a better match. My response at the sight of Lisa as she leans in close to the camera to awaken Jeff with a kiss involves an even thornier knot of affective responses: I realize that not only do I admire Kelly's sensual glamour, but I even experience something akin to desire. As she moves purposefully through Jeff's apartment, ordering a waiter while Jeff is confined to a wheelchair, Lisa is both a female object of desire to be gazed upon, and an active subject who defies passivity. Her beauty is inseparable from her assertiveness.[19]

Lisa is a double signifier. She represents the world of New York fashion, culture, and cosmopolitanism, which is gendered feminine and passive in opposition to Jeff's active, masculine world of adventure in foreign countries as a photographer.[20] At the same time, she demonstrates a courage and cleverness that Jeff lacks, as when she decides to investigate the mysterious apartment across the street by climbing up the fire escape and entering through a window. Jeff watches anxiously from his wheelchair when the apartment's occupant, who—the viewer will learn—has murdered his wife, returns unexpectedly home and confronts Lisa. In the last shot of the film, Lisa remains enigmatic. The masculine and feminine spheres as defined by this film are blurred, as she appears to be reading an adventure novel, only to set it down in order to peek at *Harper's Bazaar*. Lisa's sympathetic appeal lies in her playful disruption/ subversion of the binaries active/male-passive/female.[21]

This is not to say, however, that Lisa is a feminist heroine, nor that Hitchcock's misogyny is evident in this film, nor whether I am objectifying Grace Kelly when I admire her. Scopophilia becomes multifaceted. One may alternately pick up and then discard several pleasures throughout the viewing experience, by identifying with one character and then switching to another one.[22] How can I take pleasure in looking at Grace Kelly without objectifying her, which would be a betrayal of my feminism? I can identify with the fascinated Jeff, gazing at Lisa; then, I can identify with Lisa as she returns his gaze. Subsequently I can view the film from the critical perspective of a film student, using at once feminist, queer and psychoanalytic theories. Through nostalgia I have returned to an earlier time when I first saw this film, and therefore my own background memories mingle with my current viewing of it. Although Mulvey's theories of the male gaze and the to-be-looked-at-ness of the female object have undeniably contributed to critical studies of film, feminism, and gender theory, Berenstein's open-ended theory of spectatorship helps to understand the contradictory responses or viewing positions better than does Mulvey's theories.

If Berenstein's model of spectatorship involves the slippage between various opposing roles, performing them intermittently and countering one another, Hitchcock's characters enact a similar variety of roles within the diegeses of his films. Critics of Hitchcock's work—such as Mulvey, Modleski, Robin Wood, and Marian Keane—have discussed the various ways in which his female characters engage in performative roles, whether by assuming a false or dual identity, by disguising their bodies, modeling clothes, or playing the role of an entertainer.[23] The identities of these women are performative in the sense that they are made up of consciously and temporarily enacted behaviors and personae rather than unified by a cohesive sense of self.[24] Hitchcock's films address performativity in complex ways that remain to be explored fully. The constantly shifting identities of several Hitchcock's heroines, however—their ability to assume or reject various performative roles (as Lisa does in *Rear*

Window), as well as their entrapment within other roles and identities which they are *forced* by other characters to perform—as in *Vertigo* where Judy is forced by two different men to dress up and enact the part of Madeleine—mirrors the multivalent process of spectatorship experienced by the viewer. A Hitchcock heroine such as Madeleine/Judy in *Vertigo* may simultaneously be in and out of control of her identities, manipulating but also manipulated, until one cannot determine whether she is an object being dressed up by others or whether—and to what extent—she manipulates her performative potential to subvert the men controlling her. As Robin Wood, Charles Barr, and Marian Keane have pointed out, not only is it difficult to determine whether Judy is speaking and acting as herself or as Madeleine, but also the power dynamics in her relationship with Scottie reverse themselves, rendering Judy active participant as well as passive victim.[25] Similarly, the viewer is manipulated by the narrative's ideologies, the *mise-en-scène*, and the directorial hand. However, the viewer can circumvent these elements and can understand the film in a different manner, one that defies the logic of heteronormativity.

Consider also the final sequence of Hitchcock's 1956 remake of *The Man Who Knew Too Much*, in which Doris Day, in the role of Jo McKenna, sings "Que Sera, Sera" under the pretense of entertaining the British Prime Minister and his guests. Jo, an American singer traveling in England, chooses this song in a calculated attempt to attract the attention of her son, who has been kidnapped and is held on the second floor of the house. The woman's performative act is publicly displayed by the two men who asked her to sing: her husband and the Prime Minister, although it can also be argued that Jo exploits her own talent in order to rescue her son. Jo's double voicing is an example of how women can use performative acts to exercise power. The numerous interpretations of female performance in the film reveal not only the multi-facetedness of Hitchcock's female characters but also demonstrate the possibilities of multivalent spectatorship.

Other Hitchcock films queer gender and subjectivity in similarly compelling ways. *Rear Window* is a film that invites the viewer to adopt several subjectivities: recall that Jeff is often read as a stand-in for the film spectator[26] since he continually shifts his identifications with the various neighbors upon whom he spies. Although critics such as Robin Wood suggest that Jeff treats Thorwald, the wife-murdering neighbor, as a double onto whom he projects his own fears of commitment to Lisa, Modleski complicates this by proposing that Jeff identifies perhaps more with the bedridden Mrs. Thorwald than with her husband.[27] If Jeff identifies with both husband and wife, male murderer and female victim, then he is caught in plural gendered roles in his relationships with Lisa, his nurse Stella (Thelma Ritter) and his detective friend Doyle (Wendell Corey). At various points in his investigation into the murder of Mrs. Thorwald, Jeff positions himself *in opposition to* Stella and Lisa's ideas and opinions, as, for example, when he dismisses Stella's claim that she has "a nose for trouble" and used it to predict the 1929 crash of the stock market. At other times, Jeff aligns himself *alongside* the women (and thus in opposition to the other male characters), as for example when he and Lisa try to convince the skeptical Doyle of their suspicions. Thus, as the central figure of a film that problematizes spectatorship and identification, Jeff finds himself caught in a series of shifting gendered roles as he tries to solve the mystery of Mrs. Thorwald's disappearance. Jeff also becomes the feminized conspiracy theorist who tries to convince others that his suspicions are real rather than merely paranoia.[28]

If queer theory informs Berenstein's multivalent model of spectatorship and allows for a variety of gendered and sexed subject positions, then Hitchcock's films are ideal texts for queer and feminist viewers because of their attention to performative identity. Performativity occupies such a central place in Hitchcock's work that I propose extending the theory of the gaze in order to account for multiple gazes and multiple subject positions performed on both sides of the screen. To view Hitchcock's women only as "passive objects" or "active subjects" is to dismiss the various overlappings of the binary oppositions passive/active, gazer/gazed, and male/female that the films reflect, as well as the various overlappings of identification/objectification, desire/disinterest, and male/female experienced by the viewer. My personal experience as a lifelong fan of Hitchcock's films and especially his female characters suggests that queer theory has much to add to Hitchcock scholarship, since it allows for more diverse appreciations of his work. Queer models of reading and spectatorship allow us to move beyond a conventional or monolithic reading, viewing, and interpretation of film texts, as well as explore ways in which these conventional means of viewing and interpretation may be subverted and/or rejected.

As far as scopophilia in film is concerned, queer theory involves pleasures that go against the grain of heteronormative codings and identifications in most mainstream films. Queer theory holds useful potential for feminist theory because of its ability to conceptualize gender and sexuality in signifnicant ways. As Modleski writes in *The Women Who Knew Too Much*, "[o]ne of the problems with Mulvey's theory was that her picture of male cinema was so monolithic that she made it seem invincible, and so, from a political point of view, feminists were

stymied."[29] Queering Mulvey's theory allows for the proliferation of a wider range of viewing options, freeing all spectators from a restrictive understanding of spectatorship. Whether or not Hitchcock can be "saved for feminism," a question taken up by Robin Wood in *Hitchcock's Films Revisited*, seems to presuppose a single understanding of how his films are read and understood.[30] Rather than deciding whether Hitchcock's work is misogynistic or empowers women, I refer to Modleski's claim that Hitchcock's "thoroughgoing ambivalence about femininity" means that "the issue can never be resolved."[31]

To consider Hitchcock's work only in relation to feminism would be to lose the potentialities that queer reading adds to the study of Hitchcock's films and in particular his female characters, who, through both the queer and feminist gazes rather than the prevalent theory of the male gaze, become more than just "good-looking blondes."

Works Cited

Barr, Charles. *Vertigo*. London: BFI Publishing, 2002.

Berenstein, Rhona J. *Attack of the Leading Ladies: Gender, Sexuality, and Spectatorship in Classic Horror Cinema*. New York: Columbia University Press, 1996.

Bogdanovich, Peter. Interview. "Beyond Doubt: The Making of Hitchcock's Favorite Film." By Laurent Bouzereau. *Shadow of a Doubt*. Videodisc. Universal, 2000.

Butler, Judith. *Bodies That Matter: On the Discursive Limits of 'Sex.'* New York: Routledge, 1993.

—. *Gender Trouble: Feminism and the Subversion of Identity*. New York: Routledge, 1990.

Clover, Carol J. *Men, Women, and Chainsaws: Gender in the Modern Horror Film*. Princeton: Princeton University Press, 1992.

Doty, Alexander. "Queerness, Comedy, and *The Women*." In *Classical Hollywood Comedy*, edited by Kristine Brunovska Karnick and Henry Jenkins, 332-347. New York: Routledge, 1995.

—. "Queer Theory." In *Film Studies: Critical Approaches*, edited by John Hill and Pamela Church Gibson, 146-50. New York: Oxford University Press, 2000.

Keane, Marian. Audio commentary for *Notorious*. Videodisc. The Criterion Collection, 2001.

—. Audio commentary for *The 39 Steps*. Videodisc. The Criterion Collection, 1999.

—. "A Closer Look at Scopophilia: Mulvey, Hitchcock, and *Vertigo*." In *A Hitchcock Reader*, edited by Marshall Deutelbaum and Leland Poague, 231-248. Ames: Iowa State University Press, 1986.

Manlove, Clifford T. "Visual 'Drive' and Cinematic Narrative: Reading Gaze Theory in Lacan, Hitchcock and Mulvey." *Cinema Journal* 46, no. 3 (2007): 83-108.

Modleski, Tania. *The Women Who Knew Too Much: Hitchcock and Feminist Theory*. New York: Routledge, 1988.

Mulvey, Laura. "Afterthoughts on 'Visual Pleasure and Narrative Cinema' Inspired by King Vidor's *Duel in the Sun* (1946)." In *Feminist Film Theory: A Reader*, edited by Sue Thornham, 122-130. New York: New York University Press, 1999.

—. *Visual and Other Pleasures*. Bloomington: Indiana University Press, 1989.

Oates, Joyce Carol. "Fat Man My Love." In *High Lonesome: New and Selected Stories, 1966-2006*, 173-87. New York: Harper, 2006.

Wood, Robin. *Hitchcock's Films Revisited: Revised Edition*. New York: Columbia University Press, 2002.

Notes

[1] It is worth noting here that several of Hitchcock's films draw special attention to women's hair color and specifically the act of dyeing one's hair. In *Vertigo*, the red-haired Judy has her hair dyed blonde twice in order to resemble that of Madeleine Elster; the second time we are even given a close-up shot of her hair being rinsed in the salon sink. In *Marnie*, Tippi Hedren's hair goes from jet-black to blonde to brunette and back to blonde again; Hitchcock includes several close-ups of Marnie rinsing out the black dye in an early sequence.

[2] See Laurent Bouzereau's short documentary "Beyond Doubt: The Making of Hitchcock's Favorite Film," found on the 2000 Universal DVD of *Shadow of a Doubt*.

[3] Tania Modleski, *The Women Who Knew Too Much: Hitchcock and Feminist Theory* (New York: Routledge, 1988), 3.

[4] See, for example, Emma Newton in *Shadow of a Doubt*; Madame Sebastian in *Notorious*; Mrs. Anthony in *Strangers on a Train*; Jo McKenna in *The Man Who Knew Too Much* (1956 version); Mrs. Thornhill in *North by Northwest*; the late Mrs. Bates in *Psycho*; Lydia Brenner in *The Birds*; and Mrs. Edgar ("Mama") in *Marnie*.

[5] Modleski, 3-5.

[6] Joyce Carol Oates, "Fat Man My Love," in *High Lonesome: New and Selected Stories, 1966-2006* (New York: Harper, 2006), 173-187.

[7] Marian Keane takes special issue with Mulvey's dismissal of Madeleine/Judy in *Vertigo* in her vigorously argued response to "Visual Pleasure," "A Closer Look at

Scopophilia: Mulvey, Hitchcock, and *Vertigo*" in *A Hitchcock Reader*, ed. Marshall Deutelbaum and Leland Poague (Ames: Iowa State University Press, 1986), 231-248.

[8] Laura Mulvey, "Visual Pleasure and Narrative Cinema" in *Visual and Other Pleasures* (Bloomington: Indiana University Press, 1989), 20.

[9] Modleski, 5-9. The first half of a more recent article by Clifford T. Manlove also gives a concise summary of the history of Mulvey's essay and its influence. See Clifford T. Manlove, "Visual 'Drive' and Cinematic Narrative: Reading Gaze Theory in Hitchcock, Lacan, Mulvey," *Cinema Journal* 46, no. 3 (2007): 83-108. See also Keane's "A Closer Look at Scopophilia: Mulvey, Hitchcock, and *Vertigo*."

[10] See, for example, Mulvey's "follow-up" essay, "Afterthoughts on 'Visual Pleasure and Narrative Cinema' Inspired by King Vidor's *Duel in the Sun* (1946)," in *Feminist Film Theory: A Reader*, ed. Sue Thornham (New York: New York University Press, 1999), 122-130.

[11] Mulvey, 19.

[12] Alexander Doty, "Queer Theory," in *Film Studies: New Approaches*, eds. John Hill and Pamela Church Gibson (New York: Oxford University Press, 2000), 148.

[13] Alexander Doty, "Queerness, Comedy, and *The Women*," in *Classical Hollywood Comedy*, eds. Kristine Brunovska Karnick and Henry Jenkins (New York: Routledge, 1995), 332.

[14] See Carol J. Clover, "Her Body, Himself," in *Men, Women, and Chainsaws: Gender in the Modern Horror Film* (Princeton: Princeton University Press, 1992), 22.

[15] Modleski, 5.

[16] Rhona J. Berenstein, *Attack of the Leading Ladies: Gender, Sexuality, and Spectatorship in Classic Horror Cinema* (New York: Columbia University Press, 1996), 45.

[17] Ibid., 47.

[18] Ibid.

[19] For more on Lisa as an active rather than passive presence in *Rear Window*, see Modleski, 76-79.

[20] Ibid., 77-78.

[21] Ibid., 77-84.

[22] See Clover's work on audience identification and the slasher genre in "Her Body, Himself." It is also worth mentioning that Hitchcock gave much thought to audience identification and designed nearly all of his films with this principle in mind. Hitchcock's manipulation of audience identification occurs perhaps most obviously in *Vertigo* and *Psycho*, in which the narrative point of view suddenly shifts halfway through the film from one character to another (moving from Scottie to Judy in the former and from Marion to Norman in the latter), thus prompting the audience to reverse his or her understanding of the film and its characters.

[23] Women with false or dual identities appear in *Vertigo*, *North by Northwest*, *Notorious*, *Psycho*, and *Marnie*; women's clothing figures into the plots of *Rear*

Window, *Rebecca*, and *Vertigo*; female entertainers or performers appear in *Stage Fright* and the remake of *The Man Who Knew Too Much*.

[24] In discussing performativity, I am working out of Judith Butler's theories of gender performativity, according to which gendered identity consists of a series of repeatedly performed acts and behaviors. See Butler's *Gender Trouble: Feminism and the Subversion of Identity* (New York: Routledge, 1990), 128-141, and *Bodies That Matter: On the Discursive Limits of 'Sex'* (New York: Routledge, 1993), 223-242. For more on performativity in Hitchcock's work, see Robin Wood, "The Men Who Knew Too Much (And The Women Who Knew Much Better)" in *Hitchcock's Films Revisited* (New York: Columbia University Press, 2002), 358-370, and Marian Keane, "A Closer Look at Scopophilia: Mulvey, Hitchcock, and *Vertigo*," in *A Hitchcock Reader*, eds. Marshall Deutelbaum and Leland Poague (Ames: Iowa State University Press, 1986), 231-248. See also Keane's insightful audio essays written and recorded for the Criterion Collection DVD editions of *The 39 Steps* and *Notorious* (released in 1999 and 2001, respectively).

[25] See Wood, *Hitchcock's Films Revisited*, 108-130; Keane, "A Closer Look at Scopophilia: Mulvey, Hitchcock, and *Vertigo*"; and Charles Barr, *Vertigo* (London: BFI, 2002).

[26] Wood, 100-107.

[27] Modleski, 77.

[28] Robin Wood points out that "female" intuition is portrayed similarly in the 1955 version of *The Man Who Knew Too Much*, where Ben McKenna (Stewart) initially dismisses his wife's feelings of discomfort about the strangers they meet while traveling in Marrakech. Jo, however, "has the right instincts and perceptions and [...] makes the right decisions" as a result of them. See Wood, "The Men Who Knew Too Much (And The Women Who Knew Much Better)," 369-370.

[29] Modleski, 9.

[30] Robin Wood, "Male Desire, Male Anxiety: The Essential Hitchcock," in *Hitchcock's Films Revisited*, 371.

[31] Modleski, 3.

CHAPTER FIVE

FAMILY RESEMBLANCES: (EN)GENDERING CLAIRE DENIS, NICOLE GARCIA AND AGNÈS JAOUI'S FILM TITLES

NOËLLE ROUXEL-CUBBERLY

Even though theorists such as Jacques Derrida, Gérard Genette and Roland Barthes have extensively pondered the relationship of the title to its literary co-text, little has been written on the film title as a theoretical object of research. Composed of pictures and words, film titles[1] call for a psychoanalytic interpretation. Film titles, like psychoanalysis, rely on a principle of ipseity: titles are the expression of a specific content,[2] just as the psychoanalytic interpretation of a dream allows for the expression of a specific neurosis. Furthermore, the hermeneutic function of titles echoes the interpretative function of the dream in psychoanalysis since titles "allow...interpretative discourse"[3] and constitute the starting point of any form of interpretative comment: "titles...function as guides to interpretation."[4] Similarly, in psychoanalysis, dreams guide the patient toward an interpretation of her own words and woes.

Along similar lines as psychoanalysis, film titles display what is called regression: through a sort of linguistic regression, they lead the spectator to the very essence of the on-screen drama. Titles, like children learning to talk, tend to suppress articles and retain only one or a very small number of key-words: examples include "Chocolat," "15 août" and "Cuisine et dépendances." In discussing her film *S'en fout la Mort (No Fear No Die)*—a title that seems to insolently thumb its nose at the spectator— Claire Denis refers to the film's rehearsals as a sort of "womb."[5] This creative fusion with the "mother-work" is reminiscent of the Kristevean "prelinguistic stage"[6] evoked by film critic Georgiana Colvile in her depiction of French women's cinema and the privileged space it gives to the imaginary world. Colvile writes of "this choice place of the imaginary world which recreates the prelinguistic symbiosis with the mother."[7] If the title sketches out the "linguisticity" of the film, it also signifies the birth of the designated work. It is even its *sine qua non* condition. Without words, no psychoanalytical release is possible and the patient cannot "come out." In the same way, without a title, no release is possible and the film cannot "come out."

The titles of three contemporary female directors—Agnès Jaoui, Claire Denis and Nicole Garcia—will be analyzed through this psychoanalytic perspective. Why only women directors? First, because it is the revenge of the minority stigma: the feminine imaginary on screen has been studied more than once[8] and therefore allows for a grounded study of the correspondence between film titles and their co-texts (the film itself). Second, the themes listed by Anne Gillain in her article "L'Imaginaire féminin au cinéma,"[9] explored by these three directors, fit particularly well within the parameters of psychoanalysis: sexuality, love, parent-child relationships, and a redefinition of temporal-spatial dimensions. Third, they show a particular interest in the choice of titles they have to negotiate with producers and distributors.

As we shall see, film titles, borrowing from the techniques and goals of wit, reveal key elements from these women's works. They also express collective concerns since titles aim at engaging the potential spectator. We will attempt to define to what extent these film titles contain their author's *féminitude* and to what extent they attest to the evolution of a feminine cinema that has become "more rebellious and optimistic, post-modern and post-feminist" as suggests the feminist film critic Molly Haskell.[10]

Claire Denis, Nicole Garcia and Agnès Jaoui—selected precisely for the psychoanalytical dimension of their cinematographic *écriture* on the one hand, and for the obvious correspondence between their film titles and their cinematographic styles on the other hand—display an intriguing similarity. Their titles indeed seem to interpret, with psychoanalytic formulas, the content of the corresponding works: Claire Denis with titles carved in the rawness of the reality they describe: "J'ai pas sommeil" ("I Can't Sleep"), "S'en fout la mort" ("No Fear no Die"), "Chocolat"; Nicole Garcia with titles evoking fractured family circles: "Un week-end sur deux" ("Every Other Week-End"), "15 août" ("August 15"), "Le Fils préféré" ("The Favorite Son"); and finally, Agnès Jaoui whose playful titles blend idioms, clichés and sayings, only to better hide a bewildering seriousness: "Le Goût des autres" ("The Taste of Others"), "Comme une Image" ("Look At Me") or "On connaît la chanson" ("Same Old Song"), co-written with Jean-Pierre Bacri for Alain Resnais.

This analysis is divided in two parts: first, film titles will be compared to wit—particularly considering the pleasure they both generate—and second is a consideration of the Symbolic values film titles subvert. Film titles, and maybe even more so French women's film titles, play on words to reveal the key values of our society. Deciphering their titles should answer the following questions: to what extent does this cinematographic female imaginary—redefined through these titles beyond traditional parameters (with other forms of time, place and action)—appear in titles? To what extent does the ideology of French women's film titles challenge a Symbolic ideology of film titles and entitling?

Film Titles as Wit

Short, condensed, fragmentary, but also catchy and necessarily pictorial, both wit and film titles constitute the springboard of an intellectual gymnastics. At first, both display only part of their meanings and play on the "hidden" and the "revealed." Both become clearer only after an effort of interpretation that puts back into place elements assembled initially in an improbable order. This order seeks to be innovative while fitting into previous narrative frames.

In *Wit and its Relation to the Unconscious*[11] Freud revisits the major concepts of psychoanalysis, and more particularly the principal elements of dream works, as well as demonstrates that the benefit of pleasure generated by wit derives from the economy of "psychical expenditure." In other words, because it makes one laugh, wit allows one not to give into feelings. To illustrate this mechanism, Freud gives the example of a famous joke: a blind man asks a paralyzed man: "How is it going?" and the latter answers: "As you can see." Laughter saves us from tears: instead of sympathizing with these unfortunate characters, we revel in this economy that consists of hiding two meanings in each of these verbs: for instance, "going" refers to health and mobility. Similarly, the film title provides pleasure because it calls for a "treasure hunt," a search for possible meanings of the title. Concurrently, it promises to divert the spectator from her own "psychical expenditure."

In his definition of wit, Freud evokes two characteristics that are crucial for film titles: the effect of "sideration" and the revelation of the "hidden." The shock comes, with the film title, from words that must—or should—strike us, sometimes both graphically and semantically. Interestingly enough, these women directors often downplay the use of fancy fonts and enlarged sizes to better focus on the content of these core-words. Denis' unadorned letters for the title "Chocolat" contrasts with the mawkish culinary incentive of the rounder fonts used for Lasse Hallström's own film *Chocolat* (2000). The "hidden" is expected to be revealed in the projection space. Just like wit, the pleasure of play, search and discovery unmasks hidden treasures. For instance, Nicole Garcia's film *L'Adversaire* (*The Adversary*) conceals, in its title, another dimension of its meaning. Based on the drama that led Jean-Claude Romand—who for fifteen years pretended that he was a doctor for the World Health Organization—to kill his parents, wife and children, the film uncloaks the contender to the announced adversary: himself. The title appears on screen as the background reveals a young boy, the protagonist, trudging through the blinding snow. These very first words and images both conceal and show the essence of the drama—the protagonist being his own adversary—leaving other possible titles such as "The Murderer" to thriller versions of the story.

Jean-François Lyotard, notorious for his postmodern suspiciousness vis-à-vis the meta-narrative, has also explored what was hidden in the least common denominator of film, namely, its title. Referring to Freud's theory of the *Traumdeutung* (interpretation of dreams), Lyotard lends himself to the exercise that consists of reading "through" a title. According to Lyotard, the dream hides itself *in* the title.[12] He demonstrates this by pointing out, in Frédéric Rossif's film title "Révolution d'Octobre," that the flag's folds show only these letters: "Rév on d o r." The deciphered message "Rêvons d'or" ("Let's dream of gold") offers a compelling illustration of this characteristic. Surprisingly, Lyotard ignores another summons, just as crucial, to the spectator: "Rêvons, dors" ("Let's dream, sleep"). This invitation becomes all the more tempting as the spectators are then plunged into the "black hole" of the movie theater. These two commands, nested in the title, allow the latter to reach even more easily wit's goal: to say everything while pretending to partly hide its truth.

Once the spectator is "hooked," the title can unfold. Jaoui's "Comme une image" ("Look at Me") provides an example of a title that extends its pleasure mechanism throughout the film as the layers of the title's meanings emerge. *Comme une image* (2004) tells the story of Lolita (Marilou Berry), a young overweight voice student who lives in the denigrating shadow of her famous-author father, Etienne Cassard (Jean-Pierre Bacri). She finds solace in her singing class taught by the distant Sylvia (played by Jaoui herself) who becomes more forthcoming when she realizes the importance of her student's father. When Sylvia's writer husband finally encounters success, he seeks to impress Lolita's father. All the characters become victims of a society of image in which everybody suffers from not fitting an image modeled by that society. Lolita suffers from not looking like an image from *Elle*, while her stepmother suffers from *only* looking like an image from *Elle*. The title, with its two comparative terms, "like" and "image," refers to a *mise en abyme* of the character portraits, very much embedded in the French literary tradition. *Comme une image* depicts rebellious characters who decide not to be "as good as gold" ("sage comme une image") or fit into society's modeled images.

The problematic translation of film titles reveals the shortcomings of culturally faithful translations and yet also witnesses the title's rebirth into other cultural contexts where values expressed in the original language might not have the same currency. Transformed into "Look at me" in English as well as in German, Danish, Swedish, Norwegian, Polish and Portuguese ("Schau mich an!", "Se på mig," "Se mig," "Se meg," "Popatrz na mnie," "Olhem para mim"), "Comme une image" is translated literally in Spanish, "Como una imagen," even though there is not an idiomatic use for this phrase, as is the case in French. With "Così fan tutti" in Italian, the recycling of Da Ponte's title suggests a Mozartian transposition both tragic and light, much to the likeness of the film. The Chinese translation, "I see myself through you," pushes even further this notion of visual representation *en abyme*, but this dimension is totally abandoned in Japanese with "We are all loved by somebody." The notion of "image" disappears as the title moves eastwards, revealing a different relationship to visual references in societies fostering a different relationship to the notions of image and the self.

The recognizable wit of Jaoui's titles echoes feminist B. Ruby Rich's article on humor in feminine cinema.[13] Rich views humor as a "leaven of subversion to deflate the patriarchal order."[14] With wordplays, Jaoui fuels the pleasure mechanism of her film titles with the pleasure mechanism of wit. She thus diverts the title from its narrative function, lets it claim its independence and unleashes the spectator's imaginary by inviting her to re-create and dream around the film title.

When the title of the film is "Chocolat" the Barthesian "apéritive" function of the title[15] triggers notions of pleasure that are all the more interesting as Claire Denis' film *Chocolat* (1988) takes place in Africa where riddles commonly invite, through the symbolic transposition of banal realities, to get to the heart of things. In this film, France (Mireille Perrier), a young Caucasian woman, returns to the then-colonized Cameroon of her childhood. In a flashback, she re-experiences the cross-cultural sensory pleasures and dysfunctions of her past. When interviewed about this title, Denis referred to the 1950's expression "être chocolat": "to be had, to be cheated."[16] The mother's unfulfilled desire for her servant, while evoking the sexual commodification of the black male, echoes the title: she does not get this food which is "good but prohibited," and finds herself "chocolat," as are most of the white characters of the film. Chocolate—a colonial food—conjures up a whole racist imagery with corresponding three-syllable chocolate brands such as Bamako or Banania, and the derogatory term "chocolat," by extension, referred, until the end of the 19th century, to an African man. This film title thus speaks of the cocoa exportation through a slave system, of Europe feeding on Africa. What adds another layer to this title is that chocolate is actually never seen on screen. Not only is the morning "hot chocolate" symbolically refused by little France, the protagonist, but it is also idealized by the overtly and almost cartoonishly racist Delpich (Jacques Denis). During a meal, this coffee-planter praises the addition of bitter chocolate chips to coffee. This culinary fantasy finds a strange resonance with his sexual life since an African mistress, a "chocolat," hidden in his bedroom, spices up his libido.

With this title, Claire Denis takes from the hands of unrighteous European imperialists the colonial food that allowed them to exert their religious, political and patriarchal power for more than four centuries. Denis also questions racial identity and shows that, as Nadège Siélinou coined it, colonization also gave birth to "Noirs à la peau blanche" ("white skinned blacks").[17] *Chocolat*'s savor lies at the mythical crossroads of chocolate and Africa where the latter is exploited. A close reading allows the viewer to discover taboos more effectively denounced—as with plays on words—because their multi-layered meanings emanate from a mental gymnastics on behalf of the receiver. The pleasure goes beyond the gustative pleasure of chocolate or beyond its sheer taste. Read through the co-text, *Chocolat* tastes more like bitter chocolate as it circumscribes the desires (and failures) of characters separated by forces that dictate their desires and rule their pleasures. With this title, Denis feigns to "go back in the kitchen" to better distort the patriarchal connotations of sweetness, instant gratification and sexual pleasure that "chocolat" commonly brings to mind. In a nutshell, or in a bean, she offers a redefinition of ourselves while bringing us closer to the *jouissance* of an artistic reflection.

Another of Denis' titles that has been abundantly discussed is "Beau travail" ("Good Work"), particularly its "feminization"[18] when one of the male protagonists is called a "belle trouvaille" ("nice find"), to be discussed further. *Beau travail* (1999) is first and foremost a tribute to the work of the *légionnaires,* the soldiers of the Foreign Legion: borrowing from an unadorned and almost virile language this title transforms the soldiers' work into an aesthetic object of reflection. The title appears after a long pan revealing a fresco with vivid colors, accompanied by a male soldiers' song and a scene where a young girl dances in a club, surrounded by *légionnaires*. The ironic connotation of the title is immediately perceptible: does the title correspond to the mythical fresco, to the song or to the realities of a *légionnaire*'s life (the clubs, the girls, etc.)? "Beau travail" may also correspond to a metacommentary on the film as the product of Denis' film crew.

A very loose adaptation of Herman Melville's novel *Billy Budd, Sailor*, *Beau travail* recounts the disruption caused by the arrival of a new recruit in the life of the *légionnaires*. Sergeant Galoup (Denis Lavant) becomes jealous of the attention paid by the commanding officer to freshly debarked Sentain (Grégoire Colin). Just like Billy Budd, this new recruit is, in the commander's words, a "belle trouvaille" ("nice find") as Sentain explains that, as an infant, he was found abandoned in the stairwell of a building. The desire of the commander also ironically appears in this "palimpsest" title, as Roland-François Lack noticed[19]: "Beau travail" can be understood as a sarcastic commentary about the destruction of two men. Yet the feminization of the expression into "belle trouvaille" also generates a derogatory suffix ("-aille") that questions the beauty of the work evoked in the French title—would the film's script itself mock too boastful a title? The title, distorted by the ironic dimension of wit, leads into the homosexual subtext of the film: this play on words inserted *into* the film puts the title back on stage, literally, as if it meant to better denounce the apparent simplicity of the deictic function of the title. Through this play on the words of the title, Denis feminizes it, making it her own. However she also feigns to be "entitled" to rework Melville's novel through the tropes of a demystified intertextuality: the title Denis chose for her film shows her debt to Melville but also denounces the pretensions of a title (in the juridical sense of the word) which would mark a very illusory ownership—all the more in cinema where the title is often discussed and selected by a whole team.

This title, *Beau travail*, which discloses its "umbilical cord," with a reference to the mother work, is not foreign to the concept of the "umbilical scene" as described by Millicent Marcus. According to the theoretician of film adaptations, the "umbilical scene" reveals explicitly its affiliation with the mother work, that is to say, the literary text that inspired the filmic text.[20] More than a simple copy of Melville's novel, Denis reveals, with her title, all the filiation of this adaptation, but at the same time emancipates it from the mother work, just like a rebellious child, playing with the ironic tone of a deprecatory title. This title allows Denis to achieve the aesthetic program Marcus reads in a filmic adaptation, "that of re-writing, re-articulating, and re-proposing earlier stories in ways that allow a culture to come to know itself with respect to the past, and to take the measure of its evolution."[21]

Beau travail is a tribute to Melville but it also bears the trace of a discourse fallen out of the literary canon to better blend into today's world. Denis' allusion to this artistic genealogy in her title is all the more interesting as the French jurisdiction recognizes film title copyright protection only "if it is original."[22] The naming of this inheritor of a literary source is certainly original and, by an unexpected twist, goes over its designative function by calling its co-text "names": Beau travail! Denis' title subtly points at the illusory untouchability of the literary monument. This "nice work" does not belong to an elite: it goes from hand to hand, re-invents itself, exists in its being shared by contemporaneous spectators. This "nice work" is also the perpetual labor of artistic creation as hinted in this pun title published in the *Cahiers du cinéma*: "Le Beau travaille: esthétique contre récit?"[23]

The umbilical relation of this revisited filiation to intertextuality is not new in the field of titology. In his *Invisible Colors, A Visual History of Titles*, John Welchman suggests that "titles, textuality in general, and word-play in particular are related instances of what Matta in 1938 called the 'umbilical cords' needed to 'connect us with different suns, objects in full freedom which would be like plastic psychoanalytic mirrors.'"[24] This cord between title and visual and/or verbal texts is capital as it enables the viewers to reach into their deeper selves.

Film Titles as *Jouissance*

To go a little further in the psychoanalytic exploration of the title, let us consider its relationship to "jouissance" as Lacan describes it. The Lacanian "jouissance" goes *beyond* the pleasure principle. It sometimes approximates discomfort and implies the desire to abolish a sense of lack (*le manque*) caused by the subject's submission to the Symbolic order. Both "title" and "jouissance" relate to law. Furthermore, both have to do with the notion of "enjoying a right." With copyright protection in France,[25] film titles guarantee their creators' authorship. The title also represents a source of *jouissance*, as in the legal term "usufruct"[26] since the title lends itself to being enjoyed while belonging to somebody else— this *jouissance*, promised to the public, is even the film title's *raison d'être*. Without a title, the film cannot circulate: in order to deliver its commercial certificate to a film production company, the granting institution, the Centre National du Cinéma, requests a title among other compulsory information. The title, once attached by virtue of aristocratic privilege, refers to rights enjoyed by specific individuals. With capitalism, this enjoyment of a right has been redefined in a context of commercial exhibition, cinematographic for instance. It has become the projected *jouissance* of the Other. Titles such as these all contain a semantic promise of *jouissance*: "Vers Mathilde," "Vendredi soir" and "Chocolat" by Denis; "Le Goût des autres" and "Comme une image" by Jaoui; and finally "Place Vendôme," "Le Fils préféré," and "Un week-end sur deux" by Garcia. In an intentional *mise en abyme*, they all imply a *jouissance* of the Other but also the *jouissance* of the viewer discovering the projected *jouissance*.

One could argue that the title does not fit the Lacanian *jouissance*'s resistance to usefulness or investment since the *jouissance* is not vested with any purpose. Yet if the title calls for an investment (the price of admission into the theater for instance), it does not forcibly demand it. Moreover, its usefulness as a naming device looks sometimes like a mere excuse, a shortcut to the artistic *jouissance* certain works offer. This title then becomes a sort of *parergon* that brings the work to completion without being central nor necessary to its realization.

Finally the title relies on transgression. Because the film titles of these women directors systematically go beyond their "purely" designative function, they disobey "le nom du père" ("the name/no of the father"). Giving too much voice to the title—as Stéphane Mallarmé wrote, "ce titre qui parlerait trop haut"[27] ("this title that would speak too loud/high")— they divert it from its designative function. This allows their titles to be a path to *jouissance*, and this is a *jouissance* that might parallel the Proustian delectation drawn from cherished names. In a similar fashion, Proustian names bypass their identifying function: the reverie they engender allows the reader to reach and enjoy, through the name, the essence of the character.

For there is a pleasure attached to the title, but this pleasure should be differentiated from the *jouissance* it makes us seek, or pretends to make us seek. Flirting with destruction, the Lacanian *jouissance* borders on psychosis and neurosis. Denis' films precisely focus on these notions, leaving scant space to immediate pleasure. If her film titles exceptionally allude to pleasure ("Chocolat," "Vendredi soir"), the films themselves undermine these intentionally deceptive hooks. "Vendredi soir" ("Friday Night") tricks the spectator into anticipating pleasure, alluding to the hopes of the beginning of the week-end, while the film is really about a *jouissance* placed well beyond the sexual pleasure and sexual *jouissance* depicted in the film. *Vendredi soir* (2002) features a future doctor's wife who, trapped in a traffic jam during a strike, engages in a one-night stand

and temporarily frees herself from her bourgeois milieu. The strike, a disruption of the surrounding patriarchal order, allows her to create her own imaginary order in an unusually deserted Paris, strangely liberated from its customary hectic atmosphere. In this film, everything is "off," both in the sense of "not functioning" and "slightly displaced" into another world. If the title throws us off, so does the plot. The sensuality of the situation, played down by cold bluish tones, unglamorous characters and intentionally empty silences, dissolves into a form of unexpectedly gratuitous plenitude. But this frigid depiction of *jouissance* precisely names it without ever explicitly referring to such a notion. It is all the better hidden behind a title that seems to refer to the patriarchal time.

Jaoui's titles—"Cuisine et dépendances," "On connaît la chanson," "Le Goût des autres," "Comme une image"—also lead to a form of *jouissance*. However, unlike Claire Denis' "raw" titles, Jaoui's titles decisively take us down the merry path of wordplay with a farcical, almost "boulevardier"[28] tone. "Le Goût des autres" ("The Taste of Others"), through the different senses of the article (either definite or generic—a specific taste or the taste in general) and of the preposition (indicating either the possession or the complement of the noun), leads to a number of interpretations: what others prefer in general, what the others, as a predefined group, prefer, but also the taste for other people, or the taste or savor of other people, among various possibilities. In a country that has claimed a monopoly over taste for more than three centuries, "Taste," capitalized, also refers to Paris, the capital of France, which governs all pleasures in the name of taste. Without it, there is no hope of ever reaching the *jouissance* that taste allegedly conceals and concedes. Both a physical and aesthetic term, "taste" pinpoints the nerve center of the psychoanalytic process through which the title beguiles us: halfway between the word and the *jouissance* it evokes, "The Taste of Others" reveals all the complexities of our relationship to others' pleasure, our concern for it or rather, lack thereof, which incidentally bars our way to *jouissance*. The film denounces the diktat of a certain Parisian artistic milieu's taste unexpectedly taken on by a businessman as his petit-bourgeois interior designer wife is slowly suffocating him. Jaoui's title offers more than a pleasing "exercice de style." It invites the spectator to go *beyond* the pleasure the wordplay generates.

Film titles promise *jouissance* but often only give pleasure. But these women directors, either rebuking pleasure or, on the contrary, using it as an indirect tool, offer through their titles, revisited words that take us well beyond pleasure. Beyond the comfort zone provided by the identification and recognition stage, these titles bring the reader closer to the essence of the work. Deciphering "Chocolat" or "Le Goût des autres" allows the reader to reach further in her appreciation of the work. Just as in the Lacanian perverse structure where the subject submits to the law while making a mockery of it and disappearing in this submission, the spectator feigns to yield to the title's dictatorship, while testing it. The spectator disappears in her submission and goes to see the film, pretending to give in to the title. But her careful reading of the title allows her to access a superior form of *jouissance* since it thus enables her to better read herself.

Film theoretician Roger Odin paid particular attention to the entry of the spectator into fiction: "This moment of perceptive void represents metaphorically the spectator's crossing the screen-mirror; it is the big black hole...before the penetration into 'another world'...close to dream, the diegesis. The fade to black signs the victory of the imaginary over the Symbolic."[29] Where does the title stand in this passage? Does it reinforce the Symbolic order or, on the contrary, does it participate in this "victory of the Imaginary"?

For Jean-Pierre Oudart, the relation of the spectator to the film reflects the entry of the subject into the Symbolic order.[30] A naming agent, the title provides the work a civil status that allows it to be consumed, to become part of the Symbolic order. Raymond Queneau, referring to the phallic power of the title, talked about the "titre cache-sexe" ("G-string title").[31] Indeed, one could see in the titling practice the epitome of the inscription of a product in the Symbolic order, all the more as the title puts forward selling values. As historian Jean-Louis Flandrin noted in his study of French book titles related to sex and love during the last four centuries,[32] "these titles...reveal only the notions that a civilization dares to display"[33] and underlines the importance of the notions that do *not* appear. Hence the necessity, he suggests, to reach, through research, "the level of the unconscious."[34] This statement implies that titles express the values of a collective unconscious, but also implicitly points at the construction of this display of values. It also implies a questioning of the overarching authorities overlooking the choice of titles (in our case, film distributors and producers, among others). The title can be considered as a "hyper manifest" product, by Lacanian opposition to the production of an unconscious discourse. Its inflated size on the screen, its capitalization and its inception at the very beginning of the film bear the stamp of a guiding authority, in line with the parameters of the Symbolic order.

But at the same time, because it precedes the narration, because of its a-grammaticality, its non-temporal and non-spatial nominalization, the title escapes the Symbolic order it seems to set and follow. As a short grace period before the narrative starts, the title is also an invitation to explore an imaginary world placed at the frontier between the author and spectator.

Garcia, whose titles seem more conventional than those of Jaoui and Denis, actually reveals a subversion of the Symbolic space and time in the naming or "christening" of her films: *Un week-end sur deux* (a once-famous actress who sees her children every other week-end ends up abducting them) and *15 août* (long-time couples experience crises on the Assumption day) tell how time is problematically regulated by the Symbolic order. As for space, what title could be more patriarchal than *Place Vendôme* (1998) with its eponymous column? Once "place Saint-Louis" (Louis XIV's statue was destroyed during the Revolution), then subsequently "place des Piques"[35]—another (counter-) phallic symbol—place Vendôme becomes with Napoleon the symbol of France's military grandeur. In today's capitalist world, it is *the* most sought-after address for a French jeweler. In the film, the producers' names appear first (credit where credit is due), before the title, as if, by an ironic twist of convention, the patriarchal power blatantly displayed in this title echoed its inscription in the Symbolic order of the film credits: money first!

Yet, as in the titles of Garcia's other films, this apparent Symbolic space is a landmine: all the characters are prisoners of this prestigious square, particularly the beautiful but alcoholic wife of a famous jeweler, Madame Malivert (Catherine Deneuve), who must face her own past when her husband commits suicide. The whole drama takes place in an enclosed, suffocating space. The few outside scenes show dead-end spaces: stations are only rendez-vous places and even the road where Malivert commits suicide is blocked by a truck. The Symbolic time is also destroyed. As the film goes forward, the spectator discovers an increasingly shattered past. This square, place Vendôme, chokes its characters with its golden claws. Men—Malivert but also Madame Malivert's criminal lover who is finally arrested—have vanished in the wind blowing over this tormented and void place Vendôme, becoming themselves "vents d'homme" ("wind men"). A Rabelaisian reading[36] of this title would give a final nailing down to these patriarchal pretensions. Garcia's titles pretend to espouse the Symbolic order to actually better unleash the imaginary of the spectator. Her titles call for a feminine *jouissance*, feeding on the lack of the Other, since the co-text conceals and eventually destroys the idealized, imaginary Other. The glamorous title "Place Vendôme" actually feeds on the artistic representation of the very lack of the two Others, the suicided jeweler husband and the arrested con-man lover.

Finally, a tendency also observed in many contemporary directors—such as Quentin Tarantino in *Reservoir Dogs* (1992)—Denis, Jaoui and

Garcia's films tend to reveal their titles later, sometimes after a few scenes. Film theoretician Bruno Di Marino comments on this delayed naming and the subsequent feeling it provides to the spectator. The title appearing on the screen is "comforting from a psychological and perceptive point of view, precisely because it guarantees that we are attending a representation, distinct from the flow of images that belong to our own lives."[37] Odin notices, along the same lines, that the credits claim the enunciation that the fiction seeks to erase, making them an "essential element of the fiction effect."[38] The title epitomizes this decisive moment: when it appears, the spectator can start to believe in the fiction while also not totally buying it. Christian Metz also stresses the importance of this "feeling of not being dupes of this action: thus comforted (behind the rampart) we can allow ourselves to be a little more dupe."[39] The title, the culmination of the credits, signifies our formal adoption of the contract of fiction without which the spectator remains in a discomforting undecided position. Just as in the psychoanalytical cure and wit, decisive words allow the representation to go forward. The frontier between the two worlds is both capitalized and purposefully erased.

Denis dismantles the credits' comforting conventions: the name of the producers and actors appear at the very beginning of the film on a black screen but the title itself appears after a few scenes in most of her films. Turned into an "intruder," it appears in the eponymous film *L'Intrus* (2004) after 8 minutes and 50 seconds. Mimicking the plot's failed heart transplant, blood-red letters appear on a black background. Dimly lit by a flashlight, they evoke the incontrovertible status of these words that appear in the "heart" of the film and at the same time seem to be unburied. This exploration of the economy of the film title mimics here the film's subject and style: the heart transplant buried in a rhizomic narration. At the opposite end of the spectrum, some credit sequences become autonomous films in their own right. The opening credit sequence of *On connaît la chanson* (2004, co-written by Jaoui and Jean-Pierre Bacri), for instance, consists of a colorful animated collage of headshots roughly pasted on cut-out body shapes. Often inspired by the opening scenes designed by Saul Bass, such as for Alfred Hitchcock's *Vertigo*, these short sequences question the film-title couple. This "forced marriage" between the film and its title reflects the title's conundrum: as Leo Hoek puts it, it is "autonomous but not independent."[40] This explains the constant renegotiation that should take place between the film, the spectator and the title. It should also be an invitation to look into or beyond the face value of the title.

For these three female directors, the title reflects an intention to create another order of things, to rethink the imaginary. More than discussing common themes to the feminine imaginary—love, family, redefinition of space and time—their titles speak *against* a set order of things. As if emerging from a period of obscurity, their titles are displayed on a black screen—such as in "J'ai pas sommeil," "L'intrus," "Beau travail," "Comme une image" and "Un week-end sur deux"—and become fragmented expressions that seem to erupt from a psychoanalytic discourse.

Their titles, while using everyday language, speak *other* languages. An inheritance from her adolescent Conradian or Faulknerian readings, a third of Denis' titles are originally in English, the language of protest during her youth (1960s-1970s). As Françoise Armengaud explains: "Giving an English title is a way of severing grounded connotations of the language."[41] Moreover, the three women directors' language seems broken, as if truncated or abruptly extracted from unfinished conversations: "On connaît la chanson," "Comme une image," "J'ai pas sommeil," "L'intrus," "Beau travail" and "Selon Charlie." In an interview,[42] Denis evokes these "blocks" of impressions and words that constitute the dialogues and more generally the spurted language of her films—*Man No Run* (1989), *S'en fout la mort* (1990), *Vers Mathilde* (2005)—sometimes intentionally idiotic, keeping all the spontaneity of their orality. The three directors do not like to use the polished language of stereotypical television characters but seek to talk the language of "ordinary" people rather than use scripted dialogue, or at least, recount untold stories such as that of a forgotten actress in Garcia's *Un week-end sur deux*; an overweight teenager in Jaoui's *Comme une image*, and an immigrant raising a rooster for cock-fighting in Denis' *S'en fout la mort*. Their titles are also an incentive to rethink and question language through gender. Does not gender have a bearing on the reading of titles such as "Vers Mathilde," "L'Adversaire" or "Cuisine et dépendences"?

The final trait these titles have in common is their indirect connection with the plot itself—*Chocolat*; *Comme une image*; *15 août*—but contest a whole context of patriarchal values related here to this food, expression and date. Just like the missing tile of a mosaic, the title can help better apprehend the film and the realities it denounces. Denis' titles do not imprison a plot but rather allow her films to take off from words and images associated with titles. The three female directors' titles all display a sense of menace, of a world threatened to crumble. By diverting the title from its designative function, they manage not only to offer an alternative vision of the world but also an incentive to the spectator to create her own and thus find *jouissance*.

Armengaud concludes in her commending book on visual arts titology: "The reading of a title announces the pleasure of the image, then it *increases* it."[43] This observation confirms the importance of the affective component generated by the title's economy, not only for its reader but also for its creator. She then quotes the painter Guillaume Corneille: "I feel very uneasy when a title escapes me. The painting is right there, it is waiting, like the child who must be given a name. It must go its way, accompanied by this name."[44] These notions of necessity and pleasure associated with the idea of filiation are crucial for the three following women directors: Denis, Jaoui and Garcia who each in their own way load their film titles with the orality of film language to revisit entitling practices. Through their titles, they speak out and give an innovative shape to their take on the world.

If their titles share some family resemblances through their debt to wit and more generally to psychoanalysis, they also differ from one another through distinctive styles and loci of *jouissance*: fractured family circles deflagrating the patriarchal order; a "boulevardier" tone to denounce the overpowering pretensions of society; and broken language to present a more adequate representation of reality. The opacity of their titles might also have something to do with another fracture: the decolonization that has been an important background of each of these directors's formative years. Each of these female directors explores the themes of the feminine imaginary throughout their films and their titles already announce the problematization of specific themes: for instance, the family, with *Le Fils préféré* (*The Favorite Son*, 1994), *Un air de famille* (*Family Resemblances*, 1996), and *Nénette et Boni* (1996), as well as the importance of the past determining the present with *Chocolat* or *Selon Charlie* (*Charlie Says*, 2005). Their titles put forward values but their treatment of these values in the co-text makes us rethink the title's content. Indeed, their titles function less as set values than as changed—at least changing—values, since they engage the spectators into a different reading of the world: a female reading that, through the title's interaction with the co-text, revisits, questions and re-en*gender*s film entitling practices.

Works Cited

Armengaud, Françoise. *Titres. Entretiens avec Alechinsky, Arman, Appel, César, Marie-Elisabeth Collet, Corneille, Dolla, Hadju, Hartung,*

Helman, Herld, Jenkins, Le Gac, Masson, Philippe, Pol Bury, Pons, Sosno, Soulages, Topor, Anita Tulio, Verdet. Paris: Klincksieck, 1988.

Barthes, Roland. "Analyse textuelle d'un conte d'Edgar Poe." In *Sémiotique narrative et textuelle*, edited by Claude Chabrol, 29-54. Paris: Larousse, 1973.

Bokobza, Serge. "Déictique, énonciatrice et poétique: les fonctions du titre." *French Literature Series* 11 (1984): 33-46.

Bouquet, Stéphane, Jean-Marc Lalanne and Jérome Larcher. "Le Beau travaille." *Cahiers du cinéma* no. 545 (April 2000) : 46-53.

Colvile, Georgiana M. M. "Mais qu'est-ce qu'elles voient? Regards de Françaises à la caméra." *The French Review* vol. 67, no. 1 (October 1993): 73-81.

Di Marino, Bruno. "Ai margini della finzione. Per un'analisi dei titoli di testa e di coda." *Bianco e nero* 1-2 (2000): 74-85.

Duchet, Claude. "La Fille abandonnée et La Bête humaine: éléments de titrologie romanesque." *Littérature* 12 (1973): 49-73.

Fisher, John. "Entitling." *Critical Inquiry* 11 (1984): 286-98.

Flandrin, Jean-Louis. "Sentiments et civilisation : sondage au niveau des titres d'ouvrages." *Annales. Economies, Sociétés, Civilisations* no. 5 (20ème année, septembre-octobre, 1965): 939-967.

Freud, Sigmund. *Wit and Its Relation to the Unconscious.* Translated by A. A. Brill. New York: Moffat, Yard, and Co., 1916.

Fuller, Graham. "Must-see director—Claire Denis—French filmmaker—Brief Article—Interview." *FindArticles.com* (October 2001), http://findarticles.com/p/articles/mi_m1285/is_10_31/ai_78738609 (accessed January 7th, 2008).

Gillain, Anne. "L'imaginaire féminin au cinéma." *French Review* vol. 70, no. 2 (1996): 259.

Haskell, Molly. "Girls in Film." *The Guardian Unlimited, Arts* (March 28, 2003), http://arts.guardian.co.uk/fridayreview/story/0,,922901,00.html (accessed January 7th, 2008).

Hoek, Leo H. *La Marque du titre.* The Hague: Mouton, 1982.

Kamina, Pascal. *Film copyright in the European Union.* Cambridge: Cambridge University Press, 2002.

Lacan, Jacques. *Ecrits I.* Paris: Editions du Seuil, 1971.

Lack, Roland-François. 2004. "Good work, little soldier: text and pretext." *Journal of European Studies* 34 (2004), http://jes.sagepub.com/cgi/reprint/34/1-2/34.pdf (accessed January 7th, 2008).

Lyotard, Jean-Francois. *Discours, figure.* Paris: Klincksieck, 1974.

Mallarmé, Stéphane. "Le mystère dans les lettres." In *Œuvres complètes*, 2 vols ii, edited by Bertrand Marchal, 229–234. Paris: Gallimard, 1998–2003.

Marcus, Millicent. "Umbilical Scenes: Where Filmmakers Foreground Their Relationships To Literary Sources." *Romance Languages Annual* X. West Lafayette: Purdue Research Foundation, 1999.

Metz, Christian. *Essais sur la signification au cinéma, t. II.* Paris: Klincksieck, 1972.

Nancy, Jean-Luc. "A-religion." *Journal of European Studies* vol. 34, no. 1-2 (2004): 14-18.

Odin, Roger. "L'entrée du spectateur dans la fiction." In *Théorie du film*, edited by J. Aumont and J. L. Leutrat. Paris: Editions Albatros, 1980.

Oudart, Jean-Pierre. "Suture." Part 1. *Cahiers du cinéma* 211 (April 1969): 36-39. "Suture." Part 2. *Cahiers du cinéma* 212 (May 1969): 50-55.

Queneau, Raymond. *Bâtons, chiffres et lettres*. Paris: Gallimard, 1950.

Robin, Régine. "Pour une socio-poétique de l'imaginaire social." *Discours social* 5, no. 1-2 (1993): 7-32.

Rich, B. Ruby. "Des Mots pour nous dire." *CinemAction 9: Le Cinéma au féminisme* (1979): 166-74.

Rollet, Brigitte. 2006. "Femmes cinéastes en France: l'après-mai 68." *Clio* no. 10, *Femmes travesties: un "mauvais" genre* (May 22, 1999), http://clio.revues.org/document266.html (accessed January 7th, 2008).

Romney, Jonathan. "Claire Denis interviewed by Jonathan Romney." *Guardian Unlimited* (June 28, 2000), http://film.guardian.co.uk/interview/interviewpages/0,,338784,00.hml (accessed January 7th. 2008).

Rooney, Caroline. "From the Universal to the cosmic." *Journal of European Studies*, vol. 34, no. 1-2 (2004): 106-127.

Siélinou, Nadège. "Cameroun colonial. *Chocolat*, de Claire Denis." *Africine.org* (September 20, 2006), http://www.africine.org/?menu=art&no=6075 (accessed January 7th, 2008).

Vincendeau, Ginette. "Women as auteur-e-s: notes from Créteil," *Screen* vol. XXVII, no. 3-4 (1986): 156-162.

Welchman, John C. *Invisible Colors: A Visual History of Titles*. New Haven, Conn.: Yale University Press, 1997.

Notes

[1] "Film title" is understood here as the identifying name of a film.

[2] Claude Duchet, "La Fille Abandonnée et La Bête humaine: éléments de titrologie romanesque," *Littérature* 12 (1973): 51.

[3] John Fisher, "Entitling," *Critical Inquiry* 11 (1984): 292.

[4] Ibid., 288.

[5] Jonathan Romney, "Claire Denis interviewed by Jonathan Romney," *Guardian Unlimited*, (June 28, 2000), http://film.guardian.co.uk/interview/interviewpages/0,,338784,00.html (accessed January 7th, 2008).

[6] Georgiana M. M. Colvile, "Mais qu'est-ce qu'elles voient? Regards de Françaises à la caméra," *The French Review* vol. 67, no. 1 (October 1993): 74. All translations mine.

[7] Ibid., 78.

[8] Ginette Vincendeau, "Women as Auteur-e-s: Notes from Créteil," *Screen* vol. XXVII, no. 3-4 (1986): 156-162. Anne Gillain, "L'imaginaire féminin au cinéma," *French Review* vol. 70, no. 2 (1996): 259. Brigitte Rollet, "Femmes cinéastes en France: l'après-mai 68," *Clio* no. 10/1999, *Femmes travesties: un « mauvais » genre* (May 22, 2006), http://clio.revues.org/document266.html (accessed January 7th, 2008).

[9] Anne Gillain, "L'imaginaire féminin au cinéma," *French Review* vol. 70, no. 2 (1996): 261-263.

[10] Molly Haskell, "Girls in Film," *The Guardian Unlimited Arts* (March 28, 2003), http://arts.guardian.co.uk/fridayreview/story/0,,922901,00.html (accessed January 7th, 2008).

[11] Sigmund Freud, *Wit and its Relation to the Unconscious*, trans. A. A. Brill (New York: Moffat, Yard and Co, 1916).

[12] Jean-François Lyotard, *Discours, figure* (Paris: Klincksieck, 1974), 247-8.

[13] B. Ruby Rich, "Des Mots pour nous dire," *CinemAction 9: Le Cinéma au féminisme* (1979): 166-74.

[14] Ibid., 171.

[15] Roland Barthes, "Analyse textuelle d'un conte d'Edgar Poe" *Sémiotique narrative et textuelle*, éd. Claude Chabrol (Paris: Larousse, 1973), 29-54.

[16] Judy Stone, "'Chocolat': Bittersweet Memoir of Colonial Africa," *San Francisco Chronicle*, April 21, 1989, 47.

[17] Nadège Siélinou, "Cameroun colonial. *Chocolat*, de Claire Denis," *Africine.org* (September 20, 2006), http://www.africine.org/?menu=art&no=6075 (accessed January 7th, 2008).

[18] Roland-François Lack, "Good Work, Little Soldier: Text and Pretext," *Journal of European Studies* vol. 34, no. 1-2 (2004): http://jes.sagepub.com/cgi/reprint/34/1-2/34.pdf (accessed January 7th, 2008). Caroline Rooney, "From the Universal to the Cosmic," *Journal of European Studies* vol. 34, no. 1-2 (2004): 106-127. Jean-Luc Nancy, "A-religion," *Journal of European Studies* vol. 34, no. 1-2 (2004): 14-18.

[19] Ibid., 34.

[20] Millicent Marcus, "Umbilical Scenes: Where Filmmakers Foreground Their Relationships To Literary Sources," *Romance Languages Annual X* (West Lafayette: Purdue Research Foundation, 1999), XX.

[21] Ibid., XIX.

[22] Pascal Kamina, *Film Copyright in the European Union* (Cambridge, UK: Cambridge University Press, 2002), 105.

[23] Literally, "The Beautiful Works" which can mean, among other interpretations, "the handsome man is working" or "Beauty warps" (as metal or wood does).

[24] John Welchman, *Invisible Colors: A Visual History of Titles* (New Haven, Conn.: Yale University Press, 1997), 257.

[25] A complaint was filed after the producing company, Société Arena Films, decided to choose Agnès Jaoui's title for Resnais's film "On connaît la chanson" (*Same Old Song*). This French idiomatic expression had previously been the title of a radio program. However, the case was dismissed. See summary judgment: http://www.courdecassation.fr/jurisprudence_publications_documentation_2/bullet in_information_cour_cassation_27/bulletins_information_1998_1011/no_478_109 2/jurisprudence_1093/cours_tribunaux_1096/titres_sommaires_arrets_2724.html.

[26] According to the Merriam-Webster online dictionary, this term corresponds to "the legal right of using and enjoying the fruits or profits of something belonging to another." Merriam-Webster, *Merriam-Webster Online* (Springfield, Mass: Merriam-Webster, 1996), http://www.m-w.com/.

[27] Stéphane Mallarmé, "Le mystère dans les lettres," in *Œuvres complètes,* ed. Bertrand Marchal, 2 vols ii. (Paris: Gallimard, 1998–2003), 234.

[28] In the tradition of the theater of the "Grands boulevards," characterized by its lower-class lightness.

[29] Roger Odin, "L'entrée du spectateur dans la fiction," in *Théorie du film,* ed. J. Aumont and J. L. Leutrat (Paris : Editions Albatros, 1980), 208.

[30] Jean-Pierre Oudart, "Suture," Part 1 *Cahiers du cinéma* 211 (April): 36-39. "Suture," Part 2 *Cahiers du cinéma* 212 (May1969): 50-55.

[31] Raymond Queneau, *Bâtons, chiffres et lettres* (Paris: Gallimard, 1950), 129.

[32] Jean-Louis Flandrin, "Sentiments et civilisation: sondage au niveau des titres d'ouvrages," *Annales. Economies, Sociétés, Civilisations* no. 5 (septembre-octobre, 1965): 961-2.

[33] Ibid., 961.

[34] Ibid., 962.

[35] Pique = *pike*

[36] "Vents" in French also refers to "intestinal gas." It corresponds to the English expression "to break wind."

[37] Bruno Di Marino, "Ai margini della finzione. Per un'analisi dei titoli di testa e di coda" *Bianco e nero* 1-2 (2000): 79.

[38] Odin, "L'Entrée du spectateur," 204-5.

[39] Christian Metz, *Essais sur la signification au cinéma, t. II* (Paris: Klincksieck, 1972), 51.

[40] Leo Hoek, *La Marque du titre* (The Hague: Mouton,1982), 149.

---

[41] Françoise Armengaud, *Titres. Entretiens avec Alechinsky, Arman, Appel, César, Marie-Elisabeth Collet, Corneille, Dolla, Hadju, Hartung, Helman, Herld, Jenkins, Le Gac, Masson, Philippe, Pol Bury, Pons, Sosno, Soulages, Topor, Anita Tulio, Verdet* (Paris: Klincksieck, 1988), 276.

[42] Jonathan Romney, "Claire Denis interviewed by Jonathan Romney."

[43] Armengaud, *Titres*, 164.

[44] Ibid.

II:

THEORIZING TERROR

CHAPTER SIX

RETURN OF THE FEMALE GOTHIC: THE CAREER-WOMAN-IN-PERIL THRILLER

MONICA SOARE

The last thirty years have witnessed the rise of a new film subgenre I dub the career-woman-in-peril thriller (CWPT)[1] which challenges current theories on the relationship between female spectatorship, female subjectivity, and genre. Jonathan Demme's 1991 *The Silence of the Lambs* is the most famous example, but this subgenre extends from major works like David Mamet's *House of Games* (1987) and Jane Campion's *In the Cut* (2003) to B-movies like Sandra Locke's *Impulse* (1990) and Richard Shepard's *Oxygen* (1999). In films such as these, a woman on her own searches for love and professional success as she makes her way in the alternately frightening and exhilarating male world, whose danger is symbolized by the figure of the male serial killer. The woman at the center of these films is coded as transgressive, and her transgression is symbolized by her fascination with a possibly criminal man who is both Other and her double. The female protagonist's career has symbolic meaning, since her investigation of the mystery man is connected to an investigation of her own subjectivity. She is often a detective such as a police officer (as in *Blue Steel* [Kathryn Bigelow, 1990], *Impulse, Oxygen, Taking Lives* [D.J. Caruso, 2004], *Murder by Numbers* [Barbet Schroeder, 2003], *The Silence of the Lambs*) but sometimes another kind of "detective" such as a journalist (*Call Me* [Sollace Mitchell, 1988], *Perfect Stranger* [James Foley, 2007]); writer (*In the Cut*); psychologist (*House of Games, Never Talk to Strangers* [Peter Hall, 1995]); lawyer (*Jagged Edge* [Richard Marquand, 1985], *Guilty as Sin* [Sidney Lumet, 1993]); or anthropologist (*Candyman* [Bernard Rose, 1992]).[2] In many of these films, the heroine's ambivalent connection to the male world, with its potential for greater freedom and its threat of violence, is further signaled by her ambivalent connection to her father. She often inherits her career and sense of self from her father or a father figure, but her relationship to him is mirrored in her interaction with the criminal man, thereby showing both the problems and the possibilities of being a woman who identifies with her father both professionally and emotionally.[3]

These CWPTs are both women's films *and* horror films,[4] which fall under the rubric of the Female Gothic genre. While the term "Female Gothic" was coined in the 1970s by feminist critic Ellen Moers to describe any Gothic novel written by a woman it is now more generally used for any Gothic work that explores female subjectivity via the affect of fear.[5] Most critics also agree that the Female Gothic was invented in the 1790s by Ann Radcliffe's works *A Sicilian Romance* (1790), *The Romance of the Forest* (1791), *The Mysteries of Udolpho* (1794), and *The Italian* (1796), all of which created one of the templates for this genre: "Ann Radcliffe firmly set the Gothic in one of the ways it would go ever after: a novel in which the central figure is a young woman who is simultaneously persecuted victim and courageous heroine."[6] Most importantly for this study, Radcliffe's brand of Gothic explores the female experience— psychological and social—through the use of fear as an artistic element. Though many later Female Gothic writers were to make use of fear to explore femininity—perhaps most famously Mary Shelley, whom Moers sees as another important Female Gothic novelist working in a different vein than Radcliffe—it is Radcliffe's template that has been most influential to popular works in the Female Gothic mode. At the core of the Radcliffean model is the heroine's relationship with an attractive and dangerous man who is often doubled by her father. It is this model that was further developed by Charlotte Brontë in *Jane Eyre* (1847) which forms the basis of the most popular women's narratives of the twentieth century, from Harlequin novels to movies on the Lifetime cable network for women.[7] This narrative pattern has enjoyed popularity and longevity because it covers so much in a woman's life experience: women's romantic relationships with men, women's struggles in a male-dominated world, and women's longings for the often frightening freedom and risk-taking to which men are entitled.

In her influential 1979 essay "The Radcliffean Gothic Model: A Form for Feminine Sexuality," Cynthia Griffin Wolff argues that Radcliffe captured an inherent aspect of female sexuality in her creation of a heroine fascinated by a dangerous lover.[8] Though I agree with Wolff's emphasis on the importance of the dangerous male lover figure, I think that the Radcliffean dynamic is not concerned with sexuality alone but rather, is a complex exploration of female subjectivity and female social roles, hence its endurance and popularity. A further complication is the fact that some critics—most notably Claire Kahane—understand Radcliffean Gothic completely differently, reading it as a genre that explores women's problematic identifications with the mother. Following suggestive remarks made by Leona F. Sherman, Kahane interprets Radcliffean Gothic as the beginning of a genre that explores women's longing for unity with the mother and her simultaneous fear of this closeness.[9] Partly, of course, one's interpretation of Radcliffean Gothic depends on where one puts the emphasis, since Kahane and Wolff's templates can both be found in Radcliffe. Yet the template on which I wish to focus—the narrative of a woman whose primary relationships are with men, from the father to the dangerous lover—has been much more influential in popular women's fiction, from the already mentioned Harlequins to bestsellers by Victoria Holt, Mary Stewart, and Phyllis Whitney. In contrast, Kahane sees the influence of the template she emphasizes in the works of more literary writers such as Flannery O'Connor and Carson McCullers.[10] The greater popularity of the Radcliffean template stressed in this present study is explained by the fact that the female protagonist's fascination with the dangerous man is also an identification with the monster.

The CWPT was invented at a time when women were entering the workforce in large numbers and were thus engaging the public world, coded as male, hence this genre's focus on women's attraction to—and fear of—dangerous men.[11] The CWPTs follow the Radcliffean suggestion that the daughter's relationship with the father mirrors her relationship with the dangerous man and that these relationships allow her access to the greater opportunities of the male world. However, these opportunities/dangers of the male world create a pleasurable fear in the heroine (and by extension, the female reader or viewer). Radcliffe's narratives are fundamentally horror stories.[12] In classic Female Gothic form, then, CWPTs stage an exploration of female fantasy via the heroine's (and female spectator's) engagement with the affect of fear, becoming *de facto* horror films, and thus challenging current views on female spectatorship and genre put forth by, among others, Carol Clover, Barbara Creed, and Isabel Cristina Pinedo.[13]

A recurring scene of the CWPT is that of a single woman, alone at her desk with an alcoholic beverage, working on an investigation. In the city, depicted as dark and frightening, a male criminal is lurking. This is the underlying model that occurs in various permutations in most of the CWPTs.[14] In its purest form it is found in Philip Kaufman's *Twisted* (2004): Jessica (Ashley Judd), the heroine, sits down every evening in her big city apartment with crime scene photos and a bottle of wine. Everything in the scene is symbolic: the alcohol suggests that this woman has the freedom traditionally accorded to men, but it also hints at self-destruction. The emphasis is on the woman's involvement in the investigation; the dark city suggests adventure, excitement and danger. This iconography comes from several places such as the Female Gothic which has been kept alive in twentieth-century popular culture by writers such as Victoria Holt and Mary Stewart[15]; the single-girl-in-the-city genre (for instance, Helen Gurley Brown's 1962 *Sex and the Single Girl*) that thrived in the 1960s and 1970s[16]; noir's continuing influence on American film; and slashers popular in the 1970s and 1980s.[17] As opposed to the Female Gothic woman-in-peril thrillers of the previous decades—Alfred Hitchcock's *Rebecca* (1940) and *Suspicion* (1941), *Gaslight* (George Cukor, 1944), *Rosemary's Baby* (Roman Polanski, 1968)—the CWPT is the story of the single woman: she does not fear a husband but rather the entire patriarchal society she must encounter in her work-a-day life. But, like all Radcliffean heroines, the career woman thrives on fear; here, fear is not so much a marker of her subordinate position in the male world but of her willingness to directly engage this world as well as to explore the dark and dangerous aspects of her unconscious.

The Origins of the Career-Woman-in-Peril Thriller

The foundational Female Gothic text is Radcliffe's *The Mysteries of Udolpho*, a novel which reflects eighteenth-century interests in pleasurable fear, sadism, masochism and female subjectivity. Why is it that a two-hundred-year-old female genre continues to appeal to and haunt contemporary works about women?

As Moers argues, this novel set up a template that could be revived by 1970s feminism.[18] The heroine of *Udolpho*, Emily, is a "single girl"—a stock eighteenth-century orphan figure—in a patriarchal world. As Moers implies, this means that she could have adventures denied to married women.[19] However, before Emily is thrown out in the world to solve life-threatening mysteries all by herself, she has been indoctrinated by her father, whom she resembles. The prototype of a heroine who identifies with her father becomes a central figure in twentieth-century female-centered thrillers.[20] Emily's identification with her father is also connected to a kind of positive immaturity; it is suggested that the Female Gothic heroine refuses adult femininity because she rejects the limitations that go along with it. As Moers suggests via her discussion of the "tomboy" and of "traveling heroinism" (her term for a particular kind of agency offered women in some novels, particularly Female Gothic ones), younger women can have adventures that older women, who are expected to marry and responsibly run a household, cannot.[21] Emily's other crucial relationship in the novel is to Montoni, the male Gothic villain whose mysterious and dangerous aura stimulates her imagination. Anne Williams notes that this construction of the male as Other implies a female point of view and she dubs this archetypal figure of the Female Gothic the "Fatal Man."[22] Radcliffe's novel suggests that women can access the sublime—which in eighteenth century terminology represents visionary horror—via their engagement with the male sphere of danger, personified by Fatal Man Montoni.[23] Heightening the Freudian dynamics, Montoni is Emily's uncle, signaling the underlying symbolism: he is, as Moers points out, her father's dark *doppelgänger*.[24] When Emily's beloved father dies, then, her emotional focus is unsurprisingly transferred to Montoni, who, as the principle of aggressive male energy, is both Emily's conduit to the sublime and, because of his psychological and physical power over her, also a force of oppression.[25] Developments in nineteenth-century culture—particularly Lord Byron's writings and persona as well as Brontë's *Jane Eyre*—solidified the Fatal Man archetype, a figure that becomes a staple of Female Gothic film and literature of the twentieth century.[26] The representation of the Fatal Man plays into some female fantasies about dangerous men who are also possibly sensitive, thus fulfilling a woman's wish for freedom and safety.[27]

Films have adapted and adopted literary genres to a great extent, including the Female Gothic. Radcliffean Gothic came to the screen after Hitchcock's 1940 *Rebecca*, an adaptation of Daphne Du Maurier's eponymous novel in the Radcliffe-Brontë tradition, resulting in a group of films that are considered to be film versions of the Female Gothic.[28] Several historical and artistic developments in the 1970s and early 1980s converged and gave rise to the CWPT, a highly transformed and updated version of the Female Gothic, specifically the Radcliffean branch of this genre. Women's entry into the workforce, particularly into professions traditionally held by men, helped make the career woman a film and television staple. The rediscovery of the Female Gothic by feminist critics in the 1970s led to its dissemination for the modern woman through the cinematic apparatus.[29] The advent of the CWPT is heralded by Judith Rossner's 1975 *Looking for Mr. Goodbar*, which was filmed in 1977 by Richard Brooks. Cynthia Griffin Wolff notices this development in her 1979 article "The Radcliffean Gothic Model: A Form for Feminine Sexuality" in which she compares *Looking for Mr. Goodbar* with *Udolpho*, foreseeing how important Radcliffean Gothic still is for modern women's narrative. Wolff argues that these two texts explore the secretive and obscure nature of female subjectivity, specifically sexuality, through the devices of threatening, exciting spaces—Gothic castle and cosmopolitan city—and frightening, enticing Fatal Men. She then claims that *Mr. Goodbar*—which ends with the murder of protagonist Theresa at the hands of a stranger she met—shows the masochistic nature of female fantasy as imagined and relished in patriarchy. As opposed to misogynistic views of female fantasy, Wolff calls for women to create more positive models of female selfhood and sexuality: "It is important to recognize and acknowledge the heritage of Ann Radcliffe's Gothic tradition; it is even more important now to move on and invent other, less mutilating conventions for the rendering of feminine sexual desire."[30] However, in my study, I show that such a reading of this text and those it inspires does not do justice to the various layers of symbolism and meaning in the Female Gothic. The sexual experimentation that Theresa undertakes suggests a dangerous and painful journey of self-discovery.[31] Wolff also overlooks Radcliffe's construction of the Female Gothic heroine as father-identified (though this element is not taken up in *Mr. Goodbar*) and thus she is a figure with an already present and viable connection to the male world. Each CWPT in the thirty years following *Mr. Goodbar* stresses different aspects of this Female Gothic journey and each offers a slightly different take on the core conflicts being worked out by the heroines and, by extension, the female viewers.

The First Career-Woman-in-Peril Thrillers and the Female Gothic as Female Fantasy

While *Mr. Goodbar* advances Radcliffean Gothic by updating the heroine and the locale, the potential of the genre for modern film is not actualized until the introduction of noir and slasher film elements. As the term Fatal Man suggests, the gender dynamics in Radcliffean Gothic resemble those of film noir with the sexes reversed.[32] In noir, a male detective of dubious morality and self-destructive tendencies becomes romantically involved with a femme fatale who is both Other and his double.[33] This dynamic is perhaps best represented in Paul Verhoeven's neo-noir *Basic Instinct* (1992), which is, as Linda Ruth Williams argues in *The Erotic Thriller in Contemporary Cinema*, a synthesis of psychosexual noir themes.[34] Verhoeven explicitly sets up the overtly evil femme fatale Catherine (Sharon Stone) and the covertly evil Nick (Michael Douglas) as doubles. Nick is drawn to Catherine, even as he fears her, because she openly expresses the violent and sexual impulses that he himself expresses through his work as a police officer; thus, as a dangerous femme fatale she is still Other while also his double. The characteristics of the noir antihero match up with those of the Radcliffean heroine: the hard-living style of the noir antihero becomes the heroine's wish to access the sublime through danger, most obviously embodied in the Fatal Man. Additionally, noir, like the Gothic, uses setting symbolically: the dark city, like the sublime natural landscape created by Radcliffe, is a place of terror and adventure. The neo-noirs of the 1980s and 1990s, then, are opportune places for the Female Gothic to emerge, which explains why Joe Eszterhas, who wrote *Basic Instinct*, also wrote *Jagged Edge* (1985; henceforth *JE*), which is perhaps the initial CWPT. Eszterhas updates and rethinks noir more thoroughly than other screenwriters, so it makes sense that he would incorporate modern gender dynamics into his works. Furthermore, Eszterhas's sensibility is especially well suited for creating CWPT as a new subgenre of the Gothic: the cynical depiction of human nature and relationships in all his scripts complements the sadomasochistic mechanisms of the Gothic. Joe Eszterhas's work is relevant to the CWPT through his association with the erotic thriller.[35] As Linda Ruth Williams shows in her study of this subgenre, the erotic thriller incorporates many genres: first of all noir, closely followed by the Gothic, then pornography, and finally, horror.[36] These genres have in common the mapping of psychosexual desire. Thus, through a brief historical glance, the Gothic is interpreted as encompassing all these genres.[37] These genres flow into each other so much so that it is difficult to label them accurately. Linda Ruth Williams, however, argues that the erotic thriller is a fairly recent distinct development in film: "[the erotic thriller] did not exist prior to 1975 (though it has significant antecedents in *film noir*)."[38] In terms of how it relates to the CWPT, the most important noir element in the erotic thriller is the doubling of antihero and criminal. As Linda Ruth Williams explains, "Any number of erotic thrillers feature attraction, sex and clearly drawn similarities between criminal (or suspect) and his or her pursuer/detective/victim."[39] In a section of her book entitled "Female Point of View and the *Homme Fatal*," Linda Ruth Williams points out that several erotic thrillers focus on a woman investigating an *homme fatal* linking them to the Female Gothic film: "[the *homme fatal*] provides the basis for a shift in generic emphasis and influence, from the characteristic male-focused point of view of *noir* to a female sympathy which looks more like 1940s female Gothic."[40] Furthermore, Linda Ruth Williams considers *Looking for Mr. Goodbar* one of the first erotic thrillers ever made, calling it a "sexual-quest film,"[41] her term for a movie which connects the heroine's psychological journey to an exploration of her sexuality. Linda Ruth Williams refers to the television series *Sex and the City* as a "sexual quest narrative," which is inextricably linked to the erotic thrillers of the 1980s and 1990s, specifically those I label CWPTs.[42]

The exploration of women's psychology and social positioning through their sexuality is not a new phenomenon. Nancy K. Miller argues that this is a significant component of eighteenth-century literature written by male authors.[43] Radcliffe follows in this tradition and creates the template that becomes increasingly sexually explicit in erotic thrillers from the 1980s and 1990s.[44] Slasher films have the last influence on CWPTs: because slashers are rooted in the Gothic, they adopt some of its conventions, and become quite popular in the 1970s and 1980s, when they blend with the more traditional Female Gothic. Linda Ruth Williams also mentions the influence that slashers exerted on the erotic thriller and points specifically to the importance of the relationship between the heroine and the Fatal Man: "Films like *Guilty as Sin* are...thriller versions of Carol Clover's 'final girl' horror films, driven by a central female protagonist who...outsmarts the dark and deadly male."[45] Linda Ruth Williams sums up the various genres that create the "investigative heroine" of certain erotic thrillers: "The erotic thriller's female investigative heroine is then a hybrid figure, part *noir*ish detective woman, part horror final-girl, dominating the film's primary point of view and eliciting sympathies appropriate to both hero and quester."[46] While the protagonists of slashers tend to be pre-career women—most are adolescent girls—they are clearly Female Gothic heroines; the virginal heroine of the slasher that Clover has dubbed the Final Girl is essentially a contemporary equivalent of the Female Gothic sensitive orphan.[47] Though the Final Girl seems far-removed from the sexually adventurous modern-Gothic heroine of *Mr. Goodbar* or the hard-living woman based on the noir antihero, she also transgresses traditional gender-roles—as Clover has shown, she is coded masculine—and her transgression is emphasized through her doubling of the monster.[48] Citing the female protagonists Marti (Linda Blair) from the film *Hell Night* (Tom DeSimone, 1981) and Stretch (Caroline Williams) from *The Texas Chain Saw Massacre II* (Tobe Hooper, 1986), Clover says: "[The Final Girl] is the Girl Scout, the bookworm, the mechanic. Unlike her friends...she is not sexually active...although she is always smaller and weaker than the killer, she grapples with him energetically and convincingly. The Final Girl is boyish, in a word."[49] This fits in with her argument that "The Final Girl is...a congenial double for the adolescent male."[50] I disagree with Clover's idea that the masculinity of the Final Girl means that she represents male subjectivity. Rather, her male traits are easily explained by the history of the Female Gothic heroine: like Emily in *Udolpho*, the Final Girl retains her pre-adolescent male-identification as a form of rebellion against the constraints of adult femininity.[51] Indeed, the Final Girl has deep roots in eighteenth-century Sensibility literature, from which the Female Gothic evolves. Sensibility texts often feature a female type that Janet Todd calls "the powerful virgin"[52]: the "powerful virgin" is a heroine who, following the Sensibility doctrine, survives and even thrives in a corrupt world because of her integrity. Thus, the Final Girl's virginity—like Theresa's promiscuity in *Mr. Goodbar*—symbolizes her separation from the world, and thus her questioning of the status quo. More importantly for my argument, however, slashers explore the Final Girl's subjectivity via her fear, as do all Female Gothic narratives.

Jagged Edge is the narrative of a female lawyer with the masculine first name of Teddy (Glenn Close), who falls in love with Jack (Jeff Bridges), the criminal man whom she defends, believing he is falsely accused of having killed his wife and her maid. The attorney-client relationship mimics the relationship between two lovers, a relationship fraught with passionate tension and betrayal. The movie signals its affinities with the CWPT genre since it opens with a long shot of the Golden Gate Bridge: this is the glamorous but lonely big city of film noir. While *Jagged Edge* is influenced mostly by noir and classic Female Gothic, the first scene of the film is influenced by slashers: according to Linda Ruth Williams, "It opens, like John Carpenter's *Halloween*, with an unknown killer, whose point of view we share, enacting a sex-murder."[53] The masculine name of the heroine, which Clover shows to be one of the conventions of slashers, further suggests the influence of contemporary horror films on the CWPT.[54] Her point about slashers applies to *Jagged Edge* insofar as it allows male viewers to identify with a female protagonist who is not depicted in a traditionally feminine role. The appeal to both male and female viewers, based on this less traditionally feminine heroine, is a factor in the development of the CWPT in the 1980s/90s.[55] *JE* is engaging the female spectator via its Female Gothic as well as its CWPT dynamics. More than *Mr. Goodbar*, *JE* portrays the city and the corporate/legal world as threatening because it is masculine and its dangerous appeal is symbolized by Fatal Man Jack. Teddy becomes a *de facto* detective as she investigates a manipulative *homme fatal*.[56] At the end of the film, Jack is unmasked as the murderer of his wife and her maid as he unsuccessfully attempts to kill Teddy who kills him first. Given Eszterhas's cynical worldview, it is not surprising that this first authentic CWPT subtly suggests that women's attraction to Fatal Men is a form of masochism. Ironically, Eszterhas, whose work is often called misogynistic,[57] is, in this film, in tune with feminist Gothic critics who similarly expose the Female Gothic ideology as reactionary in suggesting that bad men are misunderstood and can be appropriated for feminist purposes.[58] In her discussion of "Modern Gothics," Joanna Russ, a feminist critic, states that the popularity of these narratives is based on their depiction of an anxiety-producing aspect of female lives: the constant need to "read" others, particularly men. As she explains, because women have less power than men, their wellbeing depends on "reading" men correctly.[59] Russ argues that Gothics romanticize this necessary and anxiety-producing aspect of women's lives by featuring a heroine who is torn between an attractive and powerful man who may or may not be a criminal and a gentler though less attractive man; she calls these figures the "Super-Male" and the "Shadow Male," respectively.[60] Russ says of the Super-Male: "The Heroine is vehemently attracted to him and usually just as vehemently repelled or frightened—she is not sure of her feelings for him, his feelings for her, and whether he 1) loves her; 2) hates her; 3) is using her; or 4) is trying to kill her."[61] The Super-Male, Russ explains, is always vindicated, while the Shadow Male turns out to be a criminal. Russ interprets this as a woman's need to believe that male aggression and violence are expressions of love: "[The Super-Male] may appear to treat me badly or brusquely; still, he loves me."[62] *JE* does not have a Shadow Male on whom the blame is thrust, but rather goes against the Gothic fantasy and constructs Super-Male Jack as guilty.[63] *JE*'s rejection of Gothic convention according to Russ is the kind of critical intervention that she, Modleski, and Massé make through their discussions of these films: they want women to realize that fantasies about bad men are masochistic and/or delusional.[64] *JE* does not place much emphasis on the doubling of heroine and Fatal Man, but it emphasizes the heroine's relationship to her father, an aspect of the Female Gothic that is important in future CWPTs.

As in following CWPTs, Teddy's law-related career is inherited from her father, a police officer. Herein lies the seed of the policewoman CWPTs, to be discussed further.[65] Additionally, Teddy's most important relationship is to her mentor and surrogate father (Robert Loggia), an alcoholic investigator. Also anticipating future CWPTs, this father figure is an ambiguous and mysterious character mirroring the Fatal Man: he is powerful though flawed, idealistic yet corrupt. Just as in *Udolpho* in which Emily is educated by her father and given access to the male world, the women heroines of the CWPTs enter the male sphere via their fathers. This differs from many films in which daughters identify with their mothers.

JE, a mainstream Hollywood film, and David Mamet's *House of Games* (1987) similarly construct a successful professional woman in the male corporate world who becomes a killer: these two female protagonists kill the men who have harmed them emotionally as well as exploited their professional skills. Like *JE*, *Games* takes a cynical attitude toward women's Gothic longings: it shows the limitations and delusions inherent in female fascination with male aggression and criminality rather than examining the creative role it plays in female self-definition.[66] *JE* and *Games*, along with *Taking Lives*—a thriller I will not explore in this analysis—all belong to a subset of CWPTs in which the woman is shown to be naïve and easily manipulated by the male criminal.

The Policewoman Thriller and the Legacy of the Father

The policewoman thriller forms another distinct subset within the CWPT: they draw a parallel between woman and monster and emphasize the relevance of the woman's father in this context. Thomas Harris's novel *The Silence of the Lambs* (1988) is the urtext in this subgenre. Harris builds a modern thriller on the model of the eighteenth-century Female Gothic novel, raising questions for feminist critics about the persistence of the Female Gothic genre into the 20th century and what this means for studies of female authorship, readership, spectatorship, and/or subjectivity. Clarice Starling (Jodie Foster), the protagonist of Demme's 1991 film adaptation, shares a special bond with Fatal Man serial killer Hannibal Lecter (Anthony Hopkins). Clarice, like *Udolpho*'s Emily, identifies with her father, who is doubled by her various male mentors, including Hannibal who allows her to access the sublime.[67] Though Harris updates the Gothic heroine/Fatal Man/father figure formula, it is Demme's cinematic version that underscores the Female Gothic aspects of the scenario. Demme's use of subjective camera brings the Female Gothic focus on female subjectivity to the film.[68] *Blue Steel* (1990) and *Impulse* (1990) anticipate many of the troubled-policewoman films to follow.[69] However, it is a later film, Philip Kaufman's *Twisted* (2004), which brings together all the elements of this CWPT sub-subgenre.

In his DVD commentary on *Twisted*, Kaufman claims that his plan was to make a noir in the Dashiell Hammett tradition.[70] As we have seen from previous CWPTs, though, noirs with female protagonists often end up becoming Female Gothics. The plot of *Twisted* epitomizes the Radcliffean structure. The policewoman protagonist, Jessica, like *Udolpho*'s Emily, is an orphan. Her police officer father was falsely accused of a murder-suicide that ended her mother's life. Jessica, a successful police officer, was raised by her father's former partner, John Mills (Samuel L. Jackson), her surrogate father and mentor. The inheritance model is clear: the daughter is the child who carries on the father's legacy.[71] This modern protagonist is the girl who replaces the son as she enters the male domain of privilege. However, this entry into a still foreign, hostile, and exclusively male space brings with it the thrilling fear that a trespasser feels. Jessica's perceptive ability is also an inheritance from her Female Gothic heroine forebears who are extremely sensitive.[72] The impressionability of the Gothic heroine has become the female cop's greatest asset.[73]

Jessica's connection to a box of mementos represents her connection to her parents. This is reminiscent of her affinities with Clover's Final Girl and with the tomboy heroine described by Mulvey.[74] In Female Gothics, the heroine often wears an idealized portrait of her mother on a necklace. In *Twisted*, Jessica looks at a picture of her mother that recalls Radcliffean iconography. Jessica's father's legacy appears more ambiguous than that of the mother, as he represents authority, criminality, and also victimization. This photograph recalls an earlier Radcliffe novel, *The Romance of the Forest* (1791) in which the heroine solves her father's murder: she finds an incomplete manuscript which tells the story of a man who was unjustly imprisoned and killed, and this man turns out to be her father. Jessica's crime scene photograph of her father is a pendant to the incomplete manuscript she must decipher to clear her father's name.

Though Jessica solves the twenty-five-year-old crime by the end of the film and proves her father's innocence, for most of the film the spectator is led to believe that he is a criminal. The convention of the transgressive heroine having a transgressive father is found in other films, especially *The Silence of the Lambs*. In "Murder and Mentorship: Advancement in *The Silence of the Lambs*," Bruce Robbins states, "Perhaps a woman needs a criminal for her mentor, and perhaps no one but a criminal will do, because of the intense moral ambiguity, from a woman's perspective, in the idea of rising into a professional world that is still very much patriarchal."[75] Robbins's claim is applicable to the CWPT in which the heroine's affinity for crime is related to her own transgression as a woman in a man's world, and, as Robbins suggests, only another transgressive figure can help her.[76] The suggestion is that a transgressive father raises a daughter who acts outside of traditional gender roles.[77] Furthermore, the heroine's criminal father symbolically empowers the heroine the same way the Fatal Man does: he allows her access to male aggression.[78] This parallel is evidenced when the killer, caught by Jessica, tells her, "you're me." Jessica not only drinks too much and has casual sex, but she cannot control her temper, severely beating up both a male criminal and an aggressive ex-boyfriend. Her appearance is stereotypically masculine, since she has short hair and usually wears dark jeans as well as a leather jacket. *Twisted* takes the identification between heroine and killer even further when it suggests that she may be a serial killer: all the men with whom she sleeps—the men she meets in bars and her male coworkers—are found dead. Yet this possible criminality does not protect Jessica; women's ambivalence about the male world means that the Female Gothic heroine fears the men in her life and fears herself as well. Thus, *Twisted*, in the more general woman-in-peril tradition, also gives us various male suspects who might pose a threat to Jessica. The question is, as Kaufman asks in his DVD commentary: "Is it her or is it after her?"[79] This doubling of heroine and criminal is again demonstrated in a dream sequence in which Jessica appears as predator instead of prey. In her dream, Jessica follows a man down an alley, apparently stalking him. The film highlights this gender reversal as the man that Jessica is following (the same man with whom she had become acquainted in a bar and who ended up dead) has long hair as opposed to Jessica's short hair. Jessica swaggers, while the man walks tentatively. She then dreams that she shoots the man, who is then replaced by other men in her life, all of whom she shoots. Jessica is masculine in that she is identified with her criminal father, but she is also feminine in that her own criminality is implicitly rooted in her feminine anger at men. The film further incorporates Female Gothic elements in having Jessica pass out every night after drinking and waking up the next morning to an announcement of a new murder. Most Gothic heroines faint and this is a sign of their great sensitivity, but the suggestion here is that these Gothic changes in consciousness are associated with crime. Jessica may transform into a Mad Woman in the Attic—to cite Sandra M. Gilbert and Susan Gubar's name for the angry alter-ego of the Female Gothic heroine—at night.[80]

The main Fatal Man in *Twisted* is Jessica's partner, Mike (Andy Garcia). The way he is presented suggests Jessica's ambivalence toward men. Mike is seen following Jessica and is set up as a suspect from the beginning. At the same time, he is the gentle suitor figure; he cooks for Jessica and offers her a romantic relationship for which the film suggests she is not ready. The resolution to Jessica's problems is ultimately related to her father. Jessica solves the case and figures out that the actual criminal is Mills, her father's partner as well as her surrogate father.[81] This is again, in the Radcliffean tradition, where the murderer almost always ends up being the heroine's uncle who, jealous of the father, kills him and steals his inheritance and his wife. Mills, who was a woman-hater, thought that Jessica's mother was promiscuous. Mills killed her and framed her husband. Moreover, Mills is the one who has been killing all of Jessica's lovers. The Freudian implications are clear: the father kills the daughter's suitors because they threaten his own power over her; the father is as much tyrant as mentor.[82] Jessica must thus kill her surrogate (bad) father and clear the real (good) father's name by exonerating him so that she can end up with the suitor figure, Mike. This is a reversal of *JE*, where the daughter kills the suitor and ends up with the father. While Jessica may be free from the oppressive influence of the father, she is now also symbolically an adult woman; this suggests a Final Girl maturation narrative that is distinctively female and counters Clover's idea that slasher-inspired films stage male maturation. But being an adult woman also brings its own oppression—for example, the suggestion is that Jessica is no longer troubled and can settle down to a more traditional lifestyle with Mike—showing that the father's legacy is a respite from this oppressive move into the adult world and is thus associated with liberation as well as oppression.[83]

The Sublimity of Female Desire: *In the Cut* and *Candyman*

While the female cop films work out some of the implications of the heroine's fascination with, and fear of, the male world through the doubling of heroine and Fatal Man and through the ambiguous legacy of the father, they generally imply that the heroine's fascination with transgression is a problem she must overcome.[84] However, two less-mainstream CWPTs, Jane Campion's *In the Cut* (2003), based on Susanna Moore's 1995 novel of the same name, and Bernard Rose's *Candyman* (1992), based on Clive Barker's short story "The Forbidden," suggest that the heroine's seemingly masochistic attraction to fear is a creative wish to push her own subjectivity to the limits and thus cross the boundaries set on women.[85] These films are also similar since they stress the importance of the sublime environment—the cityscape which is also the Fatal Man's home—in their exploration of female subjectivity. The heroine of *In the Cut*, Frannie (Meg Ryan), is a teacher and writer doing research on urban male slang: like the heroine of *House of Games*, she becomes an anthropologist in the aggressive and dangerous world of men.[86] The slang, which tends to mix violence (particularly aimed at women) and sex, is a symbol of this masculinity, and Frannie wishes to appropriate it for women by studying it and, thus, controlling it. The male world of the police figures in this CWPT as well, since some of the most misogynistic slang is used by policemen (there are no policewomen in this film) and the possible Fatal Man, Malloy (Mark Ruffalo), is a cop.[87] The other male territory is the city, something that translates especially well from book to screen.[88] The cinematography is reminiscent of the New York depicted in *Taxi Driver* (Martin Scorsese, 1977): a city of night and nightlife, with blazing neon advertisements for pornographic shows and films.[89] Though he does not mention the Gothic, Neil Young's description of the New York of *In the Cut* exemplifies why it is a sublime landscape: "Campion presents a crime-ridden metropolis full of grace notes, epiphanies, [and] the possibility of transcendence."[90] Frannie's sister (Jennifer Jason Leigh), who is more adventurous than Frannie, lives above a strip-club: like Frannie, she wants to stay close to that which could potentially threaten women, in an attempt to control and/or defy. Frannie feels close to the city and welcomes its menace and mystery: she walks as if dazed by its power and mesmerized by its grittiness.[91] She records every urban nuance as if it has special meaning for her, and, in this world of female subjectivity, it does: the poetry in transit she reads on the subway speaks to her in its symbolic language about the longing she feels.[92]

However, as in all CWPTs, the most important symbol is that of the serial killer preying on women in the city, and the danger he symbolizes is inextricably coupled with Frannie's subjectivity from the beginning. As in traditional woman-in-peril thrillers, he could be any of the men around Frannie: her ex-boyfriend, her serial killer obsessed student, or Malloy, the police officer with whom she has begun an affair. But like the policewoman CWPTs, *In the Cut* suggests that he is even closer to Frannie: he is part of her and what she desires. The film expresses this possibility with the subplot about the male student obsessed with John Wayne Gacy: the student tells Frannie that Gacy "was a victim of desire." Frannie's often reckless actions are also driven by desire. Furthermore, Campion suggests the close connection between Frannie's boundless desire and violence. Sexual acts are akin to violence—Frannie and Malloy first have sex after Frannie has been attacked in an alley, and both are aroused by reenacting the mugging—while murder has an almost sensual intimacy. Frannie asks Malloy to describe the murders in detail and she dwells on the words and the images. But the film does not suggest that Frannie, a woman living in a patriarchal society, has internalized masochism. Frannie's rejection of masochism is addressed in the novel when Frannie says, "I am no masochist. I know that."[93] Rather, *In the Cut*: allows women access to the sublime by claiming extreme feelings for them.[94] According to Camille Paglia, "There is no female Mozart because there is no female Jack the Ripper."[95] Here Paglia highlights the reason for women's fascination with serial killers—that is, with what serial killers symbolize—in these films. Paglia suggests that women cannot be excessive, and it is this excess that the Fatal Man allows the heroine to access. While Moore's novel ends with an excessive scene which re-imagines the ending of *Mr. Goodbar*—the heroine is killed, but it is represented as a daring refusal to compromise with the world and as a courageous wish to face the worst female fears—Campion's film has the heroine kill the killer. The change made in adapting novel to film resembles a change in the adaptation of Harris's *Hannibal*: both novels leave the heroines with the monsters (though in very different ways), while the cinematic adaptations have the heroines destroy or defeat the monsters. Having the dual endings for *In the Cut* is helpful in that any sort of conclusion betrays the core of the story, which is about longing and desire for its own sake. Campion's ending is more normative in that the killer is shot by Frannie, his next intended victim, and thus fits mainstream ideas of female empowerment, but it also goes against Moore's purposefully taboo-challenging vision in the novel.[96] It thus takes *Candyman*, a film that fully engages the horror genre, to truly flesh out the implications of the Female Gothic appropriation of the sublime for female fantasy.

Candyman takes one of the core ideas of *In the Cut*—that women's entry into the sublime is achieved via imagining excess, usually associated with the masculine—and literalizes it through horror motifs, a way to escape the bounds of realism still clinging to Campion's film.[97] The heroine, Helen Lyle (Virginia Madsen), is, like Frannie, a scholar of the urban, and thus the film gives her the symbolic occupation of anthropologist. She studies urban legends, particularly those about Candyman (Tony Todd), a supernatural figure with a hook-hand who is said to be responsible for killings in a housing project in Chicago. One of the ways the film shows Helen's Gothic involvement in landscape is through her fascination with the ornate graffiti in the housing projects. Graffiti resembles the Gothic motif of hieroglyphs; the intricacy and mystery of graffiti suggests a two-dimensional labyrinth, while its association with gangs makes the buildings it covers as dangerous as Gothic ruins.[98] Graffiti also acts as a mysterious signifier, lending it the imagination-stimulating quality of the sublime. Thus, the graffiti in *Candyman* plays the same role as the Poetry in Motion in the subways in *In the Cut*: both are suggestive signs that the heroines begin to take as personal messages which speak to them of their dangerous journeys.[99] Helen's subjectivity is repeatedly stressed in the film, as her eyes are shown in close-ups when she looks at graffiti or listens to horrific stories about Candyman's violent activities. Because she is so receptive to it, Helen, like Frannie, begins to feel dazed by the landscape and, like Jessica in *Twisted*, she begins having lapses in consciousness during which she may turn into a criminal. Helen's Gothic heroine receptivity also allows Candyman to possess her and put her in a trance out of which she wakes up surrounded by, and thus blamed for, his crimes. Therefore, heroine and monster are once again doubled, with Helen eventually becoming the monster, thus rendering explicit what has been implicit in most CWPTs.

While *Candyman* seems to support Creed and Pinedo's claims that women enjoy horror films in part because the genre allows women to be violent and monstrously powerful, the film actually suggests something more subtle: Candyman's monstrosity represents excess and is thus a portal to the sublime. While it seems that Helen is appropriating Candyman's phallic power—overtly represented by his hook-hand, which Helen literally inherits at the end of the film—she is more importantly appropriating the imaginative power he represents. The dynamic that Helen Stoddard finds in Charlotte Dacre's Gothic novel *Zofloya; Or, the Moor* (1807)—in which the heroine, Victoria, becomes all-powerful after she allies herself with Zofloya, a handsome Moor sent by the Devil—is at work in *Candyman*, particularly since Candyman is African-American. Before his reincarnation as Candyman, he was gruesomely lynched for having impregnated his white lover, and his hand was cut off and replaced with a hook. According to Stoddard, "Victoria encourages the dissolution of the boundary between herself and Zofloya, the sublime and demonic object...Difference and distance both eventually disappear so that she actually becomes involved with the sublime, and this is her ultimate transgression—to enter the zone of the limitless."[100] *Candyman* implies this connection between transgression and transcendence when Candyman asks Helen, "What do the good know except what the bad teach them by their excesses?" Barker echoes this concept in the DVD commentary, when he describes his own life as an artist in Romantic terms: he claims that he has always followed his muse and that it led him to the often-misunderstood horror genre. When others disapprove of his work, he reacts by making it more shocking. He sums up his artistic philosophy thus: "I was always going to be a maker of extreme things."[101] It is this access to the extreme that women are denied and that is thus symbolized by masculinity. That female fascination and identification with the Fatal Man is literalized in a horror film is especially appropriate, since the horror genre is that which is excessive in our culture and most often associated with a male audience.

It is telling that Camille Paglia—a critic who identifies horror spectatorship as feminine[102]—pinpoints some of the fascination of the CWPT for the female audience with her ideas about the male imagination and criminality. The controversial stance held by Paglia is that the aggressive and uncontrollable male libido is at the root of all innovation, and that women can be geniuses only in so far as they tap into this energy.[103] While Paglia's view is arguably misogynistic—that only men have the "divine spark" of creativity—there are ways in which this seemingly anti-feminist view can be appropriated for feminism and is being appropriated by the CWPTs. This aggrandizement of men in some respects transforms them into symbols and thus suggests a female point of view (as Anne Williams claims about the Fatal Man archetype).

Paglia, Clover, Creed, and Pinedo are reacting to a strand of feminism that sees women as constantly threatened by male violence and the male libido.[104] According to Clover, "Identifying male sadism, especially toward women, and holding men at least theoretically culpable...are major achievements of feminism. Texts like Susan Brownmiller's *Against Our Will*, which accumulates case on case of male brutality until the evidence seems crushing, have been instrumental in those achievements."[105] Clover argues that it is the feminist stake in this belief that blinds critics to the obvious nuances of the horror film: "The reason, then, for the critical eloquence on the subject of male sadism is that it holds the gender bottom line. And the reason for the virtual silence in horror film criticism and for the blank spot in film theory on the possibility of male masochism is that to broach that is...to unsettle what is apparently our ultimate gender story."[106] Though Clover's argument that the male audience of horror films identifies with the heroine rather than the killer has changed scholarly understanding of the genre, her analysis is still limited to male viewers, who, she claims, make up the bulk of the horror audience.[107] What Clover overlooks, though, is that one's attraction to a certain genre is not only based in the psychological conflicts it addresses but is also an aspect of socialization. Clover's claim that the only women she has seen at horror film screenings are there with men or in groups suggests that these women are invading male territory and must be protected.[108] It is arguable that it is still taboo for women in our culture to openly enjoy entertainment that is explicitly violent or sexual. This may explain the appeal of the CWPT inheritance model for women: a woman can more easily enter the male sphere via her father, and this is as true in horror film connoisseurship as it is in sports fandom, business or politics. While Clover stresses the male psychodrama, Creed tries to claim power for women in the horror film by showing how the feminine is itself represented as monstrous and threatening. This also suggests a masculine point of view, which Otherizes women even if it also empowers them. Furthermore, as I have argued here, the masculine is just as often depicted as monstrous, thus implying a female perspective. Pinedo, one of the few critics focusing on female subjectivity as it relates to horror film, argues that horror allows women to indulge that which is most forbidden to them: anger and violence. But this is too literal an interpretation of a symbolic genre.[109] The female spectator's involvement with fear is more complex, as my analysis of the various CWPTs has shown. Despite the complexity of an audience's interaction with any text, one of the strongest appeals the CWPT has for women is its imagining of the real world as masculine and therefore hostile and challenging. At the same time, as women obtain increased access to the male world, the formula will have to change; women's wish to possess male power will dissipate once men are no longer symbols of a separate, forbidden and intriguing sphere.[110]

Today's young women grew up with the horror movies Clover and Pinedo defended from feminist critics, and these films are thus no longer as threatening as they once were. Indeed, it seems that young women have already claimed some of this more sexual or violent entertainment. For example, Joss Whedon's *Buffy the Vampire Slayer*, a celebrated television series, is steeped in elements of the slasher; as John Kenneth Muir states in *Horror Films of the 1980s*: "One glorious day, when the eighties were just a pleasant memory, the final girl would finally transcend her origins in the derided slasher film and 'become' the thing she had always been destined to be: *Buffy the Vampire Slayer*."[111] Furthermore, "Final Girl" is now the title of a horror blog written by a woman, Stacie Ponder, and her humorous tone undercuts the possibility that 1970s and 1980s horror films are threatening to women.[112] Even more telling, perhaps, is that one of the most beloved film characters of 2007, the eponymous Juno (Ellen Page), is a fan of horror director Dario Argento.[113] What I have tried to show in this essay is that women were engaging in supposedly excessive, and thus supposedly masculine, entertainment since the Female Gothics of the 18th century. One of the most important aspects of Linda Ruth Williams's study of the erotic thriller is its revelation that the soft-core pornography direct-to-video (DTV) films of the 1980s and 1990s, a genre that would seem male-driven and male-oriented, was actually female-oriented in terms of allowing for a representation of female subjectivity and for offering women opportunities in filmmaking: "[W]e might assume that the lower and cheaper the erotic thriller is, the less positive its representation of women becomes. This is not true. The sexually strong women who populate the DTV genre...may offer a point of identification or wish-fulfillment for women in the audience."[114] Linda Ruth Williams shows how various types of DTV films—which she categorizes as "Sexual Surveillance and Female Voyeurism," "Women's Stories and Lousy Husbands," "The Undercover Heroine," and "The Strip Flick"—all feature various female (as well as male) fantasies.[115] Furthermore, some of these films were directed by women, and Linda Ruth Williams interviews two notable female directors of DTV films, Katt Shea and Anne Goursaud.[116]

Goursaud's work bridges the genres of soft-core pornography and horror; her most famous film is the Female Gothic *Embrace of the Vampire* (1995).[117] These two disreputable genres are brought together and are relegated to the margins of the film industry, but it is perhaps there, as Linda Ruth Williams suggests, that gender boundaries can be challenged. As Linda Ruth Williams shows, these DTV films are more progressive than Hollywood films in terms of representation of gender: "[U]nlike mainstream erotic thrillers such as *Fatal Attraction* or *Body of Evidence*, the low-budget versions seldom penalise women for simply possessing erotic or economic power...Here the DTV erotic thriller...seems to be doing something genuinely unique."[118]

Though female critics and artists seek to increase the female imaginative sphere, in real world terms there has been a backlash against the supposed phenomenon of women acting like men—having casual sex, putting off relationships to concentrate on a career, drinking—and several books and articles have appeared in the last few years which express ambivalence about (or even openly condemn) this equalizing tendency.[119] Perhaps it is the continued insistence of a separate sphere for men and women that keeps the CWPT vital into the twenty-first century.[120]

Works Cited

Bowman, Barbara. "Victoria Holt's Gothic Romances: A Structuralist Inquiry." In *The Female Gothic*, edited by Juliann E. Fleenor, 69-81. Montreal: Eden Press, 1983.

Brontë, Charlotte. *Jane Eyre*. 1847. Edited by Margaret Smith. Introduction and Revised Notes by Sally Shuttleworth. New York: Oxford University Press, 2000.

Burke, Edmund. *A Philosophical Enquiry into the Origin of our Ideas of the Sublime and Beautiful*. 1757. Edited and with an Introduction and Notes by Adam Phillips. New York: Oxford University Press, 1998.

Clover, Carol. *Men, Women, and Chain Saws: Gender in the Modern Horror Film*. Princeton: Princeton University Press, 1992.

Creed, Barbara. *The Monstrous-Feminine: Film, Feminism, Psychoanalysis*. New York: Routledge, 2003.

Davenport-Hines, Richard. *Gothic: Four Hundred Years of Excess, Horror, Evil, and Ruin*. New York: North Point Press, 2000.

Demme, Jonathan. "Identity Check: Interview with Jonathan Demme." By Gavin Smith. *Film Comment* (Jan.-Feb. 1991): 28-37.

Dowd, Maureen. "Bucks and Blondes: Joe Eszterhas Lives the Big Dream." *New York Times,* May 30, 1993, Film Section.

Ebert, Roger. "Review of *Music Box.*" rogerebert.suntimes.com. January 19, 1990.

Fleenor, Juliann E., ed. *The Female Gothic.* Montreal: Eden Press, 1983.

Gilbert, Sandra M. and Gubar, Susan. *The Madwoman in the Attic: The Woman Writer and the Nineteenth-Century Literary Imagination.* New Haven: Yale University Press, 1984.

Hanson, Helen. *Hollywood Heroines: Women in Film Noir and the Female Gothic Film.* London: I. B. Tauris, 2007.

Harris, Thomas. *Hannibal.* New York: Delacorte Press, 1999.

—. *The Silence of the Lambs.* New York: St. Martin's, 1989.

Holland, Norman N. and Leona F. Sherman. "Gothic Possibilities." *New Literary History* 8:2, Explorations in Literary History (Winter 1977): 279-294.

Hume, Robert D. "Gothic versus Romantic: A Revaluation of the Gothic Novel." *PMLA* 84:2 (March 1969), 282-90.

Internet Movie Database. "Bernard Rose" www.imdb.com.

—. "Candyman" www.imdb.com.

—. "In the Cut" www.imdb.com.

—. "Twisted" www.imdb.com.

Israel, Betsey. *Bachelor Girl: 100 Years of Breaking the Rules–A Social History of Living Single.* New York: Perennial, 2003.

Jancovich, Mark. Introduction to *Horror: The Film Reader,* edited by Mark Jancovich. London: Routledge, 2002.

Kahane, Claire. "The Gothic Mirror." In *The (M)other Tongue: Essays in Feminist Psychoanalytic Interpretation,* edited by Shirley Nelson Garner, Claire Kahane, and Madelon Sprengnether. Ithaca: Cornell University Press, 1985.

Massé, Michelle. *In the Name of Love: Women, Masochism, and the Gothic.* Ithaca: Cornell University Press, 1992.

Miller, Nancy K. *The Heroine's Text: Readings in the French and English Novel, 1722-1782.* New York: Columbia University Press, 1980.

Modleski, Tania. *Loving with a Vengeance: Mass-Produced Fantasies for Women.* Hamden: Archon, 1982.

Moers, Ellen. *Literary Women: The Great Writers.* New York: Oxford University Press, 1977.

Moore, Susanna. *In the Cut.* New York: Onyx, 1996.

Muir, John Kenneth. *Horror Films of the 1980s.* Jefferson: McFarland & Company, Inc., 2007.

Mulvey, Laura. "Afterthoughts on 'Visual Pleasure and Narrative Cinema' Inspired by *Duel in the Sun*." In *Psychoanalysis and Cinema*, edited by E. Ann Kaplan. New York: Routledge, 1990.

Mussell, Kay J. "'But Why Do They Read Those Things?': The Female Audience and the Gothic Novel." In *The Female Gothic*, edited by Juliann E. Fleenor, 57-68. Montreal: Eden Press, 1983.

One Page at a Time Blog. http://onepageatatime.blogspot.com/.(June 27, 2005):http://onepageatatime.blogspot.com/2005/06/monday-picks_27.html.

O'Rourke, Meghan. "Theories of the Erotic." www.slate.com (October 26, 2005), http://www.slate.com/id/2128818.

Paglia, Camille. "The Rape Debate, Continued." In *Sex, Art, and American Culture*. New York: Vintage Books, 1992.

—. "Rape and Modern Sex War." In *Sex, Art, and American Culture*.

—. *Sexual Personae: Art and Decadence from Nefertiti to Emily Dickinson*. New York: Vintage Books, 1991.

Pinedo, Isabel Cristina. *Recreational Terror: Women and the Pleasures of Horror Film Viewing*. Albany: State University of New York Press, 1997.

Ponder, Stacie. Final Girl Blog. http://finalgirl.blogspot.com/.

Praz, Mario. *The Romantic Agony*. 1933. With a Foreword by Frank Kermode. 2nd edition. New York: Oxford University Press, 1991.

Radcliffe, Ann. *The Mysteries of Udolpho*. 1794. Edited by Bonamy Dobrée. Introduction and Notes by Terry Castle. New York: Oxford University Press, 1998.

—. *The Romance of the Forest*. 1791. Edited and with an Introduction and Notes by Chloe Chard. New York: Oxford University Press, 1999.

Radway, Janice. *Reading the Romance: Women, Patriarchy, and Popular Culture*. Chapel Hill: University of North Carolina Press, 1991.

—. "The Utopian Impulse in Popular Literature: Gothic Romances and 'Feminist' Protest." *The American Quarterly* 33:2 (Summer 1981): 140-62.

Robbins, Bruce. "Murder and Mentorship: Advancement in *The Silence of the Lambs*." *Boundary 2* 23:1 (Spring 1996): 71-90.

Rossner, Judith. *Looking for Mr. Goodbar*. New York: Simon and Schuster, 1975.

Russ, Joanna. "Somebody's Trying to Kill Me and I Think It's My Husband: The Modern Gothic." In *The Female Gothic*, edited by Juliann E. Fleenor, 31-56. Montreal: Eden Press, 1983.

Smith, R. McClure. "'A Recent Martyr;' The Masochistic Aesthetics of
    Valerie Martin." *Contemporary Literature* 37:3 (Autumn 1996): 391-
    415.
Stepp, Laura Sessions. *Unhooked: How Young Women Pursue Sex, Delay
    Love, and Lose at Both.* New York: Riverhead Books, 2007.
Stoddard, Helen. "Early Female Gothic: *Zofloya* and *Manfroné; Or the
    One-Handed Monk.*"
    http://www.arts.gla.ac.uk/sesll/STELLA/COMET/glasgrev/issue2/stod
    dard.htm.
Tasker, Yvonne. *Working Girls: Gender and Sexuality in Popular Cinema.*
    New York: Routledge, 1998.
Todd, Janet. *Sensibility: An Introduction.* London: Methuen, 1986.
Williams, Anne. *Art of Darkness: A Poetics of Gothic.* Chicago: Chicago
    University Press, 1995.
Williams, Linda. "Film Bodies: Gender, Genre, and Excess." *Film
    Quarterly* 44:4 (Summer 1991): 2-13.
Williams, Linda Ruth. *The Erotic Thriller in Contemporary Cinema.*
    Bloomington: Indiana University Press, 2005.
Wolcott, James. "The Right Fluff: A Guy's Guide to Chick Flicks." *Vanity
    Fair*, March 2008.
Wolff, Cynthia Griffin. "The Radcliffean Gothic Model: A Form for
    Feminine Sexuality." *Modern Language Studies* 9:3 (Autumn 1979):
    98-113.
Young, Neil. Neil Young's Film Lounge. Review of *In the Cut.*
    http://www.jigsawlounge.co.uk/film/index.php (October 23, 2003),
    http://www.jigsawlounge.co.uk/film/inthecut.html.

Filmography

Basic Instinct. Dir. Paul Verhoeven, 1992.
The Best of Everything. Dir. Jean Negulesco, 1959.
Blue Steel. Dir. Kathryn Bigelow, 1990.
Call Me. Dir. Sollace Mitchell, 1988.
Candyman. Dir. Bernard Rose, 1992.
Crossing Jordan. 2001-2007.
Double Indemnity. Dir. Billy Wilder, 1944.
Embrace of the Vampire. Dir. Anne Goursaud, 1995.
Gaslight. Dir. George Cukor, 1944.
Guilty as Sin. Dir. Sidney Lumet, 1993.
Halloween. Dir. John Carpenter, 1978.
Hannibal. Dir. Ridley Scott, 2001.

House of Games. Dir. David Mamet, 1987.
Impulse. Dir. Sandra Locke, 1990.
In the Cut. Dir. Jane Campion, 2003.
Jagged Edge. Dir. Richard Marquand, 1985.
Juno. Dir. Jason Reitman, 2007.
Looking for Mr. Goodbar. Dir. Richard Brooks, 1977.
The Mary Tyler Moore Show. 1970-7.
Murder by Numbers. Dir. Barbet Schroeder, 2002.
My Brother's Keeper. Dir. John Badham, 2002.
Never Talk to Strangers. Dir. Peter Hall, 1995.
A Nightmare on Elm Street. Dir. Wes Craven, 1984.
Oxygen. Dir. Richard Shepard, 1999.
Perfect Stranger. Dir. James Foley, 2007.
Rebecca. Dir. Alfred Hitchcock, 1940.
Rosemary's Baby. Dir. Roman Polanski, 1968.
Saving Grace. 2007-present.
Sex and the City. 1998-2004.
The Silence of the Lambs. Dir. Jonathan Demme, 1991.
Suspicion. Dir. Alfred Hitchcock, 1941.
Taking Lives. Dir. D.J. Caruso, 2004.
Taxi Driver. Dir. Martin Scorsese, 1977.
The Texas Chain Saw Massacre. Dir. Tobe Hooper, 1974.
Twisted. Dir. Philip Kaufman, 2004.
Veronica Mars. 2004-2007.

Notes

[1] I have not seen these films categorized in the manner in which I categorize them here, nor have I seen this term used in criticism. However, Linda Ruth Williams in *The Erotic Thriller in Contemporary Cinema* (Bloomington: Indiana University Press, 2005) discusses many of these films and classifies them as erotic thrillers. In addition, I came across the term in a literature blog, onepageatatime.blogspot.com. On June 27, 2005, the writer of the blog states the following about Mary Higgins Clark: "She has her formula down pat—the strong modern career woman in peril from a seemingly benign stalker, secret admirer, or friendly neighborhood psychopath." I have also seen the term "liberated-woman-in-danger" used by film writer Neil Young to describe Jane Campion's *In the Cut*.

[2] Yvonne Tasker identified the importance of the female detective in 1980s and 1990s Hollywood films in her *Working Girls: Gender and Sexuality in Popular Cinema* (New York: Routledge, 1998). According to Tasker, "The role of prostitute/'streetwalker' allows female characters not only to inhabit urban space but to flaunt it [...] and, perhaps, to exhibit the 'toughness' through which

working-class masculinities are regularly symbolized (though just as often to be inscribed as victim/corpse) [...] [the prostitute] asserts herself within spaces from which other women are excluded," 5. Tasker's discussion of the transgressive quality of these heroines and its connection to their uneasy relationship to traditional femininity has been very influential to my analysis. After completing a draft of this essay, I came across another book—only available in the United States in February 2008—that looks at the female detective in Hollywood: Helen Hanson's *Hollywood Heroines: Women in Film Noir and the Female Gothic Film* (London: I.B. Tauris, 2007).

[3] Tasker also sees this feature of female-detective films: "the female hero may be represented as identified with the father, in search of authority and, sometimes reconciliation of authority," 69.

[4] By "woman's film," I mean a film that has a woman as the protagonist and that seeks to explore this female character's subjectivity. According to Carol Clover, "The tendency [is] to classify a plot as 'horror' when it is low budget and 'drama' or 'suspense' when it is highly produced," *Men, Women, and Chain Saws: Gender in the Modern Horror Film* (Princeton: Princeton University Press, 1992), 5.

[5] Ellen Moers, *Literary Women: The Great Writers* (New York: Oxford UP, 1977), 90.

[6] Ibid., 91. The Radcliffean heroine resembles Carol Clover's slasher film "female victim-hero," 4.

[7] The Lifetime channel is aimed at women and was indeed one of the first such channels.

[8] Wolff, *Modern Language Studies* 9:3 (Autumn 1979): 99.

[9] Kahane, "The Gothic Mirror," *The (M)other Tongue: Essays in Psychoanalytic Interpretation*, eds. Shirley Nelson Garner, Claire Kahane, Madelon Sprengnether (Ithaca: Cornell UP, 1985), 334-351: "What I see repeatedly locked into the forbidden center of the Gothic which draws me inward is the spectral presence of a dead-undead mother, archaic and all-encompassing, a ghost signifying the problematic of femininity which the heroine must confront," 336. In "Gothic Possibilities," *New Literary History* 8, no. 2, Explorations in Literary History (Winter 1977), Sherman argues: "[The castle] becomes all the possibilities of a parent or a body. It can threaten, resist, love, or confine, but in all these actions, it stands as a total environment in one-to-one relation with the victim, like the all-powerful mother of earliest childhood," 283. (Norman N. Holland co-wrote this essay.)

[10] Ibid., 343-51.

[11] Hanson argues that the working woman became an important figure in film in the 40s.

[12] Kahane notes the fact that the Female Gothic allows women to imagine a freedom not generally accorded them and usually associated with pre-adolescence.

[13] I will be engaging the best-known works of these three horror film theorists: Clover's *Men, Women, and Chain Saws*, Barbara Creed's *The Monstrous-Feminine* (New York: Routledge, 2003), and Isabel Cristina Pinedo's *Recreational Terror:*

Women and the Pleasures of Horror Film Viewing (Albany: State University of New York Press, 1997).

[14] If this sounds like a scene from the television series *Sex and the City* (1998-2004), that is because all that show needs to become a career-woman-in-peril-thriller is a serial killer.

[15] Holt's most famous work is *The Mistress of Mellyn* (1960) and Stewart's is *Nine Coaches Waiting* (1958).

[16] Other examples include Jean Negulesco's career woman melodrama *The Best of Everything* (1959, based on Rona Jaffe's 1958 bestseller) and *The Mary Tyler Moore Show* (1970-77).

[17] Tasker also argues for the hybrid nature of the female-detective film and the importance of horror and noir for this genre.

[18] According to Moers, "the Gothic fantasies of Mrs. Radcliffe are a locus of heroinism which, ever since, women have turned to feminist purposes" (*Literary Women*, 126). "Heroinism" is a term Moers coins to mean female heroism.

[19] Moers suggests this in the chapter "Traveling Heroinism: Gothic for Heroines" in *Literary Women*.

[20] For Tasker, "It is a cliché of Hollywood cinema, pulp fictions and psychoanalysis that tomboys or active heroines somehow identify with their fathers. In action films, the heroine is presented [...] as taking over/inheriting her father's position," p. 102.

[21] Regarding the popularity of the tomboy in the female imagination, Moers states, "The prohibitions on outdoor female activities must account for the proud place of the tomboy in women's literature. For in every age, whatever the social rules, there has always been one time in a woman's life, the years before puberty, when walking, running, climbing, battling, and tumbling are as normal for females as they are for males," 130.

[22] Anne Williams, *Art of Darkness: A Poetics of Gothic* (Chicago: Chicago University Press, 1995), 141. As Williams herself notes, she is here following the critic Mario Praz, who, in his book *The Romantic Agony* (New York: Oxford, 1933), identified this figure in Romanticism and dubbed him the *homme fatal*.

[23] Moers similarly argues that Montoni allows Emily access to exhilarating dangers: "In the power of her villains, her heroines are forced to do what they could never do alone, whatever their ambitions," 126. Radcliffe is also following Edmund Burke's theories on the sublime in her deployment of pleasurable fear. In his 1757 treatise *A Philosophical Enquiry into the Origin of our Ideas of the Sublime and Beautiful*, ed. and with notes by Adam Philips (New York: Oxford University Press, 1998), Burke argues that the sublime is that which is so great or mysterious that the mind cannot fully understand or contain it. The sublime is also gendered masculine by Burke: it is that which overwhelms one through its power, magnitude, or energy. While I do not have room to do justice to the gendered aspects and implications of Burke's ideas, it is important to note that Radcliffe appropriates the sublime for female subjectivity in her theory and use of terror as an artistic element.

[24] Many critics have made the connection between Emily's good and bad fathers, but Moers's analysis is particularly astute: she points out that Emily's real father "dies early in the novel, but his influence persists as a moral force forever." Moers explains Emily's father's doubling with Montoni: "Emily's father returns to play an important negative role [...] in the person of the villain Montoni [...] [Montoni] plays the bad father role in his capacity of uncle by marriage," p. 135.

[25] In *The Romantic Novel in England* (Cambridge: Harvard University Press, 1972), Robert Kiely suggests many of the same points that Moers made later.

[26] The term "supermarket fiction" is used to refer to popular literature often sold in supermarkets; another common term is "airport fiction."

[27] Michelle Massé, quoting Jessica Benjamin, makes the same point: "[The masochistic Gothic heroine's] later, dominant lover will mirror both relations and 'actually provides a dual solution, containment *and* excitement, the holding environment and the road to freedom—the joint features of both the ideal mother and father,' (120). Thus, even within the confines of masochism, the girl simultaneously seeks security *and* freedom," Massé, *In the Name of Love: Women, Masochism, and the Gothic* (Ithaca: Cornell University Press, 1992), 46.

[28] Modleski recognizes these films as important moments in Female Gothic cultural history: "Beginning with Alfred Hitchcock's 1940 movie version of *Rebecca* and continuing through and beyond George Cukor's *Gaslight* in 1944, the gaslight films may be seen to reflect *women's* fears about losing their unprecedented freedoms and being forced back into the homes after the men returned from fighting...," 21.

[29] Though there were some important critical works on the Gothic before the 1970s, a renewed interest in the genre emerged out of the growth of feminist literary criticism.

[30] "The Radcliffean Gothic Model: A Form for Feminine Sexuality," 111.

[31] Linda Ruth Williams also holds this view of *Looking for Mr. Goodbar*, calling it a "sexual quest" film.

[32] According to Murray Smith's discussion of *Deception* (Irving Rapper, 1946): "The film's interest lies in its unstable position between two popular generic forms of the Forties, two forms which are in a sense the inverse of each other—the *film noir* and the female gothic," (quoted in Hanson, 42).

[33] Tasker makes this connection to film noir, especially to *Basic Instinct*.

[34] L. R. Williams discusses *Basic Instinct* throughout *The Erotic Thriller in Contemporary Cinema*.

[35] More accurately, most CWPTs are situated between the thriller and horror genres.

[36] L. R. Williams references these various genres throughout *The Erotic Thriller in Contemporary Cinema*.

[37] L. R. Williams also points this out when discussing Steve Neale's analysis of noir.

[38] L. R. Williams, 7.

[39] Ibid., 33.

[40] Ibid., 125.

[41] Ibid., 78.

[42] Ibid., 156.

[43] See Nancy K. Miller's *The Heroine's Text: Readings in the French and English Novel, 1722-1782* (New York: Columbia University Press), 1980.

[44] Part of L. R. Williams's discussion of the erotic thriller also takes up the importance of the direct-to-video (DTV) market that developed with the VCR.

[45] L. R. Williams, *Erotic Thriller*, 127. Although many CWPTs are conventionally categorized as erotic thrillers, not all are, as a film like *Candyman* shows.

[46] Ibid., 128.

[47] The most famous Final Girl is perhaps Laurie (Jamie Lee Curtis), the heroine of John Carpenter's *Halloween* (1978).

[48] Clover explores this doubling of heroine and monster most thoroughly in the chapter "Her Body, Himself."

[49] Clover, *Men, Women, and Chain Saws*, 39-40.

[50] Ibid., 51.

[51] Laura Mulvey makes the same point—that a male-identified film heroine represents the freedom of pre-adult femininity—in her essay on female spectatorship "Afterthoughts on 'Visual Pleasure and Narrative Cinema'" in *Psychoanalysis and Cinema*, ed. E. Ann Kaplan (New York: Routledge, 1990).

[52] Janet Todd, *Sensibility: An Introduction* (London: Methuen, 1986), 114.

[53] L. R. Williams, *Erotic Thriller*, 152.

[54] Quite a few of the policewomen in CWPTs have androgynous Final Girl names, as for example Lottie (Theresa Russell) in *Impulse* and Maddy (Maura Tierney) in *Oxygen*.

[55] Hanson makes the same point about the broad appeal of the neo-noir.

[56] L. R. Williams mentions this noirish aspect, comparing this first Eszterhas film to his later more overtly noir *Basic Instinct*.

[57] L. R. Williams discusses misogyny in *Jagged Edge*: "One characteristic Eszterhas contradiction is an ability to vividly present misogynistic spectacle and then contextualize it through a gesture of feminism [...] This presentation and disclaimer usually happen at one and the same time, however, as when Teddy, *Jagged Edge*'s heroine-in-control, is misogyny's ambivalent target," 153.

[58] In *Loving with a Vengeance*, Modleski argues that this is a common female fantasy deployed in female popular culture. Michelle Massé argues in *In the Name of Love: Women, Masochism, and the Gothic* that Gothic novels appeal to women's socially-constructed masochistic fantasies.

[59] Joanna Russ, "'Somebody's Trying to Kill Me and I Think It's My Husband': The Modern Gothic," 31-56.

[60] Ibid., 44.

[61] Ibid., 32.

[62] Ibid., 51.

[63] *Sex and the City* also has these two male types in the characters of Mr. Big (Chris Noth) and Aidan (John Corbett).

[64] Hanson shows that this Female Gothic pattern was already in place to a certain extent in noirs of the 40s.

[65] Tasker points out that this relationship is seen in the early 80s television film and show *Cagney and Lacey*, 95-6.

[66] A difference between the films is that while *JE*'s Teddy has the usual father figure mentor, *The House of Games*'s heroine has an older woman as a mentor.

[67] See Bruce Robbins, "Murder and Mentorship: Advancement in *The Silence of the Lambs*," *boundary 2* vol. 23, no 1 (Spring 1996): 71-90.

[68] See Demme's interview about *Silence* in *Film Comment*, 33.

[69] See Tasker's analysis of *Blue Steel* and *Impulse*, 100-3.

[70] The DVD is the "Special Collector's Edition," distributed by Paramount Pictures (part of Viacom), 2004.

[71] See Tasker's discussion of the daughter "inheriting" the father's job in female-detective films, 102.

[72] For Tasker, "*intuition* […] can be perceived as somehow uncanny," 105.

[73] This trope is most developed in *Taking Lives*.

[74] Mulvey, "Afterthoughts on 'Visual Pleasure and Narrative Cinema,'" 130. *Impulse*'s Lottie is coded as juvenile. For example, she is repeatedly playing with a snow globe, reminiscent of the Female Gothic heroine's window, into which she stares as she daydreams.

[75] Robbins, "Murder and Mentorship," 88.

[76] The figure of the possibly criminal father occurs in mass-market Gothics (as shown by Russ). Modleski analyzes this trope in popular Gothics in her chapter "Gothic Novels for Women."

[77] Tasker makes the connection between criminality and transgression of gender norms in female detective films.

[78] According to Pinedo, women enjoy seeing horror films because of the Final Girl's aggressivity, 84-6.

[79] *Never Talk to Strangers* (1995) has the same twist: while it appears that the killer is stalking the psychologist protagonist, she herself is in fact the killer.

[80] Sandra Gilbert and Susan M. Gubar, *The Madwoman in the Attic: The Woman Writer and the Nineteenth-Century Literary Imagination* (New Haven: Yale University Press, 1984).

[81] Tasker discusses *Backstreet Justice* (1993), which has the same plot device regarding the father as *Twisted*.

[82] *Oxygen*, a policewoman CWPT, explores the legacy of the father.

[83] Mulvey suggests this in her reading of *Duel in the Sun*.

[84] One noteworthy exception is Thomas Harris's novel *Hannibal* (New York: Delacorte Press, 1999), which ends with the heroine allying herself with the criminal.

[85] These films are less mainstream because they are both experimental and therefore are not box office successes.

[86] Ian Duncan suggested the figure of the anthropologist in relation to these two texts.

[87] This fascination with the male sphere is enacted by the author Susanna Moore.

[88] Hanson points out that the female-centered 1940s noirs show the city as an intriguing place for the heroine.

[89] The DVD is the "Uncut Director's Edition," distributed by Sony Pictures, 2004.

[90] http://www.jigsawlounge.co.uk/film/inthecut.html (October 23, 2003).

[91] According to Young, "Franny is unusually receptive to her environment."

[92] The film's poster suggests female subjectivity: it shows Frannie walking down the street through the rearview mirror of a car while the hand of an unseen man is on the mirror, presumably adjusting it to get a better look at her.

[93] Moore, *In the Cut*, 188.

[94] R. McClure Smith, in "'A Recent Martyr:' The Masochistic Aesthetic of Valerie Martin," *Contemporary Literature* 37:3 (Autumn 1996), makes the same point about Martin's contemporary Gothic novel *A Recent Martyr*.

[95] Camille Paglia, *Sexual Personae: Art and Decadence from Nefertiti to Emily Dickinson* (New York: Vintage, 1991), 247.

[96] *Oxygen* problematizes the common resolution of killing the Fatal Man in these films.

[97] Tasker discusses the tendency of female-detective films to move between "realism" and "fantasy" as the conflicts they address shift or as the emphasis changes, 93.

[98] Bernard Rose makes it clear in the DVD commentary that he conceived of *Candyman* as a modern-day Gothic. He states that the housing projects in the film are the modern equivalent of a "haunted castle." Similarly, in *Gothic: Four Hundred Years of Excess, Horror, Evil and Ruin* (New York: North Point Press, 2000), Richard Davenport-Hines points to the Gothic nature of graffiti: "Gothic's obsession with decay, and its tradition of political negativity, makes it at the end of the twentieth century an aesthetic of defacement. It produces graffiti...," 3-4.

[99] In Moore's novel, Frannie says, "I have become so paranoid in the last month that I believe that the Poetry in Motion placards are messages for me," 156.

[100] Stoddard, "Early Female Gothic: *Zofloya* and *Manfroné; or the One-Handed Monk,*" www.arts.gla.ac.uk/SESLL/STELLA/COMET/glasrev/issue2/stoddard.htm. Through its use of race, *Candyman* also makes explicit what was implicit in *In the Cut*: the urban and the masculine are stereotypically coded as black. Much of the slang Frannie studies is specifically African-American, and her main informant is African-American. The rest of the men in the film also belong to ethnicities that have been stereotyped by American society as especially patriarchal and as having a machismo ethos. Malloy is Irish-American, while the murderer is Puerto Rican-American.

[101] "Special Edition" DVD, distributed by Sony Pictures, 2004.

[102] Paglia, following Edmund Burke, writes in *Sexual Personae*, "The thrill of terror is passive, masochistic, and implicitly feminine. It is imaginative submission to overwhelming superior force. The vast audience of the Gothic novel was and is female. Men who cultivate the novel or film of terror seek sex-crossing sensations," 267. Clover argues that suspense puts the audience in a masochistic position in relation to film, but though she discusses the implications of this symbolic feminization of the male audience, she does not address the way this masochism might appeal to women.

---

[103] In the article "Rape and Modern Sex War," in *Sex, Art, and American Culture* (New York: Vintage Books, 1992), Paglia claims, "I see in the simple, swaggering masculinity of the jock and in the noisy posturing of the heavy-metal guitarist certain fundamental, unchanging truths about sex. Masculinity is aggressive, unstable, combustible. It is also the most creative cultural force in history," 53.

[104] In "Rape and Modern Sex War," Paglia states that, "Feminism keeps saying the sexes are the same. It keeps telling women they can do anything, go anywhere, say anything, wear anything. No, they can't. Women will always be in sexual danger," 50. But she thinks this is inevitable and part of the thrill of sexual difference: "We cannot regulate male sexuality. The uncontrollable aspect of male sexuality is part of what makes sex interesting," "The Rape Debate Continued," in *Sex, Art, and American Culture*, 63.

[105] Clover, *Men, Women, and Chain Saws*, 226.

[106] Ibid., 227.

[107] Clover discusses this misunderstanding of horror films by feminist critics on pages 226-30.

[108] Clover, *Men, Women, and Chain Saws*, 6.

[109] Pinedo's reading of films is often too literal; see, for example, her discussion of *The Stepfather* in her chapter "... And then She Killed Him: Women and Violence in the Slasher Film."

[110] According to Paglia, women and men are biologically determined to occupy separate spheres to a certain extent.

[111] John Kenneth Muir, *Horror Films of the 1980s* (Jefferson: McFarland & Company, Inc., Publishers, 2007), 27.

[112] Stacie Ponder, Final Girl Blog, www.finalgirl.blogspot.com.

[113] *Juno* was directed by Jason Reitman but written by a young woman, Diablo Cody, who became a known author after writing her memoir of her experiences as a stripper. Female psychological journeys are often thought of in terms of sexuality.

[114] L. R. Williams, *Erotic Thriller*, 342.

[115] See L. R. Williams's discussion of DTV films in her chapter "Uncovered and Undercover: Issues in the Direct-to-Video Erotic Thriller," 331-369, where she considers Katt Shea's *Stripped to Kill*, among other films.

[116] The Shea interview runs from pages 370-375 and the Goursaud interview is on pages 409-416.

[117] The cover of the video cassette (I have not seen the DVD copy) makes it clear that this film focuses on female subjectivity/sexuality as well as provides male fantasy, since it shows the lead actress with her eyes closed in pleasure.

[118] L. R. Williams, *Erotic Thriller*, 343. This recalls Clover's argument that the more extreme and low-budget horror films allow their heroines more agency than the Hollywood films that copy them, 20.

[119] See for instance Laura Session Stepp's recent book *Unhooked: How Young Women Pursue Sex, Delay Love, and Lose at Both*. Meghan O'Rourke has an excellent discussion of this in the online magazine *Slate* (October 26, 2005, www.slate.com), in which she quotes (and then demolishes) Harvard professor

Harvey Mansfield's take on modern women: "women play the men's game, which they are bound to lose."
[120] The policewoman thriller seems to maintain its popularity on television: *Crossing Jordan* (2001-2007), *Veronica Mars* (2004-2007), and *Saving Grace* (2007-present) all have elements of the female detective CWPT.

CHAPTER SEVEN

MILLE GENRES: WOMAN AND WOMEN, HORROR FILM AND HORROR FILMS

CHUCK ROBINSON

A fundamental problem of psychoanalytically influenced feminist approaches to horror film is that they concern themselves with "the Woman." My contention is that horror film gives us *women*. Both *Silent Hill* (Christophe Gans, 2006) and *The Descent* (Neil Marshall, 2005)—which I explore in this essay—are films that problematize the nexus or knot of Truth, Being, Transformation and Gender. I have not selected these films as anomalies, however, but rather as a pair of ostensibly standard instances from a genre that has already been thoroughly theorized. As standard, contemporary instances of "The Horror Film," these two films will serve as staging grounds for a Deleuzian approach to viewing and reading horror films.

I start with three additional propositions. First, the tension between the enjoyment of horror film and its "responsibly" feminist theorization does not simply reflect a phenomenon intrinsic to horror films themselves, but rather it is the formative tension of the canon of feminist horror film criticism and the films it exposes. Second, within the discursive community of feminism(s), it is well established that essentialist pronouncements about "woman" take the first step towards reifying what Deleuze and Guattari would call a molar formation—a concept that ossifies and dictates thought, freezing becoming as being—out of what could otherwise be conceived of as a collectivity of physiologically similar becomings. Yet in attempting to theorize and criticize *the* horror film—even when breaking *the* genre into component subgenres—many feminist critics reproduce this essentialist ideology. Third, it is a critical mistake to tie down horror film, as a genre, with any universalizing accusations of misogyny; such analyses tend to ignore the multiplicity of women in horror films.

It has proven difficult for me to find the ideal path forward from these propositions for various reasons, but mainly because I do not want to find myself trapped in the territory circumscribed by them. In short, in taking on a well-established strand of feminist film theory, I find that I desire to explain myself and express my own truth in order to make an authentic argument. This commandment often experienced as an "honest desire"—like the "repressive hypothesis" so thoroughly criticized by Foucault—to "explain oneself" is a dangerous one—especially when considering *genre*.[1] Genre is the very *mise-en-scène* of non/identity, the simultaneity of similarity and dissimilarity. The confessional mode along with its inverse—the inquisition—attempts to put an end to this *mise-en-scène*. Hence, I've decided to advance by noting the frequent occurrence of the confessional opening in writings on horror film, as exemplified by Isabel Pinedo in her *Recreational Terror*:

> ...my immersion into feminism in the early eighties placed me in the compromising position of being a fan of a genre which many feminists excoriated for its depiction of violence against women. My short-lived response to this quandary was to boycott the genre. The boycott ended when I decided that my desire to indulge, what had become by then, a guilty pleasure was stronger than my political qualms. Gradually, as I came to understand the powerful and salutary role that horror played in my life, I turned back to it in good conscience. This, in turn, led me to start questioning the critical and academic condemnation of the contemporary genre and to start formulating my own questions about the cultural significance of the horror genre's popularity. And so, the work that follows stems from the confluence of my early and ongoing engagement with the genre as a fan, my concern as a cultural analyst with the meaning of popular culture, and the contradictory position this puts me in as a feminist.[2]

The confession here is followed by the recuperative explanation, as we see the "guilty pleasure" recognized for its "powerful and salutary" effects, though the "contradictory position" remains as the point of enunciation. Such apologetic confessions are to be found in many extended critical engagements with horror film, feminist and otherwise.

When the critical approach is something other than feminism, the confessional aspect wanes in favor of the apologia, which tends to address the horror film's lowbrow status.[3] On the other hand, those who see themselves as doing specifically feminist readings of the genre and its films—whether or not they confess to liking them—seek to address two key problems concerning violence and representation. Critics feel they must address the conventional understanding of violence as that which is *a priori* morally, politically, epistemologically, and aesthetically repugnant. Dealing with this repugnance produces a specific hermeneutic method with a leading question along the following lines: how can we—if it is at all possible—(re)interpret a horror film to find a meaning that overrides or eclipses the repulsive quality of its violent idiom?

A second and usually more difficult problem—this one invariably producing the mission of the book/article, as it has mine—is the worry of the seeming inability to distinguish between forms, uses, and ontological layers of violence. Is violence—whether committed by or against women—in horror films merely a matter of artful terror and meant to have a "rollercoaster" effect, offering thrills, chills, and spills? And if so, who is taking pleasure from such imaginary violence? And how? And why? Such was the controversy brought to a fever pitch by the "violence-against-women debates" of the 1970s and 1980s, exemplified in figures like Andrea Dworkin, Catherine MacKinnon, Robin Morgan and Susan Brownmiller.[4]

On the other hand, as the line of questioning and argument runs through the genealogy of "cinepsychoanalysis"[5] (Laura Mulvey, Carol Clover, and Barbara Creed), couldn't and shouldn't we see horror film and its violent idiom as an active, albeit unconscious, expression of the phallocentric discursive regime's repudiation of women/femininity/castration—that is, as an active repression, oppression, and excretion of women? From this viewpoint, the problem for "the feminist" is that horror inflicts violence on women and depicts women inflicting violence on men, and methods or perspectives for understanding this violence—*along with the act of its depiction*—as anything other than misogyny are in short supply. Theorists like Creed—the cinepsychoanalyst who I take on directly in the following pages—find in horror film the ultimate and undeniable indictment of a misogynistic and patriarchal mass culture. The psychoanalytic and narratological elements of this position have been problematized on many grounds by scholars like Steven Jay Schneider, Andrew Tudor, Michael Grant, Cynthia Freeland, and Anna Powell.

More moderate critics like Isabel Pinedo or Carol Clover see horror film as developing female resistance to the very misogynistic violence that the genre puts into play. In addition to the same assumption of misogyny, such approaches tend to see woman's agency as something that abides, survives, and perseveres rather than something that transforms its world. Furthermore, both of these strands of criticism range perilously close to a prescriptive theory of the horror genre, an understanding of genre which, in this case, often switches its "e" for an "o"—moving beyond *prescribing* the "transcendental horror film" and what individual films must do in order to be *like* a horror film to *proscribing* enjoyment and positive valuation of all horror films on the basis of the repugnance of said transcendental horror film. Though Pinedo, for her part, sets out to acknowledge the pleasure/recreational value of horror film, finding this pleasure—that is, explaining it academically—is a critical/theoretical desideratum, and not a starting position, as highlighted above.

While acknowledging the value and complexity of these traditions of feminist horror film criticism, may I suggest a return to the descriptive theory of genre that would be as rigorous as possible, a starting position that would assume horror films to be interesting and pleasurable—or at least, not worry about whether they are or not. Central to this return to the description of horror films is an application of the writings and concepts of Deleuze and Guattari, a work that Anna Powell, in *Deleuze and Horror Film*, has already begun. Just as Powell points out that "Deleuze distinguishes between a cartographic and an archaeological conception of psychic activity," I would distinguish (as countless literary critics have already done, if in different terms) between archaeological interpretation and cartographical description.[6] This description need not be devoid of interpretation, rather interpretation thereby becomes a making-available, a deterritorialization, rather than a territorialization.[7]

Simply put, there is a crucial difference between working *on* horror films and working *with* horror films. Readers who hope to do subversive, liberating, or most simply interesting new theorizing, criticizing, and enjoying of horror films need to recognize that horror films are always producing something new as well as repeating something old—this would be working *with* horror films. Explorations of this sort should lead with the question, "What is *this* horror film doing now, and how do its past and present illuminate one another?" Or, as Claire Colebrook claims, in the introduction to *Deleuze and Feminist Theory*, "rather than seek the good sense of the work, a Deleuzian reading looks at what a philosophical text creates."[8] With this in mind, I present this essay as an experiment[9] with a (hopefully acceptable) "what if" of my own: what if feminist film theory took two recent films—*Silent Hill* (2006) and *The Descent* (2005)—as its founding documents? What—if any—feminist thinking is made possible by these films?

I begin with a few answers to these hypothetical questions. First, horror films are obsessed with and obsessively ambivalent about gender and sexuality. Second, horror films place the body, gender, sexuality and discourse about them on a collision course that reflects, produces, and exploits what we commonly call "violence."[10] *Silent Hill* and *The Descent* do both. So what's new with horror film, then? To find an innovative aspect to these films entails looking at them—and perhaps all horror films—in a new way. In the following pages, I propose a few ways to do so. Turning now to *Silent Hill* and *The Descent*, I will make further theoretical elaborations *in media res,* contrasting the method and project of Barbara Creed's *The Monstrous-Feminine* with Anna Powell's *Deleuze and Horror Film*—all to discover how a certain feminist horror film criticism could think, if it follows the "lines of flight" imagined by *Silent Hill* and *The Descent.*

Creed's work in *The Monstrous-Feminine* is immediately and obviously applicable to *Silent Hill* and *The Descent.* Creed set out to explore why "woman-as-monster [had] been neglected in feminist theory and in virtually all significant theoretical analyses of the popular horror film," positing that "all human societies have a conception of the monstrous-feminine, of what it is about woman that is shocking, terrifying, horrific, abject."[11] *Silent Hill* is, apparently, not an exception to Creed's claim here, since the film involves faceless, knife-wielding nurses; a creature that sprays acid from a hole in its stomach; and a bed-ridden female burn victim who sprouts a myriad of razor-wire tentacles from her hospital bed. Nor is *The Descent* a departure from Creed's statement, since it is a film in which a group of women travel into an unexplored cave system, discovering it to be full of ravenous, naked, humanoid monsters that go straight for the jugular. When Creed speaks of "the monstrous-feminine," she has films/filmic images such as these in mind.

The term, "monstrous-feminine," and the analysis she will undertake, are both necessary, Creed argues, because

> The reasons why the monstrous-feminine horrifies her audience are quite different from the reasons why the male monster horrifies his audience. A new term is needed to specify these differences. As with all other stereotypes of the feminine, from virgin to whore, she is defined in terms of her sexuality. The phrase 'monstrous-feminine' emphasizes the importance of gender in the construct of her monstrosity.[12]

This passage points out the paramount tension in Creed's work and further why, regardless of its evident applicability to the two films under consideration, Creed's work is ill-fit to deal with horror films as a generic collective. As part of her polemics, Creed chooses to ignore her initial insight that there are both female victims and monsters, since she wants to concentrate on the monsters. That is not nearly as problematic, however, as the way essentialism slips into her semantics. It is *woman* as monster that has been neglected and "the monstrous-feminine horrifies *her* audience" in a specific, gendered way. In her introductory argument and conceptual exposition, Creed slips uncomfortably between the terms "woman," "the woman," "female," "feminine," "femininity" and "women," finally settling on the monolithic term "monstrous-feminine," which—as can be seen in the above-quoted passage—corresponds to a molar, essentialized concept of *the* woman.

This essentialism is especially contradictory as Creed goes on to describe various types of monstrous-feminine. We can see this directly in a later passage:

> In the horror films discussed above woman is represented as monstrous in relation to her reproductive and maternal functions. This occurs for a number of reasons: the archaic mother (*Alien*) horrifies because she threatens to cannibalize, to take back, the life forms to which she once gave birth; the possessed girl (*The Exorcist*) evokes a pleasurable disgust because she confronts us with those abject substances (blood, pus, vomit, urine) that signify a return to a state of infantile pre-socialization; the pregnant woman (*The Brood*) horrifies because her body houses an alien being—the infant/other; the female vampire (*The Hunger*) is monstrous because she draws attention to the female blood cycle and she reduces her captives to a state of embryonic dependency in which they must suckle blood in order to live; the young female witch (*Carrie*) evokes both sympathy and horror because her evil deeds are associated with puberty and menarche.[13]

With her glosses on *Alien, The Hunger,* and *Carrie,* Creed's theorization is self-consistent. However, her gloss on *The Exorcist* admits "infantile pre-socialization" as horrifying—not the maternal or the reproductive. Her gloss on *The Brood* is equally muddy. Both cases are interesting, because, as in *Silent Hill* and *The Descent,* little girls enter the picture—a fact that Creed must seemingly resolve either through recourse to "the infant" or "puberty."

In analyzing *Silent Hill* and *The Descent* in terms of the Deleuzian analysis recommended by Anna Powell, I note that I have only dealt with Creed briefly, and that her text is substantial, though it has been similarly criticized by Andrew Tudor and Powell.[14] Powell's general argument is that psychoanalytic film theory "treats images as static, symbolic components of underlying representational structures."[15] As a result any dynamism or vitality in the image—especially as it relates to the body's experience of flow, duration, and the unbearable—are lost. Any useful theory of horror film will be more attentive to the cinematic pleasure of fear as somatic and not merely psycho- or socio-somatic. The current critical consensus on this matter seems to be that it is not fear/terror/arousal as a feeling in itself that is pleasurable, but rather something complex related to fear through some sort of cognitive narrative structure that is essentially psychosocial—physical sensations of the body thereby discounted as something akin to symptoms.[16]

Powell suggests a Deleuzian alternative: "extreme affect can...push consciousness into an extra-mundane state where a sense of the numinous is accessed."[17] For both Deleuze and Powell, this is the "power of art to radicalise consciousness."[18] My goal is not simply to popularize Powell and denigrate Creed. Rather, I want to move away from the *a priori* meaning that critics like Creed see *engendered* in horror film, towards the concepts and the possibilities for thinking feminism that horror films *embody*. In both cases—in *Silent Hill* and *The Descent*—it is the little girl that presents herself as a radical thought-image, one which not only moves characters and plot, but which can move us beyond the commemoration, intensification, and/or interrogation of gender binaries.

The following plot summaries of *Silent Hill* and *The Descent* are given from a psychoanalytically entrenched perspective. *Silent Hill* narrates the story of Rose, a mother who braves a psychodramatic nightmare realm to save her daughter, Sharon, in order to bring her back home to the patriarchal Symbolic order. Though Rose saves her daughter from death, she cannot bring her home—at least not exactly—because, according to cinepsychoanalytic theory, Rose is a woman, and her repudiation of her husband's desires during her pursuit of Sharon should not be rewarded. Similarly, Sarah, the protagonist of *The Descent*, is punished with a horrific spelunking experience, the death of her friends, and finally, insanity—all for having failed to protect her family both from the adulterous *femme fatale* Juno, and from her own ambivalence about wifedom and motherhood, which, a psychoanalyst could, in one way or another, demonstrate as having led to the car accident which kills both Sarah's husband and their daughter. In these two films, Creed's hypothesis rings true: the woman troubles the symbolic order—for which she must be punished—and if she steps aside from/outside of it, she cannot be allowed to return, no matter how much she may desire it.

However, such summaries ignore elements—both thematic and formal—from each film that are, in Deleuze's sense "molecular," meaning in this case, tangential (and productively so) to the psychoanalytic schema. At the thematic level, most obviously, we need to pay more attention to the little girl—the fugitive protagonist (who not only needs to be found, but actually *runs away*) in *Silent Hill* and the equally, if not more perplexing daughter of *The Descent*, who appears to her mother twice after her death, bringing her a birthday cake. We must also notice the multiplicity of women in both films[19] who, in *The Descent*, literally multiply between the film's first and second nature adventures from three to six. *Silent Hill's* multiplicity of women actively depicts the multiplicity of female/feminine types, casting aspersions on each (*qua* type) in its turn, privileging only the little girl, who herself is not one single subject/identity, but the simultaneity of three becomings (becoming-demon, becoming-victim, becoming-girl). Finally, we consider both films' respective distinctions between the human and the humanoid or the human and the monstrous.

A look at all of the four formal elements will similarly yield interesting results, especially given that the feminist-psychoanalytic criticism of horror rarely does much with form, skipping as it does fairly regularly from the image—screen captures are an evidentiary mainstay in Creed's book—directly to plot. Rather than devote separate sections or arguments to theme and form I wander through each film to map their conceptual developments, not to dis-cover a meaning, but to explore each film as a way of thinking. Fundamentally, I treat *Silent Hill* and *The Descent* as similar films, though, of course, they have their differences. For my purposes, however, the films' similarities are more significant, given that (1) contributing to a descriptive theorization of a genre is my main aim and (2) the films' differences arise most clearly out of an ideological reading of their respective plots.

Silent Hill: It Takes a Child to Raze a Village

The plot of *Silent Hill*[20] revolves around Alessa/Sharon—a little girl who has split in three, as the result of a massive physical and emotional trauma. She is first ritually burned as the cult in which her mother is a member attempts to cleanse her and her mother of the sins implied by her out-of-wedlock conception. Barely alive, confined for life to a hospital room, Alessa accepts the power offered by a demonic entity, effectively splitting herself and the world surrounding *Silent Hill* into three parts. Hence, Alessa is simultaneously a charred barely-living corpse in the world of darkness, a mischievous ghost in the world of ash, and a happy little girl, oblivious of her past in the (so-called) real world, who has even managed to get out of Silent Hill, being adopted by the Da Silva family. The plot involves the coming-conscious of this little girl's memory of her other selves, though no specific motivating force lies behind this "coming conscious." There is no reason or principle behind the "return of the repressed" in this film.

The film begins with a vignette in which a frantic Chris and Rose Da Silva search for Sharon, whose sleepwalking has brought her to the edge of a waterfall. In a shot from Sharon's point of view, looking down into

the pool bellow, we see nature and water give way to an image of criss-
crossing pipes through which the camera pans, zooming in on flames and
Sharon's demonic *doppelgänger*. Moments before she collapses into this
abyss, Sharon is rescued by her adoptive mother and father, who have,
respectively, run through the forest and over the city streets to be by her
side. The evocation of dichotomy is plain here, but through the course of
this film, dichotomies are displaced, sometimes with simple multiplicities,
other times with polymorphous singularities.

Once Rose absconds with her daughter, rather than leave her in the
hands of doctors and psychologists, the spatial dichotomy of nature and
culture is replaced by the multiform layering of space in the town of Silent
Hill: the real world, the world of ash, the world of darkness, and finally—
at the end of the film—the world of fog, an alternative to the real world
that exists outside of Silent Hill and is only inhabited by Rose and Sharon.
In "reality" Silent Hill is a town in West Virginia that has been abandoned.
The men who pursue the fugitive Rose—her husband and a policeman—
are stuck in this world. Silent Hill is also a nightmare realm tied to the
same physical terrain, which—significantly—only females enter or leave
during the course of the film. The nightmare realm has two articulations.
First is the world of ash, another deserted town, with streets that end as if
they are at the edge of the world, where a constant rain of ash serves as a
reminder of "the apocalypse": a fire that destroyed the town and still burns
underground. Second, in distinction to this, there is the world of darkness:
a conversion of the world of ash as signaled by air-raid sirens and a
blanket of darkness that falls without warning. In this world of darkness,
buildings and debris take on supernaturally decrepit and disturbing forms.
The town resembles a hellish industrial park, with disfigured corpses
everywhere and strange creatures lurking about.

A passage from Powell summarizes well the temporal nature of this
triple world, though she did not explicitly have *Silent Hill* in mind:

> Several different types of horror time are operant. The personal past, with
> its traumas, and the historical past that imposes itself over the present, have
> particular generic status. Ghosts conflate past and present as they linger to
> repeat their own present, refusing to let it be past. They compel present-day
> characters to abandon contemporaneity and to experience the history of
> others by enforced overlay.[21]

Such a structure exists in *Silent Hill*, and significantly, it is three
females who move through all three phases of timespace—the little girl as
fugitive, her mother as becoming God, and the policewoman as becoming
woman. The latter two move through these phases out of concern for the

little girl's freedom to become—whereas those who seek to hold women to the molar identity "woman" are restricted in timespace. Also significant is the possibility to understand this temporality as an experience of *duration* rather than *history*—these timespaces are not flashbacks, but rather, they are durations of lived, imminent experience that *overlay* (Powell's key word) types of time as space.

The gender dichotomy of male and female is rendered prismatic by the interminable becoming of the little girl, whose threefold identity is never resolved or integrated. In the film's climax, Alessa destroys the remaining cultists, Sharon hides in her mother's arms, and the ghost seeks out Sharon to stare in her eyes. Gender is further scattered in the often androgynous, humanoid monsters of Silent Hill, which—to the exclusion of the child-creatures that pursue Rose when she first enters Silent Hill—taken together form a sort of gender continuum, that ranges from androgyneity (the Sprayer monster) to hyperbolic gender typification (the busty, faceless nurses and Pyramid head). Whereas child and woman monsters appear in groups, the two distinctively male monsters (the janitor and Pyramid Head) appear on their own, and, interestingly, are portrayed by the same actor. In this grouping of monsters, the film conceptualizes the phallic monolithia of the male which is brought to the point of hyperbole in Pyramid Head's cleaver, a heavy sword, nearly as long as he is tall, which he drags on the ground behind him, and which he often thrusts but never swings.

Given these thematic elements, it is easy to see *Silent Hill* as a film that attempts to move beyond meditations on the gender/gendering of bodies (which is frequently treated as a molar relic, viz. the monsters) toward explorations of becoming. Interesting in this regard is the film's continuous production of machinic couplings. Rose is first coupled with Sharon, and subsequently with Officer Cybil Bennett. The Rose-Sharon coupling produces flight, fleeing father, fleeing the law, while the Rose-Bennett coupling produces searching for the little girl. On the other side of reality, Chris Da Silva (Rose's husband) is coupled with Officer Thomas Gucci and their coupling produces searching for the wife and searching for the truth. Rose's coupling searches for and protects the becoming girl of the little girl, circumstantially finding the truth. Chris's coupling searches for the truth and hence finds nothing.

Much more could be said about *Silent Hill*, but most significant is its cinematographic-editing apparatus, which shows a strong formal tie with *The Descent*. In *Silent Hill*, the frenetic and typically invisible style of continuity editing can be seen as what Powell refers to as "becoming God" in her reading of *The Shining*. Common to both films, in this regard, are shots that begin as close ups and pull "up and away"—such as when a tight medium shot of Sharon's front cuts to a shot from behind her that pulls up and away to reveal the precipice at whose edge she stands. Such shots are often "apocalyptic": they reveal the hidden. Yet they also enact the moving away, the flight of God, reason, or reality from the events of the film.

We can never resolve this complex phenomenon of shot selection and editing, that as we see more panoptically, from more angles, through more montage, the diegesis and its world become more confused, confusing, and unbearable for the characters. The "cross purposes" of form and content at this juncture gives food for thought to feminist viewers: there is more (or less) to understanding than viewing and vice-versa; seeing is not believing is not being is not becoming. Though from the cinepsychoanalytic perspective, *The Descent*—as even its title suggests—is quite clearly a film "about" Woman as abject and insane, yet upon closer examination, *The Descent* is a film about transformation that occurs in a world where gender is a relic and what one is becoming is more interesting than what one is.

Reborn, Rebirthing, Becoming-birthday: *The Descent*

In as much as it can be seen as a moralizing film, *The Descent* provides an ambivalent look at a mother, Sarah, who cares more about her daughter than about anything else and Juno, an aggressive, adulterous, possibly bi-sexual extreme-sport enthusiast. In the opening segment of the film, Sarah is doting on her daughter while ignoring—or being oblivious to—her husband's affection for a *femme fatale* named Juno. Similarly, Sarah does not notice her husband drifting into the wrong lane as she lavishes all her attention on her daughter, leading to a car crash in which both daughter and husband are killed. In the following segments of the film, as the group of women-adventurers slog through a disorienting and perilous cave system, Sarah has a vision of her dead daughter several times, and each time, the daughter is carrying a birthday cake. This birthday cake image can be grouped with several other images in the film for a rather conventional reading of what already appears to be a cookie-cutter film about descent into madness/danger and the possibility of re-emergence/rebirth. At two different points in the cave ordeal, Sarah is "reborn" as she, first, falls into a pool of blood, emerging red-tinted and totally calm, ready to be an efficient killing/surviving machine, and, second, escapes the cave system, bursting forth into the surface world from the roots of a tree, head and arms first, as if clawing her way out of an earthly womb.

Most interesting about *The Descent* is that, in what I will call "becoming-birthday," who/what is reborn and who/what is doing the rebirthing become confused, intermingled, and inseparable—a subversion of the psychoanalytical dualism of "the descent into madness" vs. "the rebirth/rise of the strengthened ego." This film makes no privileging distinction between the natal, neonatal, and maieutic. In this regard, "lack of direction" is the key editing principle of this film, which—especially in action sequences—continually violates the axis of action, leaving viewers, who see all, disoriented in their all-seeing. Again, as in *Silent Hill*, having all the images does not give us truth or understanding, but rather provides us with an experience of becoming. And furthermore—also in parallel with *Silent Hill*—*The Descent* imagines becoming as interminable with the film's dual/open ending, wherein we see Sarah both *escape* from the cave, sobbing, vomiting, screaming, and finally pedal-to-the-metaling her way to freedom, and *remain psychotically trapped* in the cave, mistaking the underground bonfire she lights for her daughter's birthday cake. There's no way to decide which ending is "real" and which is "merely" an illusion—whether ours or Sarah's.

Another aspect of becoming-birthday would commonly be called selfishness. Throughout the film, Sarah is depicted as always concerned with other people before herself. After a tiring and trying rafting expedition, Sarah showers attention on her daughter, rather than securing her gear or taking a breather. After the subsequent car accident, upon awakening to find herself in a hospital bed, she pulls out her IV and detaches herself from other medical devices in order to find her daughter. Later, she elects to go spelunking to reunite her long-separated group of friends. It is only in the cave—supposedly a cave for tourists, but actually an uncharted and highly dangerous place—when confronted with both the murderous cave creatures and the murderous hypocrisy of Juno, who chose the cave as a conquest, that Sarah experiences becoming-birthday: she meets her challenges under duress, since it is her time, her day, and she will do whatever she wants. And it is in this way that, in a film in which it is difficult to keep track of character's names and faces, and close-ups of human activity are intercut with long shots of a still and uncaring nature, Sarah becomes the dominant character in the frame.

Like *Silent Hill*, *The Descent* also spatially re-imagines time—although historical time and its nuclear family are disposed with early in the film. *The Descent* is much more concerned with geological time and, in this sense, gender as a kind of fossil. The women-adventurers discover a race of humanoid beings in the cave-system they explore. These beings have what could be called gender—the many, many males aggressively pursue and attack the women explorers, while the one female creature that is shown cares for a child creature. The creatures attack in the manner reminiscent of both vampire and dog: going for the neck of their prey, chewing and ripping. Though this is clearly a feral move, this manner of attack is also bat-like and vampiric, focusing as it does on the neck from which it draws blood. Gender is hence problematized as an effect of visual apprehension—the women see the creatures, but the blind creatures do not see them—and not necessarily marked, designated, or clarified by behavior. The attack style of the creatures can be variously understood, and since the creatures are blind, at the level of their agency, the attacks cannot be gendered: "man" is not assaulting "woman," since the "man" cannot see whom he is assaulting.

Sarah's becoming-birthday can be linked with the creatures' blindness as she enacts silence, a becoming-silent that is related with the survivalist aims of her becoming-birthday. Sarah becomes a counter-cave dweller. She can dwell in the caves with the creatures, she can kill the creatures, she can escape the cave—she is indeterminant, and hence cannot receive an ending. She is no longer a molar woman—she is not a mother or a wife, she is not a feminist. She is a survivalist, a becoming-birthday, a will to realize and randomize her desires. She eventually exercises these desires against Juno—upon whom she finally enacts revenge, not killing her but making her lame and abandoning her in the caves, as a Woman, she who cannot counter-dwell, but can only dwell in the name, law, and logic of a system of naming, identity, and possession. It was Juno's idea in the first place to go to this cave, to discover it, explore it, and name it, whereas Sarah is caught inside, must deal, must dwell and counter-dwell. She does not seek to understand, to systematize, but rather to evade, deflect and disperse—to disappear in a self-affirmative way. *The Descent* suggests a way of thinking action—feminist action—that does not seek to right "masculinity" or "hegemony," but rather an agency that disperses molecularly—not one that finds the right path, but one that takes any path, every path, circuitously, not running a course, but flowing from here to there freely.

On Endings and Lying

The protagonists in both *Silent Hill* and *The Descent* can be considered feminists in a molecular sense. Both are totally unconcerned with essences—the explanation/meaning of the supernatural events they experience is irrelevant to them since they have other urgencies of action. Furthermore, though each could be seen as caught in a web of patriarchal signification (and perhaps we will never be able to completely let go of Mulvey's conviction that the cinematic apparatus itself is such a web) these heroines act on their own impulses—not only to survive, but to become, and to rescue, protect, and celebrate that which is emblematic of and empowers becoming. Both *Silent Hill* and *The Descent* conclude with images of two females together, mother and daughter, though biology is not really a factor in either case (one daughter being adopted, the other being dead). The image is incredibly dynamic in *Silent Hill*, as mother-daughter occupies the same space as father, but in separate realities. The last image in *Silent Hill* is Chris Da Silva looking out his front door to see no one—only the simultaneous sun and rain outside. This highlights the play of dualism in the world of logic, system, and patriarchy. Mother-daughter, on the other hand are left (happily) in a world of grey—or perhaps it is only grey to us from our position in the world of rain/sun.

In an earlier version, this essay was dominated by a discussion of lying. I wanted to argue that women's prime agency in horror film was to lie, to default, to sin against the molar conception of Woman. I enumerated several possible types or realms of lie and gave examples from films. I came away from this tactic however, as privileging lying as an epistemological guide still plays into the realm of truth and identity—if one can lie, one also has the option of telling the truth. But the lie is actually already in the patriarchal system of truth: that the Woman, as such, exists at all (Lacan seems to have pointed out as much). The phenomenology and agency of women in horror films frequently gives the lie to this pre-existing lie, as happens in *Silent Hill* and *The Descent*—in both of which, at a literal level, women's lies move the plot along.

To confront, discuss, and understand horror films from a feminist perspective, hence, need not be concerned with the treatment of "the Woman"—feminism always has the option of leaving the symbolic behind, of counter-dwelling like in *The Descent* or becoming-girl (becoming-becoming) as in *Silent Hill*, surpassing all the fossilized, molar genders/gender theorists. When we take Woman as a problem, and subsequently violence concerning Woman as a problem, and then phallic violence concerning Woman, with each "refinement" of the problem the definition of "a woman's" identity gets tied down a bit more—she who needs saving from a representational/political/physical/psychic factor.

To read the history of feminist film criticism is to recognize steps toward a very different way of thinking, a different way of viewing film, which is not only seen in Powell's work, but also other contemporary works on horror film and violence in association with women, like Annette Burfoot and Susan Lord's *Killing Women* and Sue Short's *Misfit Sisters*, both of which investigate feminism beyond the psychoanalytic understanding of gender difference. I hope the present work proves to be similarly valuable: as a way of doing something transformative beyond the symptomatic/ideological diagnosis of horror film. Horror films have more to give viewers, thinkers, and feminists than the same old psychoanalytic platitudes.

If we do not want to completely reject psychoanalysis and its potential for enunciating gendered violence/the violence of gender, we might— rather than considering it as a theoretical paradigm—develop a camp reading strategy. In this sense, horror films can be the beloved cultural artifacts of something we could call "psychoanalytic camp," which could go a long way towards explaining the one bodily response horror filmgoers experience which is, to my knowledge, completely neglected by horror film theorists: laughter. I remember being perplexed, while in an audience watching *Freddy versus Jason*, to hear the laughter of those around me during a particularly gruesome scene of decapitation. It would be possible, in this vein, to camp psychoanalysis—observing how phallicizing, oedipalizing, vaginalizing horror film images exposes the ridiculous, laughable, and perhaps inescapable ideologies of the gendered body. Horror film would therefore be the occasion on which horror filmgoers laugh at the melodrama of gender in horror as a means of moving beyond the horrific epistemic violence of gender.

Works Cited

Buchanan, Ian and Claire Colbrook, eds. *Deleuze and Feminist Theory*. Edinburgh: Edinburgh University Press, 2000.

Burfoot, Annette and Susan Lord, eds. *Killing Women: the Visual Culture of Gender and Violence*. Waterloo: Wilfrid Laurier University Press, 2006.

Creed, Barbara. *The Monstrous-Feminine: Film, Feminism, Psychoanalysis*. London and New York: Routledge, 1993.

Freeland, Cynthia. *The Naked and the Undead: Evil and the Appeal of Horror*. Boulder, CO: Westview Press, 2000.

Grant, Barry Keith and Christopher Sharrett, eds. *Planks of Reason: Essays on the Horror Film*. Lanham, MD: Scarecrow Press, 2004.

Pinedo, Isabel Cristina. *Recreational Terror: Women and the Pleasures of Horror Film Viewing*. Albany: State University of New York Press, 1997.

Powell, Anna. *Deleuze and Horror Film*. Edinburgh: Edinburgh University Press, 2005.

Tudor, Andrew. "Why Horror? The Peculiar Pleasures of a Popular Genre." In *Horror Film and Psychoanalysis: Freud's Worst Nightmare*, edited by Steven Jay Schneider, 55-67. Cambridge: Cambridge University Press, 2004.

Notes

[1] A word whose etymological relation to "gender" we would always do well to remember.

[2] Isabel Cristina Pinedo, *Recreational Terror: Women and the Pleasures of Horror Film Viewing* (Albany: SUNY Press, 1997), 2.

[3] As evidenced by cognitivist philosopher Cynthia Freeland's introduction to her *The Naked and the Undead: Evil and the Appeal of Horror* (Westview, 2000), where she defends horror film against accusations of shallowness/childishness. After helpfully rehearsing the cognitivist argument she states her central claim, that "in their reflections on evil, horror films often question the traditional values and gender roles associated with patriarchal institutions such as religion, science, the law, and the nuclear family" (3-4).

[4] Annette Burfoot and Susan Lord, eds., "Introduction," in *Killing Women: the Visual Culture of Gender and Violence* (Waterloo: Wilfrid Laurier University Press, 2006), xv.

[5] I am borrowing this term from Anna Powell.

[6] Anna Powell, *Deleuze and Horror Film* (Edinburgh: Edinburgh University Press, 2006), 18.

[7] To imagine territorialism in academia, one need think only of statements such as, "To understand *Alien*, you have to understand Kristeva."

[8] Ian Buchanan and Claire Colbrook, eds., "Introduction," in *Deleuze and Feminist Theory* (Edinburgh University Press, 2000), 3.

[9] For this approach I am indebted to friend and colleague Mike Dwyer.

[10] I placed "violence" in quotation marks here due to my worry over the descriptive ambiguity of the term that exists simultaneously with its assumed clarity as a critical buzzword. "Violence" always has a political agenda, sometimes an obscure one, often an auto-deconstructive one, but most synonyms prove obviously dissatisfactory: evisceration (too specific), bodily trauma (obscures agency), mortification (ideological/historical baggage abounds), etc.

[11] Barbara Creed, *The Monstrous-Feminine: Film, Feminism, Psychoanalysis* (Routledge, 1993), 1.

[12] Ibid., 3.

[13] Ibid., 83.

[14] See Andrew Tudor's "Why Horror? The Peculiar Pleasures of a Popular Genre" in *Horror Film and Psychoanalysis: Freud's Worst Nightmare*, ed. Steven Jay Schneider (Cambridge: Cambridge University Press, 2004), where he expounds upon psychoanalytic feminist film theory's hermeneutical dependence on "prior acceptance of a descriptive framework also drawn from psychoanalysis" (60). In

her *Deleuze and Horror Film* (Edinburgh: Edinburgh University Press, 2005), Anna Powell states the following about Creed: "Barbara Creed used Kristeva's psychoanalytic model of abjection to theorise *Alien* and *Carrie*. Kristeva's concept of the abject, the 'in-between [...] which disturbs identity, system, order,' has been fitted to the 'female' aspects of the monster. Despite Kristeva's suggestive exploration of the fluid nature of abjection, critical readings tend to retain a fixed dichotomy of self and other, as well as gender binaries" (16).

[15] Powell, 10.

[16] For examples we could take the positions of Dennis Giles: "Horror cinema defends viewers against their own desire" (47) and Morris Dickstein: "Fear of death is the ultimate attraction...going to horror films is a way of neutralizing anxiety" (54), both in Barry Grant and Christopher Sharrett, eds., *Planks of Reason: Essays on the Horror Film* (Lanham, MD: Scarecrow Press, 2004). Neither entertains the possibility that horror is pleasurable because a rush of adrenaline is pleasurable.

[17] Powell, 7.

[18] Ibid., 7.

[19] As Creed, for the most part, fails to do with *Carrie*—she deals with the film's eponymous protagonist and her mother in depth, but not with the gym teacher or plethora of teenage girls.

[20] I will not address this here, but it is worth noting in passing that *Silent Hill* is a film adaptation of a successful videogame franchise of the gaming genre known as "survival horror." Survival horror is a perennially popular genre, which usually features first-person or over-the-shoulder exploration of gothic-inspired environments and combat with monsters, borrowing heavily from horror film. In addition to *Silent Hill*, several other popular survival horror games have been adapted to the screen: *Resident Evil* and its sequels *Doom* and *House of the Dead*.

[21] Powell, 154.

III:

POSTFEMINIST INTERVENTIONS

CHAPTER EIGHT

A FEMINIST THEORIZATION
OF SOFIA COPPOLA'S POSTFEMINIST TRILOGY

AMY WOODWORTH

Feminist scholars ought to take interest in Sofia Coppola—perhaps the best recognized American female director in recent years and the only one, as of this writing, ever nominated for an Academy Award for Achievement in Directing (Best Director)[1]—particularly since her films have crossover appeal from the art house to the multiplex. Coppola's films are neither chick flicks nor teen films, but they represent young women's experiences and often have a "girly" or youthful focus in terms of their costumes, graphics, and soundtracks. Her pedigree as the daughter of Francis Ford Coppola, her casts of A-list actors, and her affiliation with a new generation of *auteurs*, including Wes Anderson and Noah Baumbach, give her creative freedom for her moody, impressionistic films. As opposed to academic feminism's interest in the diversity of gendered subjects who are pluralized by race, class, sexual orientation and nation, Coppola's films at best fall under the ambiguous political and theoretical umbrella known as postfeminism. Coppola's female protagonists are Caucasian girls and women who lounge about—often in their underwear—shop compulsively, and are passive-aggressive. Politically, postfeminism is either uninterested in women's rights and gender equality or takes these for granted; culturally, postfeminism embraces traditional forms of femininity and "girly" activities, such as shopping.[2] The lack of an explicit feminist agenda may render Coppola's films a postfeminist pleasure for those willing to accept unempowered women subjects.

"Nobody throws girls on pillows like Sofia Coppola," claims Nathan Lee in his *Film Comment* review of Coppola's *Marie Antoinette* (2006).[3] Indeed, the final installment of Coppola's trilogy—*The Virgin Suicides* (1999), *Lost in Translation* (2003), and *Marie Antoinette*—includes many images of reclining young women. Unlike *Lost in Translation*, *The Virgin Suicides* and *Marie Antoinette* are Coppola's adaptations of others' works, yet there is a spiritual kinship shared by the young women found throughout these three films.[4] In Coppola's own words, *Marie Antoinette* "'[is] a continuation of the other two films—sort of about a lonely girl in a big hotel or palace or whatever, kind of wandering around, trying to grow up.'"[5] Along with this return to Coppola's previous subject matter and themes, *Marie Antoinette* is marked by the idiosyncratic style developed in Coppola's earlier works. Coppola's belief is that "film is not only a visual medium but also an emotional one," according to A.O. Scott.[6] Her first three films are driven less by plot than by "moods, associations, and resonant images" of the ephemera of filmmaking, such as party scenes, diegetic sound and soundtracks.[7]

Yet many critics disparage these elements of Coppola's films, especially her controversial treatment of a historical figure such as Marie Antoinette.[8] According to Lee,

> Coppola's conception has nothing to do with thinking through the politics, history, morality, or psychology of this milieu, and everything to do with the opportunity it presents to dress up her pet tones, themes, and gestures on grand scale. Taken on her terms (of which I suspect she's only half-conscious), the only serious mistake is an extension of the narrative beyond her frame of reference.[9]

Apparently for Lee, Coppola's only frames of reference are parties, shopping, and music.

Marie Antoinette's mixed critical reception has overshadowed the success of *Lost in Translation*, which earned Coppola an Academy Award for Best Original Screenplay. Lee targets potential problems with Coppola's presentations of women that are arguably of interest for feminist film scholars. Coppola's nonverbal techniques for conveying the emotional interior of her characters, such as through body language, lighting and music are effective, although they are somewhat ambiguous.

However, attempting to categorize Coppola's work as either feminist or postfeminist means employing a set of criteria that will limit an understanding of her films. The feminist-postfeminist binary depicts feminist film theory as something static, a set of unchanging positions either to occupy or resist. Charlotte Brunsdon recently observed that just as the generation of women after second-wave feminism often distance themselves from the term feminism, so does much academic feminist practice. Postfeminism often positions itself against the "killjoy" elements of feminism whose orthodoxy means that women should not enjoy "girly" pleasures.[10] Indeed, according to critics such as Lesley Stern, Helen Grace and Laleen Jayamanne, feminist film theory—particularly psychoanalytic theory—is now treated as a "totalitarian mother" clinging to the past and no longer relevant.[11] However it is not just younger scholars who feel this way. In a special 2004 issue of *Signs: Journal of Women in Culture and Society* entitled "Beyond the Gaze: Recent Approaches to Film Feminisms" which featured a roundtable discussion on the state of film feminism, Linda Williams commented:

> Film feminisms are no longer the highest priority of my scholarship. Writing about a field that had once felt very exciting—that had uncovered galvanizing new perspectives on life, on moving images, on the dynamics of 'looking relations'—was, in the case of this essay 'assignment,' beginning to feel like an unwanted duty. Often I have the same experience teaching film theory in graduate seminars. I find I have more enthusiasm for Hugo Münsterberg than for Laura Mulvey. Where I once felt part of an exciting movement and vibrant intellectual context, I now feel weighed down by the burdens of what feels like orthodox feminist position taking.[12]

Williams sees feminism as the foundation for her work, but feels that "gaze theory" is no longer adequate for analyzing looking relations in the cinema and admits, "It *had* become boring and repetitious to see all the sensationalism of cinema motivated by castration anxiety."[13] Most problematic for Williams is that the theory of the male gaze as established by Laura Mulvey is drawn too strictly along gendered lines where all narratives seem to be about the subjugation of female characters.

While I agree with critics such as Williams that continuing to abide by and apply the theories of 1970s feminist film criticism may be limiting, abandoning those theories and feminist projects is a mistake given the state of current American cinema. The box office hit of summer 2007 was Judd Apatow's *Knocked Up* whose message seems to be that marriage and maternity are the only options for an accomplished woman who gets pregnant after a one-night stand with an unemployed male slacker.[14] In her *New York Times* review of Justin Theroux's 2007 film *Dedication*, released a few months after *Knocked Up*, Jeannette Catsoulis writes,

> That weird exhalation you hear at the multiplex these days is the sound of female characters settling for less than they deserve. Following on the wildly successful antifeminist heels of *Knocked Up*, Hollywood is falling over itself to introduce beautiful, smart young women to useless, possibly brain-damaged young men. Regular bathers need not apply.[15]

As the success of *Knocked Up* demonstrates, mainstream American film continues to portray a patriarchal fantasy. Feminist scholarship is necessary and women's filmmaking is a tool for correction. In the words of Yvonne Tasker and Diane Negra, it is necessary to "retain the strength and political commitment associated with earlier traditions of feminist writing and feminist filmmaking."[16]

Part of the process described by Tasker and Negra includes a willingness to adapt rather than reject earlier psychoanalytic feminist film theory. In the same issue of *Signs* in which Williams aligns herself with those "beyond the gaze," Mary Ann Doane expresses concern that "current film feminisms often ally themselves with the logic of the local and its corresponding suspicion of abstraction" because this approach "risks an aphasia of theory in which nothing can be said."[17] In other words, theory and the effort to localize appear to be mutually exclusive because theory's function as a totalizing explanation cannot accommodate the diversity of subjectivities for which later film feminisms argue. The universal (male) spectator has been questioned and divided into a variety of spectators by Mary Ann Doane, bell hooks, Miriam Hansen, and Jackie Stacey, among others, and many films have female characters that are active subjects rather than passive objects. Yet, virtually any encounter with the entertainment media—particularly advertising, men's magazines such as *Maxim*, and MTV—is a reminder of the prevalence of the male gaze.

Rather than discard early feminist film theory, it ought to be considered as a usable past, for while the Freudian and Lacanian theories on which it is based are often too narrow for application to all films, the patterns this criticism has found in the analysis of women onscreen are insightful.[18] In particular, early work on film form performed in negative analyses of classical Hollywood films, such as Laura Mulvey's "Visual Pleasure and Narrative Cinema" and Mary Ann Doane's "*Caught* and *Rebecca*: The Inscription of Femininity as Absence," are relevant for considering mainstream films today.

As feminist criticism turned from these negative analyses that point out the problems with male-dominated cinema towards positive analyses that examine the ways women's filmmaking constructs and addresses women as subjects—such as Teresa de Lauretis's "Rethinking Women's Cinema: Aesthetics and Feminist Theory"—scholars have spent more time studying art and independent films than Hollywood films. Scholars tend to look at films whose forms are remarkable and explicitly feminist; for example, Caroline Bainbridge's "Feminine Enunciation in Women's Cinema" examines Sally Potter's *Orlando*, Susan Streitfeld's *Female Perversions*, Marleen Gorris's *Antonia's Line*, and Jane Campion's *The Piano*.[19] While these directors are iconic examples of what feminist or feminine aesthetics are or can be, I do not think feminist criticism should limit its analyses of form to the art house. Especially since mainstream cinema often slowly adopts its style from the avant-garde, we should periodically examine what "conventional" cinema is up to and how its aesthetics are changing. As new generations of women—including those who shirk the label "feminist"—make films, they may be working with an inherited concern for how they frame and film their female characters, but without feeling wedded to a specific list of requirements based on criticism of patriarchal cinema. In other words, women directors like Coppola may show both scholars and spectators how female characters can be portrayed respectfully and their experiences treated aesthetically without the burden of all of cinema history weighing on every decision they make (though they certainly could take history and conventions into account). In *not* positioning themselves against the patriarchal tradition, women directors may have *more* creative freedom in making films about women.

Furthermore, feminist critics ought to consider the aesthetics of Hollywood films because these films appeal to and reach the general public and best function as cultural barometers. This high level of dissemination makes the entertainment film a strong agent of social and political change. As Claire Johnston first pointed out,

> In order to counter our objectification in the cinema, our collective fantasies must be released: women's cinema must embody the working through of desire: such an objective demands the use of the entertainment film. Ideas derived from the entertainment film, then, should inform the political film, and political ideas should inform the entertainment cinema: a two-way process.[20]

Johnston's call is not simply about ideologically changing the masses, but also about affirming a cinema by and for women.

The purpose of this essay is twofold: first, to offer an analysis of Coppola's aesthetic presentation of women and second, to evaluate how early feminist film criticism might be used to examine film aesthetics at the beginning of the twenty-first century. These tasks are important because as scholarship turns toward issues of postfeminism, it seems that scholars spend more time discussing character and plot than film form. A good example of this neglect of film form is *Cinema Journal*'s "In Focus: Postfeminism and Contemporary Media Studies" issue, which enlists four critics both to define postfeminism and to offer analyses of postfeminist texts. All of the essays are largely concerned with theme rather than aesthetics. The aesthetics of films that embody a postfeminist attitude may seem too conventional on the surface to be worthy of comment, such as *Bridget Jones's Diary* (2001) and *13 Going on 30* (2004). However, if a foundational belief of feminist criticism is that the aesthetic *is* ideology, analysis of film form in a discussion of the politics of content is crucial.[21] As we continue to examine images of women in film, we must continue to evaluate both change and persistence in film aesthetics, looking at the ways female filmmakers both appropriate and resist patriarchal conventions, especially those working in or reaching the mainstream.

I would like to revisit two key moments in the history of feminist film criticism that compose a two-part agenda for feminist aesthetics. The first is Laura Mulvey's "Visual Pleasure and Narrative Cinema" the best known argument for the necessity of negating patriarchal cinema. The second is Teresa de Lauretis's "Rethinking Women's Cinema: Aesthetics and Feminist Theory," a positive assertion of what feminist or feminine film might consist.[22] Both works argue that Hollywood has served as a patriarchal institution where women are the objects of the male gaze and that this power structure is created through both film form and film content. Mulvey's essay is the more canonical of the two, since it is where Mulvey first coins the term "the male gaze," and offers a structured theory for how and why Western film uses women as erotic objects. Her main point is that in classical Hollywood cinema, women onscreen resolve the male spectator's castration anxiety by either acting as an object of voyeurism, investigation and punishment to reenact the primal scene or as a fetish object to cover over and disavow castration.[23] These two functions are enabled not only by individual films' forms, but also by the cinematic apparatus itself, which positions the spectator as a voyeur while the star system contributes to the fetishization of female stars. While I am not convinced that resolving castration anxiety is the *modus operandi* of mainstream film, Mulvey is undoubtedly correct that cinema does cultivate women's "to-be-looked-at-ness" and uses them for visually pleasurable spectacle.[24] A basic list of the ways women have been objectified and controlled through formal elements of film would include fragmenting their bodies through close-ups, not just of their faces, but also of body parts such as legs; compressing the depth of field to flatten their images and reduce verisimilitude, thus turning them into icons; denying them roles as agents within the plot; and glamorizing them through special effects, such as lighting and soft focus. While Mulvey's observations tend to be fairly selective, ignoring female characters who do act as agents in the plot, such as in screwball comedies, women onscreen frequently do interrupt the narrative when they serve as spectacle: famous examples include Lauren Bacall's singing in *To Have and Have Not* (1944), Rita Hayworth's hair flip in *Gilda* (1946), and Marilyn Monroe's skirt billowing up in *The Seven Year Itch* (1955).[25]

For Mulvey, politics and aesthetics are interdependent; the mainstream film's "formal preoccupations reflect the psychic obsessions of the society which produced it."[26] Therefore, if a filmmaker wants to participate in a political revolution that overturns patriarchy, her film form must be aesthetically radical. Though Mulvey offers no clear description of what this prescribed avant-garde style should look and sound like—only that it should somehow confront and destroy mainstream film's conventions— her own films made with Peter Wollen serve as a demonstration of her theories translated to film.[27] Mulvey's avant-garde films create a cinema of pure detachment and trouble the relationship between viewer and film, but form founded on alienation and negation does not leave much pleasure for a moviegoer. By creating films for academics, Mulvey is preaching to the choir, cutting off the possibility of actually revising a mass entertainment medium as Johnston recommends with a symbiotic relationship between entertainment and politics. Focused on destroying the pleasure she associates with patriarchal cinema, Mulvey might succeed in creating *anti*-patriarchal cinema, but she neither creates a clear avenue for a positive cinema for women, nor discusses the value of one in her influential essay.

Teresa de Lauretis picks up where Mulvey leaves off and argues that the next step in feminist film criticism and filmmaking is to go beyond demystifying the mainstream film's reinforcement of patriarchal ideology and endorsing its destruction, and how to begin exploring the ways women's filmmaking can portray and address the social subject that previously had been "all but unrepresentable": women.[28] Instead of an avant-garde aesthetic of subversion that is "centered on the text and *its* effects on the viewing or reading subject—whose certain, if imaginary, self-coherence is to be fractured by the text's own disruption of linguistic, visual and/or narrative coherence," women's filmmaking must shift to an "aesthetic of reception."[29] In particular, de Lauretis discusses the ways that women filmmakers have begun to address the spectator as a female rather than a male (which Mulvey sees as typical of the mainstream film), regardless of the spectator's actual gender. To alter the subject position of the spectator, the film must "[define] all points of identification (with character, image, camera) as female, feminine, or feminist."[30] According to de Lauretis, this is partially accomplished by showing women onscreen in ways that have not been done before, particularly, as filmmaker Chantal Akerman puts it, the "'daily gestures of a woman'" that are "'the lowest in the hierarchy of film images'" (e.g., slicing potatoes rather than singing or dancing).[31] De Lauretis praises Akerman for a "pre-aesthetic" aesthetic, finding the aesthetic in the everyday, going against the norms of classical Hollywood film's glamorizing and iconizing women.

Yet creating this new subject position for women in film must go beyond content, which according to Akerman is "'the most simple and obvious thing.'"[32] Women filmmakers also must "'look for formal ways to express who they are and what they want, their own rhythms, their own way of looking at things'"; in other words, *how* things are shown is just as important as *what* is shown.[33] Akerman's way of doing this, for example, is filming at a distance that gives the woman her own space and does not fragment her. The director's form reflects her own affection for looking at women or appreciating them in a unique way. For de Lauretis, feminist aesthetics must be plural, as she writes in a moment when "radical change requires a delineation and a better understanding of the difference of women from Woman, and that is to say as well, *the differences among women.*"[34] Like Mulvey before her, she sees feminist aesthetics as a negation of the traditional aestheticization of women.[35] Each woman director's films will necessarily be personal and engage the viewer as *a* woman rather than interpellating her as Woman in a singular, essentialist way. Successful feminist filmmaking of this sort typically has been written about only in the sphere of independent or avant-garde filmmaking.

De Lauretis's later arguments about women's filmmaking are important for looking at Coppola's work because though her films are largely about women as social subjects, her formal representations of female characters often appear to correspond to the conventions chastised by earlier feminist critics like Mulvey. Coppola's films may seem politically ambiguous in terms of aesthetics, as her questionable framing of women's faces and bodies dances a fine line between duplicating and effectually exploiting the way the various social observers of her characters such as pubescent boys, older men, and the French court view women. Furthermore, her use of traditional images of women throughout her work—girls sunbathing in *The Virgin Suicides*, applying make-up in *Lost in Translation*, soaking in the bathtub (repeatedly) in *Marie Antoinette*—raises interesting questions about how feminist (or simply women) filmmakers can change the effects of conventional close-ups. All three of Coppola's films are innovative, but not in ways that would repel a mainstream audience. Rather than shocking the viewer, Coppola's work seems capable of fostering a new experience of women characters that creates empathy and understanding, and she does this through form. Over the course of her first three feature films, Coppola appears to refine her interest in and execution of conveying a woman's inner life and experience through her exterior. She not only hones in on her female subject by reducing the number of characters, but also develops her cinematography and editing to gain the most depth.

The Virgin Suicides is an impressive debut film for Coppola, since it engages some of the most important issues in psychoanalytic film criticism, particularly voyeurism and the surveillance of girls'/women's sexual behavior by men or society. The film centers on the family of the five Lisbon sisters, particularly the erotically precocious Lux (Kirsten Dunst), and their parents' effort to socially and sexually contain their daughters. One sister's suicide opens the film, and the four others' suicides close it. Despite its title, Coppola's film, like the Jeffrey Eugenides's novel on which it is based, is not so much about suicide as it is about youth and what Coppola herself calls the "'epicness' of teendom."[36] The girls' dying young embalms them forever in what patriarchal culture would consider their most exquisite form, and images of these nubile blondes will forever haunt the neighborhood boys who obsessively watch and spy on them.

The film is narrated by the collective "we" of this group of neighborhood boys, now men, remembering and imagining the mysterious lives and deaths of the five Lisbon sisters, constructing their stories through a heady mixture of clues, memory, and desire.[37] While the frame story of the boys/men discussing the past should make it clear that scenes without the boys are still products of their imaginations, Coppola emphasizes the role of fantasy by including overtly magical and dreamy sequences of the girls. In these scenes, the girls frolic with a unicorn in sunny fields, wink at the boys/camera, blow dandelions, kick their legs while swinging, and roll around in the grass. These fantasy sequences are usually prompted by the diegesis, such as a male classmate smelling a tube of lipstick in the girls' bathroom when he was invited over for dinner. The aesthetics of the fantasies render the girls mythical and idealized: they are backlit to create glowing auras, the tints are sun washed Popsicle colors, and slow motion allows the spectator to fixate on their bouncing hair and buoyant young bodies. While the fantasies are generated by onscreen male characters, they also belong to the film's audience, for these are the manifestations of a collective cultural memory of girlhood, a memory generated at the intersection of personal experience and archetypes produced by popular culture. A.O. Scott sees a partial source of the boys' fantasies as "the silent heroines of a mid-70's soft drink or shampoo commercial."[38] Likewise, the neighborhood boys have added the unicorn to their fantasy based on the cultural assumption that girls are obsessed with horses and unicorns—the unicorn a staple of 1970s fantasy poster art—and probably the exciting possibility that the unicorn does deflower the virgin with its phallic horn, as the commonly shared myth is that unicorns will only allow virgins to touch them.

Coppola implicates the viewer in these fantasies about American girls during the film's opening credits. After the title "The Virgin Suicides" repeatedly appears across a cloudy, pastel blue sky, scrawled in stereotypically girly handwriting—bubbly cursive and hearts dotting the i's, filling the screen as if filling a notebook cover while daydreaming in school—a superimposed close-up of Lux dissolves onto the sky. Lux winks at the film's viewer, her only audience, as no character is present to be associated with the camera's eye, and it is the first appearance of what will become a varying, but recurring shot. This wink sets the tone for the film, which stresses girlhood as mysterious and indecipherable to anyone but girls. After Cecilia's (Hanna Hall) first attempt at suicide, her male doctor admonishes, "You're not even old enough to know how bad life gets." Cecilia replies, "Obviously doctor, you've never been a thirteen-year-old girl." Likewise, the neighborhood boys admit, "We knew that the girls were really women in disguise, they understood love and even death, and that our job was merely to create the noise to fascinate them; we knew that they knew everything about us and that we couldn't fathom them at all." A female critic found the film's opening image of Lux finishing a Popsicle inscrutable.[39]

While the viewer sympathizes with the sisters for having severely overprotective parents, who virtually have them under house arrest by the end of the film, the viewer is somewhat emotionally distanced from them. Just as the neighborhood boys find it impossible to read the sisters' thoughts and feelings about their youngest sister's suicide and their home lives, so too does the viewer. Unlike Coppola's later films, there are not that many intimate moments with the girls in terms of how close we can get to them and identify with their individual feelings. The exceptions to this are a few scenes with Lux, most memorably when she wakes up in the football field alone, abandoned by her date, the morning after the homecoming dance—after her first sexual encounter as well as night away from home—and takes a taxi home. We watch her pain through the cab window as reflections of the neighborhood pass over it and feel her humiliation and dread of the punishment to come. This use of the close-up to convey complex emotional information through the human face will become more typical in Coppola's later two films rather than the mystery and opacity of the girls in *The Virgin Suicides*.

Lost in Translation, Coppola's most acclaimed film, is set in Tokyo and follows the brief romance between Charlotte (Scarlett Johansson) and Bob Harris (Bill Murray) who meet in a hotel. Charlotte, a recent Yale graduate, is accompanying her photographer husband who is in Japan for work and gone for days at a time. Bob, a has-been movie actor, is there to fulfill his $2 million endorsement deal for Suntory whiskey. Both characters are tired, bored, and lonely, and currently in directionless, transitional stages of life and career. The film has strong emotional texture, relying heavily on facial expression and body language to capture the mixture of ennui and confusion that structures the lives of its main characters. Unlike Coppola's other two films where the source of suffering is fairly clear to the viewer, Charlotte and Bob's problems are more subtle, and Coppola withholds many details of their lives. Though their romance eventually drives the sparse plot, they do not officially meet and have a conversation for the first third of the film. While Bob's half of the narrative consists of him shooting a commercial, drinking at the hotel bar, and humorously navigating himself through misunderstandings with the Japanese, Charlotte is mostly by herself and silent during her scenes.

The opening image of the film may be its most memorable: Charlotte's derrière seen through sheer pink panties, a medium shot of it horizontally reclining on the hotel bed. In general, Charlotte spends a lot of time in her underpants, which at first seems problematic as it fosters her "to-be-looked-at-ness," to use Mulvey's term. However, the way she lays and moves around is not performed for the male eye; she is generally without an onscreen male surrogate for the viewer, and the way she frequently folds up her body has the opposite effect of display. In fact, the moment of greatest exposure, when she briefly stands on the bed to hang a cherry blossom paper lantern, ends with her stubbing her toe getting down, undermining what may have potentially been a provocative moment. Likewise, in the scene where Charlotte performs karaoke, Johansson's singing voice (thin and stumbling) and the pink wig she wears seem to ironize or deflate what would traditionally work as erotic spectacle, drawing attention to the act of performance and masquerade.[40]

These moments of potential objectification, however, are not representative of the treatment of Charlotte throughout the film. Unlike *The Virgin Suicides*, which consists mostly of group scenes with multiple characters of interest, here Charlotte is often literally alone or moving through crowds of strangers, allowing her to be the total focus of the viewer. The increased time alone with the female protagonist is accompanied by a new type of shot used by Coppola: Charlotte seen from over her shoulder, which seems to encourage the viewer to identify with her point of view rather than objectifying her. The angles used in these shots keep her only partially in the frame so that we can see both her and what she is looking at; this framing prevents total access to her body and shows only a profile or less of her face. A good example is of Charlotte sitting on the hotel room's windowsill, looking out at the city. The camera is slightly above her, facing her back; it begins on one side of her body and moves around to her other side, creating the effect of an aerial shot, especially with the view of the city beyond her. This shot asks us to both look at Charlotte *and* with Charlotte out the window. These shots taken from over her shoulder or over her train seats or hotel room chairs do not make the viewer feel alienated from her as much as understand her own sense of alienation. As she looks at the city from the hotel window or landscapes from trains, we too feel both cut off by the glass she must look through as well as foreign from these new places. Although the viewer spends equal time with Bob and the two characters have parallel scenes, such as cab rides against the neon lights of Tokyo, Bob's scenes are generally used for comedy and we get more emotional information from him when he speaks to others than when alone. So despite the film's being a romance and a portrait of two people, Charlotte seems to preoccupy Coppola's interest. The trajectory of the trilogy brings Coppola to devote all of her attention to one woman for its final installment.

Marie Antoinette may appear to be the most intellectually lightweight of Coppola's films due to its simplified version of French politics and hot pink packaging, but it is actually the most formally preoccupied with capturing women's experiences and developing a feminist aesthetic as a means for doing so.[41] It loosely follows the notorious queen's life from her engagement to Louis XVI until the flight of all the nobles from Versailles when Marie Antoinette and Louis are left alone in the empty castle as the revolutionary mob menacingly encroaches. Their arranged marriage serves as a political alliance between France and Austria, but is a pairing that lacks basic chemistry: Marie Antoinette is pretty, charming, and vital, while Louis is timid, bland, and lacking in sexual prowess.[42] Like *The Virgin Suicides*'s 1970s America, *Marie Antoinette*'s eighteenth-century France has stiflingly rigid expectations for women. Most obvious is that female royalty function foremost as breeders. Though a woman can wield power once she has fulfilled her primary duty of producing an heir, Marie Antoinette's mother reminds her that women's value is determined by maternity: "nothing is certain about your place there until an heir is produced." There is no privacy at Versailles: royalty cannot dress, bathe, or eat unattended, and the sexual reproduction of the royal family is national business. A priest and the French court escort Marie Antoinette and Louis to their marital bed the night of their wedding, the king wishing them "Good luck, and good work." While the lack of privacy technically affects Louis as well—he receives both a doctor's visit and a pep talk on sex from his brother-in-law—Marie Antoinette receives the blame for their childlessness and is subjected to greater physical scrutiny and gossip. The

French chalk her barrenness up to frigidity: "She is Austrian, they're not exactly the warmest people," accuses one of Louis's unmarried aunts. Most intrusive is the ritual hand-over of her from Austria to France: she is stripped of all of her previous belongings, including the clothes she is wearing and her pet pug "Mops," and is possibly inspected for virginity, as Roger Ebert speculates.[43] The morning after her wedding night introduces another comparable ritual of having a large group of women wait on her and help her get dressed in the morning, a process drawn out and uncomfortable in the cold morning air. Once she has finally delivered an heir, Marie Antoinette is given a country house where she escapes the rituals of Versailles and eventually experiences sexual fulfillment through a brief love affair. Until then, she replaces sex and security with sweets and shopping, parties and champagne.

Unlike Coppola's previous two films, *Marie Antoinette* is told virtually from one character's point of view, that of the young queen. Coppola uses slightly different camera work than in the past to help create this perspective, most importantly employing a handheld camera for many point-of-view shots. The spectator learns almost nothing of Marie Antoinette's thoughts or feelings through words, probably because she has no one to talk to or ask advice in her life; she is a newcomer to Versailles, where friendships are always mixed with politics. Instead of verbal expression, facial expression provides most of the viewer's knowledge, particularly from Marie Antoinette's reactions to the letters she receives from her mother, the content of which focuses on her precarious situation as a childless queen. These scenes where she emotionally responds to the letters contain significant changes in the distance from which she is shot, either moving into a close-up or pulling away from her into a long shot, giving the viewer both a sense of her inner life and her relative isolation at Versailles. One scene filmed all in one take begins as a medium-long shot of Marie Antoinette on a balcony facing squarely toward the camera, then pulls slowly away into an extreme long shot that makes her a small speck against the enormity of the palace. Her mother's letter appears to make her shrink, and her reduced size captures her sense of powerlessness at Versailles. In an earlier scene, we watch her reactions to another letter in her mirror reflection as she herself also scrutinizes her face and body trying to determine why she hasn't charmed her husband into consummating the marriage. The camera moves slowly in on her image to echo this scrutiny, and her expression changes as she mulls over the individual words and phrases of her mother's letter, climaxing with a few deep sighs of exasperation and sadness. The camera's movement toward and away from Marie Antoinette's face in these shots is important, as it creates the cinematic illusion of a third dimension in space, breaking the two dimensional plane that Mulvey sees as responsible for making women's faces into icons.

In addition to this use of a zoom lens to create spatial depth for shots of Marie Antoinette's face, Coppola uses jump cuts to slightly disrupt images that would otherwise aestheticize her face or body. The most notable is when Marie Antoinette daydreams about her Swedish lover Count Fersen. In this scene, she flings herself across the bed with a sigh and loses herself in a private moment of rapture—eyes glazing over and drooping, hands limply resting on her chest—presumably continuing her fantasy of Fersen on horseback with canons exploding all around, a vision of masculinity as equally archetypal as the boys' fantasies of the Lisbon girls running in fields with unicorns in *The Virgin Suicides*. Marie Antoinette may lack originality, but the scene emphasizes, as the film does as a whole, her own desire as a woman. Her posture changes slightly not by moving within a shot, but by shifting the placement of her hands and head across a series of four shots. These four shots alternate camera angles and are linked by jump cuts, creating the sense of an afternoon lapsing into fantasy and intensifying the viewer's identification with the feelings of being in love. Beyond simulating restlessness and romantic agitation, the jump cuts subtly disrupt the viewer's consumption of the image of Marie Antoinette lying vulnerably on the bed. A similar use of jump cuts is found in *Lost in Translation* when showing Charlotte making herself up in the hotel bathroom. Charlotte's own contemplation of her face, application of lipstick and playing with her hair would encourage us to objectify her as well, but again, the splicing of these images through jump cuts disrupts our visual pleasure of any one image.

Along with these careful decisions for visually presenting her female characters, Coppola's trademark slow pacing, privileging of impression over plot, and development of emotional texture and mood constitute a kind of feminine aesthetic. If 1970s feminist film criticism were turned into an artistic prescription for future feminist filmmaking, the choices would be either to create formally radical avant-garde work or, at the very least, traditional narratives with women as the causal agents of plot and action, which would commandeer what Mulvey considers a male privilege of classical Hollywood film. The former would "free the look of the camera into its materiality in time and space and the look of the audience into dialectics and passionate detachment"; the latter would mobilize women into "male" three-dimensional space and linear time (which is what we typically find in mainstream films nowadays).[44] Neither quite considers appropriating what cinema has perhaps traditionally considered "female" space and time—the "no man's land" outside of the plot, according to Mulvey[45]—and I believe that Coppola works within this other dimension. I do not mean to essentialize women into having a different sense of time and space; rather, I believe Coppola's personal and idiosyncratic sense of these could be understood as *a* feminine experience of them, one that interestingly seems to correspond to those dimensions used for containing women in mainstream narratives. In this way, Coppola's use of slow pacing and flexibly compressed space to focus on the female face does set film into the materiality of time and space, just in a different way than Mulvey had in mind. Coppola's films make viewers accustomed to the pacing of mainstream films explicitly aware of time passing or, rather, not passing. Coppola's films demand surrendering to moments and relinquishing the desire to simply move forward in time and reach the end.

Thus, the most evocative scenes in Coppola's work are moments of the everyday, similar to Chantal Akerman's use of "'the lowest hierarchy of film images'" or "pre-aesthetic" images, to use de Lauretis's term.[46] In *The Virgin Suicides*, the Lisbon sisters sprawling throughout their shared bedroom, flipping through magazines, and curling up on window seats capture the weary longing of being stuck inside and grounded on a nice day. In *Lost in Translation*, Charlotte knitting a scarf, listening to self-help tapes, and putting on lipstick to amuse herself all embody the malaise of being in a hotel room away from home and the ways women fill the general emptiness of their lives. But nothing may simulate feeling more effectively than the bottom of Marie Antoinette's skirt train, seen in extreme close-up, trudging through the grass after her lover has left, and her making the long walk up the steps of Versailles back to her reality: the spectator can feel the dragging misery and heartache of the end of her affair in each step she takes. All of these small and simple actions are realistic and mundane, yet charged with emotion.

While most critics find Coppola's films to be successful as mood pieces, some are wary of her achieving this atmosphere by having female characters spend so much time on their backs or in bathtubs.[47] The Lisbon sisters lounge across beds and windowsills, stranded in their room; Charlotte nests in the hotel bed and chairs for a significant portion of her stay in Tokyo; Marie Antoinette is frequently found reclining on a fainting sofa or in the bathtub. Nathan Lee observes that Coppola's "liveliest motif is torpor—catnap, boredom, daydream, reverie—and her movies are most eloquent when they best approximate the feeling of cuddling up in a cashmere sweater."[48] Lee is concerned that Coppola's female characters come off as empty-headed since they spend a lot of time lying around and do not say anything of intellectual value, but while his observations about how female characters are visually presented across the three films is accurate, I think his conclusion about their lack of intellectual prowess is overly simplistic.

Although Coppola's female characters may talk little, this does not mean that nothing is going on beneath the surface. In fact, Coppola's quiet scenes depict scenarios where most people—women and men— realistically would be engaged in introspective reflection, especially when alone, such as the cab, train, and carriage rides found throughout all of her films. Coppola takes time with these travel scenes, which would be used as elliptical glue between the significant action in more plot-oriented films; rather than using these scenes simply to show where a character is going, she simulates the experience of staring out the window and thinking. Moreover, characters' silences in Coppola's films are often used in direct contrast to other people's talking, which is usually rather vapid, making their silence a marker of intelligence. For example, in *Lost in Translation*, the LA movie actress Kelly (Anna Farris) who is also in town to promote an action movie gushes about her interest in Japan, reducing Japanese culture to three elements: Buddhism, reincarnation and karate. Kelly's discussion of these elements of Japanese culture is sprinkled into her endless chatter about any number of shallow or trendy topics such as weight loss and detoxifying rituals. Charlotte, on the other hand, explores the country beyond Tokyo by herself, without a tour guide, and the expressions on her face during these scenes reveal an intellectual curiosity about the world around her. While she visits a Buddhist temple in search of a more authentic spiritual experience, she has the honesty to admit afterward, "I didn't feel anything." One can only imagine what Kelly would have said about the visit to this sacred place: she would have most likely given an extensive, enthusiastic and vapid commentary along the lines of "It was so amazing, what a spiritual place—I felt so...at peace there!" While Kelly does provide an alter ego for Charlotte, her role in the film seems more to generally mock the superficiality of Hollywood.

Kaja Silverman's work on the use of women's voices in the cinema has argued that they have been objectified and controlled, thus making a woman's silence a way to preserve some of her autonomy.[49] But in Coppola's work, women's silence is less about a refusal to enter the patriarchal Symbolic order according to Jacques Lacan and more about the inadequacy of words to convey feeling. In *Marie Antoinette* the Duchesse de Polignac's (Rose Byrne) gossip provides an important juxtaposition to Marie Antoinette's looking at the window, unaware of the conversation as she longs for her absent lover. This leads to the scene of her swooning and pining on her bed. Film critic Melissa Anderson approves: "I haven't seen a dreamier, more yearning look in any film this year [2006], and Dunst's ability to convey erotic reverie in this brief scene is the film's most glorious moment."[50] While Dunst deserve half the credit here, Coppola clearly needs to work expressions of emotional and intellectual information out of her actors. When asked in interview what the script says for her more impressionistic scenes in *Lost in Translation,* if it "describ[es] what Charlotte is thinking," Coppola replies, "No, because it's just for me. It would be no more than 'she wanders around' or 'she sits in her underwear and looks out the window.'"[51] Coppola's scripts are scanty, but this is because emotions are her subject matter, and emotional ideas can be communicated better through facial expressions than through speech.

Based on the conventional ways that women's faces and bodies historically have been and continue to be framed in cinema, Coppola's frequent use of close-ups could be seen as an ambiguous or controversial manner of depicting female characters in her films. Mulvey is certainly right that the close-up is an essential part of the process of aestheticizing and objectifying women in film, and no doubt, the faces of Coppola's female leads are rendered beautiful. However, the close-up is also a key part of developing sympathy and telling an emotional story, and Coppola's films collectively lead us to question our assumptions about point of view, the camera, and the look. Christian Metz's apparatus theory would have the viewer and the camera linked in terms of the look:

> When I say that 'I see' the film, I mean thereby a unique mixture of two contrary currents; the film is what I receive, and it is also what I release, since it does not pre-exist my entering the auditorium and I only need close my eyes to suppress it. Releasing it, I am the projector, receiving it, I am the screen; in both these figures together, I am the camera, which points and yet which records.[52]

Metz maps the technological cinematic apparatus onto the human body and psyche, where the viewer's point of view is always the camera's, but this is in terms of vision, not necessarily sympathy, as Nick Browne has pointed out.[53] The camera also can be temporarily associated with characters' points of view, either through shot/reverse shot editing or trick shots that simulate a character's body movement or state of mind, such as handheld camera work or upside down shots.

But very often in Coppola's films, the camera seems to represent a character's point of view in terms of sympathy even as it looks directly at that very character. This can happen both when a character is alone—such as Marie Antoinette's crying by herself when her sister-in-law bears a child before she does—or even in a room full of characters, such as the second opera scene where Marie Antoinette must withstand the court's spiteful glares. So many close-ups of Marie Antoinette's face are meant to help the viewer feel her emotions, for the viewer inhabits multiple positions while watching a film, not only identifying with the camera, but also with characters whose points of view are temporarily associated with the camera and characters being viewed, as demonstrated in the scenes where Marie Antoinette reads her mother's letters. In this respect, what Mulvey considers a cinematic tool for the fetishization of women becomes a vehicle for expression in Coppola's work. However inscrutable Lux may be in *The Virgin Suicides*, by the end of Coppola's trilogy, the faces of her female protagonists render meaning. Coppola's use of the female face demonstrates one of the ways a woman director can share her unique perspective, the project that de Lauretis and Akerman both discuss.

Marie Antoinette seems to have a fully realized feminine aesthetic based on Coppola's careful use of the camera for mediating Marie Antoinette's experience without objectifying her, and this may explain why it is her least favorably received film. The debates that *Marie Antoinette* provoked revolve around claims that Coppola privileges style over substance.[54] Unanimously acknowledged as a master of the *mise-en-scène*, critics such as Scott are pleased with Coppola's ability to capture mood via music, lighting, clothing, and sound, while others, such as Dargis and Lee, seem to think that her impressionistic films lack any real ideas, and in the case of *Marie Antoinette*, irresponsibly eschew politics. More than the film's anachronisms in music and costume, Coppola's sympathetic portrayal of Marie Antoinette has been the main target of her detractors who object that the angry mobs are only extras and want her film to deal with the French Revolution in more depth and detail.[55] But these demands seem to miss the point: *Marie Antoinette* is deliberately subjective, and again, in Coppola's own words, it "'[is] a continuation of the other two films—sort of about a lonely girl in a big hotel or palace or whatever, kind of wandering around, trying to grow up.'"[56] Even without this statement, it should be clear to anyone who has seen Coppola's previous two films that *Marie Antoinette* is another personal film interested in the experience of female adolescence and alienation. I have doubts as to what a more prominent presence the revolutionaries or a scene of Marie Antoinette's beheading would have added to the film, and I agree with Roger Ebert's defense that to make the changes prescribed by Coppola's critics would "alter its [*sic*] fragile magic and reduce its romantic and tragic poignancy to the level of an instructional film."[57]

Given the overwhelmingly favorable reception of *Lost in Translation*, also about an archetypal "poor little rich girl," perhaps there are more discontinuities between that film and *Marie Antoinette* besides the use of a historical figure rather than a fictional character.[58] There are two other qualities unique to *Marie Antoinette* that are possibly responsible for its mixed reviews. The first is that it is more critical of the male gaze than Coppola's previous two films. Both *The Virgin Suicides* and *Lost in Translation* provide male surrogates, as Mulvey would call them, for the viewer. Even if these two films are partially questioning the way women are objectified and breaking some conventions of framing women in film, enough residue of patriarchal cinema remains to which the willing viewer can cling.

Interestingly, although Coppola is already advancing in her explorations of female characters with *Lost in Translation* attempting to create more access and sympathy through the face and body language, the presence of a male counterpart seems to distract the viewer from this project. For example, in his review of *Lost in Translation*, Elvis Mitchell is drawn to the karaoke scene to discuss the lead actors' performances, which out of any scene in the film seems the closest to Mulvey's description of the dynamic of male/female relationships and women's purposes in mainstream narrative films:

> Ms. Coppola gives Mr. Murray a scene that actors dream of; he falls for Charlotte as she struggles through a karaoke version of 'Brass in Pocket,' a wisp of a smile flitting across his face as he watches her perform in a frosting-pink wig. She is his dream of an uncomplicated future, and Ms. Coppola lovingly shoots Ms. Johansson's wary, lazy eyes and lush lips—almost a parody of Japanimation.[59]

While Mitchell does pick up on the possibility of parody, his focus is primarily on Johansson as spectacle, and though she is the center of attention, the meaning of the scene resides with Murray. The female character is there to affect the male character from Mitchell's perspective. Though Murray also performs karaoke after Johansson, his performance registers as more goofy and sincere than seductive. Coppola often creates parallels for her protagonists—each has a bathtub scene, each has a phone call home—but treating their bodies similarly seems impossible, though perhaps the actors' ages and natural appearances have much to do with this. In any case, despite Coppola's experimentations with new kinds of framing and editing for Charlotte's solo scenes, Johansson's curvaceous body and the couple's romance may keep the film within proximity of patriarchal traditions.

Marie Antoinette however, does not provide male surrogates for our admiration of Dunst's body. The exception is the opening shot of the montage of her affair with Count Fersen, but their relationship is brief. In fact, the two shots of Dunst's naked backside force the viewer to identify with her exposure and vulnerability. As her nude body is shot from behind—through an extreme long shot in the hand-over scene and through a medium long shot during her first dressing ritual—the camera is associated with her point of view, and both shots have others looking at her. Particularly in the second scene where this occurs, there are approximately twelve women looking in the direction of the camera, and therefore, toward the viewer as well; this helps the viewer to identify with the woman being surveyed. Also, when Marie Antoinette performs a song in her private theater, we are less interested in the reaction of her audience than Marie Antoinette herself, and we certainly lack a male surrogate with whom our gaze can identify, since Louis is not depicted as a strong, masculine figure.

Beyond not having a male surrogate in *Marie Antoinette,* viewer discomfort also may result from Marie Antoinette's return of the gaze, which for de Lauretis is the *pièce de résistance* of feminist filmmaking. Like *The Virgin Suicides, Marie Antoinette*'s opening credits have Dunst look directly at the camera with no character present to provide an object for her look besides the film's viewer. Unlike Lux's wink in *The Virgin Suicides*, meant to either include or seduce the viewer, Marie Antoinette looks up briefly from being pampered by a servant to give what can only be described as a petulant glance at the camera; she then returns to being self-absorbed. This look tells the viewer that she already knows many in her audience will not like her and that she doesn't care; this knowledge is on behalf of not only herself, but also of Coppola, who seems to have anticipated a mixed response to the film and its protagonist.[60] This defiance is intensified by the accompanying Gang of Four song "Natural Is Not in It" and the bold, black and hot pink graphics for the credits, reminiscent of punk rock, particularly the album cover for *Never Mind the Bollocks, Here's the Sex Pistols*, and further intensified by the irony built into the contrast between punk and the frilly image of Marie Antoinette with her embracing of leisure and consumerism.

The opening credits embody the other reason for some critics' resistance to Coppola's third film: it is unabashedly girly. *Marie Antoinette* is heavily marked by Coppola's personal taste, so that if aesthetic choices for the *mise-en-scène* are meant to capture any subject accurately, that subject would be herself—or perhaps more broadly, young women today—rather than this distant historical figure. Numerous interviews and articles reveal that Coppola herself likes music, fashion, and the color pink, and the film reflects these tastes.[61] Even the designs for her films' DVD cases mark this preference; both *The Virgin Suicides* and *Marie Antoinette* have more pink and pop graphics than *Lost in Translation*, perhaps this is what alienates some of Coppola's audience who do not want the independent films they watch to be mistaken for teen girls' movies. Therefore, it is hard not to see those who reject *Marie Antoinette* as rejecting both the personal and the feminine, or perhaps more accurately, Coppola herself. Pam Cook's defense of fashion as an art of "creative reinvention" and performance reminds us that fashion, as an industry and an interest affiliated slightly more with the feminine, is considered frivolous when compared to the "real" (i.e., "masculine") fine arts.[62] Coppola's anachronistic and irreverent soundtracks, graphics, and speech/dialogue for the film likewise lead some critics to deem her frivolous as well. Best captured in *Marie Antoinette*'s upbeat shopping montage of cake and shoes set to Bow Wow Wow's iconic 1980s pop hit "I Want Candy," Coppola's films and her presence on *Vogue*'s "Best-Dressed" list make her appear to be postfeminism's poster child. Yet while Coppola's concern for style can make her seem superficial, this is belied by her film form, which shows an intense care in representing her subjects and recognition of the ideological weight of aesthetic choices. Though postfeminism is often defined as taking the gains of second-wave feminism for granted, Coppola seems actively engaged in appropriating and applying its critiques of patriarchal cinema in her own way.

Although *Lost in Translation* proves that Coppola can make crowd- and critic-pleasing films, *Marie Antoinette* shows that she is committed not so much to creating hits as to making the kinds of films she wants to make. Though she may not have an explicitly feminist agenda, I would say that her determination not to abide by any American heroic version of filmmaking—that sets the bar by male *auteurs* like her father—makes her a feminist in spirit. Coppola does achieve the goal that de Lauretis and Akerman set out: to find a film form that reflects a woman's own way of seeing and feeling. The development of Coppola's style throughout her growing oeuvre is one that works toward a personal vision and emotional experience to share with her audience, placing them temporarily in a female subject position. Most importantly, her films circulate within the mainstream and reach a broad audience. Though some might argue that mass culture always adopts avant-garde style in the search for something new and fashionable, and that some political power is lost in the process of assimilation into the mainstream, this complaint seems to miss the very wish of the critic, that the avant-garde not simply offer critique, but also promote change. Granted, the change should be in gender politics and the treatment of women in everyday life, not simply what films look and sound like. Yet Coppola's work, in its eliciting identification and empathy between the spectator and the character, could potentially effect this change by asking male viewers to occupy a feminine subject position. It is possible for the spectator to reject the position being offered, and indeed, those who did so are perhaps those who did not like *Marie Antoinette* as much as *Lost in Translation*, which offered two differently gendered subject positions. Those who did enjoy *Marie Antoinette*, such as Ebert, seemed to understand the film as being about the queen's experiences as a woman; interestingly, those who did not enjoy the film avoid discussions of women's life experiences altogether. Lee, for one, neglects to discuss Marie Antoinette's sex life or the pressure she endures to bear an heir.

Sofia Coppola's first three feature films can work as a litmus test for mainstream American cinema's taste for feminist and feminine filmmaking at the beginning of the twenty-first century. While the number of women directors is increasing (though they are still far outnumbered), there continues to be some resistance to films that want to create a feminine "aesthetic of reception," as *Marie Antoinette* seems to show. However, *Marie Antoinette*'s appearance at the local multiplex is a positive sign: its divisiveness attests to its power, and that it has reached a mainstream audience at all makes it groundbreaking. This entertainment film has inherited some of the politics of second-wave feminism, and its revisions to the camera angles, focus, and framing formerly used to objectify women seem to demonstrate the effectiveness of the dual process for which Claire Johnston had called. A full appreciation of Coppola's work, however, would be impossible without early feminist film criticism's analyses of film form, which provides critical tools that enrich readings of films today.

Works Cited

Akerman, Chantal. "Chantal Akerman on *Jeanne Dielman*." *Camera Obscura*, no. 2 (1977): 118-19. Quoted in Teresa de Lauretis, "Rethinking Women's Cinema: Aesthetics and Feminist Theory." In *Issues in Feminist Film Criticism*, edited by Patricia Erens, 288-308. Bloomington and Indianapolis: Indiana University Press, 1990.

Anderson, Melissa. "The Sun Queen: Ever-luminous Kirsten Dunst and the Eternal State of Girlhood." *Film Comment*, September-October 2006, 27-30.

Bainbridge, Caroline. "Feminine Enunciation in Women's Cinema." *Paragraph* 25, no. 3 (2002): 129-139.

Brasfield, Rebecca. "Rereading *Sex and the City*: Exposing the Hegemonic Feminist Narrative." *Journal of Popular Film and Television* 34, no. 3 (Fall 2006): 130-138.

Browne, Nick. "The Spectator-In-The-Text: The Rhetoric of *Stagecoach*." *Film Quarterly* 29 (Winter 1975-76): 26-38.

Brunsdon, Charlotte. "Feminism, Postfeminism, Martha, Martha, and Nigella." *Cinema Journal* 44, no. 2 (Winter 2005): 110-116.

—. "Post-feminism and Shopping Films." In *Screen Tastes: Soap Opera to Satellite Dishes*, 81-102. London: Routledge, 1997.

Carroll, Noël. "The Image of Women in Film: A Defense of a Paradigm." In *Feminism and Tradition in Aesthetics*, edited by Peggy Zeglin Brand and Carolyn Korsmeyer, 371-391. University Park, PA: Pennsylvania State University Press, 1995.

Catsoulis, Jeannette. "In a World of Heartbreak, He's a Catch (Quirks a Plus)." *New York Times*, August 24, 2007.

Cook, Pam. "Portrait of a Lady: Sofia Coppola." *Sight & Sound* 16, no. 11 (November 2006): 36-40.

Dargis, Manohla. "Under the Spell of Royal Rituals." *New York Times*, May 25, 2006.

De Lauretis, Teresa. "Rethinking Women's Cinema: Aesthetics and Feminist Theory." In *Issues in Feminist Film Criticism*, edited by Patricia Erens, 288-308. Bloomington and Indianapolis: Indiana University Press, 1990.

Doane, Mary Ann. "Aesthetics and Politics." *Signs: Journal of Women and Culture in Society* 30:1 (Autumn 2004): 1229-1235.

—. "Film and the Masquerade: Theorising the Female Spectator." In *Feminist Film Theory: A Reader*, edited by Sue Thornham, 131-145. New York: New York University Press, 1999.

Ebert, Roger. Review of *Marie Antoinette*, by Sofia Coppola. *Chicago Sun-Times*, October 20, 2006, http://rogerebert.suntimes.com/apps/pbcs.dll/article?AID=/20061019/R EVIEWS/610190303/1023.

Fraser, Antonia. *Marie Antoinette: The Journey*. New York: Doubleday, 2001.

Fuller, Graham. "Sofia Coppola's Second Chance." *New York Times*, April 16, 2000.

Hohenadel, Kristin. "French Royalty as Seen by Hollywood Royalty." *New York Times*, September 10, 2006.

Holmlund, Chris. "Postfeminism from A to G." *Cinema Journal* 44, no. 2 (Winter 2005): 116-121.

Johnston, Claire. "Women's Cinema as Counter-Cinema." In *Feminist Film Theory: A Reader*, edited by Sue Thornham, 31-40. New York: New York University Press, 1999.

Lee, Nathan. "Pretty Vacant: The Radical Frivolity of Sofia Coppola's *Marie Antoinette*." *Film Comment*, September-October 2006, 24-26.

Lost in Translation. DVD. Directed by Sofia Coppola. 2003; Universal City, CA: Universal Studios Home Video, 2003.

Marie Antoinette. DVD. Directed by Sofia Coppola. 2006; Culver City, CA: Sony Pictures Home Entertainment, 2007.

Metz, Christian. *The Imaginary Signifier: Psychoanalysis and the Cinema.* Translated by Celia Britton, Annwyl Williams, Ben Brewster, and Alfred Guzzetti. Bloomington: Indiana University Press, 1977.

Mitchell, Elvis. "An American in Japan, Making a Connection." *New York Times*, September 12, 2003.

Mulvey, Laura. "Visual Pleasure and Narrative Cinema." In *Feminist Film Theory: A Reader*, edited by Sue Thornham, 58-69. New York: New York University Press, 1999.

Navarro, Mireya. "On Abortion, Hollywood Is No-Choice." *New York Times*, June 10, 2007.

O'Hagan, Sean. "Sofia Coppola: Interview." *The Guardian*, October 8, 2006, http://film.guardian.co.uk/interview/interviewpages/0,,1891161,00.html.

Olsen, Mark. "Sofia Coppola: Cool and the Gang." *Sight & Sound* 14, no. 1 (January 2006): 15.

Riviere, Joan. "Womanliness as Masquerade." In *Formations of Fantasy*, edited by Victor Burgin, James Donald, and Cora Kaplan, 35-44. London: Methuen, 1986.

Scott, A.O. "Evanescent Trees and Sisters in an Enchanted 1970's Suburb." *New York Times*, April 21, 2000.

Silverman, Kaja. "Disembodying the Female Voice." In *Issues in Feminist Film Criticism*, edited by Patricia Erens, 309-327. Bloomington and Indianapolis: Indiana University Press, 1990.

Stern, Lesley, Helen Grace, and Laleen Jayamanne. "Remembering Claire Johnston, 1940-1987." *Framework* 35: 114-29.

Tasker, Yvonne and Diane Negra. "In Focus: Postfeminism and Contemporary Media Studies." *Cinema Journal* 44, no. 2 (Winter 2005): 107-110.

The Virgin Suicides. DVD. Directed by Sofia Coppola. 2000; Hollywood, CA: Paramount Home Video, 2000.

Williams, Linda. "Why I Did Not Want to Write This Essay." *Signs: Journal of Women and Culture in Society* 30:1 (Autumn 2004): 1264-1272.

Zevin, Alexander. "*Marie Antoinette* and the Ghosts of the French Revolution." *Cineaste* 32, no. 2 (Spring 2007): 32-35.

Notes

[1] As of this writing, the only two women ever nominated for Achievement in Directing (Best Director) prior to Coppola were the Italian Lina Wertmüller for *Seven Beauties* in 1976 and the Australian Jane Campion for *The Piano* in 1993.

[2] My definition of postfeminism is a synthesis of the multiple definitions offered by Yvonne Tasker and Diane Negra's introduction for the "In Focus: Postfeminism and Contemporary Media Studies" section of *Cinema Journal* 44, no.2 (Winter 2005) and Chris Holmlund's essay within that section, "Postfeminism from A to G," but I should point out this definition is of the "chick" version of postfeminism. Holmlund briefly outlines two other primary versions of postfeminism: third-wave feminism, affiliated with the Riot Grrrl movement of the 1990s, which is "politically engaged yet playful" and "happy to acknowledge the diversity among women that 'chick' postfeminism ignores," and academic postfeminism, which is "steeped in French, British, and American postmodern, postcolonial, poststructural, queer, (etc.), theory." Holmlund, "Postfeminism from A to G," 116. The "chick" version seems to be the most common one found in media studies scholarship on postfeminist texts, which until recently, has primarily focused on romantic comedies and "female-centered" genres. Good examples of this criticism are Charlotte Brunsdon's seminal essay "Post-feminism and Shopping Films" in her book *Screen Tastes: Soap Opera to Satellite Dishes* (London: Routledge, 1997) and, more recently, Rebecca Brasfield's "Rereading *Sex and the City*: Exposing the Hegemonic Feminist Narrative," *Journal of Popular Film and Television* 34, no. 3 (Fall 2006).

[3] Nathan Lee, "Pretty Vacant: The Radical Frivolity of Sofia Coppola's *Marie Antoinette*," *Film Comment*, September-October 2006, 24.

[4] *The Virgin Suicides* is based on Jeffrey Eugenides's novel of the same title; *Marie Antoinette* is based on Lady Antonia Fraser's revisionist biography of the queen, *Marie Antoinette: The Journey*.

[5] Sofia Coppola, quoted in Kristin Hohenadel, "French Royalty as Seen by Hollywood Royalty," *New York Times*, September 10, 2006.

[6] A.O. Scott, "Evanescent Trees and Sisters in an Enchanted 1970's Suburb," *New York Times*, April 20, 2000.

[7] Lee celebrates Coppola as a "legitimate genius for parties" in "Pretty Vacant": 25. In his review of *Lost in Translation*, Elvis Mitchell says, "Sound is used so beautifully, it takes your breath away..." Mitchell, "An American in Japan, Making a Connection," *New York Times*, September 12, 2003. Scott credits her

with being able to infuse 1970s songs "too lavishly gruesome even for classic rock radio" with "authentic feeling." Scott, "Evanescent Trees."

[8] Other critics who admire Coppola's talent, but see her as overly concerned with style, and who believe that she has missed the significance of Marie Antoinette as a historical figure are Manohla Dargis and Alexander Zevin. See Dargis, "Under the Spell of Royal Rituals," New York Times, May 25, 2006; and Zevin "Marie Antoinette and the Ghosts of the French Revolution," *Cineaste* 32, no. 2 (Spring 2007).

[9] Lee, 25.

[10] Charlotte Brunsdon, "Feminism, Postfeminism, Martha, Martha, and Nigella," *Cinema Journal* 44, no. 2 (Winter 2005): 112-113.

[11] Lesley Stern, Helen Grace, and Laleen Jayamanne, "Remembering Claire Johnston, 1940-1987," *Framework* 35: 119.

[12] Linda Williams, "Why I Did Not Want to Write This Essay," *Signs: Journal of Women and Culture in Society* 30, no. 1 (Autumn 2004): 1264.

[13] Williams, "Why I Did Not Want to Write This Essay," 1268.

[14] *Waitress*, an indie favorite of 2007, also avoided the dreaded issue of abortion. See Mireya Navarro's *New York Times* article "On Abortion, Hollywood Is No-Choice," June 10, 2007, on the current treatment (or lack thereof) of abortion in film and on television.

[15] Jeannette Catsoulis, "In a World of Heartbreak, He's a Catch (Quirks a Plus)," *New York Times*, August 24, 2007.

[16] Yvonne Tasker and Diane Negra, "In Focus: Postfeminism and Contemporary Media Studies," *Cinema Journal* 44, no. 2 (Winter 2005): 108.

[17] Doane, "Aesthetics and Politics," *Signs: Journal of Women and Culture in Society* 30, no. 1 (Autumn 2004): 1231.

[18] Noël Carroll offers a long rebuttal of Mulvey's theory that castration anxiety is the *modus operandi* of mainstream narrative cinema in which he heavily emphasizes the unscientific status of Freudian and Lacanian psychoanalysis. See Noël Carroll, "The Image of Women in Film: A Defense of a Paradigm" in *Feminism and Tradition in Aesthetics*, ed. Peggy Zeglin Brand and Carolyn Korsmeyer (University Park, PA: Pennsylvania State University Press, 1995).

[19] Caroline Bainbridge, "Feminine Enunciation in Women's Cinema," *Paragraph* 25, no. 3 (2002).

[20] Claire Johnston, "Women's Cinema as Counter-Cinema," in *Feminist Film Theory: A Reader*, ed. Sue Thornham (New York: New York University Press, 1999), 39-40.

[21] Although the phrase "aesthetic ideology" is most often associated with Marxist criticism, film feminism certainly recognizes that art is never outside of ideology. The early film feminisms of both the psychoanalytic and the image analysis varieties (see the next note for example of image analysis) work with the premise that film has an impact on society and vice versa; Mary Ann Doane calls this premise "the substrate of the feminist endeavor" in "Aesthetics and Politics," *Signs: Journal of Women in Culture and Society* 30, no. 1 (Autumn 2004): 1231.

[22] Obviously these two essays alone do not give a full picture of early feminist film criticism. I am deliberately not discussing "reflection theory," which analyzes images of women in film (seminal and breakthrough texts of this methodology are Molly Haskell's *From Reverence to Rape* and Marjorie Rosen's *Popcorn Venus*), because that theory remains alive and well in postfeminist criticism and because it generally does not examine aesthetics and film form. For an example, see Charlotte Brunsdon's "Post-feminism and Shopping Films" in her book *Screen Tastes: Soap Opera to Satellite Dishes* (London: Routledge, 1997). Reflection theory sees images of women in cinema as what Rosen calls a "warped mirror" held up to life and examines the sexism in stereotypes of women characters and plots; critics working in this vein argue for more positive images of women as a solution.

[23] Laura Mulvey, "Visual Pleasure and Narrative Cinema" in *Feminist Film Theory: A Reader*, ed. Sue Thornham (New York: New York University Press, 1999), 65. Mulvey's essay was first published in *Screen* 16, no. 3 (1975).

[24] Ibid., 63.

[25] For a discussion of classical Hollywood films and characters that do not work with Mulvey's paradigm, again, see Noël Carroll's "The Image of Women in Film: A Defense of a Paradigm" in *Feminism and Tradition in Aesthetics*, ed. Peggy Zeglin Brand and Carolyn Korsmeyer (University Park, PA: Pennsylvania State University Press, 1995).

[26] Mulvey, "Visual Pleasure," 60.

[27] Mulvey and Wollen's collaborative films include *Penthesilea* (1974), *Riddles of the Sphinx* (1977), *Amy!* (1979), *Crystal Gazing* (1982), *Frida Kahlo & Tina Modotti* (1983), and *The Bad Sister* (1983).

[28] Teresa de Lauretis, "Rethinking Women's Cinema: Aesthetics and Feminist Theory," in *Issues in Feminist Film Criticism*, ed. Patricia Erens (Bloomington and Indianapolis: Indiana University Press, 1990), 305. De Lauretis's essay was first published in *New German Critique*, no. 34 (Winter 1985): 154-175.

[29] De Lauretis, "Rethinking Women's Cinema," 302.

[30] Ibid., 294.

[31] Chantal Akerman, "Chantal Akerman on *Jeanne Dielman*," *Camera Obscura*, no. 2 (1977): 118-19, quoted in Teresa de Lauretis, "Rethinking Women's Cinema: Aesthetics and Feminist Theory," in *Issues in Feminist Film Criticism*, ed. Patricia Erens (Bloomington and Indianapolis: Indiana University Press, 1990), 292-293.

[32] Akerman, "Chantal Akerman," 118-119, quoted in de Lauretis, "Rethinking Women's Cinema," 293.

[33] Ibid.

[34] De Lauretis, "Rethinking Women's Cinema," 297.

[35] De Lauretis actually sees negation as the *sine qua non* of women's cinema. At the end of her essay, she points out that "most of the terms by which we speak of the construction of the female social subject in cinematic representation bear in their visual form the prefix *de-* to signal the deconstruction or the destructuring, if not destruction, of the very thing to be represented [...] There is a certain configuration of issues and formal problems that have been consistently articulated in what we call women's cinema. The way in which they have been expressed and

developed, both artistically and critically, seems to point less to a 'feminine aesthetic' than to a feminist *deaesthetic*." De Lauretis, "Rethinking Women's Cinema," 306.

[36] Graham Fuller cites Coppola as using this term in his article on the film "Sofia Coppola's Second Chance," *New York Times*, April 16, 2000. I believe "epicness" refers to what adolescence feels like while living it—in hindsight, as an adult, not that many "big" things may have happened, but while still a teenager, all those small, everyday dramas *feel* relatively important. Going to the homecoming dance is a big deal, and the Lisbon sisters are clearly thrilled that their overprotective, rule-mongering mother has agreed to let them go. A. O. Scott sees the film as successfully epic: "'The Virgin Suicides' catches both the triviality and the grandeur of youth, its prosaic details and its mythopoetic flights." Scott, "Evanescent Trees."

[37] The use of this voice is unique in this film because while the disembodied male voice usually connotes omniscience, patriarchal authority, and knowledge, according to Kaja Silverman, here it clearly connotes lack. Whereas in film noir, the voice is used to piece together a story that eventually reaches a whole and meaning, the mystery in *The Virgin Suicides* is never solved, and the disembodied male voice is always struggling to understand the girls who hold back their own knowledge. See Kaja Silverman, "Disembodying the Female Voice," in *Issues in Feminist Film Criticism*, ed. Patricia Erens (Bloomington and Indianapolis: Indiana University Press, 1990), 312.

[38] Scott, "Evanescent Trees."

[39] See Melissa Anderson's essay "The Sun Queen: Ever-luminous Kirsten Dunst and the Eternal State of Girlhood" on Dunst as a star in *Film Comment*, September-October 2006.

[40] The concept of femininity as masquerade was first theorized by Joan Riviere in her article "Womanliness as Masquerade," now anthologized in *Formations of Fantasy*, ed. Victor Burgin, James Donald, and Cora Kaplan (London: Methuen, 1986). As a psychoanalyst, Riviere discovered this mechanism of masquerade while studying intellectual or authoritative women. According to Riviere, femininity is a mask that can be put on and taken off, and women typically wear it as a defense mechanism when they have usurped "too much" masculine cultural power. For more on the masquerade as used in feminist film criticism, see Mary Ann Doane's "Film and the Masquerade: Theorizing the Female Spectator" in *Feminist Film Theory: A Reader*, ed. Sue Thornham (New York: New York University Press, 1999).

[41] By simplified version of French politics, I mean that little explanation of France's economics and international affairs that contribute to the Revolution is provided for the viewer. Louis XVI's decision to send money to American revolutionaries is made through about four sentences of dialogue. I am not implying that Coppola should have spent more time with Louis and his advisors discussing France's financial situation, or that there should have been scenes addressing the masses more explicitly, but these are common complaints made by

those critics who feel the film is politically irresponsible, such as Manohla Dargis and Alexander Zevin.

[42] Interestingly, although Marie Antoinette was released slightly before 2007's batch of films that pair talented, beautiful women with sad-sack losers, it offers the same situation from the woman's point of view (and more realistically at that). For a more detailed diagnosis of Louis XVI's sexual dysfunction, see Lady Antonia Fraser's biography *Marie Antoinette: The Journey* (New York: Doubleday, 2001).

[43] Roger Ebert, review of *Marie Antoinette*, by Sofia Coppola, *Chicago Sun-Times*, October 20, 2006, http://rogerebert.suntimes.com/apps/pbcs.dll/article?AID= /20061019/REVIEWS/610190303/1023. In Ebert's own words, "On the border for the 'official handover,' Marie is stopped, stripped and searched to ascertain, brutally, if she is indeed a virgin and, for that matter, a female. In a deal like this, it pays to kick the tires. I was reminded of the scene in von Sternberg's 'The Scarlett Empress' where Catherine arrives at the court of the Czar and the royal physician immediately crawls under her skirt to check her royal plumbing." Overall, Ebert's review is the most sympathetic to both the film and the character of Marie Antoinette, particularly in terms of the treatment of women as objects of trade.

[44] Mulvey, "Visual Pleasure," 69.

[45] Ibid., 63.

[46] Akerman, "Chantal Akerman," 118-119, quoted in de Lauretis, "Rethinking Women's Cinema," 293; De Lauretis, "Rethinking Women's Cinema," 292.

[47] Among the many critics who consider Coppola's work as successful mood pieces are the previously cited A.O. Scott ("Evanescent Trees"), Graham Fuller ("Sofia Coppola's Second Chance"), and Elvis Mitchell ("An American in Japan"), but also Mark Olsen, "Sofia Coppola: Cool and the Gang," *Sight & Sound* 14, no. 1 (January 2004).

[48] Lee, "Pretty Vacant," 24.

[49] Silverman, "Disembodying," 313.

[50] Anderson, "The Sun Queen," 28.

[51] The interviewer here is Mark Olsen, "Sofia Coppola: Cool and the Gang," 15.

[52] Christian Metz, *The Imaginary Signifier: Psychoanalysis and the Cinema*, trans. Celia Britton, Annwyl Williams, Ben Brewster, and Alfred Guzzetti (Bloomington: Indiana University Press, 1977), 51.

[53] See Nick Browne, "The Spectator-In-The-Text: The Rhetoric of *Stagecoach*," *Film Quarterly* 29 (Winter 1975-76): 26-38.

[54] Among the accusers are Dargis and Lee, with both Scott and Cook defending Coppola by refining the relation between style and substance. In Cook's words, "In Coppola's film, style is substance, a gesture that is entirely appropriate to her project and to the statement she wants to make," which is essentially that artifice is what Versailles valued, and style was a way for Marie to control what little of her life she could. Cook, "Portrait of a Lady," 40.

[55] For an extended analysis of *Marie Antoinette* in the context of French history and depictions of the queen in the arts, see Zevin, "*Marie Antoinette* and the Ghosts of the French Revolution."

[56] Sofia Coppola, quoted in Kristin Hohenadel, "French Royalty as Seen by Hollywood Royalty."

[57] Roger Ebert, review of *Marie Antoinette*.

[58] Both Dargis and Hohenadel use the term "poor little rich girl" to describe Coppola's depiction of Marie Antoinette. See Dargis, "Under the Spell" and Hohenadel, "French Royalty."

[59] Elvis Mitchell, "An American in Japan."

[60] Hohenadel, "French Royalty." According to Hohenadel, Coppola "calmly repeated in every interview [after her film was booed by some of her audience at Cannes] that a strong reaction—good or bad, anything but indifference—was what she hoped for." While this normally might sound like an idea conceived after the fact, the shot of Marie during the opening credits makes Coppola's statement seem sincere.

[61] Coppola started her own fashion line Milk Fed in 1995 and is considered designer Marc Jacobs's muse; she directs music videos for the band The White Stripes and is now married to Thomas Mars of the French band Phoenix; the dress in her photo for *Vogue*'s 2007 Best-Dressed List and the packaging for her own line of rosé are both pink. See Pam Cook, "Portrait of a Lady: Sofia Coppola," *Sight & Sound* 16, no. 11 (November 2006): 38-40; Sean O'Hagan, "Sofia Coppola: Interview," *The Guardian*, October 8, 2006, http://film.guardian.co.uk/interview/interviewpages/0,,1891161,00.html.

[62] Pam Cook, "Portrait of a Lady: Sofia Coppola," *Sight & Sound* 16, no. 11 (November 2006): 38-40.

CHAPTER NINE

LAISSE TOMBER LES FILLES:
(POST)FEMINISM IN QUENTIN TARANTINO'S
DEATH PROOF

JEREMI SZANIAWSKI

To consider that Quentin Tarantino's films adopt a postfeminist perspective may at first seem to be a foregone conclusion.[1] This does not mean that one should not call for nuances, especially since, as I will attempt to show, the conclusion is not as obvious as one might think. Tarantino, a postmodern *auteur*, has consistently challenged the spectator's expectations so much so that his films defy categorization. At first sight, Tarantino's films, especially the most recent, *Death Proof* (part of the 2007 "Grindhouse" double-bill of *Death Proof* and Robert Rodriguez's *Planet Terror*), seem to go against the grain of the feminist, anti-narrative cinema claims posited by Laura Mulvey in her groundbreaking article "Visual Pleasure and Narrative Cinema." Is *Death Proof* to be taken as a counterpoint to Mulvey's programmatic kino-utopias?[2] Or, on the contrary, does *Death Proof* constitute a subtle possibility of a (partial) answer to Mulvey, surprisingly offered through the guise of garish postmodern fare? It becomes apparent that there is more to *Death Proof* than the mere exploitation of the conventions of its "B-movie" genre as well as of its female characters.

Before proceeding further, a definition of postfeminism is required. Postfeminism is traditionally understood as a reaction against the second-wave feminism of the 1970s. Furthermore, postfeminism purports to go beyond the claims of the feminist movement(s), the latter having either won its demands or fallen short of its goals. Most importantly, in the articulation of an aesthetic discourse such as film, a postfeminist perspective operates as both an appropriation and a superseding of feminism. In this sense, postfeminism is seen as "taking feminism into account"[3]: accepting the past successes of the movement while also emphasizing that feminism "is no longer needed."[4] As Yvonne Tasker notes, postfeminist rhetoric "is inherently contradictory, characterized by a double discourse that works to construct feminism as a phenomenon of the past, traces of which can be found in the present."[5]

Feminism and postfeminism can be understood in accordance to politics, class, race, and culture. In this sense, postfeminism would appear as the capitalist, apolitical and race-free pendent to feminism. It endows women with traditionally masculine attributes,[6] and demands that they retain their youthfulness and seductive qualities, while granting them freedom of choice with respect to work, domesticity, parenting and sexual empowerment. Most importantly to this argument, postfeminism seems preoccupied with the outward appearance of women, in order to present and preserve the youthful and dynamic image of a potent consumer.[7] Indeed, like postmodernism, postfeminism involves a particular relationship to late capitalistic culture and the forms of work, leisure and, crucially, consumption that thrive within that culture.[8] This dimension of outward appearance is crucial to my argument about the postfeminist elements found in Tarantino's films, in particular, *Death Proof*. In its preoccupation with the outward and the superficial, postfeminism also paradoxically establishes a gender "equalizing" rhetoric rather than egalitarianism. By this I mean that the foregrounding of surface detracts attention from genuine gender differences and their reconciliation, while pretending, in a way, that these differences have been neutralized and therefore resolved (Ariel Levy's *Female Chauvinist Pigs* provides an eye-opening, if journalistic, discussion of this very concept). Postfeminism's preoccupation with the polished, exterior surface does not amount to a resolution of gender conflicts or issues. In this sense, postfeminism does not lead to a celebration of gender difference, but rather, eradicates difference in order for this "equalizing" to occur.

Tarantino's filmography boasts female characters who can be related to a postfeminist ethos. They are attractive, trendy and young: Mia Wallace (Uma Thurman) in *Pulp Fiction*; the Bride/Beatrix Kiddo (Uma Thurman) in *Kill Bill*; and "the girls" in *Death Proof*. Others are youthful-looking, mature, "handsome" women, for example Pam Grier in the title role of *Jackie Brown*. These female characters are often independent—or striving toward independence—therefore shunning domesticity, and are active consumers. Tarantino's cinema itself, based on a regressive, yet virtuoso sense of pastiche and recuperation of sub-genres[9]—albeit with a higher budget—retains the same degree of paradox and a-politicized excessiveness that characterizes postfeminism. However, as I argue further, to merely brand Tarantino's films as postfeminist is a reductionist view. I also ask how it is possible for Tarantino's fascination with "base" film sub-genres—such as the road race B-movie, the slasher and the horror film—to coexist with such brilliant and idiosyncratic versions.

In what follows, I situate my argument in the issue of surface, which is prevalent in discourses about both Tarantino's films and postfeminism. The term "surface" can of course be related immediately to the very surface of the cinematic screen, but also to the images on display, as well as a broader set of concepts such as superficiality, commodification, stylistic extravagance and cultural appropriation that inscribe and relate Tarantino within the broader context of postmodernism. A current, in turn, preoccupied chiefly with ironic distance, waning of affect, pastiche, narrative fracturing and the attention to surface, which closes the circle. The claim that Tarantino's cinema is preoccupied with surface and style is not new.[10] Yet in the present discussion, I show that beyond the surface to which we will be constantly referring, there lies a more complex dimension, which might surprisingly reconnect Tarantino with feminism, or at least the Feminine.

From the very onset of his cinematic production,[11] Tarantino has demonstrated that he is a stylist *hors-pair*. As his budgets grew, particularly with *Kill Bill* in 2004, Tarantino's great care with his very image(s) has only grown and refined itself. In contrast to his other films, the cinematography of *Death Proof* appears to be on a lower budget scale. Yet if the cinematography of the first part of the film appears to have been filmed with a low budget, its second half gloriously re-institutes the primacy of surface and the perfection of celluloid textures—both for the human flesh and the metal of the car. Thus, we witness the exceptional care given to minute details, such as hints of cellulite or veins bulging on the buttocks or feet of the actress Vanessa Ferlito in *Death Proof*'s first section, which is opposed to the apparently immaculate perfection of the actress Rosario Dawson's skin in its second half.

I will now closely analyze *Death Proof*'s first part, as it pertains to the surface, which I consider in relation to the simultaneously feminist and postfeminist statement that can be found in Tarantino's film. With its spectacle-driven, paper-thin narrative—a middle-aged white male psychopath stalks attractive and assertive young women before savagely murdering them with his car—*Death Proof* is structured by a series of embedding devices. Immediately after its disclaimer in the form of a cartoon alerting the audience to the film's potentially offensive contents, *Death Proof* starts with its title coming on top of the film's previous title, which is "Thunder Bolt."[12] The first shot that follows announces the nature of the film: a close-up of a young woman's feet—waving to the sound of Jack Nitzsche's song "The Last Race"—on the dashboard of a car which is moving at a leisurely pace. These shots alternate with similar shots from inside another car, this time driving much faster, on a country road. In hindsight, the spectator will identify the latter shot as being taken from inside the car of the film's psychopath, Stuntman Mike (Kurt Russell). Thus, in a simple effect of montage, Tarantino collapses the two worlds bound to collide in the film—and their similarity and interchangeability— as well as underscores and foreshadows the film's finale.

The foot fetishism of the initial shot is replaced and arguably "enhanced" by the legs and buttocks of Jungle Julia (Sydney Tamiia Poitier), as she paces through her lofty apartment, before laying down on a couch underneath a huge poster of Brigitte Bardot, whose pose, legs stretched out, she replicates. This is not only a visual pun equating Jungle Julia with Bardot, but also a device underlining the embedded, framed and therefore distanced quality of the narrative. Moreover, in the next shot, the spectator sees, in the same room, a figurine of a character evoking Jungle Julia, a reinforcement reifying, objectifying, and fetishizing the action of the film upon its characters.

The "base" nature of the Grindhouse feature is underlined again in the following scene, where bodily functions are highlighted: the camera overlaps with what we assume to be Jungle Julia's perspective, as she runs to the window, only to see her friend Arlene (Vanessa Ferlito)—a.k.a. "Butterfly"—running in short strides, in an awkward pose as she claims that she urgently needs to relieve herself. The vulgarity of the film's tone is thus set. Beyond these examples, the care with which Tarantino treats surface is apparent. This concern is homologous with the seemingly superficial aspect of the film, since, as we shall see, the script does not pretend to delve into the psychology of its characters. Through his use of the reflexive "Grindhouse" device[13] and through the referentiality incorporated within a postmodern treatment and perspective, and, paradoxically through the highlighting of surface and its relationship to the viewer, Tarantino adds a dimension to his film lacking in the B-movies to which *Death Proof* pays a vibrant homage.[14]

An ellipsis of sorts cuts from Butterfly's will to release the impending fluids as the filmstrip jumps to the streets of Austin, Texas. The jump is jarring and foregrounds one of the most conspicuous self-reflexive dimensions of the "Grindhouse" film: the print of the film appears old and scratched (although the spectator knows that the film is brand new and not damaged). The abrupt jump in the film is a wink and a nodd to those familiar with film archives—and aficionados of old 35mm screenings in general—of missing film footage. From then on, the film will constantly bring its viewers back to its very surface by reminding them of the artificiality of its device. The scratches and jumps in the image and the soundtrack, the shots going out of focus, as well as the occasional trembling of the image suggesting torn sprocket holes in the film strip help reinforce the ironic distance with the narrative, while enacting in an almost fetishistic way the viewer's nostalgia, at a time when questions of digital media and digital projection are current subjects of debate. The nostalgia, then, is for the "real" film reel, which can still be subject to decay and to the multiple alterations it can incur at the hands of unscrupulous distributors, or by chance.[15] Yet, at the same time, the nostalgia is mixed with the understanding that the film has been merely digitally manipulated so as to offer the illusion of a decayed print. This effect, alongside the errors in continuity editing spotted at various moments in the film[16] offers a commentary on the possibility for a cinema of contingency that is less perfect, and therefore more "human."

Yet it most importantly brings the spectator back to the issue of surface. It takes the viewer a moment to refocus, as it were, on the action of the film: the three girls—Jungle Julia, Butterfly and Shanna (Jordan Ladd)—are driving to a bar, cursing and talking animatedly about boys, sex, and drugs, before shouting in unison as they drive by a large billboard featuring Jungle Julia, whom the spectator realizes is a local celebrity radio DJ. Courtesy of the billboard, Jungle Julia is quite literally an icon, framed further through the publicity it gives her.

Through the girls' conversation, the spectator learns that Chris Simonson, a filmmaker visiting Austin, has "a big thing for Julia" although he never calls her. The girls also discuss Butterfly's ways of making out with boyfriends, highlighting the extent to which these women are seeking total control over their sexual drives. During this mundane discussion, the spectator is kept aware of a conflict between a desire to be intimate with these "wild" women, and the fact that the surface of the image, covered with scratches—as well as the apparent bleached out quality of the bad print—deconstructs the verisimilar illusion. The alienation is pushed further as the dialogues offer an uncanny mix of streetwise realism and the overwrought perfection that has always characterized Tarantino's writing.[17] This formalist conflict between the illusion of reality and the over-manipulation thereof will recur later in the film.

As the car passes by a third billboard—greeted again by shouts of joy, although Jungle Julia seems to have grown a bit wary of the narcissistic celebration—the image jumps and cuts again, revealing a dark vehicle, ominous yet still undefined in its very function, roaring as it drives in the same direction as the girls, who are headed to a first bar. There, Jungle Julia informs Butterfly that she has placed a bet on the airwaves. Its *enjeu* is clear: if a man approaches Butterfly and recites the well-known verse from Robert Frost's poem "Stopping by Woods on a Snowy Evening" (1922)—which is both erotic and foreboding[18]—she is supposed to perform a lap-dance for this man. The situation is fictionally rehearsed among the girls, as Marcy (Marcy Harriell), Jungle Julia's friend, impersonates the part of a fictional man named Barry.[19] The embodiment of the male fantasy through the body of the otherwise utterly feminine Marcy has a double effect. First, the female character taking on the attributes of a man evokes the interchangeability of gender, a postfeminist dimension of the film upon which its finale will be based.[20] Thus, traits and characteristics typically associated with the male, including the bet and the will to prove oneself, but most conspicuously Marcy's taking on the part of the fictitious "Barry," are embodied by female characters. On the other hand, this all-female posse in an enclosed space creates a homo-social environment in which it almost becomes logical that traits of the opposite sex would be incorporated by at least some members of the posse to compensate for the absence of men in the group. Hence, the authoritarian, almost dominatrix and "bitchy" comments made by Jungle Julia, including the reference to her promiscuity.

As Butterfly walks out onto the bar's porch, she is confronted, for the first time, with Stuntman Mike's black "death-proof" car and immediately feels unsettled by its dark and threatening appearance. A few moments later, as the girls have moved to a different bar (tended this time by Warren, played by Quentin Tarantino in a cameo role), we see an emblematic shot of Stuntman Mike, characterized not only by his car, but also by his voyeuristic function as the shot reveals him injecting drops into his eyes. This underscores his true psychopathic nature and his voyeurism. The latter is soon confirmed as he retrieves from the car's visor a series of photographs of the girls he surreptitiously took. Furthermore, it is noteworthy that this initial shot of Stuntman Mike's eyes are not framed directly, but rather are reflected in the tiny mirror of the visor. This reflexive device collapses the viewer with the voyeur. In this sense, at least from a male perspective—and this is one of the film's perverse triumphs—the spectator initially identifies more with the psychopath than with the women. This has of course to do, at least partially, with the fact that the girls constitute a posse and Stuntman Mike is alone, just as each spectator is alone in the darkness of the theater. The viewer's identification with the psychopath might actually go even further.

Stuntman Mike is defined by his calculating and voyeuristic impulse before his name or his whole face is given to the public. The way he picks up his female victims can be correlated with and seen as an outright pun upon the theories of Laura Mulvey in the voyeuristic stasis in which he finds himself observing and photographing women before enacting his murderous plans.[21] He is the active bearer of the male gaze as he objectifies and photographs the women he will eventually kill. These women are not only passive objects of his gaze, but soon also will become his passive victims, since they have no chance to defend themselves when he crushes their car and butchers them. Whereas *Death Proof* is based upon material that is opposed to the ideals of Mulvey—in the sense that it pits the spectacle of fetishized female bodies so harshly against a banal narrative—it might still contain several redeeming features. Some of these features include the varied spectatorial addresses of Stuntman Mike to the viewer, such as his winks and engaging smiles to the camera. In this respect, *Death Proof* strongly evokes Michael Haneke's *Funny Games* (1998 and 2008), with its manipulative and hyperbolic display of cruelty and playing around with the spectator's expectations of the thriller and the horror genre. The distancing, conative modes of address of Tarantino's films are discussed later on, after an examination of *Death Proof*'s diegesis.

At the Texas Chili Parlor, the girls assume a central spectacle-like position while the gazes and eyes of their male counterparts are peripheral. In an emblematic shot of Jungle Julia dancing, the head of a male bystander becomes a small, almost undefined shape at the right bottom corner of the screen, whereas another man dances awkwardly around (and behind) Butterfly, who pays little attention to his stiff moves. Horror film director Eli Roth, about whom more will follow, plays the part of Shanna's love interest.[22] He devises a strategy to get the girls so drunk that they will allow their "men" to join them later on at the lakeside house[23] owned by Shanna's father who has forbidden male guests. Although the girls champion self-sufficiency and want to avoid the company of their male partners, they are not devoid of feelings. This is highlighted in the scene where Jungle Julia sends text messages to the absent-present filmmaker, Chris Simonson. The romantic interlude (underscored in a musical theme by thriller music master Pino Donaggio) only results in Jungle Julia's hurt pride, as Chris Simonson, a Lacanian entity of unreachable plenitude—in short, the Real—will never join her at the Texas Chili Parlor.

Heavy rain starts pouring outside, establishing a parallel between the release in tension the film has been building up almost unnoticeably, and Butterfly's initial release of bodily fluids. In contrast to this narrative device, Tarantino's willingness to lay bare the threads of his film's mechanism appears nowhere clearer than in the scene where Warren asks, for no apparent reason, to turn the lights on in the parking lot adjacent to the parlor. This telescoping of the film's inner mechanisms and the use of lighting illuminates, quite literally, the dark car with which Butterfly was confronted earlier. A short, comical interlude between Butterfly and a male acquaintance (where she grants him six minutes for making out in the car and dodges a pun about not getting wet) follows, before revealing Stuntman Mike, sitting at the bar, devouring a platter of nachos, and drinking virgin piña colada. His *Icy-Hot* sponsored jacket underscores his seedy and cheap personality. To the American audience, it also evokes the pungent camphor smell of the famous brand of pain-relieving cream. Stuntman Mike, however, is not about relieving, but rather inflicting pain, although at first he will numb his victims' vigilance. In order to do so, he first approaches the posse of girls indirectly, through Pam (Rose McGowan), who, with her pale skin and bleached blond hair, appears to be the visual opposite of Jungle Julia, who was her nemesis in their school days. The snappy and wisecrack dialogue renders Stuntman Mike almost sympathetic, toning down the initial concerns the viewer might have about him and also playing with the rules of the genre, where, more often than not, the true identity of the villain is gambled with *ad infinitum* in order to deceive the audience. Yet, as the latter will soon find out, there is no deception in *Death Proof*. Stuntman Mike, in spite of his friendly smiles has steely blue eyes that will soon enough reveal his true psychotic nature. In the meantime, however, he socializes with the group of girls[24] who are smoking and drinking on the porch. Before he kills them, Stuntman Mike will also negotiate the promised lap-dance from Butterfly. The young woman, reluctant at first, eventually gives in, won over, as it were, by Stuntman Mike's arguments which include a cleverly disguised unmasking dialogue,[25] as he preys upon her hurt pride and sense of challenge. Throughout the dialogue between the two characters, images keep recurring, which further underline the film's preoccupation with surface. Stuntman Mike inquires whether Butterfly is scared of his scar, which brings his rugged features to the forefront. He then also plays upon Butterfly's lack of vocabulary, explaining to her that she is *touché*, "wounded slightly," as if, indeed, her hurt pride anticipated the genuine physical wounds to come. It is surface, here, the concern with the opinions of a third party in regards to one's image and reputation, which triumphs as Butterfly eventually concedes the lap-dance to Stuntman Mike. He claims that if she doesn't perform for him, he will write her name under the "chickenshit" category of his book in which he keeps a record of everyone he meets. A book which, the viewer imagines, might not only be a means of luring his prey, but also a sinister metonymy of the string of victims Stuntman Mike has already written down—and *off* the surface of the earth.

The long awaited lap-dance thus happens, to the tune of the Coasters' "Down in Mexico." This song, evoking exotic locales and adventures, rhythms to perfection the crowning exploitation moment in a film which is thoroughly dedicated to celebrating exploitation in cinema. The careful set-up of the following shots again highlights artifice: the focal length chosen in this scene, induced by the very wide angle lens distorting the corners of the image into a nearly circular shape, situates Stuntman Mike at the center of it. But, of course, it is Butterfly who is competing for the attention, and soon enough her suggestive gestures and provocative poses recapture the main focus. A circling tracking shot ensues, putting the two characters at the center of the image, before the frontal wide-angle long shot resumes, in which Butterfly, with her wriggling body, obliterates Stuntman Mike entirely. Then, once more, the (heterosexual) male spectator is frustrated in the visual (*scopophilia*) and auricular pleasure when another jarring cut[26] interrupts the scene midway through. This effect, as often, can be read in several ways. One is yet another self-reflexive pun made by the film and the exploitation system of the Grindhouse screenings, where a film could be chopped up, re-edited and tampered with at will by its distributor. The fact that the jump appears at what is, arguably, the most "spectacular" and erotic moment in the film so far, is also Tarantino's nod to the audience, and a wink to Mulvey's theory. A pure instance of Mulveyan spectacle, Butterfly's lap-dance constitutes an interruption in the narrative flow—to the entertainment of Stuntman Mike and at least a part of the audience (heterosexual males or those conditioned as such). In cutting straight to the next scene, Tarantino indulges in a perverse, yet clever exercise of spectacle fulfillment and frustration. The film thus moves immediately to the aftermath of the lap-dance, when the various parties are about to leave: the women going to Shanna's father's lakeside house, and Stuntman Mike giving Pam a ride "home."

The foundations of the film have been set. The following five minutes or so offer a brutal series of shocks, as Pam is crushed to death inside Stuntman Mike's car which rides wildly on the highway, before Mike engages in a violent frontal collision with the other girls in Shanna's car, not without having done away with the incriminating pieces of evidence— the girl's pictures in his car, which he throws on the road after Pam's gruesome death. The dreadful care given to detail then reaches an unbecoming peak as Tarantino perversely replays four times the death of the girls: the repetition, in slow motion, of the dismantling of their bodies, quite literally enacting Mulvey's notion of the fragmentation of the female body. The hyper-realistic details abound: Jungle Julia's leg is severed and falls flatly, a disjointed piece of meat, on the concrete, a few meters away from the car crash. Shanna meets a similar fate, as she flies through the broken windshield, while Lana is crushed by the steering wheel and Butterfly's face is torn open by one of the car's hubcaps. The audience, no doubt, is left in a state of shock. The film might as well end there, having delivered its load of adrenaline. Yet Stuntman Mike's car, is, indeed, fully death-proof for him, and the spectator then realizes that it is he who carries the film's plot, and appears as the anti-hero protagonist of the film, a subversive twist among many others.

An interlude then literally cuts the film in two. As a recovering Stuntman Mike is cleared of all suspicion by the district attorney, Sheriff Earl McGraw (a part reprised by Tarantino's regular Michael Parkes, who played the same role in *Kill Bill*) explains to his son how he suspects Stuntman Mike of being a pervert and psychotic killer.[27] The allusion, in form of pastiche, to Hitchcock's *Psycho*'s (1960) epilogue is clear, and brings a welcome moment of comic relief to the film. The sheriff ends his speech by stating that the only thing he can do is make sure Stuntman Mike leaves Texas.

Accordingly, the second half of the film takes place in another locale. The shift is not only geographic (moving from Austin, Texas to Lebanon, Tennessee), but also stylistic. For its first few minutes, the film's second half is shot in black and white. Yet it also boasts a much more careful and beautiful cinematography—and, arguably, more beautiful and immaculate female characters. The latter are four girls from the film industry who are in town for a movie shoot: make-up artist Abernathy (Rosario Dawson), actress Lee (Mary Elizabeth Winstead), and stuntwomen Kim (Tracy Thoms) and Zoë (real-life stuntwoman Zoë Bell). After a few minutes, the film resumes its colors, and we are struck by the beauty and vividness of its cinematography. The actresses' skin looks as if taken from a commercial for beauty products, and the brightness of the colors contrasts with the relatively more muddled palette and nocturnal tone of the film's first half. Clothes—such as Zoë Bell's pink T-shirt and Lee's yellow cheerleader uniform, a cliché of the cheerleader film genre—as well as shiny cars are superb, set against Stuntman Mike and his dirty dark car. The contrast will be rendered even stronger as the women trade their first car, a bright yellow one, for the white 1970 Dodge Challenger made legendary by Kowalski (Barry Newman) in Richard C. Sarafian's *Vanishing Point* (1971), yet another cinematic reference in a film already packed with them. Otherwise, the film replicates the structure of its first part: the girls indulge in idle consumption of energy drinks and fashion magazines while talking about love and sex and the absent filmmaker boyfriend. Stuntman Mike takes their pictures, unbeknownst to them, before chasing them and appearing to cause Zoë's death as she plays the dangerous "Ship's Mast" game on the hood of the car. Stuntman Mike does not realize the extent of the women's driving skills and Zoë's natural gift for dangerous stunts. After Kim has shot Mike in the arm with the gun she carries, he becomes the one who is hunted: the women regroup to successfully chase him down, crash his car, encircle him and presumably beat him to death. Note another inversion: Stuntman Mike whines and cries like a child—or an emasculated hysteric—whereas the "stuntgirls" demonstrate an aggressive, murderous instinct as they enact their revenge and destroy him. As they chase him, they reverse the anal rape imagery of the beginning of the chase, and in enacting it quite literally give flesh to the anxiety of the heterosexual male. Kim states, "you don't like it up the ass you redneck lunatic bastard," before smashing Stuntman Mike's car from behind,[28] attacking him in a choreography reminiscent of the *mise-à-mort* of the Bride in *Kill Bill*'s tragically aborted wedding rehearsal sequence. The *coup de grâce* portrays Abernathy—tamer than the stuntgirls throughout the chase—crushing Stuntman Mike's face in a point-of-view shot. This shot captures the dwarfed position of the male confronted with these empowered female figures who boast simultaneously masculine and feminine characteristics, in a climactic gesture of (post)feminist retaliation. Here I use parentheses around the "post," because, in this explosion of violence, Tarantino goes beyond the postfeminist argument, whereby women are not phallicized or masculinized, but merely "postfemininzed,"[29] according to Lisa Coulthard. Here, the solitary action and rationalized revenge is replaced by angry girl power in the form of a group of women actually reveling in their retaliation. The nihilistic and violent ending thus offers both an exhilarating and disquieting statement, with a re-establishment of feminist politics. Most significantly, the empowered postfeminist woman, with her sexual as well as girl power, is represented as having instincts that are as equally strong, evil and murderous as those of the male. Yet never have "Final Girls" (to use Carol Clover's coinage) been more seductive and more cruel than here, relishing in the retaliation with disquieting ruthlessness and joy. But again, ironic distance can be envisaged: what we see is, after all, also a striking metaphor for the younger, more sophisticated form of cinema literally taking on and squaring off with its older and less successful predecessor.

Stuntman Mike's obsession with destruction and the women's appropriation of that obsession which they turn back against him presents another set of problems for the feminist and/or postfeminist reading of *Death Proof*. Can the film be considered feminist at all? Arguments against this possibility are manifold. Tarantino's veneration for subgenres, B-movies and exploitation films—in which female figures become a masculine projection of threat, submission, and/or sexual fantasy—seems to implicate him in perpetuating this representation of female characters. *Death Proof* does little to change this perception of Tarantino's cinematic tradition. Patriarchy and capitalism, two pillars of postfeminist thinking supposedly challenged by feminism might not be undermined by this film, which is, after all, a commercialized and expendable commodity. Against this monolithic argument, one could raise another, less substantial claim, according to which Grindhouse cinema, from a feminist perspective, would be less problematic than Hollywood mainstream films. This is because Grindhouse cinema is a genuinely independent means of production. As Mike Atkinson points out: "There's no denying the attractions of this sub-culture: then as an underground alternative to Hollywood, and today as a lost swatch of cultural authenticity."[30] Indeed, Mulvey argues that the imposition of heterosexual male fantasies upon female audiences is a spurious and manipulative imprint. Hollywood, with its precise manufacturing of film-as-product (even within the framework of the co-opted "independent" film), fosters character identification for male spectators, while denying women a proper identification, rendering the cinematic apparatus a dangerous one, with potentially political and ideological ends.[31]

The less despotic discourse of the Grindhouse film—characterized by cheap, fast and piecemeal modes of production—has so many flaws and faults as a genre and as a commodity that it could hardly shape the minds of its audience in any consistent manner. This is so because it is less perfect, less hegemonic and more disorderly. Does Tarantino offer an aesthetic and political discourse alternative to Hollywood's? Jane Mills argues that he has managed to reconcile the trends of both mainstream and independent cinema and deliver his own mix of both. However, the term "independent" has suffered a co-option ever since the early 1990s in America, having to meet so many requests on the market that it is, arguably, as hegemonic (at least in terms of market distribution strategies) as the mainstream films screened in today's multiplexes.[32] Ultimately, Tarantino cannot be deemed independent, since even the most naïve filmgoer has a sense of the power of Miramax, Tarantino's financial backer and distributor. Neither can his cinema be seen as enough of an "alternative" departure from Hollywood blockbusters (that is, if alternative is to be equaled with financial non-viability, a problematic stance in its own right). Even the concern with violent banter and the carnivalesque provocation inhabiting Tarantino's films does not go much further beyond the threshold of commercialism.

In fact, some of Tarantino's advocates, in the press and other discourses, have pointed out that the mannerisms of speech and general discussion of Tarantino's female characters amount to the mere feminization of the typically male discussion of the opposite sex.[33] While Tarantino, after all hardly a realist filmmaker, is entitled to feats of poetic license and lets his remarkable dialogue skills flow, this issue leads us to another concern about the meaning of (post)feminism for *Death Proof*.

Indeed, what do we make of the viewer's—masculine or feminine— sense of unease at seeing a group of young women be reduced to pulp before the next carload of potential female prey retaliates and becomes murderous furies? Is it arguable that the malaise—specifically addressed to the "complicit" viewer I evoked earlier—is even greater in the latter instance? As the film's final close-up celebrates Abernathy's stretching skills before smashing her boot on the image, we no longer know who is the target of her strike. Tarantino plays with our expectations and sensations in a game that is both sly and brilliant. At first, the spectator will have been given the opportunity to distance him- or herself from the characters and then to sympathize and identify with them (Stuntman Mike included). As Abernathy's boot covers the entire surface of the screen, the viewer can no longer doubt that the "correction" is addressed not only to Stuntman Mike, but also to the audience. Via the device of returning the gaze of the viewer on the screen from the screen onto the viewer, the filmmaker turns the two-way mirror of cinema into a completely reflexive surface that troubles the spectator's phallus because it is *seen*. The Symbolic state is re-instituted, indeed policed onto the viewer, and, unusually, not by a father figure, but rather, by a female character (who is also a mother). Here, notions of the Lacanian *stade du miroir* and Deleuzean castrating close-ups resonate and collide with each other.[34] This scene hints at the Mulveyan definition of traditional narrative cinema that, according to her, positions the male spectator as the scopophilic voyeur of the female who is his erotic object of contemplation. Here, however, the female strikes back with a vengeance, to the literal and metaphorical voyeur's dismay.

The spectacle remains, and it seems evident that this retaliation is a game, and that the film is a pleasurable, exciting and even exhilarating ride. Ultimately, the fact is that these female characters—all imbued with to-be-looked-at-ness and empowered to match the villain's murderous skills—partake in yet another male fantasy of female castrating figuration. *Death Proof* could approximate Carol Clover's thesis on slasher[35] and "rape-and-revenge" horror films and thrillers. Clover's claim is that the female victim-hero must be the victim before she becomes the hero and therefore she always carries an element of monstrosity (the aforementioned "Final Girl").[36] Yet this is not quite the trajectory followed in Tarantino's film. To begin with, the second group of girls already carries a seed of monstrosity and ruthlessness before they meet Stuntman Mike. For instance, they have no qualms with trading Lee, one of their own, for the Dodge Challenger, leaving her at the hands of the car's owner, a lewd farmer whom they lead to believe that Lee is actually a porn actress who will accommodate him, thus tapping into his fantasies. In hindsight, it is hardly surprising that the girls would "get rid" of Lee, the only truly soft, naïve and gentle ("feminine" or "girlish" by stereotypical standards)—at the same time somewhat dull in spite of her "cuteness"—character in the group. Conversely, Abernathy, Kim and Zoë are the typical "girls with balls" from the very onset of the action, so much so that they hardly fit in with the classic notion of the "Final Girl" offered by Carol Clover. Indeed, as opposed to Clover's definition, these girls are hardly serious, work-oriented and virginal (let alone divested of any interest in sex). The only thing that connects them with the figure of the Final Girl would be the forceful and assertive demeanor they boast, more traditionally associated with male characters. But, as I mentioned, these traits are present from the start, and they are hardly prompted by the onslaught of the killer. The fact that these girls are a group, too, challenges a notion which traditionally only offers *one* Final Girl, one heroine with which the male viewer, according to Clover, can identify in spite of the initial gender difference. While Clover argues that the Final Girl is not so much a proto-postfeminist figure as a return to an earlier discourse—the "one sex reasoning" discourse challenged by psychoanalysis but prominent until the 18th century,[37] Tarantino's Final Girls seem indeed to embody and champion the truly postfeminist pendant of the concept. As so often in his productions, Tarantino enriches and complicates a well-known trope with layers of referentiality and palimpsest on the one hand, and genuinely innovates upon old concepts on the other hand, serendipitously creating a new blend with an old formula.

And yet, it is not in the film's content that one should seek redemptive markers of a feminist or postfeminist discussion about Tarantino. The film's form, "wrapping," and veneer carry the spectator toward the (post)feminist conclusion that I am embracing with all its nuances. In terms of its content, the film displays a generic coherence, within the boundaries of postmodern entertainment: the killer enacts his ruthless plan on the first group of victims, before being turned into prey through a mechanism of transfer, thus transmitting his madness and bloodlust to his would be-victims-turned-killers. While such conclusions are a cliché of typical horror films, in *Death Proof*, the characters are reduced to their surfaces to such an extent that the film's content becomes a consideration secondary to its form.

Through his stylized and seductive use of music, above all, Tarantino creates a synthesis between the form and content of *Death Proof*. The closing credits of the film roll over the French song "Laisse tomber les filles," written by Serge Gainsbourg, sung in English as "Chick Habit" and then sung in the original French by the female singer April March. Accompanying both versions is a series of flashes of young women taken from the aseptic universes of televisual targets and old commercials from the 1970s, the era to which the film refers and pays homage. The song, about a wanton male seducer who leaves a string of broken female hearts in his wake, acquires a new ironic dimension when applied to Stuntman Mike's character. In particular, the furious, vindictive lyrics of the English version basically duplicate Stuntman Mike's fate: "You're going to need a heap of glue when they all catch up with you and they cut you up in two." Although the song's lyrics are dark, the infectious rhythm of its music, its seductive aggressiveness, its sexy beat, and Gainsbourg's catchy ostinatos typical of the 1960s are in harmony with the film's shiny veneer and darker contents, as well as its generally joyful nihilistic irreverence.

One cannot help, also, to relate the figure of Serge Gainsbourg—and his self-destructive alter ego, Gainsbarre—to Stuntman Mike, since Gainsbourg was a man with rugged features and disquieting, almost evil charm, surrounded by beautiful women such as Brigitte Bardot and Jane Birkin, as well as the countless actresses and singers for whom he wrote: Isabelle Adjani, Catherine Deneuve, France Gall, and Vanessa Paradis, among others. Gainsbourg also had a voracious sexual appetite and a tendency towards self-destruction. He was simultaneously cruel and pathetic, touching and repulsive. These characteristics of Gainsbourg's are attested to in Gilles Verlant's biography, which is sympathetic to the singer while also hinting at his criminal, arsonist predilections. What kind of patrons are Gainsbourg/Gainsbarre for a film such as *Death Proof*? The French singer lends not only his sense of provocation and freedom to the film, but also his outright male chauvinism (paradoxical, in a sense, but present nonetheless). Still, the promotional materials of the film deny this perspective and interpretative line of reasoning. In the features which come along with the film's DVD, Tarantino appears as revered or at least highly respected by the actresses, and his collaboration with his long-time female editor, Sally Menke, is underscored. While the complicity between Tarantino and the actresses as well as the general female production staff transpires in the triumph that is the film, one cannot help but question the need for this promotion to counter the possible allegations of misogyny that the film raises.

Especially since the film's form does not end here: Tarantino, for the first time, is credited as his own cinematographer. He thus manipulates the lights and, most importantly, the camera, this apparatus of phallic proportions. It is interesting to point out that the faithful Sally Menke, can offer, along with her editing skills, a role that is both a counterpoint to Tarantino's possible sexism and one of troubling reversibility. If the camera is potentially mobile and open, it can also be considered in terms of the limitations it creates through framing—at times phallic, at others myopic—whereas montage, through infinite promises of spatio-temporal contiguity and scale of shots, can become the engulfing agent of all possibilities, including fragmentation. A fragment, when detached from the rest of the body in a close-up, is not necessarily gendered, since it can be potentially masculine or feminine. Similarly, the car appears as a surface whose damage can be interchangeable: after *Death Proof*'s final chase, there is very little that distinguishes the women's Dodge Challenger from Stuntman Mike's "death proof" car: they are both wrecks, both surfaces have been totaled, just as they have become connected in monstrosity through their ordeal.

Death Proof is not so much about inverting expectations of gender and genre, but rather, about the de- or a-sexualization of its content and characters as demonstrated by the primacy of the surface in the film. As Lisa Coulthard observes in her discussion of *Kill Bill*, "on the surface... the spectacle of iconicity that is primary in the film is reconfigured so as to present its violent action in a putatively gender-neutral zone."[38] In *Death Proof*, cars and characters crash into each other, neutralizing each other's effects and affects. Speed and shock, factors of progress and freedom, are prevalent over the consideration of gender binaries, however frontally showcased and omnipresent. Through speed, the contours become blurred, and eventually equalized. It is then no longer a matter of what differentiates male and female, evil and good, but simply, in a vital *élan*, to see what unites both masculine and feminine perspectives in *Death Proof*. The surface/veneer becomes paramount and seductive because of the virtuoso *mise-en-scène* and a carefully thought-out script. The primacy of the surface as it relates to gender is articulated especially well by Mary

Ann Doane in her discussion of the femme fatale, particularly of Louise Brooks in G.W. Pabst's 1929 *Pandora's Box*, a German precursor of the American film noir. In the sense that it draws attention so flamboyantly to the surfaces of things, *Death Proof* constitutes a postfeminist effort.

This concern and postfeminist tendency to "superficialize" and neutralize gender differences can also be witnessed in the films of Robert Rodriguez, but mostly in those of Eli Roth (both Rodriguez and Roth are Tarantino's male friends/protégés). The result, however, is much less compelling. In the diptych *Hostel* (2005 and 2007), Roth presents female characters as either vile temptresses or instrumentalized victims in the first installment of the film, before—in a pure postfeminist gesture—inverting the roles and making his heroine Beth (Lauren German) into a redoubtable figure. Beth is empowered by her wealth (the audience is informed early on that she is an heiress), an undeniable stand-in for the phallus, allowing her to find the only way out of the Slovakian hell in which the film is set. Beth buys her way out of the executioner's lair, before castrating her torturer (Roger Bart) with a pair of scissors, only to return, in the tradition epitomized by Carol Clover, as a vengeful killer.[39] In another scene of the film, we see a woman cut open the body of an unfortunate girl (Heather Mattarazzo), lying underneath her and bathing in her blood, before slitting her throat and climaxing as the spurting blood anoints her naked body. These sadistic actions, imparted traditionally to male figures, are in *Hostel* attributed to a beautiful woman, nodding to the Marquis de Sade as well as to the Countess Bathory and the collective myths surrounding them. These myths have produced gruesome figures such as the female vampire and Hannibal Lecter. In short, according to *Hostel*, cruelty and madness have no gender. *Hostel's* female protagonist can be perfectly inscribed within a postfeminist template, where the focus is transferred from the female victim to the female perpetrator.

In Eli Roth's case, more so than in Tarantino's, the preoccupation with de-substantiating the characters, the stripping away of the most elementary psychological traits while trying to convey a message—here, a criticism of capitalism and the woes of idle consumption—is conveyed through a gratuitous imagery, with an aesthetic that is derived from commercials, or even music videos *à la* MTV. These are paragons of surface, of which even the essence of the author—with exceptions such as Spike Jonze or Michel Gondry who have turned from videos to feature filmmaking—is taken away. For instance, at the beginning of *Hostel 2*, the scene of the auction over the future victims evokes a commercial for investment banking or financial brokerage. As for the scene in the Slovakian hot springs, it strongly evokes the universe, with its blue steams, of the Noa perfume by Cacharel. Elsewhere, the film indulges—in typical "Grindhouse-Tarantinesque" fashion—in clever pastiche. For instance, in the train sequence, which references Aldo Lado's *Midnight Train Murders* (1975)—one of Eli Roth's favorite European horror B-movies—and the cruelty of which *Hostel 2* sets out to supersede hyperbolically. At any rate, the surface and anonymous nature—possible *anomie*—of the image are here pushed to such extremes that one loses the thread between them and the formulation of the diegesis, its starting point and goal, and they thus appear as disturbing spectacular protuberances, slowing down the flow of the story, instead of being useful narrative components.

If *Death Proof* succeeds where *Hostel* fails, it is precisely because it does not try to convey a message. The former plunges merrily into a structure that is relatively self-contained, once its source material and genre are taken into account. A world where, ultimately, everything would be possible, but where "just anything" is impossible. The other, perhaps more important notion—apart from the one according to which Tarantino is a real film genius and Roth a skillful craftsman at best—would be the following: not the absence of a message in the film, but rather, its true essence. Here is my own response. In two instances of *Death Proof*, the absent male filmmaker—who, as previously mentioned, is also Jungle Julia and Abernathy's love interest—is evoked. I want to suggest that this absent filmmaker might be the overarching presence of the great image-maker—of none other than the father. According to Tarantino's biography his own father was unknown to him, and Tarantino mainly inherited his last name.

As I mentioned earlier, Tarantino's cinema endows female characters with traits generally attributed to men. In *Kill Bill*, Beatrix Kiddo (Uma Thurman) becomes a sword-wielding fury, and finds more formidable opponents in Elle Driver (Daryl Hannah) or O-Renn Ishii (Lucy Liu) than in Budd (Michael Madsen) or even Bill himself (David Carradine). In *Death Proof*, the stuntwomen Kim and Zoë are more agile and more ruthless than Stuntman Mike. As Coulthard observes: "they are never inferior to men."[40] Coulthard, a negative critic of *Kill Bill*, sees it as a celebration of the status quo in support of patriarchy and dominant capitalist ideology. For Coulthard, the ending of *Kill Bill* merely enshrines its conservative nature, as opposed to a genuine feminist violence, which would be disruptive of the narrative and truly subversive, instead of being constitutive of a linear, stabilizing narrative. This, Coulthard argues, has to do with the fact that in the patriarchal postfeminist template, the violent woman is rationalized, her violence is redemptive, and she acts alone, either shunned by the community, or justified in her acts.[41] Ultimately,

Coulthard's perspective neglects the fact that *Kill Bill* does indeed end
with the murder of Bill, who is both the male partner and father figure. Bill
is not only the father of Beatrix's daughter but also the murderer of
Beatrix's husband-to-be during their wedding rehearsal. It is worth noting
that Beatrix kills Bill by using the deadly "Five-Point-Palm-Exploding-
Heart-Technique," which she learned from another father/mentor figure in
the film, Pai-Mei (Gordon Liu) who was later on murdered by Elle. The
pattern is that the female figure takes the man's place, substitutes herself
for him and no longer needs him.[42] The film ends with a new Symbolic
order since the male/father figure is murdered and vacates the scene
altogether.

A similar case could also be made for *Death Proof.* The
postfeminist/postmodern surfaces, at work throughout both of these films
neutralize not only gender differences but also the possibility of a genuine
feminist expression. However, one knows *Kill Bill*'s ending, and its
surprising celebration of femininity and motherhood (which, in spite of
Coulthard's critical claims, in my opinion does not detract from its
emotional charge), as Beatrix collapses on the bathroom floor and cries out
at once with gratitude and happiness as well as sadness and post-traumatic
relief. Meanwhile her young daughter, apparently spared the violence of
the two films, watches cartoons on television.[43] Ironic as this ending might
be, it must be taken into account, as it constitutes a somewhat dissonant
coda to an otherwise extravagantly violent spectacle.

It is tempting to return to basics of film psychoanalysis and to interpret
Tarantino's works in terms of trauma theory and post-Lacanian
melancholy which seems to have replaced the spleen and ennui of the
nineteenth century as well as the angst of the post-World War II and
existentialist periods. The twentieth century is already distant, and yet it is
the receptacle of Tarantino's childhood, from which he draws inspiration
and cultural appropriation. What we see here, in a sense, is a Lacanian
reflex, again—to be reunited with the Real, an unreachable state—to
homage the unhomageable and recreate an unattainable past of plenitude.
There is certainly something plausible in this theoretical reference;
encrypted in it, is above all, in my opinion, the independent, strong single
mother: Connie McHugh-Zastoupil, abandoned at age 17 by her husband,
Tony Tarantino, Quentin's father and second-rate actor. She had to fend,
alone, for her genius son Quentin. We glimpse a solitary life in the legend
built around Tarantino, who, in spite or perhaps because of his high IQ,
always fled the contrivances of school and became self-taught—including
by his fabled work as a video store clerk. It is this figure of the single
mother, far more than the male father figure, who is the true place of

inspiration; she is the mother of and in these films, alive in them and through them. It would be a confusing oversimplification to characterize this relationship as Oedipal in any standard Freudian way. The films are rich in uncodified relationships of psychological subtlety and density, nowhere quite so unusual as in the familiar, final pair of *Kill Bill*: the mother overly attentive, and the daughter, tender and loving, yet at the same time strangely distant and indifferent. As for the characters of *Death Proof*, one might see their ennui as connected to the fact that they are parentless children, creatures left in the limbo of pastiche of exploitation cinema. As mentioned earlier, there is a reference made to Shanna's father early on in *Death Proof* (he owns the lakeside house that the group of girls never reach), but it is probably Stuntman Mike who is featured as closest to the incarnation of a father figure, ogre-like and incestuous—hardly wholesome, yet spuriously patriarchal.[44]

As a return of the repressed, feminism seems ultimately to re-emerge as an unexpected term in Tarantino's oeuvre—an unexpected element which might stand as a dimension of the absolute which grants its soul to this cinema otherwise so sleek and preoccupied with the surface of things. If feminism is to be seen as an absolute, we must actually relate it more to modernism than postmodernism—a gesture both surprising and that would enshrine the movement. The idea of a great autonomy of an absolute feminism is a concept and a value whose fundamental renunciation constitutes postfeminism and postmodernism. The latter, according to Fredric Jameson, would seem to have traded the eternal and posterity for the ephemerality of mass culture. This amounts to a devil's pact with the commercial, and an integration into fashion together with febrile attention to fads, marketability, novelty, and the invention of new commodities as well as a nostalgic sensibility, capable even of resurrecting simulacra of modernism itself. Is this to say that Tarantino's cinema can dodge any form of categorization, and that it can be reversibly envisaged as a (c)overt plea for feminism and female empowerment; or, rather, as the bypassing and neutralizing of the debate—and false female liberation through violence?

It is with such open questions and suggestions that I leave Tarantino for the time being, having, hopefully, done a bit more than merely stir the very surface discussed throughout this essay. Before ending, may I stress, once more, the unexpected unavoidability of such new and original contributions to the galaxy of the postmodern sphere, where *Death Proof* is an exemplary instance of the peculiar blurring of feminism and postfeminism.

Works Cited

Atkinson, Mike. "Givers of the Viscera." *Sight & Sound* 17-6 (June 2007): 19-27.

Clover, Carol J. *Men, Women and Chainsaws: Gender in the Modern Horror Film*. Princeton, NJ: Princeton University Press, 1992.

Coulthard, Lisa. "Killing Bill—Rethinking Feminism and Film Violence." In *Interrogating Postfeminism*, edited by Yvonne Tasker and Diane Negra, 153-173. Durham and London: Duke University Press, 2007.

Deleuze, Gilles. *L'Image-Mouvement*. Paris: Minuit, 1983.

Doane, Mary Ann. *Femmes Fatales: Feminism, Film Theory and Psychoanalysis*. New York: Routledge, 1991.

James, Nick. "Welcome to the Grindhouse." *Sight & Sound* 17-6 (June 2007): 16-18.

Jameson, Fredric. *Postmodernism, or, the Cultural Logic of Late Capitalism*. Durham: Duke University Press, 1991.

Lacan, Jacques. *Le Stade du Miroir. Communication donnée à Zürich, le 17 juillet 1949.*
http://pagespersoorange.fr/espace.freud/topos/psycha/psysem/miroir.htm

McRobbie, Angela. "Postfeminism and Popular Culture." In *Interrogating Postfeminism*, edited by Yvonne Tasker and Diane Negra, 27-39. Durham and London: Duke University Press, 2007.

Mills, Jane. "Catch Me if You Can, the Tarantino Legacy." *Bright Films Journal*. http://www.brightlightsfilm.com/36/tarantino1.html.

Mulvey, Laura. *Visual and Other Pleasures*. Bloomington: Indiana University Press, 1989.

Tasker, Yvonne and Diane Negra. "Feminist Politics and Postfeminist Culture." In *Interrogating Postfeminism*, edited by Yvonne Tasker and Diane Negra, 1-23. Durham and London: Duke University Press, 2007.

Verlant, Gilles. *Gainsbourg*. Paris: Albin Michel, 1999.

Notes

[1] It suffices to see the endless string of associations of his name with the concept of postfeminism, even in popular venues such as the internet.

[2] It can be argued that almost all narrative cinema goes, one way or the other, against the grain of Mulvey's argument. Her own films, of which *The Riddles of the Sphynx* (1977) remains the most famous, have enjoyed a rather unambiguous backlash in terms of popularity, both with critics and audiences.

[3] Yvonne Tasker and Diane Negra, "Feminist Politics and Postfeminist Culture" in *Interrogating Postfeminism*, ed. Yvonne Tasker and Diane Negra (Durham and London: Duke University Press, 2007), 4.

[4] Angela McRobbie, "Postfeminism and Popular Culture," in *Interrogating Postfeminism*, ed. Yvonne Tasker and Diane Negra (Durham and London: Duke University Press, 2007), 28.

[5] Tasker, "Feminist Politics and Postfeminist Culture," 8.

[6] Such as social and economic mobility, and sexual independence, set against the ticking of women's biological clocks and the anxieties of celibacy, which is alternately dreaded and celebrated (cf. Angela McRobbie's discussion of *Bridget Jones's Diary*, in "Postfeminism and Popular Culture," 36-38).

[7] Tasker, "Feminist Politics and Postfeminist Culture," 2-3.

[8] Ibid., 6.

[9] After the Asian cinemas, western and action films largely recuperated in *Kill Bill*, *Death Proof* reaches out for inspiration in the world of American B-road race movies such as *Death Race 2000* (1975), horror film atmospheres and more "respectable" classics such as *Bullitt* (1968) and *Vanishing Point* (1971).

[10] Lisa Coulthard, "Killing Bill—Rethinking Feminism and Film Violence," in *Interrogating Postfeminism*, ed. Yvonne Tasker and Diane Negra (Durham and London: Duke University Press, 2007), 158.

[11] As a director, namely for the film *Reservoir Dogs* (1992). For this and the fabled follow-up, *Pulp Fiction* (1994), Tarantino, in collaboration with cinematographer Andrzej Sekula, optioned to use extremely fast film in order to gain light and give his films the gritty quality that relates germanely to their subjects.

[12] A clear reference to the practice of distributors who, in order to enhance a film's commercial value, would re-release it under a different title, and making little changes whatsoever to the rest of the footage (with the exception of the occasional censorship). A notorious example of this would be Lucio Fulci's *The Beyond* (*L'Aldila,* 1981), re-released in the US under the title *Seven Doors of Death*. Incidentally, Tarantino promoted a re-release of the film in the 2000s, under its original title and with all the original footage restored.

[13] Reflexive, first, insofar as it is a conscious re-enactment of a long defunct practice, but reflexive also in its rich network of associations and quotations to titles and imagery of the period alluded to by Tarantino—the 1970s, with which the film establishes clear aesthetic affinities, even though its action takes place in the present day, as an ad for Sofia Coppola's *Marie Antoinette* (2006) seen at one point in the film, testifies. Interestingly enough, Sofia Coppola's film is a reflection on the late 1960s and 1970s, set in pre-revolutionary France.

[14] Since the Internet Movie Database (www.imdb.com) has a fairly comprehensive list of the "trash" films referenced in *Death Proof*, I will not enumerate them here.

[15] As was the ingenious case in Robert Rodriguez's *Planet Terror*, *Death Proof*'s companion piece, where a gigantic ellipsis is created between a lovemaking scene and a shoot'em all gorefest between humans and zombies, by simply mentioning that approximately 20 minutes in the film vanished due to a "missing reel."

[16] Nowhere more conspicuously than in the discussion at the bar between Stuntman Mike and Pam (Rose McGowan).

[17] Butterfly: 'The thing' is everything but.
   Jungle Julia: Your guys like 'the thing'?
   Butterfly: They like it better than no thing!

[18] "The woods are lovely, dark and deep, and I have promises to keep and miles to go before I sleep. Did you hear me, Butterfly? Miles to go before *you* sleep." (emphasis mine)

[19] In Jungle Julia's own terms: "a kind of cute or kind of hot or kind of sexy or better be fucking hysterically funny but not funny looking guy who you could fuck."

[20] As well as a theoretical horror/slasher film cornerstone, as Carol Clover has taught us.

[21] Just as it partakes in a long and well-known tradition of the voyeur psycho-killer, nowhere better illustrated than in the genre's founding texts: *Psycho* (Alfred Hitchcock, 1960) and *Peeping Tom* (Michael Powell, 1960).

[22] The connoisseur will have recognized the connection: Jordan Ladd played one of the main parts in Roth's breakthrough film, *Cabin Fever* (2002).

[23] A favorite locale of the slasher subgenre, ever since cult classics such as *Last House on the Left* (Wes Craven, 1972), *I Spit on Your Grave* (Meir Zarchi, 1977) or, more famously, *Friday the 13th* (Sean S. Cunningham, 1980) and its countless ersatzes and sequels, thereby swiftly alluded to in the background by one of recent American horror's most popular directors.

[24] Joined in the meantime by Lanna Frank, the posse's weed provider, played by real life stuntwoman Monica Staggs.

[25] Stuntman Mike: Do I frighten you? Is it my scar?
Butterfly: It's your car.
Stuntman Mike: It's my Mom's car.

[26] Mimicking the loss of a substantial part of footage, evoking censorship.

[27] He refers to Stuntman Mike as "Frankenstein," a direct nod to Paul Bartel's *Death Race 2000*, in which the main villain is named Frankenstein. Incidentally, this character is played by David Carradine—*Kill Bill*'s title male role.

[28] After what must be the most spectacular car chase in cinema's history, with the smashing of two R-rated (*Scary Movie 4* and *Wolf Creek*) films in the process.

[29] Coulthard,173.

[30] Mike Atkinson, "Givers of the Viscera," *Sight & Sound* 17-6 (June 2007): 20.

[31] A point Clover reprises and with which she concurs, seeing in the gender-bending implications of the slasher's Final Girl figure a more enabling and liberating device than the monolithic implications of the Hollywood machine.

[32] Jane Mills, "Catch me if you can, the Tarantino legacy,"
Bright Films Journal. http://www.brightlightsfilm.com/36/tarantino1.html.

[33] Nick James, "Welcome to the Grindhouse," *Sight & Sound* 17-6 (June 2007): 18.

[34] For a discussion of the close-up in its relationship to castration and synecdoche in Deleuze, see *L'Image-Mouvement*, 135-136. For Lacan, see his *Ecrits*, or, specifically on the Mirror Stage,

http://pagesperso-orange.fr/espace.freud/topos/psycha/psysem/miroir.htm.

[35] What difference does it make, ultimately, that the killer here swaps the knife for a car?

[36] Carol J. Clover, *Men, Women and Chainsaws: Gender in the Modern Horror Film* (Princeton, NJ: Princeton University Press, 1992), 9.

[37] Ibid., 15.

[38] Coulthard, 159.

[39] Particularly in the extensive discussion partaking to *I Spit On Your Grave* in Clover (see, particularly, pp. 114-124).

[40] Coulthard, 159.

[41] Ibid., 171.

[42] It is interesting to note, as Coulthard points out, that the murdered male characters' outer physical appearances are not altered, as opposed to the female characters, who quite literally tear each other up in grueling and bloody duels.

[43] Cartoons which do also feature, it is worth noting, stylized, seemingly innocuous scenes of violence, but violence all the same.

[44] While Stuntman Mike is also, in the slasher and psycho-killer genre tradition, an adult in body with an immature mind, twisted sexuality and probable unresolved Oedipal entanglements. After all, it his mother's car he claims to be driving. The tone of the remark may be jocular, but its Freudian implications are obviously darker and much deadlier than first meets the eye.

IV:

RE-INSCRIBING THE FEMALE SUBJECT IN HISTORY

CHAPTER TEN

DURAS RAVAGED, RAVISHED...RAVISHING

GEORGIANA M. M. COLVILE[*]

No one has captured the awful mirth of Marguerite Duras's face, the beauty of her joy.[1]
—Duras and Mazabrard

You only have to look at the Medusa straight on to see her. And she's not deadly. She's beautiful and she's laughing.[2]
—Cixous

These two epigraphs, filled with contradictions, merely skim the surface of *das Unheimliche,*[3] as it emanates from the works of Marguerite Duras. Penelope's labors, textual fabrics that fray and self-destruct at their creator's will, under the gaze of the fascinated reader-spectator. The little phonemes establishing the *différance* between destruction and deconstruction are but a starting point for the present essay. First, the complexity of the prefix *de,* from the Latin *dis,* which indicates not only distance, separation, privation, or place of origin, but also intensification. The double meaning of *con,* from the Latin *cum* (with) or *cunnus* (the female genitals), echoes this opposition. The one syllable, as paradoxical and reversible as the term *unheimlich,* from a Freudian perspective, performs absence and presence, emptiness and plenitude, feminine and masculine. It is precisely of this oppositional oscillation that Marguerite Duras's writing is born.

The case of Duras, like that of Kafka, is psychoanalytic, hard to grasp, difficult to follow. Her phenomenal corpus (around a hundred works: novels, essays, plays, screenplays, films) has inspired a metacorpus of writings almost as large and varied, mostly by women. Whether written by psychoanalysts such as Jacques Lacan and Marcelle Marini, writers or literary critics such as Julia Kristeva, Maurice Blanchot, Michèle de

[*] Université François Rabelais, Tours, France. A French version of this essay appeared in *Gradiva* 2, no. 4 (2001): 103-118. It appears here for the first time in English, translated by Gwendolyn Wells.

Montrelay, Béatrice Didier, Sharon Willis, and Trista Selous, or film critics such as Madeleine Borgomano, Marie-Claire Ropars-Wuilleumier, and Elizabeth Lyon, a dual reaction, combining fear or horror with fascination or seduction, pervades most of these metatexts: in short, the Medusa effect, to which I shall return.

The interpretation of Duras's oeuvre often seems to function like a transference between analyst and analysand, a dynamic that in turn reflects the "work" of the text. In addition to her primary drive to write almost incessantly in order to fill a void, like Blanchot, Duras regularly published interviews and autobiographical essays about her books and films, thus imparting a personal focus to this secondary production. Her own metatexts are part of an interminable process of re-membering and re-play:

> She uses the interview, that preeminent form of autobiographical confession, to express the part of experience that is irreducible to writing.[4]

Duras's corpus reads like an endless series of variations on her own version of Vinteuil's "little phrase," whose musical traces, in the form of a song by Piaf, a sonatina by Diabelli, or the lament of the Cambodian beggar woman, for example, punctuate the "search" for the prelapsarian time and place so perfectly encapsulated in Claude Roy's term, *la Durasie* ("Durasia").[5]

Specifically, Duras's quest is rooted in the time and place of her childhood in French Indochina. Her mother's Sisyphean situation already dominates one of her earliest novels, *Un Barrage contre le Pacifique* (1950; trans. *The Sea Wall*, 1967). Everyone knows the story of the widowed Madame Donnadieu, worn to the bone by work—as a schoolteacher by day, by night as the pianist at the Eden Cinema— struggling against poverty and floodtides to feed her three children, endlessly self-sacrificing, exploited by the land registry, despised by her colonial compatriots, driven half mad by chastity. This feared and adulated figure, gentle one moment and demented the next, continually haunts her daughter's fictional universe, where daily life is shaped by madness. Take, for example, the conversation between two characters in *Détruire, dit-elle* (1969; tr. *Destroy, She Said*, 1970). Stein has just met Alissa, the wife of his friend Max Thor, for the first time. Stein calmly remarks: "You didn't tell me Alissa was insane."[6] "I didn't know," replies Max Thor. Alissa/Alice. In Wonderland, the Cheshire Cat tells the little girl: "we are all mad here."[7] This is more or less what Duras's readers discover. Alice-like, Alissa manipulates the other characters like so many playing cards or pawns on a chessboard. It is she who pronounces the key word, "destroy."

The film *Détruire, dit-elle*, released shortly after the novel of the same
year, was Duras's second as writer-director. It soon became unavailable
and remained so for years. Madeleine Borgomano referred to it as "one of
Duras's lost films" and wrote:

> if cinema is considered to be an enterprise of systematic destruction, isn't it
> logical that no effort whatsoever should be made to preserve films, and that
> their fate should be to dissolve and disappear after destroying themselves?[8]

Still, a trace remained in the very title, *Détruire, dit-elle*. The film has
recently been retrieved and reprinted on DVD by Benoît Jacob Vidéo
(June 2008). The phrase, now almost synonymous with Duras,
reverberates through the corpus of criticism surrounding her work.
Blanchot, for example, in a short essay entitled "Détruire," conceives the
term as an oracle emerging out of chaos, inevitably linked with love—
"one must love in order to destroy"[9]—and mysteriously associated with
music:

> It (the word 'destroy') comes to us from far, far away, through the
> immense rumor of music that has been destroyed, perhaps deceptively, as
> it happens, too, with the beginning of all music...It is not just music
> (beauty) that proclaims its own destruction and, at the same time, its own
> rebirth. It is, more mysteriously, destruction *as* music which we both
> witness and take part in. [10]

Destruction, madness, love, and music are superimposed in a cinematic
lap dissolve, forming the fictive, fragmented portrait of the mother.
According to Cixous: "The mother, too, is a metaphor."[11] In Duras's case,
she is the metaphor of metaphors, the primal scene, the tragic flaw, the
inexhaustible source of writing and her own self-destructive force. All of
Duras's dichotomies—mobility/immobility, fear/fascination, love/hate,
Eros/Thanatos—can be traced back to the relationship with the mother, as
Kristeva indicates with regard to *L'Amant* (1984; tr. *The Lover,* 1985):

> the mother is, in fact, the archetype of the mad women who people the
> Durassian universe.... Hatred locks mother and daughter together in a vise
> of passion that emerges as the source of the mysterious silence that streaks
> through the writing.... Out of fear of her mother's madness, the novelist
> eliminates the latter, separating from her with a violence no less murderous
> than that of the mother who beats her prostituted daughter. [12]

And yet, through the reversibility that cancels out and destroys
whatever precedes it, the mother in *The Lover* is also "my mother, my

love"[13], which in *India Song* turns into "Music, my love." As Michèle de Montrelay says:

> What folly to build a wall against the sea, which will always be the strongest, which cannot *not* engulf everything.[14]

The double negative speaks volumes. The sea (*la mer*) and the mother (*la mère*) are inextricable, destruction indestructible. The sea wall at Vinh Long is set up as a screen memory. Instead of being a reassuring adult point of reference capable of helping the child pass through the mirror stage, the mother appears either as a body in pieces (in Lacanian terms) scattered throughout the daughter's specular corpus, or as the usurper of her imago, at the center of the textual mirror, as is the case with the grandmother in *Savannah Bay*. At the beginning of *The Lover*, the narrator announces: "The story of my life doesn't exist."[15] A few pages further on, she describes a photograph (probably imaginary): "My mother is in the center of the image."[16]

As a way of gauging the impact of this particular mother we may enlist André Green's theory of "blank mourning for the dead mother." Green attributes this psychic state to the child who has just lost his/her mother. Rather than her actual death or physical departure, the loss may consist of the mother's withdrawal of cathexis following a bereavement she herself has experienced, which has rendered her incapable of loving her child (Madame Donnadieu had lost her husband, her fortune, and then the younger of her two sons). As a result, the child-subject presents symptoms such as identification with the "dead" mother, feelings of guilt over her suffering, hatred, and fantasies of the primal scene, among others. The subject often finds refuge in narcissism and in sublimation through artistic creation, preferably in the form of narrative writing. It is this latter configuration that comes through in Duras's work, right down to her word choices, as Danielle Bajomée points out:

> They [Duras's words] imperceptibly build an asceticism of insignificance, bespeaking a striving toward an infinitude that is relentlessly invoked, in a trajectory that creates meaning and manifests the dread of being ripped apart, the insistence of the cut. Everywhere, morcellation, discohesion, and disaggregation dominate and are inscribed, again and again, in recurring scenes that show how the child relates to the mother and the mother to the child.[17]

The mother's influence is at the origin of the Medusa effect, which I shall discuss further on. In *Les Yeux verts* (1987; tr. *Green Eyes,* 1990), Duras tells of a meaningful dream she had of her mother:

> I said to her: "But how is that possible? You were dead." She told me: "I made you believe that to permit you to write all this."[18]

The plot of *Savannah Bay* (1982; tr. 1992) develops around a mother who really is dead. Her daughter tries to bring her back to life by seeking affection from her grandmother, who, for her part, is grief-stricken, frozen into the attitude described by Green. The play opens with a heart-rending song by Piaf after which the granddaughter cries: "she killed herself, that woman,"[19] referring to both her mother and the singer. The sound of crashing waves completes the triple maternal metaphor (via the *mer/mère* homophony). The character of the grandmother was an intentional portrait of Duras's mother, whom Madeleine Renaud, at the age of eighty-three, imitated to perfection. Duras, bowled over by the performance, thereafter referred to the actress as "my theatre mother."[20]

The personal and the political are profoundly interwoven in Duras's work. The love relationship in *Hiroshima mon amour* (1960) causes the protagonist, marked for life, to relive her individual tragic past in the context of Hiroshima, fifteen years after the war. The French woman and her Japanese lover become emblematic of Occupied France and of the Asian city pulverized by the atomic bomb. In the end, they are reduced to the names of their native cities: Hiroshima and Nevers. According to Kristeva:

> public events are depicted through the prism of madness. . . . In our time, the only event is human madness.[21]

The film *India Song* (1974) depicts the wife of the French ambassador in Calcutta, Anne-Marie Stretter, plunged into suicidal despair by the dire poverty and deterioration of India as well as by the tedium of her own decadent life. The *untouchable* Cambodian beggar woman who wanders along the Ganges, sick, starving, and singing in some incomprehensible language of her pain, her lost child, and her lost homeland, becomes the double of the ambassador's wife; together they evoke colonialism in all its horror. Later, Duras concluded that the beggar woman, with whom she was obsessed, and who figures in several works, was linked to the crematory furnaces of Auschwitz.[22] The personal/political dichotomy also stems from the mother. During a rehearsal of *Savannah Bay* Duras described her mother as being "emblematic of social injustice"—that is, similar to the beggar woman.

For all her shifts in political affiliation, on an ideological level Duras seems consistently to have favored the concept of the individual as a multiple subject, in the sense of the *schizo-analysis* posited by Deleuze and Guattari. An acute awareness of tensions between the sexes and of problems specific to women is an inherent part of the multiple subject in Duras's works.

In "Le Rire de la Méduse" (1975; tr. "The Laugh of the Medusa," 1976), her manifesto advocating a future *écriture féminine,* Hélène Cixous acknowledged three writers already engaged in this practice: Colette, Marguerite Duras, and Jean Genet.[23] Duras, like Colette, was already "writing the body" in her work well before the 1970s and the women's liberation movement. The phrase "woman is desire" often comes up in interviews with Duras, as do observations like this one: "I see the book as extracted from the body... or as an exercise of the body."[24] She firmly believed that women's writing radically differs from men's:

> We do not write from at all the same place as men. And when women do not write from the place of desire, they are in the place of plagiarism.[25]

For a deeper look into the relationship between the feminine, the sexual, and the sociopolitical, I now propose to examine two versions of a photograph of the author as a young woman that first appeared in 1975, in cropped form, in a collection of essays and interviews compiled during the final editing of *India Song.*[26] It shows Duras as an adolescent, dressed Asian-style in a silk tunic and trousers and wearing sandals, sitting at an angle on a very ornate little loveseat, her hands clasped together, looking straight into the camera, a hint of a smile on her lips. Behind her to the left stands another person whose head is cropped out of the frame. The caption reads: "Age 17, Sadec (Cochinchina)." Two years later, the same image was reproduced in Michelle Porte's illustrated interview with Duras, *Les Lieux de Marguerite Duras.*[27] This time the photograph is not cropped and shows the second person in her entirety. She is a young Vietnamese woman about the same age as the French girl, standing behind the seat with her right hand resting on the back, the other hand behind Duras's arm. Her attitude suggests a certain familiarity or even friendship. Her eyes are wide open, like her companion's, but slightly slanted, and she is looking off to the left. The two girls are dressed identically, wearing the same medallions, the same bracelets; both wear their hair pulled back. They could be twins. Only their respective positions and their gazes differentiate them. On the facing page Duras identifies and situates herself: "Here, age sixteen. This is in Sadek, along the Mekong. My dress was green."

According to Susan Sontag: "All photographs are *memento mori*"[28] and, at the same time: "Photographs shock insofar as they show something novel,"[29] which suggests that the photographic message remains current through its ability to communicate the truth. Roland Barthes, on the other hand, while establishing the relationship between the immediacy of the image and the past that it represents, defines it first and foremost as being fixed in time and space: "the photograph institutes…a consciousness of the thing's having-been-there."[30] Here, the juxtaposition of two versions of the same photograph alerts us to a lack. So, too, the V of Lol V. Stein, which Lacan interprets as a pair of scissors,[31] or the double T of Anne-Marie Stretter, a character whom Michèle de Montrelay describes as "trenchant" (*tranchant*) and whose identity fades into an incisive place-name: Calcutta. Trista Selous devotes an interesting chapter of her book to the "blanks" that play such an important role in Duras's constant replaying of the past through writing. The two adolescent girls in the photograph, placed slightly off to one side, on either side of the wing chair, leave a blank space in the middle.

In *The Lover,* Duras tells of how her mother regularly took her children to a photographer's studio.[32] Why, on this particular occasion, did the picture include a stranger, one who remains blank and anonymous, since she is not identified in any text? The resemblance between the two girls becomes all the more unsettling, uncanny. Duras made the following remark to Dominique Noguez:

> Because of my mother's profession, we were lucky enough to be relegated to the rank of the natives. That's why I wrote and watched. I didn't belong to the milieu of the important officials, I merely observed them.[33]

The absence of social status thus provided access to the dubious privilege of voyeurism. In the photograph, Duras's large, intense eyes are contrasted with the eyes of the young Asian girl—the only perceptible racial distinction between the two. They are at once the same, and other. But while Duras claims that her mother preferred the companionship of indigenous women and that she herself had only Vietnamese girl friends until the age of fifteen,[34] she also wrote that despite the family's extreme poverty, which compelled them to eat shorebirds and other game they could hunt in the marshes, those frugal meals were nevertheless prepared and served by a houseboy, and the Donnadieu children sometimes indulged in the luxury of refusing to eat their food.[35] Even if they never felt completely French, Marguerite and her brothers were never completely Vietnamese either.

The resemblance between the two girls in the photograph is heightened by their fresh complexions and silk clothes. The Chinese man in *The Lover* admires the young French girl's skin, whose softness and delicacy have been preserved by bathing in rainwater, eating a diet of fresh fish and fruit, and wearing loose clothing made of silk or cotton. By contrast, says the lover: "the women in France have hard, almost rough skin."[36] The girl was decidedly not completely French. The silk (*soie*) worn by the two girls can be interpreted as a trace of Duras's lost Vietnamese self (*soi*). In fact, her self seems to be inscribed somewhere between the little princess taken by her mother to be photographed and the Other, the nameless Vietnamese girl, in the blank space of memory, the sign of absence.

In Duras's oeuvre, the death drive is sometimes expressed through the self-destructive work of her films, and at other times through a regression toward the traumatic moment of her separation from her mother, when she was sent to France at the age of eighteen, leaving Asia forever: "I missed my mother physically, like a little girl."[37] Ever after, she sought to recreate the imaginary prelinguistic space of the lost mother-Asia—or *Merasie*.

All of Duras's heroines, like Lol V. Stein, Anne-Marie Stretter and Alissa, suffer from an atrophy of their personality beginning at eighteen, and all of them are at least partly mad. Her entire oeuvre, including her interviews and metatexts, bears the mark of *Spaltung*—splitting or dissociation—which is the crucial symptom of schizophrenia. Most of her works are psychodramas and correspond to various schizophrenic patterns.

According to Laplanche and Pontalis, the term "schizophrenia" encompasses a series of psychoses whose three main manifestations are *hebephrenia* (mental atrophy beginning in adolescence), *paranoia,* and *catatonia.* We have already invoked Green's theory in connection with the recourse to narration in the subject who has had a "dead mother." Marguerite Duras sees an analogy between "complete writing" and madness: "Only madmen write completely."[38] Genius is never far from madness. To "write completely" would no doubt mean to write outside of and beyond all language, and there are no completely mad geniuses, not even Nerval, Lautréamont, Artaud, Céline, Unica Zürn, or Duras. However, what might be seen as the eruption of partial madness in her texts explains the blanks in Duras's writing, as well as her fascination with the limits of madness and language.

"Marguerite Duras is afraid. Marguerite Duras is frightening" (*"Marguerite Duras a peur. Marguerite Duras fait peur"*).[39] "Fear" (*peur*) is in fact one of the words that Duras uses most frequently. The novel

Emily L. (1987; tr. 1989) deals mainly with the narrator's multiple manifestations of paranoia. The setting is particularly interesting, because it could contain or refer to almost any of Duras's texts. It opens: "It began with the fear."[40] And it ends:

> And I said, too, that one must write without correcting, not necessarily fast, at top speed, but at one's own pace and according to what one is experiencing at that moment, throw what one writes outside, abuse it, almost, yes, abuse it, and remove nothing from its useless mass, nothing, just leave it as part of the whole, and temper nothing, neither its speed nor its slowness, just leave it all as it first appears. (my translation)

"Self" (*soi*) and "nothing" (*rien*) are used in identical structures, in the manner of a photographic double exposure. This definition of writing is similar to the "having-been-there" that Barthes applies to photography. "Abuse" could mean cut, crop, or mutilate, which brings us back to the two versions of the photograph analyzed above, and the double linguistic message that arises out of the variant spellings Sadec/Sadek. An anagrammatic deconstruction yields, in French: *"le K(cas) Sade"*—"the case of Sade." A backwards (specular) reading of Sadec with a C gives the French *"cédas"*—"you yielded." When these two readings are juxtaposed, the resulting sadomasochistic configuration creates yet another textual mirror. The adolescent girl in *The Lover* is perceived as a child prostitute; the Vice-Consul in *India Song* is from Lahore (La Whore), and Duras referred to Anne-Marie Stretter, her favorite character, as "my prostitution." Furthermore, in her chapter on *Le Ravissement de Lol V. Stein* (1964; tr. *The Ravishing of Lol Stein,* 1966), Martha Noël Evans writes:

> In *Le Ravissement de Lol V. Stein,* as Duras uncovers and explores the indecency of female writing, she discloses that indecency as a cover for something else: the hidden whoring of language.[41]

In other words, Duras's referential conflict, between the endlessly self-sacrificing mother (Madame Donnadieu) and the dangerous whore (Elisabeth Striedter, the model for Anne-Marie Stretter), marked her passage into the symbolic and is reiterated throughout her oeuvre. This fault line becomes the underlying theme of the "Indian cycle," from the novel *The Ravishing of Lol Stein* to the film *Son Nom de Venise dans Calcutta désert* (1976). Despite the fact that the "Vietnamese" texts—*The Sea Wall, L'Eden Cinéma* (1977; tr. *The Eden Cinema,* 1988), *Savannah Bay,* and *The Lover*—are more explicitly autobiographical, Duras was passionately attached to the transposed characters of the other cycle and closely identified with the specular trio made up of Anne-Marie Stretter, the Vice-Consul, and the beggar woman.

The Indian cycle begins with *The Ravishing of Lol Stein,* and "The fear began with Lol V. Stein"[42]—to such an extent that Duras screamed as she was writing it.[43] This extraordinary novel has prompted a considerable flow of critical ink. Its title is just as famous, and even more enigmatic, than that of *Destroy, She Said.* The word "ravishing" conjoins active and passive, positive and negative, perpetuating the contradiction and self-destruction inherent in both the text and its protagonist. The verb "to ravish" can mean kidnap, rape, or cause to disappear, but also enchant, fulfill, make ecstatic. The figurine "Lou Ravi" in the Provençal crèche, transfixed in adoration, is also the village idiot, a kind of Shakespearean fool. Lacan suggests that "the ravisher is Marguerite Duras, and we are the ravished."[44] The rape of the reader seems plausible, in that ecstasy or *jouissance* is denied him or her. The protagonist's name perpetuates the process of dissociation or opposition at the level of the signifier: Lol liquified or Stein petrified.[45] Lol is short for Dolores, pain—the pain she was unable to feel at the age of eighteen as spectator of the primal scene at the ball in T. Beach, near the town where she was born, S. Thala (from the Greek *Thalassa,* or "sea"—another intimation of *mer/mère*). Lol remained frozen on the spot, until the arrival of her mother, the *primal screen,* liberated her long *primal scream,* as she watched, fascinated, the *primal scene* of her fiancé Michael Richardson dancing with the beautiful femme fatale, Anne-Marie Stretter, before leaving for India with her forever. Once the couple had vanished from her visual field, Lol fainted, went mad, and thereafter was made of stone *(Stein)*. That night, Lol's friend and alter ego, Tatiana Karl, stayed by her side all evening, a mute witness like the Vietnamese girl in the photograph.

After her supposed recovery, Lol lived at U. Bridge with her husband, Jean Bedford, and their three unnamed children, in a nondescript, orderly, dull existence, as empty as the postmodern profusion of signifiers formed by the endlessly repeated given names. Ten years later, we return to S. Thala. There Lol meets Jacques Hold, who reveals his identity, hitherto concealed in the anonymous, unreliable narrator. Lol renews her acquaintance with Tatiana Karl, who is now Madame Pierre Beugner and Jacques Hold's mistress. All these names/non-persons intercirculate constantly. Jacques Hold, ravished by Lol, wants not only to ravish her body, but also to take *hold* of the past and the young woman's lost/stolen identity. It is Lol, however, who will make use of him to reproduce the primal scene of the ball, in order to project for herself the lack she had become that night, the unpronounced word, the absent sign, caught between language and madness, on the screen of the "cinema of Lol V. Stein,"[46] which Duras turned into *India Song* ten years later. Lol regularly goes and lies down in the nearby rye field to watch the lighted window of the hotel room where the specular couple, Tatiana Karl and Jacques Hold, make love. Jacques spies the spy from the window. He then conceals Tatiana's head under the shroudlike sheet and takes possession of the decapitated object of his desire: Lol V. Stein. Jacques and Lol (the non-couple) make a pilgrimage to T. Beach, the site of the ballroom. They finally make love in a hotel—or rather, Jacques Hold rapes Lol, who remains more *Stein* than ever. After this double fiasco, they return to S. Thala and shut themselves in with Tatiana, he in a hotel room, she by proxy in the rye field, thus reconstituting the infernal triangle of their intrapsychic cinematic apparatus. Evidently afflicted with *hebephrenia*, Lol suffers an attack of *paranoia* during the trip to T. Beach, before falling back into her habitual state of *catatonia*. The constant shifting of verb tenses, between the perfect, preterite, and imperfect past tenses and the present, muddles the registers of the narration, story and discourse, further undermining the credibility of Jacques Hold's narrative, which is largely dependent on what he has been told by others, sowing doubt and lack throughout the text of the novel.

Andrew Wyeth's well-known painting, *Christina's World* (1948), provides a perfect iconographic mise-en-abyme of Lol V. Stein's desire. The figure of the disabled young woman lying in a field, seen from behind, straining toward a house on the horizon, is an exact re-presentation of Lol focalized by the lens of an omniscient camera, the eye of Duras or the implied reader—Lol observed from behind, as she observes the lovers. The desire of Lol (whose infirmity is mental) is situated precisely there, in the impossibility of seeing herself, the absent sign, as excluded from the love scene, just as Michael Richardson and Anne-Marie Stretter saw her, at the very moment they left the ball and Lol forever.

Duras later made the connection between Lol's primal scene and her own: some time between the ages of seven and eleven, she learned that a young man had committed suicide because of Elizabeth Striedter, the model for Anne-Marie Stretter. This female figure was thus a "giver of death," as well as a seductress who experienced sexual pleasure, *jouissance,* unlike Duras's mother, who lived in abstinence. The tension between Eros and Thanatos, in the form of a direct connection between love and murder, is a constant throughout Duras's oeuvre.

The *Ravishing of Lol Stein* serves as a prologue to the "Indian cycle." The next novel, *Le Vice-consul* (1965; tr. *The Vice-Consul,* 1968), is the first in which the action proper takes place in India. This novel prefigures the screenplay for *India Song* (1973) and the film made the following year. This series of works is structured around Anne-Marie Stretter's deadly dull daily life, and then her premature death, in Calcutta, as well as a new character, the Vice-Consul, with his shady past and mad passion for Anne-Marie Stretter expressed in a long, inhuman scream. He too will die of love. The beggar woman's sad, mad song, emblematic of the obscene poverty constantly present behind the scene in India, punctuates the film with an intensity that becomes almost obsessive.

In the third novel, *L'Amour* (1971), Michael Richardson returns to S. Thala after Anne-Marie Stretter's death. There he finds Lol V. Stein, now an errant old madwoman who, like Truffaut's Adèle Hugo (*L'Histoire d'Adèle H.*, 1975), no longer even recognizes the object of her former passion. This novel also prefigures the film *La Femme du Gange* (1973). Duras claimed each film destroyed the corresponding novel. She completed the obliteration of the entire cycle by making the final film, *Son Nom de Venise dans Calcutta désert* (1976). The title refers to the Vice-Consul's scream and Anne-Marie Stretter's Venetian origins.

Duras made that experimental film by combining the sound track from *India Song,* intact, with new footage shot at the old Château de Rothschild, which had been abandoned after Goering occupied it during the war and was later gutted. The film is a series of close-up shots of cracked walls, broken mirrors, gaping doors, windows, and fireplaces—in short, empty spaces devoid of human presence, with the exception of a brief appearance by three women toward the end. Already, *India Song* had a schizophrenic structure in which sound and image were dissociated. There, the characters move like so many zombies, especially when they dance at the reception, in a continuation of Lol V. Stein's ball. A whole range of disembodied voices—those of the characters, the female narrators, and unidentifiable others—indicates that they are all dead, mere images, a rhythmic restaging of the past before a mirror. It is a fresco of the colonial decadence of India, on the verge of dissolution, reminiscent of Fellini's *Roma* (1971). *India Song* achieves aesthetic perfection and fascinates the viewer, with its effect of symmetry created by the omnipresent mirror, the harmony of colors, the retro 1920s décor, the deathly beauty of the characters, Carlos d'Alessio's delicious blues, and the exotic song of the unseen beggar woman. *Son Nom de Venise* erases all that beauty and novelistic reverie; like the opening scenes of Resnais's *Nuit et brouillard* (1955; *Night and Fog*), this film brutally inscribes the traces of death. Duras expressed her own fear in the face of the destructive mechanism unleashed by her films:

What a career I would have if each time I make something, it kills whatever precedes it—dreadful.

Quelle carrière je ferais si à chaque fois que je fais quelque-chose, ça tue la précédente, affreux.[47]

One is struck by the shifting verb modes and tenses and the use, in the French, of *ça*—the *id:* desire kills. After *Les Enfants* (1984), Duras made the decision not to shoot any more films:

I said to myself that that was enough, what with my films in tatters, dispersed, without a contract, lost—that it wasn't worth making a career of negligence to that extent.[48]

It is interesting to note that it is a character in a film, the Vice-Consul, a sort of Shakespearean fool and a projection of the *corps morcelé,* a body "made out of bits and pieces... a bit like a Picasso,"[49] who, for an instant, manages to "write completely" through his madman's scream.

In an attempt to avoid falling into the trap of a mimetic Durassian replay, I propose a final mise-en-abyme. At the opening of *The Lover,* a longtime friend, a man, upon seeing the narrator–implied author for the first time in years, remarks upon her *ravaged* face. He recalls her past beauty, but declares: "Rather than your face as a young woman, I prefer your face as it is now. Ravaged."[50] The adjective echoes and evokes the faceless film, *Son Nom de Venise dans Calcutta désert.* After this unusual homage, the narrator/Duras describes the sudden, premature aging of her face when she was eighteen, as happens to Lol's face, then returns abruptly to the present: *"j'ai un visage détruit"*—"I have a ravaged face."[51] These two faces—the ravishing and the ravaged—are superimposed in most of Duras's female characters.

In French, *le cas ravage* ("the case of 'ravage'") might allude to Duras's ravaged face and also, by homophony, to the sixteenth-century Italian painter Caravaggio (known in French as "Le Caravage"), who painted a self-portrait in the guise of Medusa. Louis Marin's ingenious study, *Détruire la peinture* (1977; tr. *To Destroy Painting,* 1995), has provided me with a new ruse, a shield of Perseus that will enable me to penetrate a bit further into the enigma of Duras without fear of being turned to stone. Marin's title takes up Poussin's disdainful witticism summing up Caravaggio's aspirations. The similarity between *Détruire la peinture* and the *Détruire dit-elle* that critics constantly apply to Duras is readily apparent. As we have already seen, Duras, like Anne-Marie

Stretter, often played the role of a "giver of death" in and with regard to her own oeuvre.

Barthes likens Medusa to the *Doxa,* or public opinion[52] that is, to a generalized reflection or echo. In the Greek myth, the Gorgon Medusa, unlike her two sisters, was mortal. Originally, she was ravishing, stunningly beautiful thanks to her incomparable tresses, later to be turned into snakes. Tatiana Karl, in *The Ravishing of Lol Stein,* and the narrator of *The Lover* are both endowed with lavish, silky locks. The hair of the narrator in *The Lover* was cropped before she began to write. Marin cites Ovid, who explains that the legendary Medusa was first considered a monster, and then as the victim of a metamorphosis, a punishment by Athena whose jealousy she had aroused. Marin emphasizes Medusa's hybridity:

> We have, then, two Medusas in one: a horrible monster as well as a striking beauty: the fascination of contraries mixed together.[53]

Freud had already interpreted Medusa's petrifying effect as the meeting point between the paralysis of terror and the erection of fascination and desire.[54] According to Michèle de Montrelay, Jacques Hold is stunned—*médusé*—upon meeting Lol V. Stein, just as Lol herself was turned to stone at the sight of the dancers in the primal scene. Perseus was able to decapitate Medusa, without looking at her, thanks to the ruse of using his shield as a reflective screen, forcing the monster to see her own image and fall into the trap of self-petrification. Marin maintains that Caravaggio captured the very instant of her metamorphosis, in which she sees herself and reproduces the same expression of horror she has seen on the faces of her victims at the moment of death:

> She bears the same terrifying gaze that these victims did not have time to perceive; she voices the same savage cry that they did not have time to hear.[55]

Marin rightly emphasizes the fact that Caravaggio's "Gorgon who has just petrified herself" is a self-portrait. Under the tangle of snakes is the artist's face, his terrorized/terrifying eyes gazing simultaneously straight ahead and slightly off to the side. The expression is freshly fixed in time and space, for the head has just been severed, in a powerful evocation of castration, like the concealed head of Tatiana in *The Ravishing of Lol Stein* and the cropped hair of the narrator in *The Lover.* According to Jean Clair:

The violent gesture of decapitation is the very process of identification, that of the individual's maturation, inasmuch as he must necessarily go through the paranoid act of having to slay the Gorgon.[56]

Returning to Caravaggio's painting, the open mouth recalls the impotent screams of Lol and the Vice-Consul, inscribing the feminine *non-dit*—the unsaid, unsayable—an O between two L's. It is tempting, in retrospect, to read in Caravaggio's painting a silent avowal of his own feminine nature, condensed with fear of the *vagina dentata.*

Commissioned by Cardinal del Monte, the painting was executed on an actual shield, just as in the myth, the head of the dead Medusa was reproduced on Athena's shield at the goddess's demand. Metaphorically speaking, Duras tirelessly painted and repainted her Gorgon's face on the empty page or screen, shields on which the dazzling beauty of the author as a young girl and the portrait of the (rav)aged novelist meet and merge. The Medusa effect of this hybrid face stems in part from the artist's constant replaying of it:

> The very movement of reflection, revision, reconsidering, thus produces a sense of malaise, disquiet, strangeness, that comes from the fact that what we discover by going back, by reconsidering, rather than delighting us, stuns and paralyzes us.[57]

The reader-spectator is maintained in the role of Jacques Hold. Women painters have long turned to self-portraiture as a way of countering their negative inscription, by society and psychology, as absent. Athena used her petrifying shield to protect herself from her enemies. Duras used hers in an interminable attempt to exorcise the dual mother/whore specter. Marin deciphers Caravaggio's iconic text as a condensation of enunciated and enunciation, form and content.[58] Representation, like Perseus' shield—and in this case, the representation *is* a shield—confronts Medusa's ruse with a counter-ruse. The ephemeral, the unnameable, and the petrification process can thus be captured and communicated through art.

The beauty of Marguerite Duras's language wards off and transcends the petrifying madness inscribed in her texts. The destruction perpetuated from one film to the next occurs as swiftly as the mortal blow delivered by Perseus, and yet, each time, the precursor text remains, a trace of the fatal moment, like the head on the shield...

Translated from the French by Gwendolyn Wells

Works Cited

Translator's Note: Many of the French references cited in this article have been translated into English, and quotations here have generally been excerpted from these published translations. In a few instances when the discussion required a very close rendering of the French, I have modified an extant translation or substituted my own, so indicating in parentheses.

L'Arc 98 (1985). *Marguerite Duras.*

Armel, Aliette. "Dossier Marguerite Duras et interview de l'écrivain." *Magazine Littéraire* 278 (1990): 16-59.

Bajomée, Danielle. "Veiller sur le sens absent." *Magazine Littéraire* 278 (1990): 32-34.

Barthes, Roland. "Rhétorique de l'image." Translated by Richard Howard as "Rhetoric of the Image" in *The Responsibility of Forms,* 27-30 (New York: Hill and Wang, 1985).

—. *Roland Barthes par Roland Barthes.* Paris: Seuil, 1975. Translated by Richard Howard as *Barthes by Roland Barthes.* New York: Farrar, Straus, and Giroux, 1977.

Borgomano, Madeleine. *L'Ecriture filmique de Marguerite Duras.* Paris: Albatros, 1985.

Carroll, Lewis. *Alice's Adventures in Wonderland and Through the Looking Glass.* New York: Bantam Classic Edition, 1981.

Clair, Jean. *Méduse.* Paris: Gallimard, 1989.

Cixous, Hélène. "Le Rire de la Méduse" (1975). Translated by Keith Cohen and Paula Cohen as "The Laugh of the Medusa." *Signs* 1, no. 4 (Summer 1976): 875-893.

Duras, Marguerite. *L'Amant.* Paris: Minuit, 1984. Translated by Barbara Bray as *The Lover.* New York: Random House, 1985.

—. *Un Barrage contre le Pacifique.* Paris: Gallimard, 1950. Translated by Herma Briffault as *The Sea Wall.* New York: Farrar, Straus & Giroux, 1985, c. 1952.

—. *Détruire, dit-elle.* Paris: Minuit, 1969. Translated by Barbara Bray as *Destroy, She Said.* New York: Grove Press, 1970.

—. *Détruire, dit-elle* (film). Ancinex, Madeleine Films, 1969.

—. *L'Eden Cinéma.* Paris: Minuit, 1977. Translated by Barbara Bray as *The Eden Cinema,* in *Eden Cinéma, version scénique.* Paris: Actes Sud-Papiers, 1988.

—. *Emily L.* Paris: Minuit, 1987. Translated by Barbara Bray as *Emily L.* New York: Pantheon Books, 1989.

—. *India Song* (film). Sunchild Productions, Valio, 1975.

—. *Le Ravissement de Lol V. Stein*. Paris: Gallimard, 1964. Translated by Richard Seaver as *The Ravishing of Lol Stein*. New York: Grove Press, 1966.

—. *Savannah Bay*. Paris: Minuit, 1982. Translated by Howard Limoli as *Savannah Bay*, in *Agatha, Savannah Bay: Two Plays by Marguerite Duras*. Sausalito, CA: Post-Apollo Press, 1992.

—. *Les Yeux verts*. Paris: Cahiers du Cinéma, 1987. Translated by Carol Barko as *Green Eyes*. New York: Columbia University Press, 1990.

Duras, Marguerite, et al. *Marguerite Duras*. Paris: Albatros, 1975.

Duras, Marguerite, and Xavière Gauthier. *Les Parleuses*. Paris: Minuit, 1974. Translated by Katharine A. Jensen as *Woman to Woman*. Lincoln and London: University of Nebraska Press, 1987.

Duras, Marguerite, and Michelle Porte. *Les Lieux de Marguerite Duras*. Paris: Minuit, 1978.

—. *Marguerite Duras filme*. Televised interview at a rehearsal of *Savannah Bay*. 1982.

Duras, Marguerite, and Dominique Noguez. "*India Song* la couleur des mots." In *Marguerite Duras oeuvres cinématographiques*, annotated videographic edition, 21-33. Paris: Ministère des Relations Extérieures, Bureau d'Animation Culturelle, 1984.

Duras, Marguerite, and Colette Mazabrard. Interview. *Cahiers du Cinéma* 426 (1989): 65.

Evans, Martha Noël. *Masks of Tradition*. Ithaca: Cornell University Press, 1987.

Freud, Sigmund. "Medusa's Head." In *Sexuality and the Psychology of Love*, edited by Philip Rieff. New York: Simon and Schuster, 1997: 202-203.

—. "The Uncanny" (*Das Unheimliche*, 1919). In *On Creativity and the Unconscious: Papers on the Psychology of Art, Literature, Love, Religion*, edited and with an introduction by Benjamin Nelson, 122-161. New York: Harper Colophon Books, 1958.

Green, André. "La Mère morte." In *Narcissisme de vie, narcissisme de mort*, 222-253. Paris: Minuit, 1983. Translated by Andrew Weller as "The Dead Mother." In *Life Narcissism, Death Narcissism*. Translated by Andrew Weller. London and New York: Free Association Books, 2001.

Kristeva, Julia. "The Pain of Sorrow in the Modern World: The Works of Marguerite Duras." *PMLA* 102, no. 2 (1987): 38-52.

Lacan, Jacques. "Hommage fait à Marguerite Duras, du ravissement de Lol V. Stein." In *Marguerite Duras*, edited by François Barot and Joël Fargues, 93-99. Paris: Albatros, 1975.

Marin, Louis. *Détruire la peinture*. Paris: Galilée, 1977. Translated by
Mette Hjort as *To Destroy Painting*. Chicago and London: University
of Chicago Press, 1995.
Montrelay, Michèle de. *L'Ombre et le nom*. Paris: Minuit, 1977.
Selous, Trista. *The Other Woman*. New Haven: Yale University Press,
1988.
Sontag, Susan. *On Photography*. New York: Dell, 1977.

Notes

[1] Marguerite Duras and Colette Mazabrard, "Interview," *Cahiers du Cinéma* 426
(1989), 65.
[2] Hélène Cixous, "Le Rire de la Méduse" (1975). Translated by Keith Cohen and
Paula Cohen as "The Laugh of the Medusa," *Signs* 1, no. 4 (Summer 1976): 885.
[3] See Sigmund Freud, "The Uncanny" (*Das Unheimliche*, 1919), in *On Creativity
and the Unconscious: Papers on the Psychology of Art, Literature, Love, Religion*,
ed. Benjamin Nelson. New York: Harper Colophon Books, 1958: 122-161.
[4] Aliette Armel, "Dossier Marguerite Duras et interview de l'écrivain," *Magazine
Littéraire* 278 (1990): 16.
[5] *L'Arc*, "Marguerite Duras," 1985 (98): 7.
[6] Marguerite Duras, *Destroy, She Said*, trans. Barbara Bray (New York: Grove
Press, 1970), 21.
[7] Lewis Carroll, *Alice's Adventures in Wonderland and Through the Looking Glass*
(New York: Bantam Classic Edition, 1981), 47.
[8] Madeleine Borgomano, *L'Ecriture filmique de Marguerite Duras* (Paris:
Albatros, 1985), 58.
[9] Marguerite Duras and others, *Marguerite Duras* (Paris: Albatros, 1975), 100-103.
[10] Ibid., 103.
[11] Cixous, 881.
[12] Julia Kristeva, "The Pain of Sorrow in the Modern World: The Works of
Marguerite Duras," *PMLA* 102, no. 2 (1987): 46.
[13] Marguerite Duras, *The Lover*, trans. Barbara Bray (New York: Random House,
1985), 23.
[14] Michèle de Montrelay, *L'Ombre et le nom* (Paris: Minuit, 1977), 17.
[15] Duras, *The Lover*, 8.
[16] Ibid., 14.
[17] Danielle Bajomée, "Veiller sur le sens absent," *Magazine Littéraire* 278 (1990):
32.
[18] Marguerite Duras, *Green Eyes*, trans. Carol Barko (New York: Columbia
University Press, 1990), 86.
[19] Marguerite Duras, *Savannah Bay*, trans. Howard Limoli as *Savannah Bay*, in
Agatha, Savannah Bay: Two Plays by Marguerite Duras (Sausalito, CA: Post-
Apollo Press, 1992), 127.

[20] *Marguerite Duras filme.* (Televised interview with Michelle Porte at a rehearsal of *Savannah Bay* 1982).

[21] Kristeva, 43.

[22] Duras and Mazabrard, 63.

[23] Cixous, 878-879, note 3.

[24] Duras and Porte, film.

[25] Marguerite Duras and Michelle Porte, *Les Lieux de Marguerite Duras* (Paris: Minuit, 1978), 102.

[26] *Marguerite Duras,* 96.

[27] Duras and Porte, *Lieux,* 45.

[28] Susan Sontag, *On Photography* (New York: Dell, 1977), 15.

[29] Ibid.,19.

[30] Roland Barthes, "The Rhetoric of the Image," trans. Richard Howard in *The Responsibility of Forms,* (New York: Hill and Wang, 1985), 33.

[31] Jacques Lacan, "Hommage fait à Marguerite Duras, du ravissement de Lol V. Stein," in *Marguerite Duras,* eds. François Barot and Joël Fargues (Paris: Albatros, 1975), 93.

[32] Duras, *The Lover,* 95-96.

[33] Marguerite Duras and Dominique Noguez, "*India Song* la couleur des mots," in *Marguerite Duras oeuvres cinématographiques,* annotated videographic edition, (Paris: Ministère des Relations Extérieures, Bureau d'Animation Culturelle, 1984), 21-22.

[34] Duras and Porte, *Lieux,* 56.

[35] Duras, *The Lover,* 7.

[36] Duras, *The Lover,* 98.

[37] Duras and Porte, film.

[38] Marguerite Duras and Xavière Gauthier, *Woman to Woman,* trans. Katharine A. Jensen (Lincoln and London: University of Nebraska Press, 1987), 30.

[39] Armel, 30.

[40] Marguerite Duras, *Emily L.,* trans. Barbara Bray (New York: Pantheon Books, 1989), 3.

[41] Martha Noël Evans, *Masks of Tradition* (Ithaca: Cornell University Press, 1987), 124.

[42] Duras and Gauthier, *Woman to Woman,* 4.

[43] Duras and Porte, *Lieux,* 102.

[44] Lacan, 93

[45] Montrelay, 22.

[46] Marguerite Duras, *The Ravishing of Lol Stein,* trans. Richard Seaver (New York: Grove Press, 1966), 49.

[47] Duras and others, *Marguerite Duras,* 90.

[48] Duras, cited by Armel, 31.

[49] Duras and Gauthier, *Woman to Woman,* 124.

[50] *The Lover,* 3

[51] Marguerite Duras, *L'Amant* (Paris: Minuit, 1984), 10, translation mine.

[52] Roland Barthes, *Barthes by Roland Barthes*, trans. Richard Howard, (New York: Farrar, Straus, and Giroux, 1977), 71.

[53] Louis Marin, *To Destroy Painting*, trans. Mette Hjort (Chicago and London: University of Chicago Press, 1995), 114.

[54] Sigmund Freud, "Medusa's Head," in *Sexuality and the Psychology of Love*, Philip Rieff, ed., New York: Simon & Schuster, Touchstone edition, 1997: 202-203.

[55] Ibid., 136

[56] Jean Clair, *Méduse* (Paris: Gallimard, 1989), 62.

[57] Ibid., 37

[58] Marin, 138.

CHAPTER ELEVEN

VARDA: *THE GLEANER* AND THE JUST

SANDY FLITTERMAN-LEWIS*

Within the extraordinary richness and variety of Agnès Varda's protean oeuvre there remains a consistent authorial signature, one that explores feminine identity within the social complex and ceaselessly, one might say increasingly, establishes that identity as a function of History. Through the stories she gathers and the diverse materials that she gleans, Varda has made a heterogeneous body of films that merge documentary and fiction, each redefining the parameters of cinematic language, the fixed categories of generic forms, the concepts of cinematic writing, authorship, and spectatorship, and even the notion of subjectivity itself. In my book *To Desire Differently: Feminism and the French Cinema*[1] I argued that Varda's authorship presented a series of "laboratories" in which she blended the dual concerns of film language and feminism in order to arrive at a concept of feminine cinematic writing (*filmer en femme*). More recently she has applied her inventive, collage-type signature beyond the strictly cinematic, first to an illustrated autobiography, *Varda par Agnès*,[2] and now to installations in which the actual film is only a part of the total work—three-dimensional viewing situations that create a contemplative space in which the "spectators" are free to wander, experience a range of feelings, and reflect or dream about the varied forms of representation surrounding them.[3]

At first glance, it seems possible to trace a trajectory in Varda's work from subjective interiority toward increased historical and social commitment, especially if one considers the dazzling lyricism of *L'Opéra-Mouffe* (1958) as the personal and intimate vision of a pregnant woman, and the deft sociology of *Daguerréotypes* (1975), *Sans toit ni loi* (1985),

* Sandy Flitterman-Lewis presented a version of this essay in French as "Varda, Glaneuse d'histoire(s)" at the Université de Rennes for the international conference "Le Cinéma d'Agnès Varda" (November 2007). It appears here for the first time in her own English adaptation.

and *Les Glaneurs et la glaneuse* (2000) as evidence of more objective explorations of the material social world. However, I am suggesting another conclusion, one that finds a continual interchange between historical context and issues of the female self in society at every stage of Varda's work. This becomes obvious as soon as one considers the hauntingly beautiful installation that Varda created for the dedication ceremony at the Panthéon in Paris for a plaque honoring the Righteous of France during World War II. From this perspective, it is no longer a question of simple teleology or linear progression, but of a perpetual and reverberating dialectic. For within the very personal vision of *L'Opéra-Mouffe* there is an almost hyper-realistic story of daily life—scruffy *clochards*, stout wrinkled women with kerchiefs and shopping carts, drunkards and beggars, women gossiping and children playing on the cobblestones—while with the very public and official ceremony for the *Hommage aux Justes de France* in the Panthéon, there is an unexpected intimacy that derives from a profoundly personal vision of the emotional lives not only of those French citizens who saved Jews from extermination, but of those, practically all very young, who were protected by their efforts.

It can be argued that the persecution of Jews in France during the German Occupation amounted to a veritable war against children.[4] According to French lawyer and historian Serge Klarsfeld (and himself a hidden child), of the 11,403 Jewish children deported from France, a mere 300 survived. The number of casualties among Jewish children increases when those who died in French detention centers such as Drancy and Beaune-la-Rolande, for example, are included. One can determine the exact date when the fate of French Jewish children was sealed—the 16th and 17th of July, 1942, the infamous Vel d'Hiv roundup. The name is shorthand for the Vélodrôme d'Hiver (Winter Cycling Stadium), where the over 14,000 Jews detained by the French police were held before being shipped to their inevitable deaths in Auschwitz by way of Drancy, just outside of Paris and known as the Antechamber of Death. Because this was the first time that entire families were arrested—where previously only "suspect" men were sought for deportation—among the nearly 14,000 detainees in the Vel d'Hiv, two thirds were women and children. In fact, the vision of so many terrified youngsters had its effect: even the celebrated Catholic novelist François Mauriac would write years later, in his preface to Elie Wiesel's *La Nuit*,

> I confided to my young visitor that nothing I had witnessed during that dark period had marked me as deeply as the image of cattle cars filled with Jewish children at the Austerlitz train station…Yet I did not even see them

with my own eyes. It was my wife who described them to me, still under the shock of the horror she had felt.[5]

At any rate, from this point on, networks for rescuing Jewish children were organized, clandestine safehouses were formed, and relays of escape and underground flight were mapped out. Moreover, there were numerous French individuals of all faiths, origins, and social classes—organized or not—who were moved to take moral action themselves by hiding these children, putting their own lives and safety at terrible risk.

The title "Righteous Among Nations" is given by the Memorial of Yad Vashem in Jerusalem (created in 1953) to those who took on great personal peril in order to save Jewish lives during World War II. Simone Veil, President of the Fondation pour la Mémoire de la Shoah, has put the figure of the Righteous in France at 2740. When the Élysée Palace wanted to recognize these rescuers (both known and unknown) in the name of France, they decided to place a plaque in the crypt of the national hall of honor, the Panthéon. The inscription on the marble tablet reads:

> Beneath the heavy weight of hatred in the dark night that fell on France during the years of the Occupation, millions of lights refused to be extinguished. Named 'Righteous Among the Nations,' or remaining anonymous, these men and women, of every origin and from every area of society, saved the Jews from anti-Semitic persecution, and from deportation to the extermination camps. Braving the risks inherent in their acts, they became the manifestation of French honour, embodying its values of justice, tolerance and humanity.[6]

The plaque was installed in the crypt during an official ceremony on January 18, 2007, presided over by the then President Jacques Chirac, during which time Varda's audiovisual installation was on display for the visitors. The temporary installation was to remain over the weekend, but lasted ten more days due to public demand; Varda subsequently organized a version of it for the Festival d'Avignon in July 2007.

For her installation, Varda avoids all forms of "schindlerism" through a multifaceted and varied strategy, typical of her oeuvre, that fragments images and sensations to create an environment that reverberates with simultaneous impressions: 1) Three hundred archival photographs of the known French Righteous, 2) Two films on four screens, projected in a loop every fifteen minutes (two of them in black and white, in the style of Occupation newsreels, two in color, made up of fictional and fleeting vignettes of scenes of rescue), and 3) A large tree projected on a screen at the back of the nave of the Panthéon. Through this *"double récit"*—the Righteous and the children, photo-portraits and cinema, vibrant nature and solid marble—Varda succeeds in creating an evocative, fragmented vision, one that she describes in this way: "Memories, faces, landscapes, feelings. Yesterday, and today as well."[7] In the program for the ceremony, she adds, "While they are watching this double film on separate screens, I wanted [the visitors to the Panthéon] to experience many fragmented feelings, bits of emotion linked to both History and to certain key images of our collective memories."[8]

It is through this dynamism put into play in the Panthéon—a dialectic that is at once personal and historical, individual and social, a process in which the present moment combines with an unknown, forgotten, or hidden past—that Varda arrives at a new conception of the subject, what might be called historical and ethical subjectivity. Beyond that, in the very heart of the grand patriarchal institution par excellence (*"To great men, a grateful nation/Aux grands hommes la patrie reconnaissante"* declaims the western façade of the building), Varda has found a way to insinuate the idea of a feminine consciousness, one based on a vision of relations of compassion that are at the base of all human interaction. The invisible links of human responsibility that form the social community are emphasized by this installation whose images and sounds remind us that human generosity appears even (or perhaps especially) in the darkest of circumstances. I note as well that these films provoke reflection on the subtle attention to small details, the often unnoticed little gestures, the warm memories of a gentle caress or an act of compassion—those little gestures of care (*des petits soins*) that, for example, allowed Charlotte Delbo and her fellow survivors to leave Auschwitz with their spirits intact.[9] Testimony to the capacity to triumph over the most horrible circumstances if one can find the tiniest gesture of compassion, Delbo's *Le Convoi du 24 janvier* contains the remembered portraits of the two hundred and thirty women deported to Auschwitz on this single convoy, written by the fifty of them who survived.

It is here in the Panthéon that we can see most clearly that Varda's trajectory does not simply move from interiority to social commitment; rather, she historicizes feminine subjectivity in keeping with her concerns throughout her career. With *L'Hommage aux Justes* Varda recasts History in feminine terms while she simultaneously conceives of the feminine in historical context. In these relational values there is something of what could be called a feminine sensibility, and it is through this sensibility that Varda combines "the Jewish memory of the Shoah" with the historical memory of the Righteous of France, thereby producing a new conception of the collective memory and of the social imaginary. By reformulating interiority in socio-historical terms and conceiving History along more intimate lines, Varda provides us with a new understanding of the individual, one defined by affective relations and concern for others. By giving us a feminine vision of these relations, a vision that recognizes equality between men and women, she posits the historical feminine subject, and the reductive binary of the personal and the social is thereby eliminated.

Coincidentally, with *L'Opéra-Mouffe*, made almost a half-century earlier, we are not very far from the Panthéon. This short black and white film, a visual notebook of the vibrant market on the rue Mouffetard that Varda calls a "subjective documentary," begins with a written title that immediately places us in the presence of this imposing institution: "Behind the Panthéon between the churches of Saint Étienne du Mont and Saint Médard, the rue Mouffetard crosses the neighborhood to which she has lent her name."[10] With a montage of photo-portraits of ordinary people of this actual social milieu—the beggars, drunkards, old people, and anxious drifters who populated this impoverished place at the time, all taken from Varda's own photos without sentimentality and in the tradition of the great realist photographers such as Brassaï, Doisneau, and Cartier-Bresson—we are not too far from the *"double amour"* that Varda is able to accomplish in the Panthéon fifty years after *L'Opéra-Mouffe*. In *Varda par Agnès* she says:

> Photography and Cinema…these two ways of capturing life, one immobile and silent, the other in motion and sound, are not really enemies but simply different, even complementary. With photography we have movement that has been stopped, or inner movement immobilized. On the other hand, the cinema gives us a series of successive photographs in a length of time that animates them. But there is another way of combining these two visions: you could film the photographs themselves and show them on the screen. You can add to the fixed image the possibility of seeing them in a determined length of time. Make what is fixed come alive by the active gaze.[11]

It is in the Panthéon in 2007 that Varda is able to realize her ambition to *"faire vivre"* the photographic image, for with her installation she animates the photo-portraits of the Righteous and their epoch in an exceptional way. Among the archival black and white photographs placed on the floor or posed like open books, there are other photo-portraits that are in color; Varda combines the archival photos with those taken from the fictional recreations in the projected films. She explains:

> There are portraits of the Righteous taken from diverse archives, including the incredible collections of the Mémorial de la Shoah; these are both

single portraits or photos of groups. Their names are written below the photos. And, since I filmed short fictional moments of scenes of the period, I mixed in photos of the people/characters in my own evocation of that period. These people, with faces reflecting simple goodwill or strong determination, represent—without their names appearing on the portraits—the thousands of anonymous people during the 1940s who have no official portraits, and thus they are the Unknown Righteous.[12]

As Walter Benjamin has said, "To honor the memory of the unknown is a more arduous task than to honor that of the famous. The idea of historic construction is dedicated to the memory of the unknown."[13] It is this "memory of the unknown" that Varda brings to life in the Panthéon, with a particularly astute awareness of the fact that history is most often made in the invisible corners of humanity.

When the Minister of Culture and Communication, Renaud Donnedieu de Vabres, commissioned Varda to create an installation for the nation's Hommage to the Righteous of France, she pointed out that there was a large number of anonymous rescuers who had not been officially designated. I would add that the names of the thousands of hidden children in France were unknown as well, an idea to which Varda was obviously sensitive. It is here that we can see Varda's extraordinary accomplishment; she inverts the traditional meaning of the place dedicated to "great men" through the invention of a new kind of spectatorship, one which traverses a mental space crisscrossed by fragmented perceptions from one reality to the other. She, as "author," sees herself as a sort of "intermediary who gives voice to those who have none," including the Jewish children whose stories have never seen the light of official recognition. Because of this, the visitor to the Panthéon is subject to multiple, diverse looks and feelings dispersed among both the protectors and those in need of that protection.

By means of a visual and sensory apparatus that represents both the hidden children as well as their rescuers, Varda makes us experience, either through memory, psychology, or empathetic identification, the emotional atmosphere of the period. The spectator's look is dispersed between fiction and historical reality in a three-dimensional expression of subjective memory. In the installation, Varda makes the portraits of actual rescuers come alive at the same time that she evokes almost imperceptible feelings, sensations barely understood but recognized from our collective memory of childhood. Situations of daily life and symbolic images blend in these two nine-minute films. On two of the screens, black and white images "realistically evoke the German Occupation, the persecution of the Jews and the shelter of Jewish children," with recognized symbols such as the swastika, black boots, the yellow star, administrative stamps, the roundups, and then the false baptismal certificates, the hiding places in the country, the attics, the catholic schools. The two screens projecting color films show "more or less the same scenes, the same tragic or quotidian moments, but filmed and treated differently," with details of tree trunks, rough stones, wooden shoes, grain sacks and other elements signifying the texture of country life. The television station France 2 showed a synthesized version that is available for viewing at the Institut National de l'Audiovisuel, as well as in schools.

Color film. Unexpected, fragmented projection. On two of the four screens that hide the statues surrounding the central space of the Panthéon—a circular parquet where the Foucault pendulum usually swings, now filled with photo-portraits of the Righteous—there is a stream of moving images, almost dreamlike in their progression. Thirteen vignettes take place in the blink of an eye. Each of the circumstances demonstrates an action of the Righteous, and practically all of them involve the rescue of children. Each episode ends on a portrait, the fictive incarnation of one of the Righteous, framed by a thin black line; this is immediately transformed into the real archival black and white photo of the actual person. Of the eighteen Righteous portrayed, eight are included in the book *Les Justes de France*[14] whose publication preceded the ceremony in the Panthéon; two more of them are represented in the program for the dedication of the plaque. The others are truly "the unknown," found in forgotten archives by Varda, a *cinéaste* on the hunt. Their names are as follows: Sister Marie-Paule, Germaine Ribeire, Angèle Marseille, Monsignor Gabriel Piguet, Marie-Louise Siauve, Gabrielle Chignaguet, Pierre Marché, Father Pierre Chaillet, Pastor André Trochmé (the most well-known), Paul Larchet, Antoine Beille, Lucien Flachot, Jeanne Acgouan, Jeanne Vallat, Jean Kroutz, François Lafaye, Marie-Rose Gineste, Émile and Félice Treyture. In the thirteen vignettes we find 1) a little boy hidden under the protective sleeve of a nun; 2) a young mother with a suitcase who leaves her two small children at a house in the country; 3) a baptismal certificate signed by a priest; 4) young women students chatting while a man registers as a Jew at the city hall; 5) two children shaking their head "no" in silence to some inquiring gendarmes; 6) the passage of baskets filled with food in the mountains; 7) a little girl given to the protective arms of a peasant woman; 8) children playing in a huge tree in the country; 9) adults talking in front of a church while a man gets on his bicycle; 10) the warning from village to farm by the man on his bicycle; 11) children on a playground being told to hide; 12) children on a farm hiding in the hayloft; 13) the arrival of the Gestapo, the capturing and deportation of two trapped children, and the arrest of their protector.

In these thirteen episodes, each ending with a photograph of one of the Righteous, and sketched out with an almost poetic minimalism, how is it possible that Varda is able to suggest the perspective of Jewish children in danger? In fact, it is through the smallest gesture, the tiniest detail barely seen from an oblique glance, thanks to the arrangement of screens and photos, that our consciousness is touched. Furthermore, through a combination of memory, vision, and imagination, Varda succeeds in avoiding conventional cinematic voyeurism while maintaining the powerful effect of the visual image. The actors are no longer "characters," but they are attitudes, gestures, and ideas concretized in the space of an instant. For example, the violin music that functions as a sort of punctuation helps to attain this effect. Varda says,

> I wanted to tell this story with a certain naturalness, making the viewer feel the childhood of these little ones, their loneliness, the omnipresent fear, but also the discovery of the countryside. Violaine Sultan's work on the music is very beautiful; she suggested a minimal composition based on a Yiddish song. She sings alto.[15]

This music functions as an invisible thread that links the diverse places and situations. Yiddish can also be found in the barely perceptible refrain heard or imagined by the boy sitting high up in the branches of a tree. The term in Yiddish, "Mameloshn"—the maternal language of a vanished culture—suggests all the childhood memories of maternal lullabies. On the other hand, the soundtrack also contains, with subtlety and off screen, brutal symbolic reference to the persecution of the Jews during the Occupation: whistles, shouts, scuffles, boots, trains, children crying, typewriters clacking, telephones ringing, and stamps pounding out the designation of Jews as prey. But also present in this choreography of sounds are other noises: the sound of insouciant childhood (a stick clacking across an iron grille) and the idyllic life in the country (chickens and dogs, church bells, sonorous rhythms of the countryside), and it is through this complex weave of the soundtrack that Varda gives us the *double reality* of the Righteous and the Jews.

Most of all, it is on the image-track that we find the Jewish presence, an evocation that transforms this official homage into an appeal against anti-Semitism and intolerance. The first section of the color film ends with a newsreel image that shows a telephone booth "Forbidden to Jews," symbol of the process of social exclusion that normalized the isolation of Jews under the Occupation. This is followed by a close-up of a yellow star being hand-sewn onto a garment, a black and white image that transforms into vibrant color, marking the beginning of the thirteen vignettes of rescue. This yellow star (imposed by the Decree of May 29, 1942, and setting up the conditions for the Vel d'Hiv roundups in July) also indicates an artistic strategy of Varda's, for after this "key image" (Varda's term), she shows us two simultaneous actions—the arrest of a Jewish tailor and his wife, and the protection of a little boy by a nun (one of the Righteous named in the book). This structure is maintained; the humiliating situation at the city hall where the identity card is stamped "Jew" and the false baptismal certificate, the pursuit by the Gestapo (aided by the French police) and the comforting breast of the peasant woman, the bicyclist who warns the villagers and a small child's hand in that of an adult. There are also more subtle evocations of Jewishness, such as the tree with scarlet leaves that calls to mind the Burning Bush, and the face of a young girl that evokes Marguerite Duras's Aurelia Steiner, the child hidden by an old woman in her war memoir, *La Douleur*. At any rate, the last sequence of the film reminds us that the history of the Righteous is also, and always inevitably, the history of the Jews. This last sequence contains the only sentence spoken on the soundtrack by one of the actors in the imagined scenes: "We've been told that you are hiding Jewish children." The horrifying scene that follows—the hidden children being forced out of the cellar, the arrest of the bourgeois man in his tailored suit, all in silence, the handcuffs in close-up and the off screen whistle of a train calling to mind both deportation and extermination—immediately makes us understand how "Jewish Memory" and French history are linked in a complex reciprocal process, across generations and for all time.

For my interpretation of this fragmentary film, a film that is a single fragment of the total installation, an installation that is itself made up of fragments—bits of gestures, of expressions, of views, of emotions—I return to Varda's film *Les Glaneurs et la glaneuse*. Here I am speaking specifically of a gleaner whose name is not pronounced in Varda's film.[16] I am referring to the biblical Ruth, the most famous gleaner in Jewish liturgy and literature. The Book of Ruth has another title, The Book of Chesed (Loving kindness, Caritas, Compassionate tenderness—there is no exact translation) because it is about relations of generosity and kindness among human beings, inspired in the Book of Ruth by women's caring for each other. In fact, the most famous biblical phrase—*"Whither thou goest I will go; and where thou lodgest I will lodge"*—is not a declaration of conjugal love, as has sometimes been assumed. Rather, it is a manifestation of Ruth's devotion to her mother-in-law Naomi when she wants to follow her from Moab to Judah. Ruth recognizes her responsibility not to turn away from this woman, not to abandon her; she knows that they are bound morally by bonds of caring. Thus in the midst of the patriarchal stories of the Bible we can find a feminist ethic and aesthetic based on empathetic relations, connections that suggest that the human community is formed in affective bonds among people. The psychologist Carol Gilligan has called this "ethic of care" the basis of women's moral vision, noting that feminine identity is inextricably formed in relation to others.[17] The Book of Ruth (there are only two books of the Bible which bear a woman's name, the Book of Esther being the other) emphasizes relations of fidelity, generosity, and kindness; in this book, the Divine presence is manifested in relations of caring, in attentiveness to others as to oneself, and not in dramatic dreamlike or symbolic revelation. In the biblical story Ruth transforms her suffering into song; while she gleans she sings in the wheat and the corn, fabricating a work of art that exalts relations of the heart. Her song emphasizes the value of friendship (the name Ruth means "friend"), and her relational moral perspective tells us that true knowledge comes when one listens to the voice of the other.[18] For the poet and midrashist Alicia Ostriker the Book of Ruth is profoundly optimistic, with "an optimism generated…by looking at the possibilities of *chesed*, or loving kindness—lovingly generous human behavior at the most intimate of levels."[19]

Yet there is another reference to gleaning in the Bible and it is found—coincidentally—at the entrance to the permanent exhibition at the Mémorial de la Shoah in Paris. It comes from Leviticus (19:9-10):

> *9. And when ye reap the harvest of your land, thou shalt not wholly reap the corner of thy field, neither shalt thou gather the gleaning of thy harvest. 10. And thou shalt not glean thy vineyard, neither shalt thou gather the fallen fruit of thy vineyard; thou shalt leave them for the poor and for the stranger.*

Leviticus is the Book of the Law, and it is notably the law of the patriarchs. One is commanded by an authoritarian voice, even if (and this is the case of the Memorial exhibition) this voice requires vigilance against all forms of intolerance. In contrast, with *L'Hommage aux Justes de France*, Agnès Varda has produced her own song of Ruth, a song which has its origin in the final image of *Les Glaneurs et la glaneuse*, where two almost identical women hold each side of a large painting in the wind, and we understand immediately the sacred importance of empathetic reciprocity. Rabbi Harold Schulweis has spoken of those who saved persecuted Jews as "sparks of the Divine in the ashes of atrocity,"[20] while Sir Martin Gilbert has said that their efforts are "a pointer to what human beings are capable of doing—for the good—when the challenge is greatest and the dangers most pressing."[21] With her installation, Varda has combined both sentiments (and others as well), by giving the ordinary spectator of an unknown or suppressed history, an immersion in *lived history*, a glittering sensation of the past in the present moment.

Works Cited

Delbo, Charlotte. *Le Convoi du 24 janvier*. Paris: Les Editions de Minuit, 1965.

Flitterman-Lewis, Sandy. *To Desire Differently: Feminism and the French Cinema*. New York: Columbia University Press, 1996.

Gilbert, Sir Martin. *The Righteous: The Unsung Heroes of the Holocaust*. New York: Henry Holt and Company, 2003.

Gilligan, Carol. *In a Different Voice*. Cambridge and London: Harvard University Press, 1982.

Guéno, Jean-Pierre. *Paroles d'étoiles: Mémoire des enfants cachés (1939-1945)*. Paris: Radio France, 2002.

Hommage de la Nation aux Justes de France (Panthéon, Thursday 18 January 2007).

Les Justes de France (Mémorial de la Shoah ; Musée, Centre de Documentation Juive Contemporaine ; Fondation pour la Mémoire de la Shoah, janvier 2007). Program published in conjunction with the exposition Les Justes, 9 mai—24 octobre, 2006.

Klarsfeld, Serge. *Mémorial des enfants juifs déportés de France*. Paris: Fondation Beate Klarsfeld, 1994.

Ostriker, Alicia. *For the Love of God: The Bible as an Open Book*. New Brunswick, New Jersey: Rutgers University Press, 2007.

Schept, Susan. "*Hesed:* Feminist Ethics and Jewish Tradition." *Conservative Judaism* 57:1 (Fall 2004).

Varda, Agnès. "Création pour le Panthéon," *Dossier de presse*.

—. *Hommage aux Justes de France*, program for installation in Avignon, July 7-27, 2007.

—. *Varda par Agnès*. Paris: Editions Cahiers du Cinéma, 1994.

Wiesel, Elie. *Night*. Translated by Marion Wiesel. New York: Hill and Wang, 2006.

Notes

[1] Sandy Flitterman-Lewis, *To Desire Differently: Feminism and the French Cinema* (New York: Columbia University Press, 1996).

[2] Agnes Varda, *Varda par Agnès* (Paris: Éditions Cahiers du Cinéma, 1994).

[3] These installations are: *Patatutopia* (2002, Venice Biennale), *L'Ile et elle* (2006, Fondation Cartier, Paris), *Hommage de la Nation aux Justes de France* (2007, Panthéon, Paris).

[4] See Serge Klarsfeld, *Mémorial des enfants juifs déportés de France* (Paris: Fondation Beate Klarsfeld, 1994). Klarsfeld has published a dozen books on the fate of French Jewry during World War II and has been active in bringing Nazi and Vichy officials to trial for the crimes they committed. He is president of the organization Sons and Daughters of the Jewish Deportees of France.

[5] The novel *La Nuit* (*Night*) by Elie Wiesel, the most famous testimony of the Shoah, was almost not published: first written in Yiddish under the title *And the World Was Silent*, then translated into English and French, it was rejected everywhere. Finally, the famous Catholic novelist François Mauriac was able to have it published at Les Editions de Minuit in 1958, and English translation and publication followed some fourteen years later.

[6] This translation of the inscription on the plaque is taken from the January 15, 2007 press release of the Foundation for the Memory of the Shoah.

[7] Cited by Armelle Héliot, "Les Justes au Panthéon," *Le Figaro,* 22 December, 2007.

[8] *Hommage de la Nation aux Justes de France* (Panthéon, Thursday 18 January 2007), 7.

[9] Charlotte Delbo, *Le Convoi du 24 janvier* (Paris: Les Editions de Minuit, 1965).

[10] Agnès Varda, *L'Opéra-Mouffe*, 1958.

[11] Agnès Varda, *Varda par Agnès* (Paris: Editions Cahiers du Cinéma, 1994), 130. This last sentence reads: "*Faire vivre ce qui est fixe par la vie du regard.*"

[12] Agnès Varda, "Création pour le Panthéon," *Dossier de presse*, 8.

[13] Walter Benjamin, cited by Dani Karavan in his installation *Passages* at Port Bou, Spain, May 15, 1994.

[14] *Les Justes de France* (Mémorial de la Shoah; Musée, Centre de Documentation Juive Contemporaine; Fondation pour la Mémoire de la Shoah, janvier 2007). Program for the exposition Les Justes, 9 mai—24 octobre, 2006.

[15] Agnès Varda, *Hommage aux Justes de France*, program for installation in Avignon, July 7-27, 2007.

[16] Jules Breton's painting *La Glaneuse*—which is reproduced by Varda in her film—is said to represent biblical Ruth, but her name is never pronounced. Therefore, the reference is very subtle, and subtextual.

[17] Carol Gilligan, *In a Different Voice* (Cambridge and London: Harvard University Press, 1982), 7-8.

[18] Susan Schept, "Feminist Ethics and Jewish Tradition," *Conservative Judaism* 57:1 (Fall 2004): 27.

[19] Alicia Ostriker, *For the Love of God: The Bible as an Open Book* (New Brunswick, New Jersey: Rutgers University Press, 2007), 40.

[20] David Grubin, *The Jewish Americans*, PBS Broadcast, February 2008.

[21] Sir Martin Gilbert, *The Righteous: The Unsung Heroes of the Holocaust* (New York: Henry Holt and Company, 2003), 443.

CHAPTER TWELVE

'NO WOMAN WOULD DIE LIKE THAT': *STAGE BEAUTY* AS CORRECTIVE-COUNTERPOINT TO *OTHELLO*

ELIZABETH GRUBER

How can a verbal or visual artistic representation be both aesthetically pleasing and morbid, as the conjunction of beautiful women and death seems to imply?
—Elisabeth Bronfen, *Over Her Dead Body*

Bronfen's observation indicates that spectators want to have their corpses and enjoy them too. Which is to say: violence and murder sometimes generate oddly approving responses. Consider, for example, that in its August 1990 "women-we-love" issue, *Esquire* magazine featured on its cover actress Sheryl Lee, who had garnered fame for her star turn as a corpse on the television show *Twin Peaks*.[1] While it is always risky to assume the portability of cultural ideals, appreciation for dead women would appear to forge connections across different cultures and eras.[2] Is this because (female) corpses approximate, or incarnate, a feminine ideal? Shakespeare's *Othello* engages precisely this question, and arguably dabbles in necrophilia, in its presentation of Desdemona's murder. In a moment described by Edward Pechter as "overtly necrophiliac,"[3] Othello stands over the inert, sleeping Desdemona and declares, "I will kill thee/And love thee after."[4] Desdemona will evidently be at her most desirable once she is dead. In death, it seems, Desdemona conforms to the image set forth by Renaissance conduct books, which frequently exhorted women to be "silent, chaste, and pleasing to look at."[5] This trio of "virtues," collectively endorsing female passivity, may help to explain the propensity to aestheticize, or fetishize, dead women.

The conjunction of violence and eroticism, or morbidity and aesthetics, propels *Stage Beauty* (2004), directed by Sir Richard Eyre, a film that joins the ever-growing number of *Othello's* progeny. Set in the

Restoration, *Stage Beauty* capitalizes on a key development in English theater, wherein women were allowed to take the stage as actresses. Not incidentally, Desdemona was one of the first roles to be performed by a woman acting on a public stage. In fact, Shakespeare's character is a fitting precursor to the newly emergent heroines of she-tragedy, a sub-genre of plays, as Jean I. Marsden has commented, which showcases "the suffering and often tragic end of a central, female figure."[6] *Stage Beauty* calls attention to the ways in which Restoration drama transformed the material conditions sustaining theatrical productions. Accordingly, the film depicts the entwining fates of two actors: Ned Kynaston, whose brilliant success playing Desdemona defines his stage career, and his one-time dresser/assistant, Maria, or Mrs. Hughes, who has her own aspirations of acting in public theaters. Ned and Maria are both based on historical figures: the former was one of the last "female impersonators," or Restoration actors who enjoyed success playing female roles, whereas the latter was a trailblazing actress of the period. In the film, Ned, played by Billy Crudup, is devastated when he is forced to relinquish the role of Desdemona. Conversely, Maria, who is played by Claire Danes, is catapulted into the spotlight when she appears on stage as Desdemona. In its dramatization of a contest for ownership of Desdemona (the role, that is), *Stage Beauty* permits fresh consideration of the scopic economies, and attendant gender politics, delineated in *Othello*. In so doing, *Stage Beauty* also serves as the perfect vehicle for reconsidering basic elements of feminist film theory.

The advent of actresses during the Restoration might seem, initially, to be an unequivocal boon for women. But the cultural and political implications of women acting on public stages are rather complex. As Marjorie Garber has pointed out: "Transvestite theater recognizes that all of the figures onstage are impersonators," a point that tends to undermine rigid dichotomizations of masculine and feminine.[7] But drama is the genre of the body—and the bawdy, admittedly, which was particularly true of Restoration productions, with their often excessive corporeal displays. In a study that emphasizes the importance of women as a material presence in Restoration theaters, Marsden comments that actresses "made possible the use of female sexuality not simply as discourse but as genuine spectacle, and playwrights and theater managers were quick to take advantage of this new opportunity."[8] Marsden adds: "the advent of the actress presented an opportunity for visual representation" of the "homosocial exchange" of women.[9] Looked at in this way, actresses reinforced the commodification of women. In this sense, the novelty of actresses may have worked to the detriment of women.

Sometimes, it seems, the presence of women onstage has diminished the impact of theatrical productions. By way of illustration, we might consider the transformed status of *Peter Pan* when the title role was restored to a male actor. Garber observes that it was customary for women to play the title role in *Peter Pan*, but in 1982 the Royal Shakespeare Company broke with this tradition and accorded star billing to a male actor. This casting innovation, reports Garber, was seen as "making the play a tragedy" and "elevating it from the ghetto of children's theater into a national masterpiece."[10] And she observes that, "Like *Hamlet, Peter Pan* could be a national masterpiece of tragic drama; all it needed was the RSC and a star with a phallus. It was a matter of putting the 'peter' back in Peter Pan."[11] This example, and Garber's witty assessment of it, serves as an important reminder that drama is a fleshly genre; as such, it feeds on, and also nourishes, cultural assumptions regarding gender and sexuality.

Responses to and evaluations of the gender of *Peter Pan*'s star reinvigorate questions about how spectators apprehend the fit (or gap) between actors and the characters they play. Such inquiries are of particular relevance to *Stage Beauty*, of course, since the play is set at a transitional moment in theater history, when assumptions about gender and performance were necessarily in flux. We cannot know for certain how Renaissance audiences responded to male actors playing female roles, although we do know that contemporary anti-theatricalist writers frequently decried the transvestism of the theater. For instance, William Rankins, one of the most prolific of the anti-theatricalist writers, persistently criticized the theater for its promotion of "monstrousness." As Jonathan V. Crewe points out, Rankins was particularly troubled by "the players' tendency to forget themselves and become what they act," which he feared led to "profoundly threatening cultural and individual metamorphoses as well as unprecedented boundary crossings."[12] Rankins, therefore, focused mainly on material practices and theatrical conventions, with the "boundary-crossing" or gender-bending actors playing female roles deemed especially threatening. Reflecting on the significance of all-male acting troupes, Jean E. Howard writes: "at some level boy actors playing women [in Renaissance plays] must simply have been accepted in performance as a convention."[13] Of course, "accepting conventions" does not mean ignoring them, and it is certainly possible that the familiar convention of men playing women was a reliable source of provocation *and* titillation—a source of anxious pleasure, that is—for Renaissance audiences.

By contrast, the first Restoration productions to feature women in their casts exploited the novelty of the practice. For example, in his prologue to a Restoration adaptation of *Othello* (1660), Thomas Jordan announces that a woman is readying herself to take the stage as Desdemona and professes to have seen her "drest" (i.e., in the act of dressing...or undressed). This moment of voyeurism, as Marsden suggests, is designed to provide a tantalizing glimpse of what is in store for audiences.[14]

Economies of spectatorship forge intriguing connections between Restoration drama and contemporary film. Building on Laura Mulvey's ground-breaking essay, "Visual Pleasure and Narrative Cinema,"[15] feminist film theorists have convincingly shown how scopic politics reinforce cultural assumptions regarding gender and sexuality. A deceptively simple equation emerges: to look is to be a masculine (desiring) subject; to be looked at is to be a feminine (desired) object. Or, as Kaja Silverman writes: "It is by now axiomatic that the female subject is the object...of the gaze in mainstream narrative cinema."[16] E. Ann Kaplan concurs, writing: "the dominant cinematic apparatus is constructed by men for a male spectator."[17] But perhaps Kaplan's most important point is this: "Men do not simply look; their gaze carries with it the power of action and of possession that is lacking in the female gaze."[18] In this formulation, gazing connotes power and effects a symbolic colonization; trapped within this system, the female spectator cannot arrogate to herself the power or prerogatives of looking.

Undeniably, many contemporary films (like Restoration plays) depict women as spectacles designed to appeal to implicitly male viewers. But there are certain dangers in adhering too rigidly to the masculine-looker/feminine-object schema. An especially cogent critique of this formulation is presented by Jane Gaines, who argues: "the male/female opposition, so seemingly fundamental to feminism, may actually lock us into modes of analysis which will continually misunderstand the position of many women."[19] Gaines's work shows how visual dynamics and scopic pleasures are constituted within specific social matrices, which are not always reducible to the polarities of masculine and feminine.[20] As Gaines suggests, theorizations of gazing have tended to "reinforce white middle-class values" and they have often failed to acknowledge the position of lesbian spectators.[21] Gaines's essay usefully advances the feminist work preceding it by urging reconsideration of the basic relations between observer and observed. If gazing can be read as an act of hostility or aggression that freezes its object, it likewise has the potential to transfix observers. A paradigmatic illustration of these complexities is to be found, of course, in the myth of Medusa (and in responses to it): in this case, it is the looker who is immobilized and imperiled.[22]

Stage Beauty's main conflict, the contest between Ned and Maria, reinvigorates questions about the power infusing visual transactions. Taking its cue from *Othello*, which uses voyeurism as an important trope, *Stage Beauty* repeatedly scrutinizes scopic power. In one scene, Maria watches in fascinated horror as Ned has sex with his male lover. Positioned as an on obsessed spectator, Maria steps into Othello's role: in Shakespeare's play, the hero initially demands "ocular proof" if he is to accept the case against Desdemona. Knowing he cannot provide this, Iago asks Othello: "Would you, the supervisor, grossly gape on, behold her topped?" (3.3.395-96). Here, Iago may be chiding the audience, as well as Othello, for desiring to become an illicit observer. In the film, Maria cannot avert her gaze even though the sight of Ned with another lover is painful to her. Her agonized spectatorship complicates notions of gazing as, inherently, assertions of power.

Stage Beauty complicates the argument that objects of visual pleasure necessarily experience powerlessness. This point is made in the play's opening scene, which essentially picks up where *Othello* concludes. The camera shows Ned preparing to go on-stage as an about-to-be-murdered Desdemona. The audience within the film is clearly primed for this scene and knows what to expect, although this preparation does not seem to dampen their pleasure. Ned's performance of death is highly stylized. When the actor playing Othello raises the pillow to smother him, Ned displays an exaggerated non-resistance. His Desdemona does not so much surrender to death as welcome it. Although Shakespeare's play proceeds from Desdemona's murder to the hero's recognition of having been duped, and his subsequent suicide, in *Stage Beauty* audiences who attend *Othello* try to ensure that it concludes at the moment of Desdemona's death through their enthusiastic and sustained applause. Ned's Desdemona steals the show, and he seems entirely in command of the audience's response. To be sure, he is a beautiful and enticing Desdemona, and his death holds the audience in rapt attention. As the object and source of visual pleasure, Ned-as-Desdemona controls and shapes his audience's reactions, even—or especially—when he succumbs to murder and is thus silenced and immobilized (not to mention "pleasing to look at"). In highlighting enthusiastic reactions to Desdemona's murder, *Stage Beauty* invites us to consider: What is so appealing, exactly, about the simulation of murder and its after-effects? One answer is provided by Bronfen, who surmises: "Representations of death in art are so pleasing, it seems, because they occur in a realm clearly delineated as not life, or not real, even as they refer to the basic fact of life we know but choose not to acknowledge too overtly."[23]

Bronfen is convincing in her argument that representations of death "both articulate an anxiety about and a desire for death."[24] Her position does, however, rest on maintaining clear distinctions between representation and reality. *Othello*, by contrast, has vexed critics and theorists who wish to promote properly "distanced" or dispassionate readings. Notably, for example, when Wayne C. Booth articulates the problems of "under-distancing"—a response one might also characterize as over-empathizing—the text he calls upon is *Othello*. Booth writes: "[I]f a man who believes that he has reason to be jealous of his wife attends *Othello*, he will be moved too deeply and in a manner not properly aesthetic."[25] *Stage Beauty* lends credence to Booth's position. After watching Ned's portrayal of Desdemona, two female fans wish to escort the actor on a drive through the countryside, and they desire him to remain in female clothing, makeup, etc. As the two "gentle ladies" ultimately confess to Ned, they are intent upon determining whether he is actually male or female so that they might settle a wager. As they are concluding their business, Ned and his curious fans are approached by Sir Charles Sedley, played by Richard Griffiths, who, initially, believes that all three are (female) prostitutes. Ned's fans are affronted at being thought prostitutes and promptly leave. Ned does not, however, make his own getaway as quickly. In fact, Sir Charles is only dissuaded from "seducing" Ned when he tries to grope under the actor's skirts and encounters what Ned calls "a guardian at the gates."

Sir Charles's mistake (or, if one prefers, Ned's ability to "pass") underscores the artifice or orchestration of femininity. That is, the film presents gender as a fluid set of signs rather than a fixed system anchored by immutable biological difference. More important, the theme of Ned's desirability affirms the love-and-death nexus that is so important in *Stage Beauty*. In presenting Ned as an object of desire with cross-gendered appeal (as was supposedly the case with the historical Kynaston), *Stage Beauty* illuminates one of the chief fears associated with the all-male theater of the Renaissance.[26] Stephen Orgel's research on anti-theatricalist writings discloses that major objections to Renaissance theatrical productions were couched in terms of the effects of lust on male spectators. Orgel points out that the major polemics against theater always associated it with sexuality, specifically, with desire. Summarizing such attitudes, Orgel writes: "Women are dangerous to men because sexual passion for women renders men effeminate."[27] For the polemicists, the phenomenon of boy actors deepened this threat. As Orgel puts it: "It is argued [by theater's detractors] first that the boys who perform the roles of women will be transformed into their roles and play the part in reality" and that "Male spectators...will be seduced by the impersonation [of women by boys], and losing their reason will become effeminate," which means not only that they will desire women, but that they will desire the boys playing women—thereby themselves inhabiting the female role.[28] In these documents, desire—especially when provoked by the beauty of the transvestite—is identified as a deadly weapon, one presumed capable of annihilating manhood.

In her comprehensive study of the cultural valences inflecting cross-dressing, Garber argues that "the appeal of cross-dressing is clearly related to its status as a sign of the constructedness of gender categories."[29] And she cautions that "the tendency on the part of many critics has been to look *through* rather than *at* the cross-dresser, to turn away from a close encounter with the transvestite and to want instead to subsume that figure within one of the two traditional genders."[30] Following Garber, instead of reading Ned as female when he is cross-dressed, it may be more useful to grasp the ways in which he can incarnate, simultaneously, traits deemed "masculine" and "feminine"—thus is binary logic disrupted. If such disruption has radical or revolutionary potential, it is often difficult to achieve or maintain. For example, in *Stage Beauty*, Ned's male lover George Villiars emphasizes that, for him, gender and sexuality work in tandem. George tells Ned: "When I did spend time with you I always thought of you as a woman." As George further notes, their sexual relationship was always conducted in a bed on a stage-set, and the theme of masquerade defines their relationship. When the two have sex, George asks that Ned wear a wig. George explains his request by commenting: "I like to see a golden flow as I die in you." Here, of course, the film plays on the Renaissance equation of orgasm and death. Once again, desire is most forcefully expressed in terms of its annihilative effects. George's request also indicates (the deconstructive magic of the transvestite notwithstanding) that when he is with Ned he still imagines his partner as a woman. To George, Ned is desirable precisely because the latter can convincingly perform as a woman.

At times Ned seems to apprehend the theatricality of desire, and the attendant fluidity of gender roles. For instance, when Ned is confronted with the news that Maria wishes to act, and to take on female parts, his rather contemptuous response is: "A woman playing a woman, where's the trick in that?" As Maria prepares for an audition, Ned asks her: "Do you know the five positions of feminine subjugation?" From this perspective, femininity is acutely stylized, emerging as a series of specific practices and gestures, a point that tends to corroborate the constructedness of gender roles.[31] On the other hand, Ned veers into essentialism when addressing Maria's question about his refusal to play men. Ned argues: "Men aren't beautiful. Women do everything beautifully. Especially when they die." Not incidentally, Ned's assertion would seem to affirm the notion that Desdemona is at her most appealing when she has been turned into a corpse. In any case, Ned's complicated feelings about performing as a woman intensify rather than resolve questions about the basis or source of gendered behavior. Working through the consistent (and startlingly cross-cultural and trans-historical) appeal of beautiful dead women, Bronfen writes: "Death and femininity are culturally positioned as the two central enigmas of western discourse."[32] As "enigmas," they are, obviously, "unknowable," but representation momentarily captures them, freeze-framing them and allowing for their scrutiny. It seems, as a man playing a woman, that Ned both recognizes the (putative) eternal mysteriousness of women and relishes being inside, or embodying, it.

When Ned is hired as Maria's acting coach, she takes the opportunity to challenge his assumptions about women, especially those demonstrated through his female impersonations. Maria tells Ned: "I always hated you as Desdemona. You never fought! You just died, beautifully. No woman would die like that, no matter how much she loved him! A woman would fight!" This exchange marks one of the film's strongest correctives to the trajectory of murder, and concomitant aesthetic, of *Othello*. If Ned's Desdemona exhibits pliancy or surrender, perhaps this is because he adheres closely to the text of *Othello*, which does indicate the heroine's acquiescence to her murder. "Desdemona," says Alan Sinfeld, "never manages much opposition to her death."[33] And, of course, when Shakespeare's character momentarily revives, she uses her dying breath to try and deflect suspicion away from the man who has just murdered her. If this is to be read as a supreme demonstration of love, it is one rooted in masochism so extreme that it culminates in a death wish.

Maria's passionate declaration regarding how women *would* die rejects female passivity and emphatically contradicts the notion that there is anything serene or beautiful in murder. This transformation of *Othello* can be understood as a feminist intervention, although it must be acknowledged that *Stage Beauty* does not present a tidy set of precepts (such as a coherent feminist agenda) and sometimes the disparate arguments it generates are in conflict. Earlier in the film, for example, Maria has expressed unqualified admiration for Ned's performance as Desdemona.[34] Such contradictions are unsurprising, given that the purpose of a film is not to advance a coherent political (or ideological) platform. In any case, I suspect that Robin Wood's observation regarding the uneasy fit between feminism and film still holds. Wood argues: "In order to be admitted to the Hollywood cinema at all, feminism had to undergo drastic changes, the fundamental one, from which all the rest follow, being the repression of politics."[35] On the other hand, *Stage Beauty* sheds light on the politics of aesthetics, particularly as this relates to gender. Notably, Maria does not want to change the outcome for Desdemona but, rather, the means by which it is attained. Although Maria couches her objections to Ned's performance in terms of verisimilitude, it seems that she actually wishes the death-scene to correspond to her fantasy of domination. For, as Linda Williams has commented: "even in the most extreme displays of masochistic suffering, there is always a component of either power or pleasure for the woman victim."[36] Williams calls for feminist analyses that attend to women's participation in masochistic structures, or what she terms "what is in masochism for women."[37] Following Williams, the pleasure Maria derives is expressly connected to resisting—but ultimately succumbing to—victimization.

Maria's corrective to *Othello*: "No woman would die like that," foregrounds an important problem in feminist studies of film. As Diane Waldman reminds us, it is difficult to use the generation of (positive) female images as the baseline by which to judge the implications and effects of contemporary cinema.[38] Waldman asks: "Do [films] depict things as they really are, or as we think they should be?"[39] She also wonders: "How do we deal with the reality of sexism as it currently exists?"[40] If films (and analyses of them) are to propel cultural transformation, they must both confront what is and be equipped to imagine what could be.

Cinematic images will always negotiate between the "real" and the "ideal"—a point beautifully made in Maria's critique of Ned's performance. Even when the two are simply rehearsing, the murder scene is marked by reciprocal physicality and aggression. Following this volatile exchange, Ned informs Maria that he "blames her for [his] death." In the wake of this declaration/accusation, the two prepare to take the stage as Othello and Desdemona. The camera, which can assume the role of Iago in the film by enlisting our complicity in intended malevolence, pans to Ned, who sits at a mirror and applies make-up for his role. As he does so, he recalls lines from one of Othello's speeches. Specifically, Ned utters Othello's justification for murder, stating: "It is the cause, it is the cause, my soul" (5.2.1). These are the words Shakespeare's hero delivers just prior to killing Desdemona. When Ned and Maria perform the murder scene for a live audience, he initially seems intent on turning the drama into a snuff-play. The audience, readily perceiving that Maria's struggles and cries for help seem genuine, is both transfixed and horrified. Maria seems to be dead—she is a truly convincing corpse, if not a well-groomed and beautiful one. After an agonizingly suspenseful pause, Maria raises her head and delivers Desdemona's final (Othello-exculpating) line. Once they are back stage, Ned and Maria embrace and kiss. She asks why he didn't finish her off, to which he replies: "We finally got the death scene right." The eroticism that clearly infuses the final encounter between Ned and Maria in no way obviates the possibility of future violence, and maybe it is just this prospect that always invigorates performances of *Othello*.

Maria's corrective to Ned—and, by implication, to Shakespeare's play—attempts to recast erotic politics such that Desdemona is not consigned to a pliant and passive role. While it is not necessarily the case that an actively resistant Desdemona constitutes a feminist revision of *Othello*, her forceful rejection of passivity may dislodge the masochism that otherwise tinges her death. In her study of the dead woman as spectacle, Bronfen wonders "whether every representation of dying is not violent precisely because it implies the safe position of a spectator ('voyeur') and because a fragmentation and idolization of the body...is always built into such images."[41] According to Bronfen, this "places us as spectators in the interstice between an aesthetic and an empathetic response."[42] One of the pleasures of art is, perhaps, that it offers a place from which to escape the demands of empathy—the often painful necessity of coping with another's suffering. On the other hand, art can be an immensely powerful empathy-trigger. A Desdemona who passionately fights against her murderer, thereby expressing an unequivocal will to live, complicates our retreat to the haven of aesthetics. This may be the most effective means of lifting the veil of sentimentality that shrouds murder in *Othello*.

Works Cited

Artel, Linda and Susan Wengraf. "Positive Images: Screening Women's Films." In *Issues in Feminist Film Criticism*, edited by Patricia Erens, 9-13. Bloomington and Indianapolis: Indiana University Press, 1990.

Booth, Wayne C. *The Rhetoric of Fiction*. 2nd Edition. Chicago: The University of Chicago Press, 1983.

Bray, Alan. "Homosexuality and the Signs of Male Friendship in Elizabethan England." In *Queering the Renaissance*, edited by Jonathon Goldberg, 40-61. Durham: Duke University Press, 1994.

Bronfen, Elisabeth. *Over Her Dead Body: Death, Femininity and the Aesthetic*. New York: Routledge, 1992.

Butler, Judith. *Bodies That Matter: On the Discursive Limits of 'Sex.'* New York: Routledge, 1993.

Creed, Barbara. *The Monstrous-Feminine: Film, Feminism, Psychoanalysis.* London: Routledge, 1993.

Crewe, Jonathan V. "The Theater of Idols: Theatrical and Anti-theatrical Discourse." In *Staging the Renaissance: Reinterpretations of Elizabethan and Jacobean Drama*, edited by David Scott Kastan and Peter Stallybrass, 49-56. New York: Routledge, 1991.

Davis, Nick. "Review of *Stage Beauty*" *Nick's Flick Picks.* (2004). www.nicksflickpicks.com/movarchs.html. (Accessed July 25, 2007).

Doane, Mary Ann. "Film and the Masquerade." In *Issues in Feminist Film Criticism,* edited by Patricia Erens, 41-57. Bloomington: Indiana University Press, 1990.

Esquire. August 1990.

Gaines, Jane. "White Privilege and Looking Relations: Race and Gender in Feminist Film Theory." In *Issues in Feminist Film Criticism*, edited by Patricia Erens, 197-215. Bloomington: Indiana University Press, 1990.

Garber, Marjorie. *Vested Interests: Cross-Dressing and Cultural Anxiety.* New York: Routledge, 1992.

Hodgdon, Barbara. *The Shakespeare Trade: Performances and Appropriations.* Philadelphia: University of Pennsylvania Press, 1998.

Howard, Jean E. *The Stage and Social Struggle in Early Modern England.* London: Routledge, 1994.

Hull, Suzanne W. *Chaste, Silent & Obedient: English Books for Women 1475-1640.* San Marino: Huntington Library, 1982.

Kaplan, E. Ann. "Is the Gaze Male?" In *Oxford Readings in Feminism: Feminism and Film*, edited by E. Ann Kaplan, 119-138. Oxford: Oxford University Press, 2000.

Marsden, Jean I. *Fatal Desire: Women, Sexuality, and the English Stage 1660-1720.* Ithaca: Cornell University Press, 2006.

Mulvey, Laura. "Visual Pleasure and Narrative Cinema." 1975. In *Literary Theory: An Anthology*, edited by Julie Rivkin and Michael Ryan. Malden, MA: Blackwell, 1998.

Orgel, Stephen. *Impersonations: The Performance of Gender in Shakespeare's England.* Cambridge: Cambridge University Press, 1996.

Pechter, Edward. *Othello and Interpretive Traditions.* Iowa City: Univ. of Iowa Press, 1999.

Shakespeare, William. *Othello*. *The Riverside Shakespeare 2ⁿᵈ Edition*, edited by G. Blakemore Evans, 1251-1296. Boston: Houghton Mifflin, 2000.

Silverman, Kaja. "Dis-Embodying the Female Voice." In *Issues in Feminist Film Criticism*, edited by Patricia Erens, 309-27. Bloomington and Indianapolis: Indiana University Press, 1990.

Sinfeld, Alan. *Faultlines: Cultural Materialism and the Politics of Dissident Reading*. Berkeley: University of California Press, 1992.

Waldman, Diane. "There's More to a Positive Image Than Meets the Eye." In *Issues in Feminist Film Criticism*, edited by Patricia Erens, 13-18. Bloomington and Indianapolis: Indiana University Press, 1990.

Williams, Linda. "Film Bodies: Gender, Genre and Excess." In *Feminist Film Theory: A Reader*, edited by Sue Thornham, 267-281. Washington Square, NY: New York University Press, 1999.

Wood, Robin. "Images and Women." In *Issues in Feminist Film Criticism*, edited by Patricia Erens, 337-352. Bloomington and Indianapolis: Indiana University Press, 1990.

Notes

[1] See *Esquire*'s August 1990 issue. Although Lee's character, Laura Palmer, always appeared as a corpse, she was tremendously popular with audiences.

[2] In *Over Her Dead Body: Death, Femininity, and the Aesthetic* (New York: Routledge, 1992), Bronfen identifies numerous compelling examples of corpse-worship, and her incisive analysis has shaped my own thinking about gender, aesthetics, and death.

[3] Edward Pechter, Othello *and Interpretive Traditions* (Iowa City: Univ. of Iowa Press, 1999), 144.

[4] Shakespeare, *Othello*. *The Riverside Shakespeare*, ed. G. Blakemore Evans (Boston: Houghton Mifflin, 1997), 5.2.18-19. All subsequent quotations from *Othello* are cited parenthetically in the text.

[5] In *Chaste, Silent & Obedient: English Books for Women 1475-1640* (San Marino: Huntingdon Library, 1982), Suzanne Hull shows how codes of conduct regulating female behavior were discursively constituted. The three attributes named in her title powerfully underscore the ways in which women's passivity, in varying contexts, was certified as a cultural ideal.

[6] Jean I. Marsden, *Fatal Desire: Women, Sexuality, and the English Stage 1660-1720* (Ithaca: Cornell Univ. Press, 2006), 65.

[7] Marjorie Garber, *Vested Interests: Cross-Dressing and Cultural Anxiety* (New York: Routledge, 1992), 40.

[8] Marsden, 3.

[9] Marsden, 8.

[10] Garber, 165.

[11] Garber, 165.

[12] See Jonathan V. Crewe, "The Theater of the Idols: Theatrical and Anti-theatrical Discourse," in *Staging the Renaissance: Reinterpretations of Elizabethan and Jacobean Drama*, ed. David Scott Kastan and Peter Stallybrass (New York: Routledge, 1991), 53.

[13] Jean E. Howard, *The Stage and Social Struggle in Early Modern England* (London: Routledge, 1994), 128.

[14] Marsden, 1-3.

[15] Laura Mulvey, "Visual Pleasure and Narrative Cinema," 1975, Rpt. in *Literary Theory: An Anthology*, ed. Julie Rivken and Michael Ryan (Malden, MA: Blackwell, 1998). Mulvey's work is of continued importance to feminist film studies because of its cogent analysis of scopic economies and gender politics.

[16] Kaja Silverman, "Dis-Embodying the Female Voice," in *Issues in Feminist Film Criticism*, ed. Patricia Erens (Bloomington and Indianapolis: Indiana Univ. Press, 1990), 309.

[17] E. Ann Kaplan, "Is the Gaze Male?" in *Oxford Readings in Feminism: Feminism and Film*, ed. E. Ann Kaplan (Oxford: Oxford Univ. Press, 2000), 122.

[18] Ibid., 121.

[19] Jane Gaines, "White Privilege and Looking Relations: Race and Gender in Feminist Film Theory," in *Issues in Feminist Film Criticism*, ed. Patricia Erens, (Bloomington and Indianapolis: Indiana Univ. Press, 1990), 210.

[20] *Othello*, and its critics, continue to reveal much about the politics of gazing. For example, as Barbara Hodgdon argues in *The Shakespeare Trade: Performances and Appropriates* (Philadelphia: Univ. of Pennsylvania Press, 1998), readings and productions of *Othello* have, historically, emphasized the hero's blackness, especially vis-à-vis spectators' (presumed) whiteness. As Hodgdon states: "*Othello* represents a site through which the problem of the black body in the white imaginary becomes a visible, even tangible, body of evidence" (43).

[21] Gaines, 198-200.

[22] Barbara Creed's study of femininity and monstrousness, *The Monstrous-Feminine: Film, Feminism, Psychoanalysis* (London: Routledge, 1993), reconsiders the meaning and significance of Medusa's warning. Creed points out that Freud construed Medusa's warning in terms of female castration (read as a kind of monstrousness), with the snakes of her head representing female genitals. By contrast, Creed raises the possibility that Medusa is meant to signify a castrating female power.

[23] Bronfen, x.

[24] Ibid.

[25] Wayne C. Booth, *The Rhetoric of Fiction*, 2nd ed., (Chicago: Univ. of Chicago Press, 1983), 122.

[26] See Alan Bray, "Homosexuality and the Signs of Male Friendship in Elizabethan England," in *Queering the Renaissance*, ed. Jonathan Goldberg (Durham: Duke Univ. Press, 1994), 40-61, for an examination of the ways in which the images of the "masculine friend" and the "sodomite" convey Renaissance assumptions about male-male relationships. Bray notes that "the image of the masculine friend was

an image of intimacy between men in stark contrast to the forbidden intimacy of homosexuality" (42).

[27] Stephen Orgel, *Impersonations: The Performance of Gender in Shakespeare's England* (Cambridge: Cambridge Univ. Press, 1996), 26.

[28] Ibid, 26-27.

[29] Garber, 9.

[30] Ibid.

[31] Judith Butler's work on gender and performativity, especially in *Bodies That Matter: On the Discursive Limits of "Sex,"* (New York: Routledge, 1993), is especially relevant to *Stage Beauty*. Butler is always careful to point out that performativity is not synonymous with voluntariness, a caveat echoed in the film. Likewise, Mary Ann Doane's work on the "masquerade" that femininity requires or necessitates helps to contextualize the themes grappled with in *Stage Beauty*. See "Film and the Masquerade," in *Issues in Feminist Film Criticism,* ed. Patricia Erens (Bloomington and Indianapolis: Indiana Univ. Press, 1990), 41-57.

[32] Bronfen, 255.

[33] Alan Sinfeld, *Faultlines: Cultural Materialism and the Politics of Dissident Reading* (Berkeley: Univ. of California Press, 1992), 53.

[34] For a witty and caustic review of *Stage Beauty*'s internal contradictions, see Nick Davis's Web site, *Nick's Flick Pick* (*www.nicksflickpicks.com/movarchs.html*). Acknowledging the film's ambitious scope, Davis nonetheless faults it for failing to make a coherent statement about gender and sexuality.

[35] Robin Wood, "Images and Women," in *Issues in Feminist Film Criticism*, ed. Patricia Erens (Bloomington and Indianapolis: Indiana Univ. Press, 1990), 337-52.

[36] Linda Williams, "Film Bodies: Gender, Genre, and Excess," in Feminist Film *Theory: A Reader*, ed. Sue Thornham (Washington Square, NY: New York Univ. Press, 1999), 274.

[37] Ibid., 273.

[38] Diane Waldman's essay, "There's More to a Positive Image Than Meets the Eye," in *Issues in Feminist Film Criticism*, ed. Patricia Erens, (Bloomington and Indianapolis: Indiana Univ. Press, 1990), 13-18, is positioned as a response to a collaborative piece by Linda Artel and Susan Wengraf. Their essay, published in the same volume, pp. 9-13, provides a useful catalogue of women's films. However, I share Waldman's contention that the adjective "positive" is nebulous, which renders it an ineffectual criterion by which to judge films. And, as noted in the body of my essay, cinematic productions cannot simply depict utopian visions if they are to have any transformative potential.

[39] Waldman, 14.

[40] Ibid.

[41] Bronfen, 45.

[42] Ibid., 44.

CHAPTER THIRTEEN

DIS-ABLING THE SADISTIC GAZE AND DEAF PROSTITUTES IN ALEKSEI BALABANOV'S *OF FREAKS AND MEN* AND VALERII TODOROVSKII'S *LAND OF THE DEAF*

IZABELA KALINOWSKA

In previous epochs, Soviet cinema's portrayal of women provided an indication of changing ideological and aesthetic styles. As Lynn Atwood has pointed out: "One of the distinctive features of Soviet cinema has been the symbolic use of the human form to convey certain abstract ideas: the motherland, liberty, Bolshevism, and so on."[1] The overt politicization of the body in Soviet cinema that began already with Eisenstein allows one to chart the dominant ideological assumptions, adjustments and shifts throughout Soviet history by analyzing, in particular, the images of women, their appearances, and the physical transformations they undergo. Throughout the years of Soviet rule, screen constructions of women's bodies provided both a reinforcement and an indicator of the reigning ideological constructions: from Lyubov Orlova's classic metamorphoses in Grigoriy Aleksandrov's *Circus* (1936) and *The Shining Path* (1939), through the controlled dishevelment of Vera Alentova in Vladimir Menshov's *Moscow Does Not Believe in Tears* (1980) to Natalya Negoda's unabashed nudity in the title role of *Little Vera* (Vasili Pichul, 1989). During the first post-communist decade—when questions continued being asked about Russia's past and future, old ideas were being reevaluated and new ideas were being forged amidst the ongoing search for a new aesthetic—two of the more significant films to come out of Russia in 1998, Aleksei Balabanov's *Of Freaks and Men* and Valerii Todorovskii's *Land of the Deaf,* foreground looking at women. But if the classic Soviet paradigm employed the transformation of the central female figure as a metaphor for the strides made by the Soviet system, these two films have consistently reversed the previously employed trajectory. In Balabanov's and Todorovskii's pictures, the foregrounded feminine body effectively subverts the dominant political/social/symbolic order. At the same time, each film leads the viewer to radically different conclusions concerning woman's power to undermine the ruling forces of patriarchy. For Balabanov, the spectacle of the feminine body represents the epicenter of a brewing disaster, while Todorovskii transforms the display of feminine beauty into a site of positive identity building.

In *Of Freaks and Men*, a complex and disturbing film, Aleksei Balabanov offers his own version of the advent of moving pictures in Russia. The questions he thereby poses interrogate the medium and its social impact. The use to which the photographer/filmmaker puts the female body forms the central issue in Balabanov's recasting of the history of the moving pictures. Cinema begins, according to *Of Freaks and Men*, as a calculated appeal to voyeuristic desire. In spite of the film's involvement with history, the conclusions Balabanov reaches do not pertain to the time of cinema's inception. Rather, both his diagnosis and the film's political message bear witness to contemporary Russia.

Balabanov's film, attractively self-reflexive in form as well as in content, starts with a black and white account of the arrival of Yohan (Sergei Makovetskii) to St. Petersburg. He comes from abroad, from an unspecified place, carrying just a small, checkered suitcase. As the story, filmed in sepia and punctuated with intertitles, unfolds, Yohan establishes an illicit pornographic business, where he employs a young photographer. The photographer—dressed in checkers from head to toe, as if he had sprung from Yohan's bag—takes pictures of women in different stages of undress, in poses that convey strong sadomasochistic overtones. One frequent set-up involves women with exposed buttocks who are subjected to a thrashing. Yohan's business eventually progresses from still photography to moving pictures.

The birth of cinema as narrated by Balabanov appears at first to be consistent with the way in which the classics of feminist film theory described the structures underlying the functioning of mainstream cinema. Voyeurism is one of the key concepts in feminist explications of the mechanisms that come into play when a male spectator watches a female image. As Suzanna Walters summed up:

> The darkened room of the movie theater sets in motion a set of psychic responses that encourage both a voyeuristic/scopophilic attitude and an ego identification with the characters on the screen. Mulvey argues that woman is created as a spectacle for male desire through the gaze of the camera

(seen here as a phallic substitute), the gaze of the men within the narrative, and the gaze of the male spectator.[2]

Balabanov exposes the relations of power present in gendered looking in a manner akin to second-wave feminism. In his show of illicit attractions, the filmmaker includes a woman who does not see, but who is looked at by voyeuristic, pleasure-seeking males. The blind wife of the respectable doctor Stasov, Ekaterina Kirilovna (Lika Nevolina) becomes seduced by the voice of a certain Victor Ivanovich (Viktor Sukhorukov), Yohan's accomplice, who invades her apartment in search of her adopted Siamese twin sons. She willingly raises her skirt to display her private parts for his viewing pleasure. He later has her disrobe, places her in front of a camera and a silent male audience, and subjects her to a whipping administered by her own servant girl.

In a similar vein, Balabanov presents women who are conditioned to become consumers of pornographic pictures. The corruptive power of the images transforms some of the film's female protagonists into objects of sexual exploitation and abuse. They must fancy themselves as actors in the dominance-submission patterns of the photographs, and, consequently, those who at first only look at the pictures are drawn to reenact the same scenarios for male audiences. In the film's exposition, Liza, the daughter of engineer Radlov, is a timid five-year-old posing for a family picture. The narrative then jumps to the story's present, when a teenage Liza (Dinara Drukarova), who after the death of her mother lives with her father, dreams of traveling to the West, as she watches trains arrive and depart from a railroad water pump outside the apartment's window. Radlov invites a young man named Putilov to dinner, and introduces him to Liza. Beneath the smooth surface of proper bourgeois life and of Liza and Putilov's budding youthful infatuation lie the young couple's dark secrets. In order to gain the financial means necessary to establish himself as a photographer, Putilov lends his skills to the dirty business of commercial pornography. When engineer Radlov foretells the advent of a new era that will be due to the development of cinema and its potential to "reveal the truth to the simple people," Balabanov's viewer already knows that Putilov's creative energy has been channeled elsewhere. Liza, on the other hand, has already become a consumer of the products that the young photographer helps put on the market; she secretly buys Yohan's "dirty" pictures from Victor Ivanovich. For this reason, Putilov's question whether she likes photography makes her feel uneasy. Liza likes photography in ways that are not sanctioned by official culture.

Yohan, the mastermind behind Russia's adventure with (pornographic) photography, is himself fascinated with the Russian virgin Liza. His offer of marriage gives her father a heart attack. When the housekeeper who happens to be Yohan's sister shows the pictures hidden in Lisa's closet to the father, the latter dies. The door is now open for Yohan to move from the underworld into Liza's apartment and for him to take possession of her life. To complete the cycle of perversity, Putilov, the infatuated youth, will be the one to film Liza's entrance onto the scene of pornographic spectacle. His excitement over the ability to work with the "cinematograph" mixes with consternation and shame due to the fact that he is filming a scene in which the naked Lisa is subjected to "punishment" in the form of a whipping administered by an older woman whom we know as Yohan's nanny.

Thus, looking in cinema means primarily gazing at women and it is a process that is uniformly exploitative in nature. The entire world within Balabanov's film becomes corrupted by pornographic images of women. A diegetic audience of silent, middle-class men becomes a predictable element of the unseemly spectacles. Yet, the perfunctory similarity between Balabanov's "message" and the classical feminist argument stops here. Balabanov does not present an indictment against patriarchy. The evils he associates with pornographic pictures—both still and moving—are not a by-product of the established social order, but rather, they work to undermine the patriarchal status quo. The two ineffective but otherwise nearly ideal patriarchs in the film, Liza's father and the doctor, fall victim to the increasingly powerful underworld. The father dies when he is exposed to the pornographic pictures. Their manufacturer shoots and kills the doctor. Yohan and his retinue easily corrupt women and children such as the doctor's Siamese twins. Even though Victor Ivanovich eventually becomes one of the victims of the violence he helped unleash, while Putilov, Liza, and the twins liberate themselves from Yohan's tyrannical grip, the poison that spread from Yohan's checkered suitcase has already thoroughly contaminated Russia's "innocents." The "good" fathers are defenseless against the gang's machinations.

Since the film does not critique the structures of patriarchy, what happens here in terms of suture, or "the procedures by means of which cinematic texts confer subjectivity upon their viewers"[3]? Balabanov quite clearly does not invite his audience to appropriate the "gaze" of either Yohan or Victor Ivanovich. The two fathers, Radlov and Stasov, refuse to be drawn into the spectacle. The diegetic audience is not sufficiently individuated and it therefore remains without identity. This emergence of various masculinities, and the consequent fragmentation of the male subject position is for Balabanov symptomatic of a crisis that afflicts the dominant, male/patriarchal identity. Implied in the filmmaker's diagnosis of a society in decline is a judgment. The only male characters who inspire sympathy in this picture are, in fact, the pillars of the existing order, the fathers. The exploitative "gaze" originates at the fringes of established society. Thus, wholesome values are associated with patriarchy and their erosion is due to the evil influence of "strangers" and an inherent weakness of character in women, who are thus ultimately responsible for the collapse of the good old world around them.

Carried by a train, whose speed might denote her youthful energy and a desire to start anew, Liza leaves for the "West." What was hidden from public view or accessible only to initiated audiences in St. Petersburg exists here, in the unidentified place in which she arrives, in the public sphere. She walks along a street of a red-light district. A couple of prostitutes look at her from their displays, and a grinning young man dressed in black leather beckons her. As she hesitates, Putilov, in a speeding car, tries to evade a crowd of young women following him. Liza chooses the grinning gigolo over Putilov. She enters the display and submits herself to a whipping. In direct contrast to the previous sadomasochistic scenes, she now faces the camera. This type of framing seems to emphasize the element of choice. Liza acts out a sexual fantasy; she is no longer a victim of circumstances beyond her control.

St. Petersburg, the "dead city" as Liza refers to it, with its deserted streets and multiple waterways, figures very prominently as the background for the story the filmmaker tells in *Of Freaks and Men*. The atmosphere of Russia's northern capital brings Pushkin's "Bronze Horseman" to mind. Had Putilov not sold out to commercial filmmaking, he too—just as the protagonist of Pushkin's poem—would probably roam St. Petersburg blaming the mighty Peter for his personal catastrophe. The city that was to serve as Russia's window to Europe provides a perfect location for Balabanov's re-telling of the story of cinema's arrival from the West to Russia.

The presence of clear references to cinematic beginnings in *Of Freaks and Men* adds to the picture's meta-cinematic quality. The trains arriving and departing from the pump as seen through the window of the Radlov residence are a reminder of one of the first Lumière films, *The Arrival of a Train at La Ciotat Station*, which first "arrived" at the Grand Café in Paris in 1895, and ushered the age of the moving pictures. Does Balabanov comment on the path taken by Western cinema? Quite paradoxically for someone who is a filmmaker himself, he certainly seems to be commenting on the negative influence this Western invention has had and continues to have on Russia's society.

In the film's final sequence, Yohan steps on a floe of ice on the Neva and drifts off. This sequence is reminiscent of another classic of early cinema, D.W. Griffith's *Way Down East* (1921). In Griffith's melodrama the heroine, mother of an illegitimate child who is therefore deemed a "fallen woman," is cast away by the father of a man whom she loves. In the film's concluding sequence she finds herself on a floe of ice moving towards a waterfall. In *Cinematernity* Lucy Fisher analyzes the metaphoric implications of this sequence. She emphasizes the association of aquatic metaphors with feminine sexuality. On the one hand, "fragmentation of the river's surface" may correspond to the themes of "female erotic transgression, defloration, and illegitimate birth."[4] Griffith's heroine "is positioned on the water for the sin of having 'broken' maternal 'waters.'"[5] On the other hand, "the fact that ice thaws under Anna's body—following a scene in which she challenges patriarchal categories of 'good' and 'bad' girls—seems suggestive of a certain power in woman to render solids fluid."[6] By analogy, when Balabanov unites Yohan with the river at the end of *Of Freaks and Men*, he emphasizes, on the one hand, the "stranger's" questionable masculinity, and on the other, his ability to shatter the legitimate social order determined by bourgeois values.

After the first film shoot with Liza in the main role, an intertitle informs the viewer that Liza has become a woman. But Yohan never even tries to physically approach her; he has her violated literally through his nanny's whip and figuratively through the camera's lens. These "paraphernalia" serve as substitutes for a "proper" consummation of their relationship. It may also be that while watching the scene of her beating, Yohan does not strive to possess Liza, but, rather, he identifies with her. Yohan employs his own nanny to perform the role of the executioner in what seems to be a reenactment of Freud's "a child is being beaten" fantasy. In addition, the shot reverse shot formation at the center of this sequence raises important questions concerning the subject/object relationship. The first shot of the sequence, Yohan's point of view, frames the scene of the beating. The second one consists of a close-up of Yohan's strangely inert, entranced face. This shot bears a resemblance to the close-up of Liza's face at the time when she subjects herself to the beating by the "western" hired man. Even though Yohan is positioned as the viewer (subject) within the formation, through the strangely passive expression of his face he transforms himself into a mere object of our gaze. This peculiar process of identification contributes to the confusion of sexual difference. It also makes the hypothetical male viewer's identification with Yohan's "gaze" problematic. Moreover, if Yohan's strangely colored suitcase stands for the "disease" which he imports into Russia, then cinema may also be conceptualized as a child to which he gives birth, a child stamped with a stigma of illegitimacy due to its uncertain origins.

Ice breaks on the water when Yohan first arrives in St. Petersburg. Yet since he is the one responsible for completing the disintegration of the city's bourgeois establishment, the breaking ice on the Neva in the film's concluding sequence suggests that Yohan has effectively subverted the world as it had existed prior to his appearance. As Eliot Borenstein has demonstrated,

> On a scale surpassing both the libertinism of the fin-de-siècle 'boulevard' and the eroticized battlefield of the Russian Civil War and New Economic Policy, Russian culture in all its manifestations would appear to have become thoroughly and overtly sexualized...Many voices have spoken against the sexual saturation of Russian popular culture. One man's utopia is another's apocalypse, and the numerous critiques of sexual 'excess' suggest that it is only a small step from scatology to eschatology. [7]

Balabanov joins in with those who are apprehensive of the danger associated with the prevalence of overtly sexual imagery in Russian popular culture. *Of Freaks and Men* seduces its viewers with an artsy and sexy appearance, only to make them aware of the evil resulting from such seduction. Likewise, Balabanov steps outside the boundaries of "legitimate" gender constructions in order to reaffirm a desired ideal, a fiction of a native realm that is free of the polluting influence of strangers and governed by traditional values.

As Helena Goscilo has explained,

> With desovietization and the indiscriminate enthusiasm for things Western among a significant portion of its urban population, Russia in the early 1990s began shedding its identity of virtuous self-denial for 'the good life' and a 'beautiful style.' [8]

The dominant drive to appear beautiful has been fueled by popular magazines, Western films, and television. [9] Aestheticization of the female body presents one of the surface manifestations of the search for a new aesthetics that is quite apparent in recent Russian cinema as well. While some aestheticized images of women conform to the dominant trend of celebrating the "fantasy universe of stylish well-being," [10] others redefine old paradigms in provocative ways. In the remaining part of this essay I focus on Valerii Todorovskii's *Land of the Deaf* (1998) as a picture in which the centrally situated female body also threatens to undermine the established social order. Unlike Balabanov, Todorovskii sets his story within the realities of contemporary Russia, in the context of the new consumer culture so aptly diagnosed by Goscilo. In contrast to Balabanov's film, in *Land of the Deaf*, the transformation of gender-related social roles produces a destabilizing effect that in turn leads to questioning of the status quo.

Todorovskii constructs the film's two female protagonists in a way evocative of both feminine myths of previous epochs and contemporary socio-cultural paradigms. He then leads the two women along a path of self-discovery and liberation from these oppressive stereotypes. Rather than continue in the roles imposed on them by the dominant culture, the protagonists of *Land of the Deaf* escape into their own perception of themselves as beautiful.

In *Dehexing Sex*, Goscilo discusses the "Romantic" habits that dominated the gendered representation of nineteenth-century Russian and twentieth-century Soviet literature:

> Generalized into a vague blur of ethereal beauty, in Russia as elsewhere, woman's form was reduced to symmetry, delicacy, and harmony, its specifics carefully confined to large, expressive eyes ('mirror of the soul'), porcelain pallor, and clouds of hair. While religious icons (angel, virgin Mary) dominated the conceptualization of womanhood, euphemism and lyrical effusions desexed any bodily part associated with potential sensuality (e.g. breasts, hips, feet).[11]

Goscilo points out that "Soviet literature adapted the Romantic aesthetic of the preceding century to the pseudomodern Russian context."[12] This type of external form narrated female virtue. On the opposite side, an emphasis on a woman's physical presence signaled experienced sexual predators.

The opening shots of *Land of the Deaf* suggest a standard use of the female as a trope. In the very first shot we see a serious, pensive female figure in a medium close-up, with a male figure seated in the background. This shot privileges a female perspective but the following shot undermines this assumption by reversing the perspective. The big-eyed, icon-like Rita (Chulpan Khamatova) is now pushed to the side while her boyfriend Alesha (Nikita Tyunin) occupies the center of the frame. Rita's words establish her as the embodiment of a specifically Russian type of femininity. "They will kill me," says Alesha. "Let them try," answers Rita. "I will shelter you with my own body. Let all the bullets hit me." Rita loves selflessly and unconditionally. She will willingly sacrifice herself in order to save Alesha, an unrelenting gambler who is seriously in debt to a mafia boss. Rita will even, in accordance with a Dostoevskian variant, use her body to "save" him by becoming a prostitute. She will accept the highest degree of degradation in order to fulfill her role of savior.

In the following sequence, the director appears to be working towards the establishment of the—once again—familiar and universal dichotomy between the virginal beauty and the whore. The sequence starts with the shot of a stripper, Yaya (Dina Korzun), dancing in a bar. Just as in the case of women who were the objects of Yohan's photographs in Balabanov's film, Yaya's back is turned towards the audience, and her face, in contrast to the opening shot of Rita, is at first not visible at all. Thus limited in her existence to the parameters of her body, she becomes a commodity subjected to the scrutinizing gaze of the diegetic audience: the bar's predominantly male clientele. As the camera pans out to include Rita and her boyfriend in the picture, the dark-haired stripper and the blond self-sacrificing girl stand in clear opposition to one another. While one disrobes her body to satisfy base masculine instincts, the other displays with modesty the purity of her soul—made bare in the innocent, wide-eyed expression on her face. Whereas the stripper's body is a site of illicit pleasures, Rita's face holds the promise of redemption. But the simple dichotomy breaks down when the stripper slaps, in his face, one of the men in the audience. Yaya thereby breaks the boundary between herself— the spectacle—and the male spectator. She refuses to remain contained within the role of a projection of male fantasies by destroying the comfort of male specular indulgence. More importantly, her action effectively undermines the paradigms of corrupted versus pure and redeeming femininity. Her sudden departure from the stage exposes the performative character of feminine roles sanctioned by the dominant culture. The same gesture of rejection in turn provides the starting point of the two women's relationship.

It has to be noted that the female dichotomy set up at the outset of *Land of the Deaf* goes beyond the superficial opposition of the virgin and the whore. The film juxtaposes an elevated ideal of femininity: the mythical figure of the woman who is there to save and redeem the man with the reality of female exploitation that in the years following the collapse of the Soviet Union has become synonymous with the transformation of women into commodities. As Goscilo observed, already late Soviet culture saw "Exploitation of women's bodies as marketable commodities and objects of displaced male violence (which) suddenly found unsavory expression in diverse aspects of late Soviet culture."[13] Right after Rita and Yaya meet, Yaya, the deaf stripper, identifies the most important factor that unites them: "You are in danger. You are threatened by men."

As the narrative unfolds, Todorovskii continues to allude to the theme of the whore—virgin dyad. The two women find refuge from the threatening outside world in the studio of a sculptor who has gone to a monastery in search of inspiration. The sculpture for which Yaya had served as a model presents a deformed female figure that menacingly stretches three pairs of hands (which could alternatively be interpreted as an image of a kind of non-Christian deity). Rita's image framed in a mirror is, on the other hand, closer to that of the virgin Mary. If the model of femininity represented by Rita is consistent with the Russian/Soviet tradition of ideologically pious and sexually restrained womanhood, Yaya's character grows out of the hedonism and the related commodification of female bodies in post-Soviet times. To confirm this, Yaya convinces Rita that the only way to obtain the money Rita desperately needs in order to save her boyfriend is to get it "from men." Yaya, one could argue, corrupts Rita by presenting prostitution as a viable option for dealing with one's financial problems. One might surmise that—just as in the case of Balabanov's film—corruption and moral degeneration will spread like waves from this stone thrown by the corrupted Yaya into the pond of Rita's pure soul.

Yet Todorovskii refers to the two feminine types only in order to allow his protagonists to overcome them. Katerina Clark identified the prostitute as "the figure of culture during late perestroika." "Why the prostitute? How could a prostitute signify a struggle about Culture?" asks Clark. "No doubt this was because she traffics in her body, one of the most overused symbols in moral, political, and even aesthetic discourse."[14] Pyotr Todorovskii the elder transformed the prostitute into a filmic icon of such late Soviet anxieties in his cinematic adaptation of Vladimir Kunin's *Interdevochka* (1989). Yet the son, Valerii Todorovskii, moves beyond the discourse perpetuated by his father. The original breach of conventions signaled by Yaya's slapping of the customer in *Land of the Deaf* represents what the film as a whole accomplishes: a move away from determined models of femininity and cultural iconography sanctioned by the dominant culture towards a female rediscovery of the self as a subject articulating meaning and searching for means of self-expression.

The emphasis on the self, evident in the name the heroine chooses for herself: "Ya–ya" ("I–I"), finds expression in both Yaya and Rita's emphasis on shaping their own images. The main principle guiding them in this process is a search for beauty. The two women begin to play "dress-up" in order to enhance their images in ways that may please men. Their attitude once again exposes the performative character of gender norms. Gradually they move towards the realization that they want to be beautiful for themselves. Within the space of the sculptor's studio they begin to mold their images by trying on different outfits. They look at each other and at their own reflections in the mirror. This preoccupation with their own images adds emphasis to the narcissistic focus on the self that was already signaled by the name Yaya had chosen for herself. Within the walls of the artist's studio, the mirror does not represent a private, enclosed space, the traditional domain of the feminine. Neither does it function as a guardian of an officially sanctioned image of female beauty. Instead, reflected images open up the possibility of once again putting stress on the self. They enable the protagonists to break free from the roles imposed on women by social conditioning. Taking pleasure in sculpting their own images becomes a source of empowerment for Yaya and for Rita.

When Yaya, who constantly emphasizes the need to appear beautiful, encourages Rita to eat for the sake of preserving and enhancing her beauty, Rita asks: "Why?" "In order to be liked," Yaya responds. "Why?" persists Rita. "In order to live..." answers Yaya. Implied in the last statement is something other than the ability to attract the attention of men. At this point in the narrative an aestheticized feminine body has been freed from its function of attracting the male gaze. "Consider gender...as a corporeal style, an 'act,' as it were, which is both intentional and performative, where 'performative' suggests a dramatic and contingent construction of meaning,"[15] challenged Judith Butler in *Gender Trouble*. The female protagonists of *Land of the Deaf* seem to be responding to this type of challenge. Consequently, they are able to distance themselves from the world of male desire. Instead, their search for beauty becomes synonymous with an ontological quest for self-definition.

The two women plan an escape to the Land of the Deaf, a warm island where everybody is nice and one does not have to worry about money, and where, as Yaya says, "we will buy the most beautiful swim suits and we will be the most beautiful on the beach." The contrast between this dream of an escape and the reality of the deaf mafia, which operates on the same principles as the hearing criminal underworld, precludes the possibility of such an easy way out. Rather than present a realistic plan of action, Yaya's utopia stands for the necessity of searching for a refuge from an oppressive reality. The island of the deaf materializes in the two women's relationship.

Todorovskii manages to create his two female characters as beautiful by unorthodox means. Medium close-ups of the two women predominate—their bodies are not fragmented or overtly sexualized. Through the use of light and color he renders them aesthetically appealing.

Numerous shots include both of the women within the frame. At first, there is a male perspective implied, but the viewer is left with a strong impression of the two women looking at themselves and at each other. As a result, the two protagonists become liberated: they are no longer constrained to perform the roles imposed on their bodies by patriarchal ideology, socialist or otherwise.

The outside world intervenes to crush this oppositionist union and to destroy the two protagonists' resolve to live their lives beautifully. Alesha once again squanders the money earned by Rita to bail him out. Yaya breaks down and informs on him only to trap Rita and herself in the clutches of the angered mafia boss. By appealing to the deaf mafia boss for help, Rita pits the two groups against each other. Only Yaya and Rita escape with their lives from the final shoot out. In the film's final sequence we see the two women squatting beneath an embankment. The violence they witness seems to reduce them: it forces them to assume fetal-like positions and gone is their gracious confidence. The world has collapsed around them, yet the bond they had previously established is now even stronger because of Rita's trauma-induced loss of hearing. It will enable them to get up and to continue living their lives on their own terms.

In *Ideology of the Aesthetic*, Terry Eagleton points to the contradictoriness of the aesthetic which he identifies at once as "inseparable from the construction of the dominant ideological forms of modern class society," and at the same time harboring the possibility of posing "an unusually powerful challenge and alternative to these dominant ideological forms."[16] Autonomous vis-à-vis the surrounding reality, the domain of the aesthetic "provides a central constituent of bourgeois ideology," yet, simultaneously

> It also marks an emphasis on the self-determining nature of human powers and capacities which becomes, in the work of Marx and others, the anthropological foundation of a revolutionary opposition to bourgeois utility.[17]

The Polish poet Zbigniew Herbert recognized in his own way this opposition's potential of the aesthetic when in "The Power of Taste" he attributed Solidarity's successful challenge to the established order of drab Communist reality to the latter's striking tastelessness.

A post-communist impulse may also play a role in determining the shape of the two protagonists' search for self-expression in Todorovskii's film since the way they dress and sculpt their images is strikingly different from the communist norm. But Rita and Yaya seek refuge from the social realities of contemporary Russia in their beautiful Land of the Deaf. The aesthetic creates an area of opposition and free expression in a world in which patriarchy is still the easily identifiable enemy, where social and legal inequities are still very much a part of female experience. The aesthetic does not serve as a justification for the dominant ideological forms; it provides a method for the construction of an alternative, feminine subject: internally conflicted but still striving for agency and opposed to the patriarchal enemy.

Both films, *Of Freaks and Men* and *Land of the Deaf*, place the figure of a crippled woman at their centers. However, the ideological resonance of each of them is very different. In Balabanov's film, the blindness of Dr. Stasov's wife serves as an external sign of her flawed character. She is not only physically, but also spiritually crippled: not able to appreciate the humane qualities of her husband, she is easily seduced by Viktor Ivanovich and drawn onto a path that destroys her as well as her entire family. In *Land of the Deaf*, Yaya's loss of hearing results from the abuse she suffered as a child. But female bodies in Todorovskii's film no longer "document" their owners' suffering and degradation."[18] Instead, Yaya views herself as different rather than crippled. She transcends her handicap by embracing everything that she defines as beautiful. Her choice is synonymous with a striving towards defining the world independently of the oppressive social circumstances.

In both films the narrative develops towards a fracturing of the established order. In *Of Freaks and Men* this fracturing validates the order of the bourgeois family as Balabanov casts a nostalgic even if slightly ironic glance at the old world. In *Land of the Deaf*, on the other hand, there is only a vague yet welcome promise that something positively new will replace the world that has been fractured. The juxtaposition of the two pictures adds up to create an image of a society in flux, torn by often contradictory impulses. Unlike in previous times, the performance of gender no longer yields a unified view of an officially sanctioned social matrix.

Works Cited

Atwood, Lynne. *Red Women on the Silver Screen*. London: Pandora, 1993.

Borenstein, Eliot. "About That: Deploying and Deploring Sex in Postsoviet Russia." *STCL* 24 no. 1 (Winter 2000): 51-83.

Butler, Judith. *Gender Trouble. Feminism and The Subversion of Identity*. New York: Routledge, 1990.

Clark, Katerina. "Not for Sale. The Russian-Soviet Intelligentsia, Prostitution, and the Paradox of Internal Colonization." In vol. 7 of

Stanford Slavic Studies: Russian Culture in Transition. Stanford: Stanford University Press, 1993, 189-205.

Eagleton, Terry. *The Ideology of the Aesthetic*. Cambridge, Mass.: Basil Blackwell, 1990.

Fisher, Lucy. *Cinematernity: Film, Motherhood, Genre*. Princeton: Princeton University Press, 1996.

Goscilo, Helena. *Dehexing Sex. Russian Womanhood During and After Glasnost*. Ann Arbor: University of Michigan Press, 1996.

Goscilo, Helena. "Style and S(t)imulation: Popular Magazines, or The Aestheticization of Postsoviet Russia." *STCL* 24, no. 1 (Winter 2000): 15-49.

Silverman, Kaja. *The Subject of Semiotics*. New York: Oxford University Press, 1983.

Walters, Suzanna Danuta. *Material Girls. Making Sense of Feminist Cultural Theory*. Berkeley: University of California Press, 1995.

Notes

[1] Lynne Atwood, *Red Women on the Silver Screen* (London: Pandora, 1993), 18.

[2] Suzanna Danuta Walters, *Material Girls. Making Sense of Feminist Cultural Theory* (Berkeley: University of California Press, 1995), 56.

[3] Kaja Silverman, *The Subject of Semiotics* (New York: Oxford University Press, 1983), 195.

[4] Lucy Fisher, *Cinematernity: Film, Motherhood, Genre* (Princeton: Princeton University Press, 1996), 66.

[5] Ibid., 66.

[6] Ibid., 64.

[7] Eliot Borenstein, "About That: Deploying and Deploring Sex in Postsoviet Russia," *STCL* 24, no.1 (Winter 2000): 55, 61.

[8] Helena Goscilo, "Style and S(t)imulation: Popular Magazines, or The Aestheticization of Postsoviet Russia," *STCL* 24, no.1 (Winter, 2000): 17.

[9] Ibid., 17.

[10] Ibid., 18.

[11] Helena Goscilo, *Dehexing Sex. Russian Womanhood During and After Glasnost* (Ann Arbor: University of Michigan Press, 1996), 88.

[12] Ibid., 88.

[13] Ibid., 13.

[14] Katerina Clark, "Not for Sale. The Russian-Soviet Intelligentsia, Prostitution, and the Paradox of Internal Colonization," in *Russian Culture in Transition*, vol. 7 of *Stanford Slavic Studies* (Stanford: Stanford University Press, 1993), 191.

[15] Judith Butler, *Gender Trouble. Feminism and The Subversion of Identity* (New York: Routledge, 1999), 177.

---

[16] Terry Eagleton, *The Ideology of the Aesthetic* (Cambridge, Mass.: Basil Blackwell, 1990), 3.
[17] Ibid., 9.
[18] *Dehexing Sex*, 89.

CHAPTER FOURTEEN

CHANTAL AKERMAN'S CINEMATIC TRANSGRESSIONS: TRANSHISTORICAL AND TRANSCULTURAL TRANSPOSITIONS, TRANSLINGUALISM, AND THE TRANSGENDERING OF THE CINEMATIC GAZE

SHARON LUBKEMANN ALLEN

In a June 2001 discussion "On Absence and Imagination in Documentary Film" linked to lectures on "Crossing Cinematic Borders," Chantal Akerman speaks of her work in spatial terms, as transgressive cinema, crossing geo-cultural borders and challenging cinematic boundaries.[1] It is transgressive in both chronotopic and socio-ideological senses of deviance, digression, and dissent. Delineating aesthetic deviations, Akerman descries violent breaks with cinematic conventions, pushing shots to a point of "unbearable" pressure and only then releasing the viewer to another shot, thereby doing a kind of "violence" to or even "violating" the viewer, while pursuing a particular view of society and aesthetic mode of vision to the point that cinematic genres "implode."[2] We might understand Akerman's disruptive work in terms of the explosive, but creatively productive "ruptures" and "travesty" described by Lotman in his dialectic analyses of cultural formation[3] and his work on "dialogue mechanisms" defining dynamics along the boundaries within and between cultures.[4] The latter offers a model of dialogue in which travesty and translation are essential and transformative for cultural consciousness,[5] in which cultural (re)construction is contingent on the "alien" word, "double-voicing," and "rejoinder" described by Bakhtin in his analysis of dialogic discourse in the novel and "speech genres,"[6] but also in which dialogue, even as it respects autonomy also reflects asymmetry and enacts a kind of violence or deconstruction, a Derridean decentering, in order to redirect or re-conceive the cultural sphere. Lotman's complex model of the semiosphere, operative at every level of culture and consciousness may further elucidate the interplay of discourses in Akerman's work and its relation to larger cultural spheres. Akerman's cinema demarks "extreme edges" of the semiosphere where dialogue is "incessant" as well as internal boundaries which are also among the "hottest spots for semioticizing processes"[7]:

> The entire space of the semiosphere is transected by boundaries of different levels, boundaries of different languages and even of texts, and the internal space of each of these sub-semiospheres has its own semiotic 'I' which is realized as the relationship of any language, group of texts, separate to a metastructural space which describes them.[8]

Akerman's films demonstrate the essential "heterogeneity" of her personal aesthetics, of cinematic discourse, of larger socio-political and cultural semiospheres,[9] of the many "speech genres" and cultural discourses at play in her work,[10] or of the linguistic or semiotic "polysystems" in which her work participates.[11] They offer a dialogic model for the cinema, marked by that conscious attentiveness to discrete voices, viewpoints, modes of speech and vision, available only by inhabiting and crossing thresholds.[12] That is, her work occupies the "boundary" that is always "bilingual and polylingual"[13] and, like "minor literatures," it "work[s] over its material...in a relation of multiple deterritorializations with language."[14] So Akerman's is consistently a "border cinema" in which the borders crossed are often literally geographical, national, linguistic, or cultural (as in *Je, tu, il, elle* (1974), *Les Rendez-vous d'Anna* (1978), *D'Est* (1993), *Un divan à New York/A Couch in New York* (1996) and *De l'autre côté* (2002)). But these borders are also imagined and/or remembered distances (registered in the layered longings of *News from Home* (1976) and *Histoires d'Amérique* (1988)), apparent historical differences (linking lynchings in the American South to the Holocaust and Stalin's purges in *Sud* (1999)), and always socio-ideological boundaries and cinematic conventions. Most audibly and visibly to critics of her early work, Akerman has crossed boundaries by attending to the discourses of women's everyday existence and articulating a new kind of feminine cinematic discourse. But at the same time, her work represents a translingual and transhistorical as well as transgendered authority and authorship.

The interrelated crossings of Akerman's work owe a great deal to what Alisa Lebow defines in her 2003 analysis of *D'Est* as "Memory Once Removed: Indirect Memory and Transitive Autobiography."[15] That is, the personal network of investigations openly and obliquely pursued in Akerman's work at once confirms Lotman's claim that "the boundary of the personality is a semiotic boundary"[16] and complicates the notion of boundary by giving that cinematic semiotic boundary the dynamic dimensions of a continually decentered, deconstructed, and dialogically redefined semiosphere or polysystem. More than many other filmmakers, Akerman has been "an artist committed enough to ask questions in different idioms."[17] If those questions are consistently concerned with identity, particularly that of the female subject and of the female filmmaker, especially as exile or postmodern nomad, they are investigated in terms of a vast variety of what Bakhtin recognizes as personally, socio-ideologically and aesthetically differentiated "speech genres" that call for a careful and complex analysis in terms of "sociological stylistics."[18] Akerman's work is always positioned at those cultural, historical, aesthetic "crossroads" that Bakhtin finds essential to the "dialogic" novel as the genre of modernity. And, participating in a more postmodern aesthetic, the crossroads she investigates retain their "open-endedness" by tracing convergences and digressions in cultural and personal memory, inviting dialogue between apparently incommensurate cinematic conventions, and investigating connections between self-conscious filmmaking and spectatorship. That is, her creativity is contingent on her work's consistent positioning on a threshold, from which multiple horizons are held in view. It is "avant-garde" in terms of both the political-ideological authenticity and realist aesthetic recognized by Lukács in works that critique current social tendencies and types and anticipate alternative realities,[19] but also, paradoxically, in terms of a modernist aesthetic rejected by Lukács but recognized by theorists such as Adorno and Horkheimer as maintaining autonomy in the context of a homogenizing culture industry.[20] Both Akerman's political and aesthetic (re)vision push beyond the viewer and culture's "horizon of expectations."[21] So Akerman's work is transgressive insofar as it extends that horizon or widens threshold space so that different social perspectives, historical moments, cultural histories, cinematic discourses, and languages enter into contact.

In an aesthetic sense, Akerman's work transgresses by turning inward, exploring paradoxes in cinematic consciousness and exposing problematics in a cinematic unconscious across generic boundaries. Her work also transgresses as it turns outward, most often into the modern city or pursuing cross-country trajectories, violating cultural conventions, not only by dis-covering uncharted cultural domains but also by refracting conventional domains of cinema—in both cases, often domains inhabited by women—through an unsettling cinematic gaze and disjuncture between sound and image. Akerman further compounds these dislocations by crossing between distant cultures within and across her works, discovering both points of connection and incommunicability. At the same time, she recovers historical connections and disconnect, navigating difficult domains of personal and cultural memory. It is this increasingly complex and creative defamiliarization of cultural domains and cinematic devices, past and present, that is Chantal Akerman's great contribution to cinema in general and feminist cinema, criticism and theory in particular. Her work relies on that concomitant "defamiliarization" or "estrangement" (*ostranenie*) of the habitual in our social existence and of habitual ways of seeing—i.e. it renders both social and literary/cinematic convention tangible in ways noted by formalists such as Shklovsky, Eikenbaum, and Tynianov.[22] So Akerman's work transgenders the camera, as it were, through its redirected and formally redefined focus on women's everyday existence, no less in later documentaries such as *Sud* as in early "feminist" films such as *Je, tu, il, elle* and *Jeanne Dielman*, but only and increasingly as she also transposes the cinematic gaze, exploring its potential in translation and as translingual, transcultural, and transhistorical traveler.

Feminist film criticism and theory has been most interested in Akerman as a filmmaker attentive to overlooked domains and dynamics of women's everyday existence, and attentive to these through a distinctly feminist lens—challenging conventional constructions of predominantly female protagonists and the spaces they inhabit and cross by using such strategies as long, low-angle, static shots associated with "objective realism."[23] As Catherine Fowler notes in her brief overview of Akerman's significance to cinematic practice, Akerman's early work was recognized for an "interrogation of film language" akin to that of modernist or avant-garde filmmakers, but anomalously achieved "without actually interrupting the fictional world," instead still "telling a story" while shifting the construction of meaning "from narrative to other aspects such as time, space, ritual and repetition."[24] Her cinema is read as resisting voyeurism and freeing the gaze, her redirection of the camera and refusal of the directives issued by different camera "angles and movements, point-of-view shots and close-ups" requiring of the spectator a new kind of critical attentiveness to cinematic "attractions" as well as an active wandering within the frame, responding to "Mulvey's call in her famous article "Visual Pleasure and Narrative Cinema" to "free the look of the camera into its materiality in time and space."[25] This attentiveness, too, might be understood in terms of Bakhtin's definition of dialogic authorship—whose utterance or work is one always attentive to distinct voices, preserving their autonomy, and requiring a "rejoinder" from the reader[26] (or in this case, viewer). Lotman similarly recognizes this active co-operation between originary and "receptive" consciousness or culture— though he recognizes more fully the invasive and reactive, disruptive and explosive, as well as creative dynamics inherent in that necessarily shifting asymmetrical relationship.[27] His model is somewhat closer then to Bakhtin's characterization of carnival, also associated with dialogic discourse, but more clearly marked by potentially violent inversions and reversals. But like Bakhtin's dialogic author, whose interest guarantees a maximum of freedom and evokes voluntary response, Akerman seems to seek to guarantee filmmaker, cinematic subject, and audience the sort of freedom and responsibility ascribed to author and reader by Sartre in his "Why Write?"[28]

Foregrounding women as subjects and forging a new mode of seeing women on screen, Akerman's early films, from her debut film *Saute ma ville* (1968) to *Jeanne Dielman, 23 Quai du Commerce, 1080 Bruxelles* (released in 1975, the year Mulvey's renown article was published) and *Les Rendez-vous d'Anna* (1978) were recognized as paradigms of a "feminist film practice" and "female aesthetic,"[29] emancipating a "female subject."[30] Films such as *Je, tu, il, elle* and *Jeanne Dielman* offered sustained and restrained (fixed rather than fixated and fetishizing) gazes at women's lives, in real time and in overlooked or marginalized contexts. They foregrounded the everyday—forcing the viewer to watch women waiting (for a teapot to boil, for words) and going through routine gestures of preparing a meal and eating packets of sugar. Akerman also re-inscribed such acts as lesbian intercourse within the everyday and re-valued conventionally climactic and pleasurable cinematic events (such as Jeanne's murder of the john), rendering them no more significant and less suspenseful and violent than the clinking of dishes, boiling of the pot, and related disruptions of routine. And Akerman forced the viewer to confront the opaque, if apparently introspective, gaze of her protagonists, preserving what Bakhtin might recognize as their autonomy and "unfinalizedness" relative to the viewer. She was lauded by feminist critics for "her decoding of oppressive cinematic conventions and her invention of new codes of non-voyeuristic vision."[31] That is, Akerman's "unwavering gaze" was read as a means of representing women in humanizing terms. And while admittedly "violating" the viewer or the viewer's cinematic expectations, her films do not de-humanize the viewer. Instead, by forcing the viewer to endure a new kind of tension and engage as active subject through a new kind of attentive, open-ended, unfinalizing gaze, Akerman incited consciousness. At the same time, "her reintroduction of narrative and characters into the avant-garde's otherwise de-humanized world led the way for an alternative practice which would challenge mainstream cinema on its own ground."[32] Until recently, however, both feminist and broader film criticism failed to recognize the extent of this challenge to both mainstream and avant-garde cinema, partly by focusing only on Akerman's early films, closest in their play with cinematic conventions to avant-garde paradigms of feminist critique, and partly by scrutinizing these through reductive critical lenses, privileging the "'negative' function of film language" and thereby excluding considerations beyond the bounds of binary opposition to cultural and cinematic norms.[33]

Recent studies—most notably Ivone Margulies's *Nothing Happens: Chantal Akerman's Hyperrealist Everyday* (1996), Veronica Pravadelli's *Performance, Rewriting, Identity: Chantal Akerman's Postmodern Cinema* (2000), and the collection of essays *Identity and Memory: The Films of Chantal Akerman* (2003) edited by Gwendolyn Foster—have significantly complicated and clarified contexts, concerns, and connections within Akerman's *oeuvre*, charting her complex cultural critique and cinematic (re)construction in relation to shifting landscapes of cinematic, cultural, and feminist theory. Margulies challenges formal and feminist analyses of Akerman's early cinema by recontextualizing her concern with the quotidian lives of women. Not only is Akerman's aesthetic derived from and in dialogue with Neorealist and feminist realist representational strategies, "descriptive impulse" and "humanist interest" in the "underrepresented," but it also creatively and critically engages both American modernist and Brechtian aesthetics (Warhol and Snow's hyperrealist minimalism, "Warhol's 'literal' mode and 'indifference' toward any 'human interest,'" and Godard's symbolic representation).[34] Margulies' analysis of films such as *Jeanne Dielman* demonstrates how Akerman's cinematic bricolage pushes beyond an "essentialist" image of either particular character or social type and refuses to reduce the image to either literal or symbolic signification.[35] Further, Margulies aligns Akerman's consistently "antinaturalistic use of dialogues and monologues" with a "nondidactic strand of European modernist realist cinema,"[36] exemplified by filmmakers such as Bresson and Dreyer. The "intensification" of elements rather than evocation of "metaphoric associations" results in a far more open-ended, ambivalent discourse, defined as much by "rhythmic and non-verbal qualities" as by its "communicative function,"[37] as well as by the disjuncture between sound and image. Margulies finds a continuous concern with rhythm across Akerman's films, in the form of serial and cyclic structures, cliché and repetition. Finally, Margulies links Akerman's aesthetics to a "politics of the singular" rather than a feminist politics of "representativeness," based on Akerman's attentiveness to the difference between reality and representation and her concern with identity continually challenged by diverse forms of displacement (sexual, geo-cultural, etc.).[38] This difference must be understood again in both synchronic and diachronic terms, in terms of a complex dialogue, marked by distance and deferral, *différence* and *différance*.

Building on Margulies' work, critics such as White [39] and Pravadelli also "reappraise the role of gender" in Akerman's aesthetic, while seeking to recuperate Akerman's direct engagement with gender politics, address more than "residual" aesthetic traits in Akerman's later films, and investigate alternative points of reference—cinematic, more broadly aesthetic, and philosophical.[40] If American feminist critics such as Bergstrom and Johnston[41] offered early compelling arguments for a feminist reading of films such as *Jeanne Dielman* in terms of political modernism, aligning cinematic choices such as the refusal of reverse shots with a more conscious involvement of the viewer and a cognitive feminist critique of social constructions, Pravadelli complicates these readings by contending that Akerman's engagement of the viewer operates alternately through "sensory and cognitive processes" achieved partly through "the contrastive function of the visual track—especially the articulation of its spatio-temporal coordinates—and verbal language" and partly through calculated shifts between discontinuity and continuity editing.[42] Pravadelli's study re-examines Akerman's "core" cinematic concerns of female and Jewish identity and desire through the lens of "postmodern aesthetics," reconsidering her films in terms of "performance," "phenomenological" rather than cognitive spectatorship, and "rewriting."[43] She reads Akerman's work as revision of multiple mainstream and avant-garde cinematic models (Minimalism, Structural-materialist cinema, French New Wave, and various documentary traditions, including American "personal" cinema of "self-expression").[44] Pravadelli argues that Akerman's "eclectic style" "confront[s] issues of female representation, sexuality, and subjectivity in ways that the avant-garde did not" and "complicates any easy identification of her films as explicitly feminist"; Akerman concerns herself with "the performative nature of the human body and the nomadic constitution of female identity, thematics that ultimately offer ambiguous and contradictory notions of gender,"[45] inextricably linked to complex notions of ethnicity.[46] Positing "a *convergence* between formal and epistemological categories, between *aesthetics* and *ideology*,"[47] Pravadelli analyzes Akerman's work through parallel postmodern conceptions of *style* and *subjectivity*: both are "enmeshed" in the present in ways charted by Jameson's analysis in "Postmodernism and Consumer Society"[48] and "privilege the flowing of time, the 'happening of the event', and the 'time-image'" as defined by Lyotard and Deleuze.[49] Performative rather than expressive, Akerman's style and subjectivity likewise privilege direct and plural sensory experience over critically distanced intellectual interpretation, as delineated in Sontag and Kaye's analyses of postmodernism.[50] That style and subjectivity are, finally, "nomadic," citational and reflexive, attending to what "escapes signification and meaning," and breaking beyond modernist concerns with otherness or outsideness only "in terms of its potential representation."[51]

The implications of this "nomadism" for Akerman's cinematic configuration of the female subject, author, spectator are particularly significant since nomadism involves that continual reconstruction and deconstruction of identity through a Bakhtinian "double-voiced discourse" or those "deterritorializations of language" described by Deleuze and Guattari, associated by Pravadelli also with Cixous's postmodern feminist practice and theory of *écriture féminine*.[52] Citing Akerman's expressed reservations about associating her cinematic vision with a nomadism defined in terms of an attempt at "finding one's place"—"I don't know if you ever find your place...I think that goes back to my Jewish origin"— Lebow concurs that "the only place in which Akerman is fully identified is a textual one: the site of her own work."[53] This is explicitly the case in Akerman's citational *Chantal Akerman par Chantal Akerman* (1996), representing autobiography and aesthetic vision through re-edited clips, framed by brief ruminations on the process of writing/rewriting. But, as Lebow notes, all of Akerman's work may be read as "transitive autobiography," understood in terms of "detours to the self (as a daughter, as a Jew, as a filmmaker)" and "as an elaboration of her (and her generation's) post-Holocaust Jewish identity." That elaboration is marked by a continual return to what Akerman herself calls her "primal scene"— "images of evacuation," displacement, disoriented or directionless and disorienting movement—against which Akerman also focuses on "faces" that "still" "offer themselves, occasionally effacing a feeling of loss, of a world poised on the edge of the abyss" though "flickering between robust life and the possibility of a death which would strike them down without their having asked for anything."[54] Akerman offers this disorienting displacement and such potentially redemptive faces in works as apparently distant in subject and stylistically discrete as *Jeanne Dielman* and *D'Est*, or as she herself notes at the conclusion of her monologue for *D'Est*, indicating the contiguity of her work, "So that's what it was: that again."

Akerman's works, while seeming to reflect distinct "avant-garde/structuralist, counter-cinema/deconstructionist, and conventional art film" "stages" in her filmmaking, are actually rooted in "similarly radical aesthetic and political assumptions," demonstrate a truly avant-garde commitment to "raise, across a variety of forms, common questions that touch the core of both cinematic aesthetics and feminist political practice," and question narrow definitions of feminist engagement through "(supposedly) politically or aesthetically purified form," as noted by White in his analysis of Akerman's "Revisionist Aesthetics."[55] Building on Margulies' claim that "no formal strategy can be essentially feminist, anti-illusionist or political,"[56] White's close analysis of *News from Home, Les Années 80*, and *Un divan à New York/A Couch in New York* charts formal and feminist challenges issued by Akerman's works' central concern with a voiced female subjectivity and "uneasy—and very Barthesian—tension between textual pleasure and critical distance."[57] Works such as these are "most significant in the ways [they] depart" from structuralist or modernist, postmodernist, and mainstream models, by respectively evoking an unanticipated emotional intensity through modernist materialist explorations, demonstrating "alternate forms of narrative pleasure" in "deconstructed images and illusionist narrative" and using postmodern playfulness as a means of political critique "evoking the fragmented subjectivity available to women within a patriarchal society," as well as "injecting avant-garde strategies" such as "long takes and flattened dialogue" into conventional Hollywood narrative. Operating in discrete genres, Akerman relocates "the rigorous" in traditionally closed and purely pleasurable narrative as well as the "pleasurable in the rigorous and openended."[58] Through formal discontinuities "Akerman dissolves categories of *différence* central to dominant theories of film—documentary/fiction, rigor/lyricism, nonlinear/linear movement"—and engages instead in free play with multiple modalities."[59] At the same time, she dissolves the distance between textuality or self-referentiality and context or political engagement. Thus, in *Les Années 80*, which deconstructs Akerman's already reflexively postmodern musical *Golden Eighties* (or *Window Shopping*), the two-part structure of the film (fragmenting and then reconstituting the rehearsals for the musical), cinematographic shifts between video and 35 mm handheld and stationary camera work, and alternation between documentary and melodrama serve "to evoke the filmmaker's historical and cultural moment, explaining (or 'translating' [to use Barthes term]) social and political concepts, building community, and providing narrative pleasure."[60] The self-referential duration of Akerman's shots in films as aesthetically and temporally distant as *News from Home* and *A Couch in New York*, together with the flattening of dialogue in the later work and disjuncture of sound and image in the earlier film, "serve not only as meditations on cinema, but also as evocations of a deepening melancholy—an emotion that occupies the core of Akerman's *oeuvre*."[61] And, as Margulies notes in her analysis of *News from Home*, that "alienation between image and sound," which is "a common tactic in structuralist minimalist film," furthers Akerman's "subversion of a fixed locus for the 'I'" and "parallels the disjunction between the mother's space of letter writing and Akerman's space of performance—between the foreign reality and New York."[62] All these films explore subjectivity, and specifically female interiority, in the context of external pressures, particularly those associated with displacement, as well as through aesthetic discontinuities or dialogue. While White echoes Tarantino in describing Akerman's work in terms of a consistent "dialectic of form and content," we might again rather describe this in terms of Bakhtinian dialogue and "double-voicing," holding in suspension in the work itself a multiplicity of intentions. White aptly notes Akerman's "aesthetic eccentricities that draw on a wide number of traditions, refusing any kind of either/or assessment,"[63] or, again, in other terms notes Akerman's nomadism, postmodern bricolage, dialogism, and open-endedness.

Recognizing critical insights into Akerman's aesthetics offered by Anglo-American critics' layering of semiotic, psychoanalytic, and feminist lenses, Pravadelli's analysis draws additionally from what she defines as a contrastive, ethnically rather than sexually defined cultural difference and Jewish rather than Hegelian dialectic model informing Franco-Belgian deconstructive analyses of Akerman's films. As a way of reconsidering Akerman's dissenting aesthetics, she notes that "in Jewish thought, 'law' and 'transgression' are not mutually exclusive, since each pole *signifies* only in relation to the other. Thus, the subject can make sense of the world only if s/he posits the two terms as necessarily co-present."[64] Analyses by critics such as Veillon and Narboni, respectively noting sustained thematic and structural tensions between law or constriction and transgression in *Jeanne Dielman* and "stasis and seclusion" and "erratic wandering" in *Je, tu, il, elle* suggest this alternate dialectic to Pravadelli, who notes intersections between this aesthetic and the thematics of Akerman's later films.[65] Yet again this might be better understood in terms of a Bakhtinian "dialogic" aesthetic, particularly insofar as Akerman's films challenge chronotopic conventions, refusing traditional cinematic realizations and finalization, while insisting on the "outsideness" that Bakhtin considers essential to dialogue and understanding.[66] Rather than linear, the structure of Akerman's work is cyclical, recursive, refractive, and reflexive. Or, as Pravadelli also notes, Akerman's work "deconstructs the very notion of dialectic"[67] and lends itself to reconsideration as paradigmatic of postmodern rather than modernist sensibilities, the former necessarily incorporating the latter. In an aesthetic sense, then, Akerman's films can be aligned with her thematics of otherness and open-ended identity, both sexual and ethnic or cultural.

Alongside Pravadelli and Lebow's reconsiderations of Akerman's aesthetics and politics, numerous recent essays including Vojkovic's "On the Borders of Redemption: Recovering the Image of the Past" (1999), Zelechow's "The Formalist Film-Maker with a Subtext: Chantal Akerman" (1999), Diaconescu-Blumenfeld's contrastive analysis of *D'Est* and *Lamerica* (2000), Cerne's "Writing in Tongues: Chantal Akerman's *News from Home*" (2002), and Liénard's analysis of *Sud* as "espace de mémoire" (2006) emphasize the formative function of ethnic otherness. Zelechow argues that Akerman uses formalist tropes of "linguistic homelessness and silence" to represent the shoah as "the central traumatic event" across her work, while "subsum[ing] the question of Jewish identity in Europe in the closing decades of the century under the general problematic of postmodern identity crisis"[68] and exploring that postmodern crisis through diverse cinematic forms. If, "typically," Akerman's "films emphasize nonlinear narrative, discontinuity of thought and action, the illusion of real time, and the random inscrutability of a surface image," "offering a simulacrum of unorganized, meaningless phenomena lacking teleological significance" and functioning rather "self-referentially," Zelechow contends that, like "formalist" fiction, both her avant-garde and more apparently conventional films render present that which they seek to repress as well as the repression they "examine" in order "to re-inscribe."[69] Through these tropes, Akerman constructs for the viewer in general "an experience of fractured identity, the pain of the harrowing past, the gulf separating the generations and the resulting vacuum,"[70] but both her evacuation of history and oblique historical references point to a particular past. Thus, Zelechow reads the explicit Jewish subtexts in films as diverse as *Les Rendez-vous d'Anna* and *Window Shopping*, in which there is inter-generational dialogue and silence surrounding experiences of the Holocaust and diaspora, as interrelated investigations of post-Holocaust impossibilities of language and love.[71] Similarly, he reads Akerman's *Je, tu, il, elle* and *Un divan à New York* as investigations of an anonymous and homeless "Jewish identity that is lacking either Zionist or religious content."[72] These oblique investigations might be analogous to the Jewish identity that Akerman herself reads as pretext and context for her documentary *D'Est* and as subtext for *Sud*, as discussed by Liénard in her analysis of *Sud*, Akerman's documentary on the American South, as "une histoire de territoire et de terre" or "espace de mémoire."[73]

In her own commentary on *Sud*, distributed in a brochure at the Festival de Cannes in 1999, Akerman notes not only literary subtexts (Faulkner and Baldwin) for her representation of the American South, but also transcultural and transhistorical connections to cultures and violent practices of exclusion: "*À notre époque et plus que jamais, il y a de la purification dans l'air.*" ("In our times, and more than ever, purification is in the air"). Lingering on solitary trees at crossroads, her camera seeks to remind us of a history of lynching in the South, but also of all sorts of suffering, particularly in Europe, both past and contemporary. For Akerman, these multivalent signs explicitly recall the concentration camps and the gulag. Liénard charts how Akerman's camera respectively recovers "terre" (or terrain) and "territoire" (territory, history) through its double focus on landscape and testimony, "devenant à la fois témoin et accusatrice. Elle montre pour démontrer, voire démonter."[74] ("Becoming at once witness and accuser. She shows in order to show, even in order to take it apart").

Akerman explicitly seeks to echo Baldwin's description of the South in *Harlem Quartet*, noting in her commentary on the film: "Le silence du Sud. Un silence lourd, tendu. Un silence de plomb. Un silence qui devrait être, mais qui ne l'est pas. On guette le cri qui va briser ce silence. On redoute le jour qui vient."[75] ("The silence of the South. A heavy, tense silence. A silence as heavy as lead. A silence which should have been, but which is not. We wait for the scream that will break this silence. We fear the coming day"). Here again, we note silence/absence/presence that recall other silences/absences/past/present.

Focusing on *D'Est*, Vojkovic, too, emphasizes the superimposition of past and present.[76] But he notes how the relation between the two is dynamic, any reading of history "dependent on the dialectics of seeing" and on a "discourse of redemption" contingent on reflection, not only in Lukács's representational sense of the term, but also in the sense of consciousness or coming face to face with oneself. Building on Benjamin's work, Vojkovic examines the "discrepancy between the film's social function and its semiotic function," noting that cinematic choices such as the "slow and long movements of the camera or static shots where the camera stares at people, waiting for something to happen" (but always only waiting, or following movement across an extreme distance and duration, but without clarifying point of departure, destination, or even directionality), intensify the representation of disintegration, disorientation, insignificance, and "entrapment in a state of permanent transition." If this "perpetual deferral of the resolution" "increases the sense of unease and underscores the impossibility of redemption," the "focus on separate faces can be read as Akerman's attempt to 'save' as many people as possible from anonymity, from the fate which makes them invisible" as well as to "recover" "the impossible image of horror from the past" specifically by using these gazes to construct the "phatic calling" of the work for an "encounter" or rejoinder in the present.[77] Arriving at similar conclusions though examining the film through alternate critical lenses, Diaconescu-Blumenfeld contrasts a modernist "illusion of origins" and "nostalgia for purity" in Pasolini and Amelio's work, with the "maximum of space for reflection" in Akerman's *D'Est*, as film and installation. Through the latter "Akerman succeeds in integrating all the awareness [...] of the other, of the representation of the other, of the medium itself," much like other women filmmakers such as Trinh T. Minh-ha in *Re-assemblage* and Ulrike Ottinger in *Superbia*, working in hybrid genres and similarly questioning notions of culture and temporality, history, urgency, purity.[78] In her review of the installation, Butler likewise considers how Akerman's feminist focus in the film can be connected to how her installation "re-poses questions about the cinematic process and the construction of filmic documents through a different physical and ideational space," so that as "viewers move forward through the installation" they "move conceptually backward through a deconstruction of the filmmaking process." As an installation, *D'Est* is contingent on "a principle of deferment" of meaning or closure, and it "renounces the authoritative voice of the documentary." Through the disjuncture between sound and image, plurality and positioning of images, and "deliberate" and "impartial eye" of the camera, Akerman refuses to build or allow the viewer to construct any consistent or coherent narrative, inviting instead constant questions and re-visions, which continue to re-present the work. Comparing Akerman's work to films by Duras, Resnais and Lanzmann, Butler notes how Akerman's treatment of "personal crisis in the midst of social upheaval, of disaster and its aftermath, as well as the personal stakes of remembering and/or forgetting that upheaval," "of passing time, of waiting, and of the uncertainty born of daily life in the midst of despair" involves a redirected gaze at "moments preceding or following the event of daily life" and a reversal of "the hierarchy of public and private" that Akerman links explicitly with feminism. Thus, like Diaconescu-Blumenfeld's comparison, Butler's analysis points to the essential interconnectedness of feminist and ethnic questions of identity and aesthetics in Akerman's work, explored further in Cerne's analysis as well as those collected by Foster in *Identity and Memory* (2003).

Akerman's focus on those spaces of everyday encounter and alienation, on very specifically located private domains such as Jeanne Dielman's apartment or the rooms inhabited by named and anonymous figures interviewed in *D'Est* and *De l'autre côté*, as on unmapped public waystations, crossroads, fences, horizons, and landscapes transected by roads or lights, equally serve to "evacuate" cinema of its conventional form and meaning, to displace the viewer into a domain in which a disoriented and dislocated gaze must wander and find its own way, navigating this terrain through personal and historical association, cinematic cross-reference and spectatorial self-consciousness. There are historical and personal markers in terms of which this new cinematic trajectory or terrain can be charted. As Margulies notes in her analysis, "Echo and Voice in *Meetings with Anna*," history and personal memory are inscribed in both place and space.[79] But those markers, as Akerman's aesthetic or cinematic orientations, derive from what criticism often delineates as discrete domains. Akerman's cinema might be understood in terms of the "cosmopolitanism" and "world culture" associated with exilic figures such as Osip Mandel'stam and Joseph Brodsky, for whom "cosmopolitanism" figured a dissenting transhistorical and transcultural aesthetic, dislocating and defamiliarizing Russian reality, even as it functioned as a masked political accusation (standing in for anti-semitism and used broadly in the context of Stalin's and later purges against Jews, gays, and other targeted social, cultural, and ethnic minorities). Cosmopolitanism marked a double-voiced, dialogic consciousness, both deconstructive and constructing an alternate vision of culture or of a "civilization" that is "the sum total of different cultures animated by a common spiritual numerator" whose "main vehicle—speaking both literally and metaphorically, is translation." In Brodsky's analysis of Mandel'stam's poetry, "the wandering of a Greek portico into the latitude of the tundra is a translation,"[80] transforming both the literal and literary, socio-political and cultural landscape as "a wandering structure."[81] All of these dynamics of cosmopolitan translation and transformation figure essentially also in Akerman's films—audibly in those "accented films"[82] such as *News from Home*, *Les Rendez-vous d'Anna*, *D'Est*, *Sud* and *De l'autre côté*, explicitly concerned with transcultural displacement, but even in those, such as *Jeanne Dielman*, in which transposition seems to have little to do with cinematic or thematic tensions and transgressions.

Jeanne Dielman is one of the few films among Akerman's oeuvre that is famously and firmly linked to one persona but also located in one particular place, the eponymous address of the title, *Jeanne Dielman, 23 Quai du Commerce, 1080 Bruxelles*. The viewer explores Jeanne's apartment and street through her routine trajectories through those spaces, from the vantage point of a largely static (read rooted) camera that forces the viewer to follow and wait for her and to explore these spaces without her, without a focusing gaze. Thus, this space is estranged or defamiliarized, as much as Jeanne is herself, through the apparent disinterestedness and duration of the shots, through routine sounds and switching on and off of lights. This place is also, like Jeanne, increasingly invaded by tension, not because of an invasive camera or an increased tempo in shot montage, ordinary cinematic devices for the construction of narrative cinema, but rather because of those subtle shifts this space undergoes in real time. We see this space in different lights and in terms of different discourses or kinds of encounter that dislocate or disorient the viewer—prostitution as much a part of this place as single-mother parenting and meal preparation, and each of these represented as routine and disrupted by equally violent acts (murder no more so than the making of meatloaf). One of the more often overlooked "events" in this film that connects it to Akerman's other works is the reading of a letter, through which the viewer is privy to another perspective of Jeanne and to another place and experience of displacement that also reorients us to her place in the world and the space she inhabits. This letter, read in real time to her son at the conclusion of a dinner, projects an alternate life for Jeanne in emigration, imagines her displaced and defined by other attachments. She reads it without apparent irony or desire, her disinterested double-voicing allowing for the maximal potential meaning to be read into the letter. Thus, it suggests the ambivalence of the dialogue, double-voicing, and displacement at the core of all self-constructions in Akerman's films.

One of the central concerns and strategies of Akerman's cinema is silence. Her films suggest the limits of speech and of diegetic sound. The disjuncture between sound and image through devices such as Akerman's dispassionate voice-over reading of her mother's letters in *News From Home*, disconnected from the flow of images of the city, suggest incommunicability. Or at least, authority does not lie in diegetic discourse between characters but in cinematic constructions, in the distances, differences, and silences that surround discourses and moments of dialogue, in the disjunction between sound and image and often between voice-over narrative and the narrative or impression produced by images, long shots, sequences. There is a continual deferral of definite meaning achieved also through "austere visuals," "matter-of-fact and emotionless voice," and postponement of dialogue and writing that Naficy finds characteristic of accented epistolary structures. "Psychologically, the interrupted structure of seriality intensifies the desire for more letters, and the successive addition of each letter"—letters which also "continually complain of the infrequency and late arrival of her daughter's letters"— "builds a palimpsestic narrative structure."[83] This palimpsest layers traces, constructing, rather than uncovering places and personas: "each letter compels viewers to revise their earlier hypotheses about the writer(s), addressee(s), and reciter(s) of the letters, the world they inhabit, and the desires and prohibitions under which they are attempting to connect"— resulting in a "spectatorial" experience analogous to that of the displaced filmmaker/character, "result[ing] from the inability to close the gap of exile."[84] Akerman compounds that palimpsest structure also through the introduction of diegetic sound. Cars, such as those we hear almost constantly throughout *News from Home* and *De l'autre côté*, "speak" as clearly (or ambivalently) and significantly as human conversations and voice-over commentary in many of Akerman's fictions and all her documentaries. As Margulies declaims, we might read this "general awkwardness in address as the only appropriate form for a thematics of displacement."[85]

Akerman's films must be understood in terms of displacement, actual and imaginary. In many cases her films foreground literal travel, emigration, or exile, all attended by discontinuities of landscape, language, etc. Yet each of these kinds of displacement is defined by different exigencies. Travel not only assumes a home, but also the possibility, likelihood, and even necessity of return to that point of departure. Conversely, emigration suggests a more permanent departure or the unlikelihood of return except in the context of travel from a new home. Exile, in contrast to both of these, implies forced departure from a home that continues to function as such, but only as absence, as a place permanently fixed in the past or "at the moment of departure,"[86] as object of nostalgia or an impossible return. And within each of these categories, as Eva Hoffman notes in her lecture/essay "The New Nomads," there are wide variations in the experience of displacement, dependent on discrete political, socio-economic, and cultural contingencies.[87] Akerman's films foreground these differences as well as the commonplaces of exile, emigration, diaspora, and nomadism and the ways in which "dislocation, disorientation, self-division" have become commonplace. That is, her work, accepted as avant-garde, confirms Hoffman's claim that "at least within the framework of postmodern theory, we have come to value exactly those qualities of experience that exile demands—uncertainty, displacement, the fragmented identity." At the same time, Akerman also challenges notions of exile as "sexy, glamorous, interesting" and nomadism and diaspora as "fashionable terms in intellectual discourse"[88] by confronting it with that cinematic gaze that displaces narrative pleasure and discomfits the viewer. If "these days we think the exilic position has precisely the virtues of instability, marginality, absence, and outsiderness," offering thereby "a real description of our world, which indeed has become more decentered, fragmented and unstable," what Akerman's cinematic representation of displacement does is also realize these positions for the viewer, refusing the viewer a safe distance from "the human cost of actual exile as well as some of its psychic implications."[89] Further, rather than "detachment" from place, Akerman's fictions and documentaries function more through the interpolation of places and moments, cultures and histories, remembered and imagined, like Aciman's "shadow cities."[90] So the displacement narratively and cinematically realized in Akerman's work makes her viewers neither "less space-bound" nor "free of time"[91] but bound to the interplay of spaces and temporalities or semiospheres—with their historical, psychological, gendered, linguistic, and aesthetic boundaries.

Several of Akerman's films can be understood in the context of the "road movie," though more a subversive European variant determined by "experiences of emigration, exile, and exclusion" than the American paradigm, playing out the "mythology of the frontier."[92] In a comparative analysis focused through a close reading of Friðrik Þór Friðriksson's *Cold Fever*, Everett discusses this variant as one that internally redirects this "fluid and open-ended genre which uses the narrative trajectory of road as an extended metaphor of quest and discovery through which to approach fundamental concepts of identity" and concomitantly "self-consciously explores the relationship between the spatial and temporal displacement of journey and the discourse of film itself."[93] While maintaining the convention of "home as a structuring absence," European filmmakers such as Friðriksson, Wenders, and Angelopoulos fundamentally challenge the road movie's conventional notions of "home as a locus of certainty and definition."[94] Similarly, while the road still determines the "film's narrative trajectory," "this fundamental marker is portrayed as erratic and problematical," its alignment with "escape and freedom" and the "mythology of the frontier" rendered ambiguous. The car, which conventionally "represents a clear sense of male identity for the protagonist through its status as an object that combines technology and modernity," instead offers "ironic resistance to its traditional filmic status as symbol of American culture, at least as defined by Baudrillard as 'space, speed, cinema, technology'" by functioning unpredictably and unreliably, demonstrating the contingency of any control.[95] Likewise, the car refuses to function traditionally (like home) as "protective shell," or as representation of "simultaneous stasis and movement."[96] Instead, the car becomes emblematic of how spaces and boundaries become porous. The car forces contact, at the very least as a material object that "has punctures, breaks down, and needs petrol," and mediates that self-awareness "predicated upon awareness of the other" as well as the realization that "centre and periphery" are "relative and unstable concepts."[97] If the car breaks down psychological and cultural boundaries, it also breaks through cinematic boundaries insofar as it "functions as cinema," offering its windshield as "the wide screen of the cinema, advancing the filmic narrative and alternating with the reflective and retrospective viewpoint provided by the smaller 'screen' of the rear mirror."[98] Baring their devices and foregrounding cinematic differences, European variants of the road movie redefine movement "from home to homelessness, from closure to openness, from certainty to insecurity," towards the realization "that the journeys that really matter are those that cannot be described or defined; that are unmappable" and "that it is traveling, rather than the destination, that counts, since identity is open-ended and mobile; a process, not a state."[99] Everett aligns this redirected movement with film's inherently deconstructive representation of "identity" as "a constant state of movement and insecurity," which she sees as "articulat[ing] the fundamentally 'discontinuous state of being' which is one of Edward Said's definitions of exile."[100] Akerman's films similarly redefine the road and subvert the conventions of the road movie. As early as *Je, tu, il, elle*, the road is rendered ambiguous as a space for self-definition and as narrative determinant. Because of the circularity of the narrative, point of departure and destination are rendered ambiguous. Further, in Akerman's films, the road is a space of contingency, forced confrontation with inscrutable other and self, the collapse of myth, the realization of contradiction, unanticipated connections and essential disconnect, necessary communication and incommunicability.

The road is realized in these terms in fictional films such as *Je, tu, il, elle* and *Les Rendez-vous d'Anna* partly through narrative "plotting" and in documentaries such as *News from Home*, *Sud*, and *D'Est* partly as a function of relatively open-ended narrative, directed by discovery in the process of filmmaking. In both kinds of film, the road is rendered ambiguous also through the disjuncture between sound and image, suggesting spatial and temporal, physical and psychological discontinuities or discontinuous associations. Several of Akerman's films may be described in the terms Lupton uses for Chris Marker's *Sans Soleil*, in which "narration and images drift apart. Each provides its own distinct itinerary of the rediscovered city, and to the extent that the two accounts hold together, it is by subliminal affinity rather than descriptive anchorage."[101] In Akerman's films there is often not only disjuncture between sound and image, but disjuncture within sound—double-voicing, transhistorical, transcultural, intertextual references, commentary, polyphony. Thus, in *News from Home*, the lack of clear differentiation in Akerman's and her mother's respective reading of her mother's letters results in a complex dialogue not only between mother and daughter, but also between sound and images—the letters are not just the daughter's internal points of reference as her gaze wanders through the New York cityscape. Their distance from that landscape varies.

Each of these films—*Je, tu, il, elle*; *News from Home*; *Les Rendez-vous d'Anna*; *Sud*; *D'Est*; *De l'autre côté*—represents, at least in part, the traveler, whether protagonist or filmmaker free (and even forced by economic or psychological necessity) to return home, but also never at home, representative of a postmodern homelessness. Yet like Marker's work, Akerman's oeuvre may be read as ultimately representing an exilic rather than what might be a more apparently nomadic cinema. On the one hand, there is a crucial, critical difference and distance between the camera or cinematic gaze (or filmmaker foregrounded through devices such as voice-over) and the object of that gaze on the road. There is a marked otherness, sometimes foreignness—an explicitly as well as implicitly "accented" cinema, with difference marked both audibly and visually. This difference might be understood in terms of the "social privilege, based in class, gender, nationality and language" associated with the "modern nomad" who is "also accused of objectifying, exoticizing and then abandoning host cultures, trading in a spectacle of Otherness which avoids any genuine engagement with cultural and racial diversity."[102] We note, for instance, Akerman's admission or assertion of her European identity in *Sud* as well as the arbitrariness and temporariness of her engagement with the American South. However, this noted European difference is deconstructed by being made explicit; it is further subjected to self-critique through her explicit identification with the Other, both victim and aggressor, insofar as Akerman attests that as she registers racial divides in the American South, she is both recalling Stalin's purges and the Holocaust as well as speaking to contemporary racism in Europe. Further, Akerman's indifferent, static camera registers both the subjectivity and cultural contingency of the cinematic gaze, subjecting it to scrutiny by rendering it as a fixed perspective, even as the fixing of that perspective allows the object of its gaze freedom of movement in and out of the frame, and shifts both object and audience into the position of subjects. At the same time, that "fixed" or static gaze is not associated with any particular subjectivity or any individual figure (character or author), even as it does not consistently coincide with sound, narrative voice-over, etc. It can be understood in terms of the "analogy between nomadism and the constructed identity formations of postmodern and post-structuralist philosophy: the notion that the self is not essential and fixed but perpetually in process, not self-generating but 'always-already' written by pre-existing cultural and social practices, in relation to which subjectivity operates in open-ended dynamic tension."[103] Like Marker's *Sans Soleil*, the "endlessly multiplied voices and personae" and "fondness for verbal and visual quotation" in Akerman's road films defer any fixed notion of self, with determined "origins" and "destination."[104]

On the other hand, despite the multiplication of perspectives and personae, and though as a filmmaker Akerman continually travels and appears to be at home in every place and genre, in fact, her films everywhere represent an exilic attachment to a particular home/past and a diasporic attachment to a dispersed community.[105] If there is no "individuation" in her films, despite their focus on individual faces, events, stories, etc., discrete cultures nevertheless re-call the viewer to a transhistorical, transnational recognition of an experience, particularly a feminine experience, of recent Jewish history, of Jewish aesthetics and philosophy. Across Akerman's films, the road is a space of return and recovery, discovering new landscapes to be sure, but also recognizing distant cultures and moments in that landscape and re-covering the past. If "one of the characteristic shots featured in the road movie is the direct cut between map and the territory it represents," partly in order to demonstrate the degree to which "the two tend to be mutually elusive," in Akerman's films, there is scarce reference to literal or narrative maps, little attempt to "establish some sort of rational control over natural chaos" or over disorienting human (re)construction.[106] Rather her films often foreground human disorientation with respect to place and past—documentaries such as *D'Est* and *De l'autre côté* focusing on the disorientation of both displaced filmmaker and of displaced figures, on their partial points of reference, potential for misunderstanding, uncertainty, and opacity—the ways in which their gaze can become a space into which viewers can project what they know, but in which they must also confront the unknown, unspeakable, and forgotten. We might then understand home and identity in Akerman's films partly in Angelopoulos's terms "as 'a car passing through a landscape,'"[107] or, like Chris Marker's, as a roving, remembering gaze, particularly focused on gaps, "the non-place and the public space."[108]

But Akerman also explores interior spaces, those "conventional domestic spaces—homes, private interiors, personal belongings, any sense of enclosure, ownership and rootedness" such as are "extremely rare in *Sans Soleil*" and this is true not only in films such as *Jeanne Dielman* but also in her road fictions and documentaries such as *Sud* and *D'Est*. Akerman directs a similarly focused, unwavering gaze on these interiors as on the road—a decentered gaze, displacing also interior horizons and our "horizons of expectation" with respect to these inhabited spaces (especially inhabited by women), waiting for rather than following the movement of their inhabitants (like her cinematic gaze watches people waiting and walking, watches cars enter and depart the frame without pursuing point of origin or destination). Constructing these interior spaces with the same indifference and attentiveness with which she constructs larger landscapes, Akerman introduces a similar kind of restlessness for the viewer, whose gaze has to find its own interior trajectory in terms of which to make sense of this place, of particular personas, of the modern feminine psyche, which Akerman explores in terms Sarraute might associate with the surfaces of Kafka's fiction rather than Dostoevsky's psychological realism.[109]

Akerman's films could be said to chronicle violence, though not in any ordinary sense of violence in the movies. Akerman wholly de-sensationalizes violence, depriving it of its sensual seductions, of its privileged status in terms of plot (climax) or the camera's gaze—as calm as ever as it confronts the violent act. While violence may be significant in Akerman's films (as narrative aim in *Saute ma ville*, as intervention disrupting routine in *Jeanne Dielman*, instigating Jeanne's finally impenetrable introspection), it is not legible in conventional cinematic terms. Akerman's camera looks at violent or traumatic disruption as it looks at the everyday, with that "unwavering" gaze, both attentive and indifferent, fixed, hence partly averted or rather redirected, refusing direction from the object of the gaze. The way in which violence is represented is not mere cinematic effect, a sort of presentation through a refusal to look, but rather insistence on a different kind of looking at this violence in the context of the everyday, with its many, seemingly insignificant, acts—in *Jeanne Dielman* the act of murder is attended by less suspense than the tensions inherent in brewing tea and the moments of reflection around the murder (literally mirrored reflection, introspective reflection) no more significant than those attending the reading of a letter, these other events registered in real time. More than explosive, murderous, passionate moments, what Akerman chronicles with a dispassionate gaze are traces of violence inherent in the everyday lives of women and men, inherent in monological cultural constructions, in fragmented historical and personal memory. These more essential traumas, generally invisible, can only be observed through such an unwavering gaze. More than a depiction of historical events, everyday time can register these historical traces of women's lives, of exiles' and illegal immigrants' lives, of all sorts of lives on cultural margins. This registration, particularly in Akerman's documentary films and documentary-like fictions, could be read as social critique. Akerman herself attests to this function of her films in her commentary on *Sud*, for instance. Her films are also admitted attempts at registering a fugitive reality, both external and internal—thus, she discusses *Sud* in terms of the literal landscape, a literary one linked with cultural memory, and an internal landscape of personal memory projected onto this place. The figures in her films represent both their own and displaced memory, whether as objects (the trees in *Sud* that remind us of the Holocaust) or subjects: memory is read in and onto the gazes of the people Akerman films. That is, Akerman's objects/subjects remember their own histories but Akerman's own cultural memory is also re-membered through actors and alternates, relocated on distant landscapes. In some senses, this makes Akerman's films akin to fictions such as Kundera's, in that they experiment with gestures, speech genres, cinematic discourses. As Kundera attests in one of the metatextual moments of *The Unbearable Lightness of Being*, the life that one can actually live out only once in time, in the context of art, becomes possible to live in multiple times, places, modes. Akerman herself describes her filmmaking as this sort of "eternal return" to the same questions about identity, and with a degree of regularity, directly inserts her own voice, persona, figure into her films. But if Marker's characters in films such as *Sans Soleil* and *La Jetée* attempt to "shield" themselves "from loss, from the unthinkable and unrepresentable"[110] and from "the amnesiac present"[111] with "the memory image,"[112] only to ultimately discover the "impossibility" of memory, its annihilation of time and of the "subject who exists in time and remembers,"[113] and the impossibility and undesirability of "going back," Akerman's films represent neither such illusions nor disillusionment. Rather, Akerman's "exilic optic" (to borrow Bhabha's formulation) recovers both "social and psychic repressed knowledge," not through "'a simply 'negative', or negating, glance'" but an "'*at once* contiguous, and *in that flash*, contingent" vision of "'the realms of human consciousness and the unconscious, the discourses of history and psychoanalysis.'"[114] It employs this optic differently than as defined in Lupton's analysis of

Marker's work, in which such an "oblique lens" is contingent partly on the "separation of the voice-over from the images, and the pervasive uncertainty about their precise relationship to each other" as in Akerman's films, but also on "perpetual shocks and displacements of the montage."[115] In place of this montage, of flickering images that "do some of the work of unveiling otherness within the memory image," Akerman offers her almost unbearably static or slow moving gaze. In doing so, she registers even more insistently "the working of history as an active, insistent pressure;" represented as "violent rupture and discontinuity, and as the savage movements of re-inscription that obliterate one version of the past in favor of another,"[116] but in real time, in traces that the viewer must read.

As Lieve Spaas notes, Akerman's works "attempt to engage the viewer in a twofold struggle against exile, operating on both the aesthetic and formal level of the film and on a historical level foregrounding the effect of memory."[117] Analyzing the ways in which the viewer is engaged by the static camera and duration of the shot in films such as *Hôtel Monterey* (1972), *Jeanne Dielman*, and *Les Rendez-vous d'Anna*, Spaas affirms Akerman's own claims about the impossibility of escaping the image.[118] By foregrounding the camera, making "viewers very conscious of the loss of a real image" she argues "Akerman's cinema [...] aims at repairing the viewers' exilic experience from their own vision."[119] "Exile" in this sense is metaphysical or psychological, that modern condition involving distortions "imposed" by "technological advances"—a loss of distance from the image, of self-conscious perspective, of autonomy. Akerman's postmodern corrective is achieved through delay and distanciation, through the "disorienting" duration of her static or slow panning shots, recuperating the act of seeing as such and aiming for "an image that is not endowed with multiple [defined] points of view and does not attempt to force meaning."[120] This aesthetic "corrective" for internal exile or alienation is linked to Akerman's historical relation to physical exile. But in this case, her films are not exactly struggling "against exile" as Spaas claims, but within it, in their attempt to recuperate memory—"memory as personal and cultural history, memory as inscribed in objects and memory as part of a process of making meaning in the work."[121] As Spaas notes, Akerman contends "with and against exile" in her cinema, confronting her own displacement vis-à-vis her mother and a Jewish mandate to remember but not re-member through images. She seeks to recuperate her mother's repressed memories of Auschwitz and engages in an admittedly "willful transgression of the Biblical command" against graven images.[122] Akerman's project seems to be precisely to re-member the past in the present and the present in relation to the past through a decentering gaze, deconstructing internal and external cultural margins—literal ones such as the waiting rooms and walls, fences and horizons of *D'Est, Sud, De L'autre côté*, or historical ones, as in *Histoires d'Amérique* (1989), actual or fictional, as in *News from Home* and *Les Rendez-vous d'Anna* and *Un divan à New York*. Filming on the margin of genres and along overlooked internal cultural margins, she redefines both margin and center, with a wholly unsentimentalized but also engaging elucidation of problematic assumptions about women, cultural community, history, language, and cinematic discourse. Akerman's transgressive cinema, "explosive" and "implosive," ultimately not only transgenders the cinematic gaze, but also transforms it through translingual, transnational, and transhistorical turns that offer the viewer not a reinforced sense of modern disconnect, but a more nuanced understanding of our connectedness.

Works Cited

Aciman, André, ed. *Letters of Transit: Reflections on Exile, Identity, Language, and Loss*. New York: The New Press, 1998.

Adorno, Theodor, and Max Horkheimer. *Dialectic of Enlightenment*. Translated by John Cumming. New York: Herder and Herder, 1972.

Akerman, Chantal, Catherine David, and Michael Tarantino. *Bordering on Fiction: Chantal Akerman's D'Est*. Minneapolis: Walker Art Center, 1995.

—. "À propos de *Sud*." Press-book for the film presentation at Cannes Film Festival. 1-7. May 1999.

Bakhtin, Mikhail. *Art and Answerability*. Edited by Michael Holquist and Vadim Liapunov. Translated with notes by V. Liapunov. Austin: The University of Texas Press, 1990.

—. *The Dialogic Imagination: Four Essays by M.M. Bakhtin*. Edited by Michael Holquist. Translated by Caryl Emerson and Michael Holquist. Austin: The University of Texas Press, 1981.

—. *Problems of Dostoevsky's Poetics*. Edited and translated by Caryl Emerson. Minneapolis: The University of Minnesota Press, 1984. Originally published as *Проблемы творчества Достоевского*. Kiev: Next, 1994.

—. *Speech Genres and Other Late Essays*. Edited by Caryl Emerson and Michael Holquist. Translated by Vern W. McGee. Austin: The University of Texas Press, 1978. Originally published as *Эстетика словесного творчества*. Moscow: Искусство, 1979.

Barker, Jennifer M. "The Feminine Side of New York: Travelogue, Autobiography and Architecture in *News from Home*." In *Identity and*

Memory: the Films of Chantal Akerman, edited by Gwendolyn Audrey Foster, 41-58. Carbondale: Southern Illinois University Press, 2003.

Bergstrom, Janet. "Chantal Akerman: Splitting." In *Endless Night: Cinema and Psychoanalysis, Parallel Histories*, edited by Janet Bergstrom, 273-90. Berkeley: University of California Press, 1999.

—. "Invented Memories." In *Identity and Memory: the Films of Chantal Akerman*, edited by Gwendolyn Audrey Foster, 94-116. Carbondale: Southern Illinois University Press, 2003.

—. "*Jeanne Dielman, 23 Quai du Commerce, 1080 Bruxelles* by Chantal Akerman." *Camera Obscura* 2 (Fall 1977): 114-18.

Bhabha, Homi. "Arrivals and Departures." In *Home, Exile, Homeland: Film, Media and the Politics of Place*, edited by Hamid Naficy, viii-xi. London and New York: Routledge/AFI Film Readers, 1999.

—. *The Location of Culture*. London and New York: Routledge, 1994.

Boym, Svetlana. "Estrangement as a Lifestyle: Shklovsky and Brodsky." *Poetics Today*, vol. 17, no. 4 (Winter 1996), 511-530.

Butler, Kristine. "Bordering on Fiction: Chantal Akerman's *D'Est*." Exhibit Review. *Postmodern Culture* 6.1 (September 1995). http://infomotions.com/serials/pmc/pmc-v6n1-butler-bordering.txt.

—. "Bordering on Fiction: Chantal Akerman's *From the East*." In *Identity and Memory: the Films of Chantal Akerman*, edited by Gwendolyn Audrey Foster, 162-78. Carbondale: Southern Illinois University Press, 2003.

Capp, Rose. "Akerman Resists Southern Comfort." Review of *Sud (South)*. *Senses of Cinema*. 1999. http://www.sensesofcinema. com/contents/00/6/south.html.

Cerne, Adriana. "Writing in Tongues: Chantal Akerman's *News from Home*." *European Studies* 32 (2002): 235-47.

Daney, Serge. "Écriture du désastre" and "Toute une nuit." In *Ciné Journal 1981-1986,* 131-32. Paris: Editions Cahiers du cinema, 1986.

David, Catherine. "*D'Est*: Akerman Variations." In *Bordering on Fiction: Chantal Akerman's D'Est*, edited by Kathy Halbreich and Bruce Jenkins. 57-64. Minneapolis: Walker Art Center, 1995.

Deleuze, Gilles. *Cinema 2. The Time-Image*. Translated by Hugh Tomlinson and Robert Galeta. Minneapolis: University of Minnesota Press, 1989.

Deleuze, Gilles and Félix Guattari. *Kafka: For a Minor Literature*. Translated by Dana Polan. Minneapolis: University of Minnesota Press, 1986. Originally published as *Pour une littérature mineure*. Paris: Éditions de Minuit, 1975.

—. *A Thousand Plateaus: Capitalism and Schizophrenia.* Translated by Brian Massumi. Minneapolis: University of Minnesota Press, 1987. Originally published as *Capitalisme et schizophrénie. T.2. Mille plateaux.* Paris: Editions de Minuit, 1980.

Derrida, Jacques. *Dissemination.* Translated by Barbara Johnson. Chicago: University of Chicago Press, 1981.

—. *Positions.* Translated by Alan Bass. Chicago: University of Chicago Press, 1981.

Diaconescu-Blumenfeld, Rodica. "*Lamerica,* History in Diaspora." *Romance Languages Annual* XI (2000): 167-73.

Even-Zohar, I. "Polysystem Theory." *Poetics Today* 1:1-2 (1979): 287-310.

—. "Polysystem Theory." *Poetics Today* 11:1 (Spring 1990): 9-26.

Everett, Wendy. "Leaving Home: Exile and Displacement in Contemporary European Cinema." In *Cultures of Exile: Images of Displacement,* edited by Wendy E. Everett and Peter Wagstaff, 17-32. New York: Berghahn Books, 2004.

Foster, Gwendolyn Audrey, ed. *Identity and Memory: the Films of Chantal Akerman.* Carbondale: Southern Illinois University Press, 2003.

Fowler, Catherine. "Chantal Akerman." In *The Oxford Guide to Film Studies,* edited by John Hill, 489-91. New York: Oxford University Press, 1998.

—. "*All Night Long*: The Ambivalent Text of 'Belgianicity.'" In *Identity and Memory: the Films of Chantal Akerman,* edited by Gwendolyn Audrey Foster, 77-93. Carbondale: Southern Illinois University Press, 2003.

Jameson, Fredric. "Postmodernism and Consumer Society." In *The Cultural Turn: Selected Writings on the Postmodern, 1983-1998.* London and New York: Verso, 1998.

Jauss, Hans Robert. "Literary History as a Challenge to Literary Theory." Translated by Timothy Bahti. In *The Norton Anthology of Theory and Criticism,* edited by Vincent B. Leitch et al, 1550-64. New York and London: W.W. Norton & Co., 2001.

Jayamanne, Laleen. "Modes of Performance in Chantal Akerman's *Jeanne Dielman, 23 Quai du Commerce, 1080 Bruxelles.*" In *Towards Cinema and its Double: Cross-Cultural Mimesis,* 149-60. Bloomington: Indiana University Press, 2001.

Johnston, Claire. "Towards a Feminist Film Practice: Some Theses." In Vol. 2 of *Movies and Methods,* edited by Bill Nichols, 315-27. Berkeley: University of California Press, 1985.

Kuhn, Annette. *Women's Pictures: Feminism and Cinema*. London, Boston, and Melbourne: Routledge, 1982.

Kinsman, R. Patrick. "She's Come Undone: Chantal Akerman's *Jeanne Dielman, 23 Quai du Commerce, 1080 Bruxelles* (1975) and Countercinema." *Quarterly Review of Film and Video* 24.3 (May 2007): 217-24.

Lebow, Alisa. "Memory Once Removed: Indirect Memory and Transitive Autobiography in Chantal Akerman's *D'Est*." *Camera Obscura* 52:18.1 (2003): 35-84.

Levinas, Emmanuel. *Totality and Infinity: An Essay on Exteriority*. The Hague & Boston: M. Nijhoff Publishers, 1979.

Levitin, Jacqueline, Judith Plessis, and Valerie Raoul, eds. *Women Filmmakers: Refocusing*. New York: Routledge, 2003.

Liénard, Marie. "*Sud* de Chantal Akerman ou une Histoire de Territoire et de Terre: *Le Sud* comme Espace de Mémoire." *Anglophonia : French Journal of English Studies* 19 (2006): 131-38.

Lotman, Iurii. «Семиотическои пространство, Понятие границы, Механизмы диалога, Семиосфера и проблема сюжета, & Символика пространство» in *Внутры мыслящих миров, Семиосфера*. *Семиосфера*. Saint Petersburg: изд. «Искусство-СПБ», 2004.

—. «Система с одним языком» and «Прерывное и непрерывное.» *Култура и взыв*. Moscow: изд. «Гнозис», 1992.

—. *The Universe of the Mind: A Semiotic Theory of Culture*. Translated by Ann Shukman. London: I. B. Tauris & Co, Ltd., 1990.

Lukács, György. *Essays on Realism*. Translated by Rodney Livingstone. Cambridge: MIT Press, 1981.

Lupton, Catherine. "The Exile of Remembering: Movement and Memory in Chris Marker's *Sans Soleil*." In *Cultures of Exile: Images of Displacement*, edited by Wendy E. Everett and Peter Wagstaff, 33-48. New York: Berghahn Book, 2004.

Lyotard, Jean-François. *The Postmodern Condition*. Minneapolis: University of Minnesota Press, 1984.

—. *Toward the Postmodern*. Atlantic Highlands: Humanities Press, 1993.

MacDonald, Scott. "Chantal Akerman (on *D'Est*, *Sud*, and *De l'autre côté*)." In *A Critical Cinema 4: Interviews with Independent Filmmakers*, 258-73. Berkeley: University of California Press, 2005.

Margulies, Ivone. "Echo and Voice in *Meetings with Anna*." In *Identity and Memory: the Films of Chantal Akerman*, edited by Gwendolyn Audrey Foster, 59-76. Carbondale: Southern Illinois University Press, 2003.

—. *Nothing Happens: Chantal Akerman's Hyperrealist Everyday.*
Durham: Duke University Press, 1996.

Martin, Angela. "Chantal Akerman's Films: Notes on the Issues Raised for
Feminism." In *Films for Women*, edited by Charlotte Brunsdon, 62-71.
London: British Film Institute, 1986.

Mellencamp, Patricia. *Indiscretions. Avant-Garde Film, Video, and
Feminism.* Bloomington: Indiana University Press, 1990.

Mulvey, Laura. *Visual and Other Pleasures.* Bloomington: Indiana
University Press, 1989.

Naficy, Hamid. *An Accented Cinema: Exile and Diasporic Filmmaking.*
Princeton: Princeton University Press, 2001.

Pravadelli, Veronica. *Performance, Rewriting, Identity: Chantal
Akerman's Postmodern Cinema.* Torino: Otto Editore, 2000.

Pursley, Darlene. "Moving in Time: Chantal Akerman's *Toute une nuit.*"
Modern Language Notes 120 (2005): 1192-1205.

Rich, B. Ruby. *Chick Flicks: Theories and Memories of the Feminist Film
Movement.* Durham: Duke University Press, 1998.

—. "In the Name of Feminist Film Criticism." *Movies and Methods.* In
Vol. 2 of *Movies and Methods*, edited by Bill Nichols, 340-58.
Berkeley: University of California Press, 1985.

Rosen, Philip. "Border Times and Geopolitical Frames. The Martin Walsh
Memorial Lecture 2006." *Canadian Journal of Film Studies/Revue
Canadienne d'Etudes Cinématographiques* 15.2 (Fall 2006): 2-19.

Said, Edward. *Reflections on Exile and Other Essays.* Cambridge: Harvard
University Press, 2000.

Sarraute, Nathalie. "De Dostoïevski à Kafka." In *L'Ere du soupçon*, 13-55.
Paris: Editions Gallimard, 1956.

Sartre, Jean-Paul. *What is Literature?* Translated by Bernard Frechtman.
New York: Harper & Row, 1965.

Shaviro, Steven. "Clichés of Identity: Chantal Akerman's Musicals."
Quarterly Review of Film and Video 24 (2007): 11-17.

Shklovsky, Victor. "Art as Technique." In *Russian Formalist Criticism;
Four Essays*, translated by Lee T. Lemon and Marion J. Reis, 3-24.
Lincoln: University of Nebraska Press, 1965. Originally published as
"Iskusstvo, kak priyom." *Sborniki*, II (1917).

—. *Theory of Prose.* Translated by B. Sher. Elmwood Park: Dalkey
Archive Press, 1990.

Sontag, Susan. "Against Interpretation." *Against Interpretation and Other
Essays.* New York: Farrar, Strauss & Giroux, 1966.

Spaas, Lieve. "Chantal Akerman: A Struggle with Exile." In *Cultures of Exile: Images of Displacement*, edited by Wendy E. Everett and Peter Wagstaff, 87-94. New York: Berghahn Books, 2004.

Vincendeau, Ginette. "*Night and Day*: A Parisian Fairy Tale." In *Identity and Memory: the Films of Chantal Akerman*, edited by Gwendolyn Audrey Foster, 117-31. Carbondale: Southern Illinois University Press, 2003.

Vojkovic, Sasha. "On the Borders of Redemption: Recovering the Image of the Past." *Parallax* 5.3 (1999): 90-101.

Walsh, Maria. "Intervals of Inner Flight: Chantal Akerman's *News from Home*." *Screen* 45.3 (Autumn 2004): 190-205.

White, Jerry. "Chantal Akerman's Revisionist Aesthetic." In *Women and Experimental Filmmaking*, edited by Jean Petrolle and Virginia Wright Wexman, 47-68. Urbana: University of Illinois Press, 2005.

Williams, Bruce. "A Transit to Significance: Poetic Discourse in Chantal Akerman's *Toute une nuit*." *Literature Film Quarterly* 23:3 (1995): 216-22.

—. "Splintered Perspectives: Counterpoint and Subjectivity in Modernist Film Narrative." *Film Criticism* 15:2 (Winter 1991): 2-12.

Yervasi, Carina. "Dislocating the Domestic in Chantal Akerman's *Jeanne Dielman*." *Sites: The Journal of Twentieth-century Contemporary French Studies* 4:2 (Fall 2000): 385-97.

Zelechow, Bernard. "The Formalist Film-Maker with a Subtext: Chantal Akerman." *Applied Semiotics/Sémiotique appliquée* 8 (1999): 441-8.

Filmography

Saute ma ville (1968)
L'enfant aimé ou je joue à être une femme mariée (1971)
La Chambre 1 (1972)
La Chambre 2 (1972)
Hôtel Monterey (1972)
Le 15/8 (1973)
Hanging Out Yonkers (1973)
Je, tu, il, elle (1974)
Jeanne Dielman, 23 Quai du Commerce, 1080 Bruxelles (1975)
News from Home (1976)
Les Rendez-vous d'Anna (1978)
Toute une nuit (1982)
Les Années 80 (1983)
J'ai faim, j'ai froid (1984)

Seven Women, Seven Sins (1987)
Letters Home (1986)
Mallet-Stevens (1986)
Le Marteau (1986)
La Paresse (1986)
Histoires d'Amérique (1988)
Les Trois derniéres sonates de Franz Schubert (1989)
Trois strophes sur le nom de Sacher (1989)
Contre l'oubli (1991)
Nuit et Jour (1991)
D'Est (1993)
Portrait d'une jeune fille de la fin des années 60, à Bruxelles (1993)
Un divan à New York/A Couch in New York (1996)
Chantal Akerman par Chantal Akerman (1996)
La Captive (2000)
De l'autre côté/From the Other Side (2002)
Demain on déménage/Tomorrow We Move (2004)
Là-bas/Over There (2006)
Tombée de nuit sur Shanghai in *O Estado do Mundo/State of the World* (2007)

Notes

[1] Chantal Akerman, "On Absence and Imagination in Documentary Film," *Crossing Cinematic Borders*, European Graduate School (EGS), http://www.egs.edu/faculty/akerman/akerman-absence-and-imagination-2001.html
[2] Ibid.
[3] Yuri Lotman discusses the potential explosion (*vzryv*) created by the "interruption" and "intersection" or "overlap" (*peresechenie*) of sign systems, languages, and ideas in "Система с одним языком" and "Прерывное и непрерывное," *Кулътура и взыв*, (Moscow: Gnozis/Progress Publishing, 1992), 12-16 and 25-34
[4] Yuri M. Lotman, "Dialogue Mechanisms," in *The Universe of the Mind: A Semiotic Theory of Culture*, trans. Ann Shukman (London: I. B. Tauris & Co, Ltd., 1990), 143-50.
[5] Lotman, *Universe*, 143-5, 126.
[6] Cf. Mikhail Bakhtin, "Discourse in the Novel," in *The Dialogic Imagination: Four Essays by M. M. Bakhtin*, ed. Michael Holquist, trans. Caryl Emerson and Michael Holquist (Austin: The University of Texas Press, 1981), 259-422; *Speech Genres and Other Late Essays*, ed. Caryl Emerson and Michael Holquist, trans. Vern W. McGee (Austin: The University of Texas Press, 1978).
[7] Lotman, *Universe*, 136.
[8] Ibid., 138.
[9] Ibid., 125.

[10] Bakhtin, *Speech Genres*, 60.

[11] I. Even-Zohar, "Polysystem Theory," *Poetics Today* 11:1 (Spring 1990): 12.

[12] Bakhtin, *Discourse in the Novel*, 296-302, and *Speech Genres*, 1-7; Lotman, *Universe*, 167-68.

[13] Lotman, *Universe*, 136.

[14] Gilles Deleuze and Félix Guattari, *Kafka: Towards a Minor Literature*, trans. Dana Polan (Minneapolis: University of Minnesota Press, 1986), 19.

[15] Alisa Lebow, "Memory Once Removed: Indirect Memory and Transitive Autobiography in Chantal Akerman's *D'Est*," *Camera Obscura* 52: 18.1 (2003): 35-84.

[16] Lotman, *Universe*, 136.

[17] Jerry White, "Chantal Akerman's Revisionist Aesthetic," in *Women and Experimental Filmmaking*, ed. Jean Petrolle and Virginia Wright Wexman (Urbana: University of Illinois Press, 2005), 46.

[18] Bakhtin, *Speech Genres*, 79; *Discourse in the Novel*, 300.

[19] Gyorgy Lukács, "Realism in the Balance," in *Essays on Realism*, trans. Rodney Livingstone (Cambridge: MIT Press, 1981).

[20] Theodor Adorno and Max Horkheimer, "The Cultural Industry: Enlightenment as Mass Deception," in *Dialectic of Enlightenment*, trans. John Cumming (New York: Herder and Herder, 1972).

[21] Hans-Robert Jauss, "Literary History as a Challenge to Literary Theory," trans. Timothy Bahti, in *The Norton Anthology of Theory and Criticism*, ed. Vincent B. Leitch (New York and London: W. W. Norton & Co., 2001), 1550-64.

[22] Victor Shklovsky, "Art as Technique," and Boris Eichenbaum, "The Theory of the 'Formal Method,'" in *Russian Formalist Criticism; Four Essays*, trans. Lee T. Lemon and Marion J. Reis (Lincoln: University of Nebraska Press, 1965), 3-24, 99-139; Yuri Tynianov, "Достоевский и Гоголь: к теории пародии," in *Тынянов Ю. Н. Поэтика. История литературы. Кино* (Moscow, 1977), 198-226.

[23] Catherine Fowler, "Chantal Akerman," in *The Oxford Guide to Film Studies*, ed. John Hill (New York: Oxford University Press, 1998), 489.

[24] Ibid., 489.

[25] Ibid., 490; Laura Mulvey 1979), 18, quoted in Fowler, "Chantal Akerman," 490.

[26] Cf. Bakhtin, "The Dialogic Novel" and *Speech Genres*.

[27] Lotman, *Universe*, 146-47.

[28] Jean-Paul Sartre, "Why Write?," in *What is Literature?*, trans. Bernard Frechtman. (New York: Harper & Row, 1965).

[29] Janet Bergstrom, "*Jeanne Dielman, 23 Quai du Commerce, 1080 Bruxelles* by Chantal Akerman," *Camera Obscura* 2 (Fall 1977): 114-18; Annette Kuhn, *Women's Pictures: Feminism and Cinema* (London, Boston, and Melbourne: Routledge, 1982), 173-4; Fowler, "Chantal Akerman," 490.

[30] Veronica Pravadelli, *Performance, Rewriting, Identity: Chantal Akerman's Postmodern Cinema* (Torino: Otto Editore, 2000), 6.

[31] B. Ruby Rich, "In the Name of Feminist Film Criticism," in *Movies and Methods*, vol. 2, ed. Bill Nichols (Berkeley: University of California Press, 1985), 340-58; quoted in Pravadelli, *Performance*, 10.

[32] Fowler, "Chantal Akerman," 490.

[33] Pravadelli, *Performance*, 9-10.

[34] Ivone Margulies, *Nothing Happens: Chantal Akerman's Hyperrealist Everyday* (Durham: Duke University Press, 1996); quoted in Pravadelli, *Performance*, 17-19.

[35] Margulies, *Nothing Happens*, 140-43.

[36] Ibid., 11.

[37] Pravadelli, *Performance*, 19.

[38] Cf. Margulies, *Nothing Happens*, 109-27; Pravadelli, *Performance*, 21.

[39] Jerry White, "Chantal Akerman's Revisionist Aesthetic," in *Women and Experimental Filmmaking*, ed. Jean Petrolle and Virginia Wright Wexman (Urbana: University of Illinois Press, 2005), 47-68.

[40] Pravadelli, *Performance*, 22.

[41] Claire Johnston, "Towards a Feminist Film Practice: Some Theses," in *Movies and Methods*, vol. 2, ed. Bill Nichols (Berkeley: University of California Press, 1985). 315-27.

[42] Pravadelli, *Performance*, 12.

[43] Ibid., 2.

[44] Ibid., 40.

[45] Ibid., 6-7.

[46] Ibid., 42.

[47] Ibid., 23.

[48] Ibid., 25; cf. Fredric Jameson, "Postmodernism and Consumer Society," 125.

[49] Ibid., 36-37; cf. Lyotard, "The Sublime and the Avant-Garde," and Deleuze, *Cinema 2. The Time-Image*.

[50] Ibid., 30-31; cf. Susan Sontag, "Against Interpretation" and Kaye, *Postmodernism and Performance*.

[51] Ibid., 37-38.

[52] Ibid., 42-43.

[53] Lebow, "Memory Once Removed," 39.

[54] Ibid., 39, 41-42; citing Akerman's *Bordering on Fiction: Chantal Akerman's D'Est* installation monologue.

[55] White, "Akerman's Revisionist Aesthetic," 46-49.

[56] Margulies, *Nothing Happens*, 7.

[57] White, "Akerman's Revisionist Aesthetic," 46.

[58] Ibid., 46-66.

[59] Ibid., 58.

[60] Ibid., 60.

[61] Ibid., 52.

[62] Margulies, *Nothing Happens*, 152.

[63] White, "Akerman's Revisionist Aesthetic," 48.

[64] Pravadelli, *Performance*, 13.

[65] Ibid., 14.

[66] Bakhtin, *Speech Genres*, 7.

[67] Pravadelli, *Performance*, 15.

[68] Bernard Zelechow, "The Formalist Film-Maker with a Subtext: Chantal Akerman," *Applied Semiotics/Sémiotique appliquée* 8 (1999): 441.

[69] Ibid., 441.

[70] Ibid., 441.

[71] Ibid., 444-45.

[72] Ibid., 441, 446.

[73] Marie Liénard, "*Sud* de Chantal Akerman ou une Histoire de Territoire et de Terre: *Le Sud* comme Espace de Mémoire," *Anglophonia : French Journal of English Studies* 19 (2006): 131-38.

[74] Ibid., 132.

[75] Qtd. in Liénard.

[76] Sasha Vojkovic, "On the Borders of Redemption: recovering the Image of the Past," *Parallax* 5.3 (1999): 91.

[77] Ibid., 93-94.

[78] Rodica Diaconescu-Blumenfeld, "*Lamerica*, History in Diaspora," *Romance Languages Annual* XI (2000): 171-72." cf. Kristine Butler's exhibit review, "Bordering on Fiction: Chantal Akerman's *D'Est*," *Postmodern Culture* 6.1 (September 1995).

[79] Ivone Margulies, "Echo and Voice in *Meetings with Anna*," in *Identity and Memory: the Films of Chantal Akerman*, ed. Gwendolyn Audrey Foster (Carbondale: Southern Illinois University Press, 2003), 59-60.

[80] Joseph Brodsky, *Less Than One: Selected Essays* (New York: Farrar, Straus, & Giroux, 1986), 139.

[81] Svetlana Boym, "Estrangement as a Lifestyle: Shklovsky and Brodsky," *Poetics Today* vol. 17, no. 4 (Winter 1996): 523.

[82] Hamid Naficy, *An Accented Cinema: Exile and Diasporic Filmmaking* (Princeton: Princeton University Press, 2001).

[83] Naficy, *Accented Cinema*, 113.

[84] Ibid., 114.

[85] Margulies, "Echo and Voice," 67.

[86] Svetlana Boym discusses this notion derived from Herzen's *From the Other Shore* in "Estrangement as a Lifestyle: Shklovsky and Brodsky," *Poetics Today* vol. 17, no. 4 (Winter 1996), 525.

[87] Eva Hoffman, "The New Nomads," in *Letters of Transit: Reflections on Exile, Identity, Language, and Loss*, ed. André Aciman (New York: The New Press, 1999), 40.

[88] Ibid., 44.

[89] Ibid., 45.

[90] André Aciman, "Shadow Cities" in *Letters of Transit: Reflections on Exile, Identity, Language, and Loss*, ed. André Aciman (New York: The New Press, 1999), 15-34.

[91] Hoffman, "The New Nomads," 44.

[92] Wendy Everett, "Leaving Home: Exile and Displacement in Contemporary European Cinema" in *Cultures of Exile: Images of Displacement*, ed. Wendy E. Everett and Peter Wagstaff (New York: Berghahn Books, 2004), 30.

[93] Ibid., 19.
[94] Ibid., 20.
[95] Ibid., 24-25.
[96] Ibid., 25.
[97] Ibid., 26.
[98] Ibid., 25.
[99] Ibid., 29.
[100] Ibid., 30; citing Edward Said, *Reflections on Exile and Other Essays* (Cambridge: Harvard University Press, 2000), 177.
[101] Catherine Lupton, "The Exile of Remembering: Movement and Memory in Chris Marker's *Sans Soleil*," in *Cultures of Exile: Images of Displacement*, ed. Wendy E. Everett and Peter Wagstaff (New York: Berghahn Books, 2004), 34.
[102] Ibid., 39.
[103] Ibid., 38.
[104] Ibid.
[105] Ibid., 36.
[106] Everett, "Leaving Home," 23.
[107] Ibid., 31.
[108] Lupton, "Exile of Remembering," 37.
[109] Nathalie Sarraute, "De Dostoïevski à Kafka," in *L'Ere du soupçon* (Paris: Editions Gallimard, 1956), 13-55.
[110] Lupton, "Exile of Remembering," 43.
[111] Ibid., 46.
[112] Ibid., 43.
[113] Ibid., 41.
[114] Ibid., 44; citing Homi Bhabha, "Arrivals and Departures," in *Home, Exile, Homeland: Film, Media and the Politics of Place*, ed. Hamid Naficy (London and New York: Routledge/AFI Film Readers, 1999), xi.
[115] Ibid., 44.
[116] Ibid., 45.
[117] Lieve Spaas, "Chantal Akerman: A Struggle with Exile," in *Cultures of Exile: Images of Displacement*, ed. Wendy E. Everett and Peter Wagstaff (New York: Berghahn Books, 2004), 88.
[118] Ibid., 89; citing Aubenas 1995:6.
[119] Ibid., 90.
[120] Ibid.
[121] Ibid., 91.
[122] In the soundtrack to the *D'Est* installation, Akerman reads Exodus 20:4, first in an accented Hebrew and then in fluent French; cf., Spaas, "Struggle with Exile," 94.

AFTERWORD TO THE SECOND EDITION

FROM THE PAINTER'S BRUSH
TO THE MOVIE CAMERA

MARCELLINE BLOCK

> Cinema and philosophy are brought together in a continuing process of intercutting. This is philosophy as assemblage, a kind of provoked becoming of thought.
> —Hugh Tomlinson and Robert Galeta

Since my edited collection entitled *Situating the Feminist Gaze and Spectatorship in Postwar Cinema* was published in 2008, Kathryn Bigelow (b. 1951) received the Academy Award for Achievement in Directing for *The Hurt Locker* (2008) on March 7, 2010. *The Hurt Locker* was also awarded the Oscar for Best Picture. Bigelow is the first female film director to be granted these distinctions. Before Bigelow's groundbreaking victory, only three women—Lina Wertmüller, Jane Campion,[1] and Sofia Coppola[2]—had ever been nominated for the Academy Award for Achievement in Directing.

In the early 1970s—*toujours* the 70s, the long 1970s, as if today's intellectual climate had sprung from that time period—Bigelow came to Manhattan from the San Francisco Art Institute after being selected for the prestigious Independent Study Program at the Whitney Museum of American Art. Bigelow, in a 1995 interview with Gavin Smith for *Film Comment*, discussed her experience at the Whitney:

> I came to New York through the Whitney Museum in the early 1970s. At that time they gave fifteen people scholarships every year to come to New York and get your own studio...So I did that for a year and a half. At the end you had a piece of your work shown in the Whitney. Which was amazing. The art world at the time became very politicised, conceptual art moved into a political arena, so the work was more and more aggressive. I started working with Art and Language, a British-based group of conceptual artists, and we had a piece at the Venice Biennale one year.[3]

Bigelow's training as a painter shapes her films: "'I was an abstract expressionist,' [she] says. 'My paintings definitely reflected a sense of light, but they were dark and frenzied.' And so are her films."[4] Robert Bresson, Maurice Pialat,[5] and many other cineastes also began their careers as painters, whereas Jean Renoir started in ceramics. In the case of Fernand Léger who wrote and co-directed the iconic film *Ballet mécanique* (1924; with a musical score by American composer George Antheil), his interest in cinema nearly led him to leave painting for filmmaking: he exclaimed that "before I saw it in a film, I did not know what a hand was!"[6] Yet, Léger did not abandon painting for cinema, perhaps because, in his estimation, cinema could be credited with only one single invention: the close-up.[7] The intersection of painting with the moving image has long been pondered and interrogated by many, including Gilles Deleuze. In the introduction to Deleuze's *Cinema 2: The Time-Image*, Hugh Tomlinson and Robert Galeta, who translated it from the French, state:

> What makes cinema of special interest is that, as with painting, it gives conceptual construction new dimensions, those of the percept and affect— which should not be confused with perception and feeling. 'Affect, percept, and concept are three inseparable powers going from art to philosophy and the reverse.' Cinema and philosophy are brought together in a continuing process of intercutting. This is philosophy as assemblage, a kind of provoked becoming of thought.[8]

From her painter's studio in the 1970s, courtesy of the Whitney, Bigelow transitioned into the movie studio, such as Warner Bros. and Summit Entertainment. Her cinematic style is not only informed by her painter's background, but also by critical theories, the politics of reading, and semiotics, which infused the zeitgeist of the long 1970s, both in France and in New York. For Deleuze,

> The cinema seems to us to be a composition of images and of signs, that is, a pre-verbal intelligible content (*pure semiotics*), whilst semiology of a linguistic inspiration abolishes the image and tends to dispense with the sign. What we call cinematographic concepts are therefore the types of images and the signs which correspond to each type.[9]

This period also witnessed the coming of age of second wave feminism,[10] with groundbreaking works by Laura Mulvey, Hélène Cixous,[11] and Chantal Akerman, as well as Lizzie Borden's dystopian *Born in Flames* (1983), in which Bigelow herself was cast as a newspaper editor: "'I've never seen it...I played one of three somewhat militant girls in a scene,'" she recalls.[12] Yet Bigelow's spectatorial gaze encompasses the broadest horizon of film production. Upon entering Columbia's film school, she "'just dived into film, all periods...I'd see everything...*Year of 13 Moons*, I thought I'd died and gone to heaven when I saw that film.'"[13]

In Bigelow's words,

> This was the late 1970s when conceptual art mutated through a political phase into a French structuralist phase. There was a kind of natural evolution...[her first film, *Set Up*] was a really very overtly political piece and incendiary in its own small context...*The Village Voice* called it the first skinhead movie. One guy was calling another a fascist, the other's calling him a commie...then the same images are deconstructed in voice over, by these two philosophers, Sylvère Lotringer and Marshall Bronsky [*sic*]*...and...Sylvère talking about the fact that in the 1960s you think of the enemy as outside of yourself...but that's not really the case...fascism is very insidious, we reproduce it all the time.[14]

Bigelow, the painter turned cineaste, was also a participant in the poststructuralist, deconstruction and semiotics debates at Columbia, where she was an associate editor who also designed and illustrated the 1981 issue of Sylvère Lotringer's journal, *Semiotext(e)*, entitled *Polysexuality*, which was edited by François Peraldi, featuring texts by Roland Barthes, Gilles Deleuze, Jacques Lacan, Jean-François Lyotard, Michele Montrelay, Alain Robbe-Grillet, and Paul Virilio, all literary household names.

Bigelow's attraction to violence in "'high-impact, high-velocity filmmaking'"[15] leads her to describe her film style as "'a fatalism combined with an adrenalin aspect.'"[16] Before starting at Columbia, Bigelow shot her first film, *Set Up* (1978), of which she states: "'on the surface, it's these two guys who beat each other up...getting bloodier and bloodier...I almost killed them.'"[17] Bigelow directs adventure, action and war movies whose originality resides not in sexualizing violence, but rather in a stylized approach to it. Her *Blue Steel* (1990) is exemplary of the career-woman-in-peril thriller, as discussed by Monica Soare in the sixth chapter of this collection. For Bigelow, *Blue Steel* is "'a tough piece...Women who have seen it see Jamie [Lee Curtis, who plays protagonist Megan Turner] as a role model. There are very few women in films they can identify with, and they like to see women take charge.'"[18]

Bigelow's Oscars reward a female director's work in "male-dominated" genres, and who thus rescripts spectatorial expectation about gender. In

---

* This ought to read: Marshall Blonsky.

her own words, "'people expect fairly tame movies from women. I don't know why that should be gender-related, but we have to work against those preconceptions.'"[19] Bigelow's filmography is launched upon cutting-edge political and philosophical concepts that she had first tackled with her painter's brushes and later with her editorial pen at *Semiotext(e)*: from the Whitney to *Polysexuality* to *The Hurt Locker*, she maintains integrity, commitment and her conceptual artist's vision.

Standing at the threshold of a new era in film directing, women are reterritorializing a field in which a female director, Alice Guy Blaché[20] (1873–1968) directed what is considered the first narrative film, the sixty second long *La fée aux choux* (*The Cabbage Fairy*, 1896). Although Alice Guy Blaché had been almost entirely forgotten—in spite of making over 1,000 films—a retrospective entitled "Alice Guy Blaché: Cinema Pioneer" was held at the Whitney (November 2009-January 2010), thus beginning the process of rehabilitating her and inaugurating a return to the origins of narrative cinema through a "Woman with a Movie Camera."[21]

—Marcelline Block
Manhattan, Spring 2010

Works Cited

Block, Marcelline. "'The Shock of the Real' in Pialat's *Van Gogh* (1991): Trauma and The Red Vineyard." *Excavatio: Realism and Naturalism in Film Studies*, Vol. XXII (Nos. 1-2, 2007): 234-250.

Coburn, Marcia Froelke. "Revamping Vampires: Erotic Thriller Moves Locale to the Midwest." *The Chicago Tribune*, 11 October 1987: n.p.

Deleuze, Gilles. *Cinema 1: The Movement-Image*. Translated by Hugh Tomlinson and Barbara Habberjam. Minneapolis: University of Minnesota Press, 1986.

—. *Cinema 2: The Time-Image*. Translated by Hugh Tomlinson and Robert Galeta. Minneapolis: University of Minnesota Press, 1989.

Love, Barbara, ed. *Feminists Who Changed America, 1963-1975*. Foreword by Nancy F. Cott. Urbana: University of Illinois Press, 2006.

Mills, Nancy. "*Blue Steel:* Kathryn Bigelow in Action." *American Film*, September 1989 (vol. 14, no. 10): 59.

Serota, Nicholas, ed. *Fernand Léger: The Later Years*. Munich: Prestel-Verlag; London: Trustees of the Whitechapel Art Gallery, 1987.

Smith, Gavin. "'Momentum and Design': Interview with Kathryn Bigelow." Reprinted in *The Cinema of Kathryn Bigelow: Hollywood Transgressor*, edited by Deborah Jermyn and Sean Redmond, 20-31. London and New York: Wallflower Press, 2003.

Notes

[1] See chapter six, "Return of the Female Gothic: The Career-Woman-in-Peril Thriler," by Monica Soare.

[2] See chapter eight, "A Feminist Theorization of Sofia Coppola's Postfeminist Trilogy," by Amy Woodworth.

[3] Gavin Smith, "'Momentum and Design': Interview with Kathryn Bigelow," in Deborah Jermyn and Sean Redmond, eds., *The Cinema of Kathryn Bigelow: Hollywood Transgressor* (London and New York: Wallflower Press, 2003), 28.

[4] Nancy Mills, "*Blue Steel:* Kathryn Bigelow in Action," *American Film*, September 1989 (vol. 14, no. 10): 59.

[5] For a discussion of Pialat's art, see Marcelline Block, "'The Shock of the Real' in Pialat's *Van Gogh* (1991): Trauma and The Red Vineyard," *Excavatio: Realism and Naturalism in Film Studies*, Vol. XXII (Nos. 1-2, 2007): 234-250.

[6] Fernand Léger quoted in *Fernand Léger: The Later Years*, edited by Nicholas Serota (Munich: Prestel-Verlag; London: Trustees of the Whitechapel Art Gallery, 1987), 20-21.

[7] Ibid.

[8] Hugh Tomlinson and Robert Galeta, "Translators' Introduction," *Gilles Deleuze, Cinema 2: The Time-Image*, trans. Tomlinson and Galeta (Minneapolis: University of Minnesota Press, 1989), xv.

[9] Gilles Deleuze, "Preface to the English Edition," *Cinema 1: The Movement-Image*, trans. Hugh Tomlinson and Barbara Habberjam (Minneapolis: University of Minnesota Press, 1986), xi.

[10] See *Feminists Who Changed America, 1963-1975*, ed. Barbara Love, foreword by Nancy F. Cott (Urbana: University of Illinois Press, 2006).

[11] On May 15, 2010, the 35th anniversary of Hélène Cixous's "Le Rire de la Méduse" was celebrated in Paris at the Bibliothèque François Mitterrand. Actress Emmanuelle Riva's readings from Cixous's text were interspersed with interventions and commentaries by Catherine Nesci, Jean-Michel Rabaté, Frédéric Regard and Martine Reid.

[12] Smith, 29.

[13] Ibid.

[14] Ibid.

[15] Marcia Froelke Coburn, "Revamping Vampires: Erotic Thriller Moves Locale to the Midwest," *The Chicago Tribune* (October 11, 1987), n.p.

[16] Ibid.

[17] Smith, 29-30.

[18] Mills, 59.

[19] Ibid.

[20] See Joan Simon, ed., *Alice Guy Blaché: Cinema Pioneer* (Yale University Press in association with the Whitney Museum of American Art, 2009). My upcoming article on Alice Guy Blaché is set to appear in a fall 2010 anthology.

[21] "Woman with a Movie Camera: Alice Guy Blaché Symposium" was held on November 14, 2009 at New York University. It was co-sponsored by the Whitney's Education Department and the Department of Cinema Studies, Tisch School of the Arts, New York University.

CONTRIBUTORS

Sharon Lubkemann Allen is Assistant Professor of Comparative Literature and Theory at the State University of New York, Brockport, where she teaches modern Slavic, European, Latin American and transnational literature, film, and theory. She received her PhD in Comparative Literature from Princeton University, where she taught writing, Russian and European literature. She also studied at the Sorbonne, the Ecole Normale Supérieure, Petersburg State University, the International Dostoevsky Museum in St. Petersburg, and the University of Lisbon. She held a Mellon Postdoctoral Fellowship in 2004-2005 at the Penn Humanities Forum at the University of Pennsylvania. Her published work is in modern European literature, with emphasis on geographical, historical, and generic dimensions of modernist narratives. Her forthcoming book is titled *EccentriCities: Writing in the Margins of Modernism, St. Petersburg to Rio de Janeiro* and her manuscripts in progress concern shifting architectonics of cultural memory in the Paris text and transnational transformations of literary and cinematic *topoi*.

Marcelline Block received a BA in History and Literature from Harvard and an MA in French from Princeton, where she is finishing a PhD and is receiving Graduate Certificates in the Study of Women, Gender and Sexuality as well as Media and Modernity. She taught French, English, comparative literature, women's studies and political science, among other subjects, at Princeton since 2003. Among her articles are "'The Shock of the Real' in Pialat's *Van Gogh*: Trauma and *The Red Vineyard*" in *Excavatio: Realism and Naturalism in Film Studies* (2007; archived in CNRS, 2008) and "'Mother Figure': Photographic Representations of the Maternal in Georges Perec's *W ou le souvenir d'enfance*," in *The Harvard French Review* (2007). She is co-editor of *Critical Matrix: The Princeton Journal of Women, Gender and Culture* and text editor of *LINE: The Journal of the Richard and Mica Hadar Foundation*. She is also a referee for *Working Papers in the Romance Languages* (University of Pennsylvania). She published reviews of Jean-François Sirinelli's *Les Vingt décisives: le passé proche de notre avenir, 1965-1985* in French in *XXème Siècle: Revue d'histoire* (2007); Susie Hennessy's *The Mother Figure in Emile Zola's Les Rougon-Macquart* in *Women in French Studies* (2008) and Ada Uzoamaka Azodo's *Emerging Perspectives on Aminata*

Sow Fall in *Women in French Studies* (2009). Forthcoming: *Prescribing Gender in Medicine and Narrative* (Co-editor, Cambridge Scholars Press, 2009) and *The International Encyclopedia of Revolution and Protest, 1500 to the Present* (Editor, contributor, and translator; Blackwell, March 2009). She organized panels at the NeMLA convention about feminist film theory; gender and medical narrative; the 30th anniversary of Susan Sontag's *On Photography*; and postfeminism. She organized a seminar at the 2009 ACLA about media studies and medical narrative and read papers at the American Comparative Literature Association (2006); the American Society of Geolinguistics in 2007 (about Kassovitz's film *La Haine*) and in 2008 (about Sofia Coppola's film *Lost in Translation*); at Columbia University in 2008 (about Sophie Calle's video installation *Pas pu saisir la mort/Couldn't Capture Death*). She gave papers at graduate student conferences at Brown, NYU, Princeton, and Harvard.

Georgiana M. M. Colvile is Professor Emeritus of Anglophone Studies at the University of Tours, France. She has taught French, Francophone and Comparative Literature and Film at the University of Colorado, Boulder, among other American universities. She specializes in Francophone and Anglophone Avant-Garde and Contemporary Literature, Art and Film, particularly by women. Her four latest books focus on women surrealists: *Scandaleusement d'elles* (anthology: Jean-Michel Place, 1999); editions of the works of Valentine Penrose (Joëlle Losfeld, 2001) and Simone Kahn-Breton (Joëlle Losfeld & Gallimard, 2005) and with Katharine Conley, *La Femme s'entête* (proceedings of their 1997 Cerisy conference *La Part du feminin dans le surréalisme*: Lachenal & Ritter, 1998).

Lisa DeTora is Assistant Professor of English and the Assistant Director of the College Writing Program at Lafayette College in Easton, Pennsylvania. She earned a PhD in English and a graduate certificate in Women's Studies from the University of Rochester, Rochester, New York. DeTora's scholarly interests include media, popular culture and discourses of science and medicine. Her prior publications have appeared in *Modern Language Studies* and various medical and clinical pharmacology journals. At Lafayette, her course offerings include "Influenza Pandemics and Other Anxieties," "Writing Science," and "Writing About Food."

Sandy Flitterman-Lewis is Associate Professor at Rutgers University where she teaches Cinema Studies and Comparative Literature. She is the author of *To Desire Differently: Feminism and the French Cinema* (expanded edition, Columbia University Press, 1996) and co-author of

New Vocabularies in Film Semiotics (Routledge, 1992). A founding co-editor of both *Camera Obscura* and *Discourse*, she has chapters in numerous anthologies and articles in a wide range of journals. Her current work, *Hidden Voices: Childhood, the Family, and Anti-Semitism in Occupied France* continues the research from a conference she organized at Columbia University.

Elizabeth Gruber completed her PhD in English at the University of Nevada, Reno (2002). Since 2003, she has been Assistant Professor, in English, at Lock Haven University in Lock Haven, Pennsylvania. She has published articles on Shakespeare and Shakespearean adaptation, and is particularly interested in feminist appropriations of Shakespeare. Currently, she is working on a book-length study of the mechanics of adaptation.

Izabela Kalinowska is Associate Professor in the Department of European Languages, Literatures, and Cultures at Stony Brook University. She works in the areas of Polish and Russian literatures and cinemas. She is the author of *Between East and West: Polish and Russian Nineteenth-Century Travel to the Orient* (University of Rochester Press, 2004) and of several articles dealing with issues of gender and nation in Polish cinema. A recent publication is "Polanski's Iconoclastic Journeys in Time: *When Angels Fall* and *Bitter Moon*" in Elzbieta Ostrowska and John Orr, eds., *The Cinema of Roman Polanski: Dark Spaces of the World*.

Jean-Michel Rabaté, Vartan Gregorian Professor in the Humanities at the University of Pennsylvania, has published over fifteen books on Samuel Beckett, Thomas Bernhard, Ezra Pound, James Joyce, psychoanalysis and literary theory, including *The Ghosts of Modernity* (University of Florida Press, 1996), *Joyce and the Politics of Egoism* (Cambridge UP, 2001), *Jacques Lacan and Literature* (Palgrave, 2001), *Logiques du Mensonge* (Calmann-Levy, 2005), *Given: 1° Art, 2° Crime* (Sussex University Press, 2006), *1913: The Cradle of Modernism* (Blackwell, July 2007), and *The Ethic of the Lie* (The Other Press, 2008), among others. His edited collections of essays include *Writing the Image After Roland Barthes* (University of Pennsylvania Press, 1997), *Jacques Lacan in America* (The Other Press, 2000), *The Cambridge Companion to Jacques Lacan* (2003), *The Future of Theory* (Blackwell, 2002), *On the Diagram: the Art of Marjorie Welish* (2004 Palgrave), *Advances to James Joyce* (2004), *Architecture Against Death: On Arakawa and Gins* (two volumes), *William Anastasi's Pataphysical Society* (Slought, 2005), and *Hélène*

Cixous—On Cities (Slought, 2006).

Rachel Ritterbusch joined the Modern Languages faculty at Shepherd University in 2004 after teaching French and German in the St. Louis area. She holds an MA in French, German and Spanish from the University of Munich (1993). She received a PhD in French from the University of Wisconsin-Madison (dissertation topic: Marguerite Duras). Her areas of specialization include 19th- and 20th-century French literature, French and Francophone culture, and film studies. She is also interested in the application of second-language acquisition theory to the classroom and has published a study on difficulties experienced by native English speakers learning the German case system. Her recent articles focus on contemporary French filmmaker Anne Fontaine.

Chuck Robinson is a PhD student in English Language and Literature at Syracuse University, and received an MA in the Humanities from the University of Chicago. An Americanist specializing in the 19th Century, Chuck teaches film and American literature at Syracuse University. His research interests also include American gothic in all its forms; contemporary American popular culture; Southern literature and other regionalisms; globalization studies; and poststructuralist modulations of Spinoza, Hegel, Marx, Nietzsche and Freud. He recently published "Mommy, Baby, Ghost: the Technological Chain Letter and the Nuclear Family in *The Ring*," in the anthology *Heroes and Homefronts,* edited by Lisa DeTora.

Noëlle Rouxel-Cubberly received an MA (maîtrise) in American Literature and Linguistics as well as in French as a Foreign Language at the Université de Tours, France. She is currently completing a PhD in French at the City University of New York. Her dissertation, "A(voir) le titre: économie et évolution du titre de film français depuis 1968/(En)titling: Economics and Evolution of the French Film Title since 1968," seeks to define the relations between French film titles and their co-texts and to weigh the importance of the values they shape and convey to the public. A former faculty member of the Regional Center for Languages and Cultures at Bennington College, Noëlle returns to Bennington each summer to teach the course in French language, culture, and pedagogy for the Master's in the Arts of Teaching a Second Language program. Noëlle's current projects include a French second-year textbook series edited by Isabelle Kaplan and an article on film title semiotics. She serves as a Technology Fellow for CUNY's Research Foundation where she assists foreign language faculty in the development of online courses.

Monica Soare, a PhD candidate in English at the University of California, Berkeley, is working on her dissertation, "Female Fantasy and the Gothic," which examines how the actual and imagined female audience shaped the rise of the Female Gothic genre in the late eighteenth/early nineteenth centuries and how it informs women and horror entertainment today. She studies horror stories from eighteenth century women's magazines to late twentieth-century B-movie thrillers within a scholarly framework.

Jeremi Szaniawski, originally from Brussels, Belgium, is a PhD candidate in the joint Slavic Languages and Literatures and Film Studies program at Yale University. He is the co-founder of Yale's film club, the Cinema at the Whitney (www.yale.edu/cinema), and lead curator of Yale's Slavic Film Colloquium. His dissertation topic is Russian filmmaker Alexander Sokurov, and his fields of interest include contemporary art-house cinema at large, modernism and postmodernism in film, Georges Bataille and Surrealism, Slavic cinema of the Thaw and Horror films (which he taught at Yale during the Summer Film Institute, 2008). Publications include an interview with Alexander Sokurov in *Critical Inquiry* (2006); articles on Sokurov in English, Russian and Japanese; a discussion of the canon in contemporary film theory; and the resurgence of modernism in contemporary cinema, entitled "Transmodernism." He is also an independent filmmaker and screenwriter.

Ian Scott Todd is a graduate student at Ohio University, where his research interests include 20th century literature, film, gender and queer studies. He teaches literature, writing, and film, including the Western, and is writing about Mark Ravenhill's plays.

M. Hunter Vaughan received his PhD in French Cinema and Philosophy from the University of Oxford, and is currently Lecturer of Film and Media Studies at Washington University in St. Louis. His primary areas of interest include ideological and philosophical problems of audio-visual representation, interdisciplinary approaches to film aesthetics, new media studies, and American and European cinemas.

Gwendolyn Wells is a freelance writer, translator, and editor in a variety of fields. She edited a book on Albert C. Barnes and the Barnes Foundation. She was one of twelve collaborating translators for a three-volume reference work, the *International Dictionary of Psychoanalysis*, edited by Alain de Mijolla (Thomson Gale, 2005). She was translations editor at Fitzroy-Dearborn, a reference press in Chicago (2000-2002). She taught French language, literature, and culture at Duke University, Kenyon College, l'Université de Paris VII-Denis Diderot, and the University of Pennsylvania, where she received her PhD in Romance Languages.

Amy Woodworth is a doctoral candidate in the English Department at Temple University. She holds a BA from New York University and an MA from Rutgers University (New Jersey). Her areas of research are 20th Century American Literature, Film, and Women's Studies.

INDEX

A

G